THE BOOK OF SCSI
A GUIDE FOR ADVENTURERS

PETER M. RIDGE

WITH

DAVID A. DEMING

STEFAN GROLL

JOHN HEIM

GERHARD ISLINGER

JOHN LOHMEYER

no starch press
daly city, california

Publisher **WILLIAM POLLOCK**

Project Editor **DEBORAH COGAN**

Production Assistance **VICKI FRIEDBERG**

Cover Illustration **ALAN OKAMOTO**

Cover and Text Design **CLOYCE WALL**

Compositor **STEVEN BOLINGER**

Copyeditor **KATHRYN HASHIMOTO**

Proofreader **LINDA MEDOFF**

Indexer **MATTHEW SPENCE**

**Library of Congress
Cataloging-in-Publication Data**

Ridge, Peter M.
    The book of SCSI : a guide for adventurers /
Peter M. Ridge.
        p.   cm.
    Includes index.
    ISBN 1-886411-02-6
    1. SCSI (Computer bus). I. Title.
TK7895.B87R53   1995
004.6'2dc20
                                    94-44670

Distributed to the book trade in the United States and Canada by Publishers Group West, 4065 Hollis, P.O. Box 8843, Emeryville, California 94662, phone: 800-788-3123 or 510-548-4393, fax: 510-658-1834.

For information on translations or book distributors outside the United States, please contact No Starch Press directly:

No Starch Press
1903 Jameston Lane
Daly City, CA 94014-3466
Phone: 415-334-7200; Fax: 415-334-3166;
E-mail: nostarch@ix.netcom.com

The information in this book is distributed on an "As Is" basis, without warranty. While every precaution has been taken in the preparation of this work, neither the author nor No Starch Press shall have any liability to any person or entity with respect to any loss or damage caused or alleged to be caused directly or indirectly by the instructions contained in this book or by the computer software or hardware described in it.

Grateful acknowledgment is
made for permission to reproduce:

Chapter 6 ("How the Bus Works"). Copyright 1994, 1995 ENDL Publications and David A. Deming. All rights reserved. Reprinted here with the permission of David A. Deming and ENDL Publications.
Chapter 7 ("A Look at SCSI-3"). Copyright 1995 John Lohmeyer. All rights reserved.
Appendix B figures B.3 through B.12 and B.18 through B.26. Copyright 1992 and 1993 by Amp Incorporated. All rights reserved. Reprinted here with the permission of Amp Incorporated.
Appendixes D ("A Profile of ASPI Programming") and **K** ("Q&A from Adaptec"). Copyright 1994, 1995 Adaptec, Inc. All rights reserved. Portions reprinted with the permission of Adaptec, Inc.
Appendixes E ("Future/CAM Developer's Reference Manual") and **J** ("Q&A from Future Domain Corporation"). Copyright 1995 Future Domain Corporation. All rights reserved. Reprinted here with the permission of Future Domain Corporation.
Appendixes F ("IDE Versus SCSI"), **G** ("Building Fast SCSI Subsystems"), **H** ("An Introduction to RAID"), and **I** ("Q&A from Distributed Processing Technology"). Copyright 1995 Distributed Processing Technology. All rights reserved. Reprinted here with the permission of Distributed Processing Technology.

Printed in the United States of America

2 3 4 5 6 7 8 9 10—99 98 97 96 95

 Printed on acid-free recycled paper.

Trademarks

Trademarked names are used throughout this book. Rather than use a trademark symbol with every occurrence of a trademarked name, we are using the names only in an editorial fashion and to the benefit of the trademark owner, with no intention of infringement of the trademark.

Your Tour Guides

This book is the work of many hands and has been guided by many minds. Whether you're a computer novice or a seasoned expert, these contributors will help you make the most of your SCSI hardware and supply you with a wealth of practical know-how and reference material.

Peter Ridge

Peter is the Engineering Manager at Creative Labs, Inc., home of the Sound Blaster sound card. With nine years of technical experience in the computer industry, he has contributed to several books on computer and multimedia hardware and software including *Sound Blaster: The Official Book* (Osborne/McGraw-Hill) and *The Business Week Guide to Multimedia Presentations* (Osborne/McGraw-Hill). Although working and writing books takes up his free time, he also enjoys programming and playing on keyboards (both computer and musical).

David A. Deming

Dave (author of Chapter 6, "How the Bus Works") is an independent consultant and founder of Solution Technology, with over 15 years of experience designing many software and hardware courses covering a wide variety of programming languages and operating systems for testing and development. Dave is an active member of the X3T10 (SCSI-3) and X3T10.1 (Serial Storage Architecture) Standards committees. Dave has conducted hundreds of training courses worldwide and trained thousands of engineers on SCSI-related topics.

Stefan Groll

Stefan (author of Chapter 5, "Troubleshooting," and a contributor to Appendix B, "All-Platform Technical Reference") was born in Munich, Germany. After finishing school and a long stint in sports, he began work in freelance software development with a security services company. In 1986 he began his study of electronics. While developing diagnostic systems and self-test software, he acquired PC and UNIX know-how, which resulted in his troubleshooting security products for these environments. After some time in the publishing business developing electronic books and retrieval systems, he returned to security management, where he currently works in a mixed mainframe and workstation environment.

John Heim

For the past ten years, John (co-contributor to Chapter 4, "Adding SCSI to Your PC") has been working as a software engineer and computer consultant specializing in image storage and retrieval. He is currently on the staff of the Division of Information Technology at the University of Wisconsin. John's initial interest in SCSI came when he was asked to help build a PC that could fool a medical scanner into thinking it was talking to a SCSI hard drive.

Gerhard Islinger

Gerhard (co-author of Appendix B, "All-Platform Technical Reference," a general contributor to several sections of the book, and all-around technical editor) was born in Grafenau, Lower Bavaria, Germany. After playing with a Wang 2200 at school, he made computers his hobby and later his profession. In 1982 he began working for Siemens as a service technician, first on HELL typesetting systems, then for two years on the OEM'ed Xerox Star workstations. After two years of PC support, freelance projects brought him to a collaboration on a European ESPRIT-based project called CIMple (CIM Implementation Toolkit). He is currently back at Siemens handling network and end-user support.

John Lohmeyer

John (author of the Foreword and Chapter 7, "A Look at SCSI-3") is a senior consulting engineer with Symbios Logic in Colorado Springs, Colorado. He began his involvement with SCSI when it was still called SASI in the summer of 1981. Since then, John has contributed to the SCSI effort as a member of the design team on the first SCSI chip (NCR 5385), technical editor of SCSI-1, and chair of the X3T10 committee (formerly X3T9.2), which is responsible for the ANSI SCSI standards. He also operates the SCSI Bulletin Board System to disseminate information about SCSI and other I/O interface standards.

BRIEF CONTENTS

CONTENTS IN DETAIL

Acknowledgments

The Book of SCSI: A Guide for Adventurers would not be possible without the labors of many hard-working people. First, thanks to Dave Deming, Stefan Groll, John Heim, Gerhard Islinger, and John Lohmeyer for their invaluable contributions to the book. Their experience and wisdom allowed this book to reach a broader audience.

For all the technical information in the appendixes, thanks go to Adaptec, Inc., Future Domain Corporation, Distributed Processing Technology, and Amp, Inc.

Thanks to No Starch Press and the book team: Steve Bolinger, Debbie Cogan, Vicki Friedberg, Kathy Hashimoto, Linda Medoff, Alan Okamoto, and Cloyce Wall.

FOREWORD

Finally, here is a practical book about SCSI aimed at helping the real users of SCSI—a book on SCSI that is chock-full of helpful hints on making SCSI work for you. You'll find arcane SCSI concepts explained simply and clearly. Whether you already have SCSI on your PC or are contemplating adding it, this book is definitely worth reading.

You will find discussions on terminating your SCSI bus (not with a gun); setting SCSI IDs; choosing cables; choosing host adapter (controller card) features; setting up I/O addresses, IRQs, and DMA channels; installing device drivers; and more. You'll also find a hefty listing of SCSI vendors complete with addresses, phone numbers, BBS numbers, etc.

I have personally installed SCSI on quite a few PCs, both at work and at home. Beyond getting the SCSI hardware installed right, I still had to get the PC hardware and software installed right—tasks that are not always easy. This book makes those tasks much simpler by explaining what your choices are and how to make them.

You may have heard a lot of hype about Intel/Microsoft's Plug-and-Play (PnP) making installation easier. It will. But Plug-and-Play will not happen overnight, and it does not address everything you may need to know about SCSI—particularly if you want to mix your current SCSI devices with your PnP SCSI devices. In fact, PnP SCSI, while solving most installation problems, may create a new problem: SCSI IDs are no longer fixed. Adding a tape drive to your system *could* cause your drive letters to be rearranged unless the future releases of the operating systems are modified to compensate. So, protect yourself. Learn what is going on in the hardware.

Now a couple of notes about standards committees. Standards committees are often accused of being slow and plodding organizations. We often are—for good reason. We are required to achieve consensus on highly technical concepts, and our only resources are volunteers. Our employers may pay our travel and give us some time to work on the standards, but much of the work is actually accomplished evenings and weekends by some rather dedicated individuals who want to have an impact on the industry. The standards process is designed to prevent litigation. We have a lot of rules that prevent sneak attacks—but they can also slow down legitimate work. That is why most companies cannot wait for final approval on standards before beginning product development.

Also, the fact is that users can't afford to attend standards committee meetings, or they are not inclined to because their investment in SCSI is relatively small. As a result, users tend to be underrepresented in the SCSI development process. But there is a way that you can have input into the development of SCSI standards without having to appear at meetings and spending a lot of money. All standards go through a public review process that allows for input on all pending standards. You can find out about these public review periods by dialing into the SCSI BBS at 719-574-0424. Once on the BBS, look for information on subscribing to the SCSI Reflector mailing list (you can reach many committee members using this mailing list), read any bulletins, and look for X3 Press Releases on Public Review Periods.

If, in spite of the foregoing, you are still interested in participating in the standards development process, I urge you to contact the X3 Secretariat in Washington, DC for more information. They can be reached by Internet at x3sec@itic.nw.dc.us or voice at 202-737-8888.

John Lohmeyer
Chair X3T10
Symbios Logic Inc.
1635 Aeroplaza Drive
Colorado Springs, CO 80916

INTRODUCTION

This guide began with a fundamental goal: to teach users about SCSI and show users how to work with SCSI, without all the hard-to-understand language prevalent in the computer industry. It wasn't an easy undertaking. As time passed, the book grew and matured. As a result, it now appeals to a broader audience than just the average user. With contributions from John Lohmeyer, Chair of the ANSI X3T10 committee on SCSI, and Dave Deming, founder of Solutions Technology, this book provides the in-depth information about SCSI that advanced computer users search for. In addition, the twelve appendixes, chockfull of reference material, will save many of you the arduous process of hunting for that elusive table of SCSI commands or cable connector specifications.

This book is a guide for adventurers of all levels. The first four chapters are for everyone. If you're in a hurry, no problem—here's a quick rundown of where to begin. For those who aren't familiar with SCSI or who would like a refresher course, Chapters 1 and 2 are the place to start. If you own a PC and you're ready to install your SCSI interface card, read Chapter 4, then continue with Chapter 3, which contains more general explanations of SCSI concepts. Otherwise, you can start connecting your devices by jumping right into Chapter 3.

Chapter 1 begins with a short history on *the birth and development of SCSI*. Beginning with the Shugart Associates Systems Interface, you'll tag along with us to the land of SCSI. Once we're there, you'll see all the great things you can do with SCSI and learn why it's the interface of choice for today's high-performance computer systems.

Chapter 2 takes a closer look at *the parts that make up a SCSI system and how they work*. Not to worry, we'll be venturing through this area carefully, and we'll explain everything we come across. You'll learn the fundamentals of SCSI technology, such as device IDs, parity checking, and transfer modes.

In *Chapter 3*, we take a break from our scenic tour with the beginning of the hands-on portion of the journey. You'll learn about *cables, connecting internal and external SCSI devices, what terminators are and how to use them, and how to configure SCSI devices to get them to work properly in your system*. This chapter is not machine-specific, but relates to any machine with SCSI capability. It also has several illustrations of SCSI systems and hardware, which make it a more scenic, hands-on segment.

Chapter 4 is specifically for all the *PC users* out there. In this chapter, we talk about the SCSI interface card, CD-ROM drives, and other SCSI devices. You'll learn how to configure the board, configure and install the proper software, and turn your PC into a SCSI machine.

If you run into trouble, *Chapter 5* (by Stefan Groll) is your safety net. Here you'll find a plethora of helpful hints and *troubleshooting* tips to get you up and running again quickly.

For all you techie adventurers, Dave Deming takes a look at *how the SCSI bus works* in *Chapter 6*. You'll learn how SCSI really operates, down to the messages sent between devices and the control signals used to make it all happen.

As the chapters draw to a close, John Lohmeyer peers into his crystal ball (*Chapter 7*) to gaze upon the next generation of SCSI and what we can expect to see in the near and distant future. He covers the many aspects of the *SCSI-3* standard, which, as you'll see, is actually many standards rolled into one.

Appendix A shows you *where to find all the great hardware and software that works with your SCSI system*. It should be but a starting point for your own personal quest.

Appendix B (by Gerhard Islinger and Stefan Groll) holds *everything you've misplaced about cables, connectors, terminators, and bus timing*. This appendix also contains numerous diagrams and tables reproduced courtesy of the Amp Corporation.

Appendix C lists some *common configurations for PC cards* to help you avoid problems when adding your SCSI interface.

Programmers and the programming-curious will enjoy *Appendixes D and E, overviews of the ASPI and CAM interfaces* which are used to write applications that can communicate with SCSI hardware. These appendixes are contributed by Adaptec and the Future Domain Corporation, respectively.

For hardware gurus, DPT (Distributed Processing Technology) was kind enough to let us reproduce or adapt several of their publications for your information. *Appendix F* shows you *the real difference between SCSI and IDE*, the popular, low-cost alternative. Then, to really soup up your setup, *Appendix G* shows you what it takes to *build really fast SCSI subsystems*. And finally, to ensure that your data is as safe as it can be, *Appendix H* introduces you to *RAID* (Redundant Array of Inexpensive Disks).

Appendixes I, J, and K present the *most frequently asked questions and answers from DPT, Future Domain, and Adaptec*. So, before you call technical support, check these appendixes.

Finally, *Appendix L lists online services, BBSs, and Internet sites*.

And now, let's get going!

1

We begin this adventure with a lay of the land, so to speak. A short background on the birth of SCSI (pronounced "scuzzy"), what it is, and where it's going. Since this may be the first time you've ventured into SCSI territory, here are a few terms you'll need to be familiar with before we embark.

bus: The bus is the path or channel that carries data between the computer and other devices (like a printer or scanner) or between a series of devices. Cables, wires, and optical fiber are components commonly used to form a bus. The bus itself is not a physical object that you can hold in your hand. Rather, it is the entire collection of cables and wires used to make up the communications pathway. The size of the bus changes in direct proportion to the number of connections.

bus slots: Bus slots are connectors inside the computer that are used for attaching add-on cards (like sound or video cards) and devices to a bus.

controller card: Controller cards are circuit boards that plug into the motherboard on the computer. They allow the computer to communicate with and control devices. SCSI, IDE, and ESDI cards are examples of hard disk controller cards. Some printers and scanners require their own controller cards, separate from the computer's. Controller cards are often referred to simply as controllers.

data transfer rate: Data transfer rate is a measure of how quickly information can be passed between the computer and another device or between devices. The higher the data transfer rate, the less you'll have to wait for data to get to its destination.

device: Device generally refers to hardware that can be connected to the computer (such as printers, hard disks, scanners, and modems), though sometimes the computer itself is referred to as a device as well. Devices can also be interface cards, such as video cards, SCSI cards, and sound cards.

hardware interface: A hardware interface consists of the electronics necessary to communicate with and control devices. When you put these electronics on a card you have an interface card, also known as a controller card. In this book, we'll often refer to the hardware interface as simply the interface.

multitasking: Multitasking simply means performing more than one function simultaneously. Multitasking operating systems, such as Windows 95, OS/2, and UNIX, can run many programs simultaneously. When your software or devices are multitasking, they don't have to wait for one program to finish before they can do their work—they all work simultaneously. And, as a user of a multitasking system, you don't have to wait, either.

IDE: Integrated Drive Electronics, or IDE, is a common, parallel bus standard for hard disk drives. All the control electronics for IDE reside on the hard disk drive, not on the interface card. Since IDE is not an intelligent bus, simpler, low-cost electronics can be used. The low cost of IDE, coupled with its support for hard drives only, makes it an ideal interface for the mass-market.

EIDE: Enhanced IDE is an updated version of IDE that improves on IDE's speed and includes support for CD-ROM drives in addition to hard drives.

THE BIRTH OF SCSI

SCSI began life in 1979 as the Shugart Associates Systems Interface (abbreviated SASI and pronounced "sassy"). SASI was the first small-scale intelligent hard disk interface designed to work with smaller mini-computers. SCSI's birth was a major leap forward in hardware interfaces. Interfaces prior to SCSI were not intelligent; they were designed specifically for a device, so they required particular interfaces for each different device, such as a hard disk interface for a hard disk. SCSI, on the other hand, defined a standard interface for all devices, so that only one controller was required. Intelligent interfaces, like SCSI, know what types of devices are connected to the computer and how to deal with each. As an intelligent interface, SCSI allows users to mix and match devices on one controller rather than needing a separate controller for each device.

But in order to get everyone to use SCSI, and to make sure that every company's devices would be compatible with it, a SCSI standard had to be defined. And so, in 1981, Shugart and NCR (National Cash Register) presented their SASI proposal to the X3T9.2 committee for a standard to be published by the American National Standards Institute (ANSI, pronounced "anssy"), the standard-setting organization in the U.S. After many long years of debate on the exact specifications for this new bus, ANSI finally gave its approval in June, 1986. The new standard, document X3.131-1986, was named the Small Computer System Interface (SCSI), and thus SCSI was born. That first version of SCSI is now referred to as SCSI-1, because newer standards have been released since 1986.

SCSI-1 defined a universal parallel, system-level interface for connecting up to eight devices along a single cable, called the SCSI bus. Parallel devices (such as the majority of printers) send a group of bits (binary digits) at a time, as opposed to serial devices (such as modems and mice), which send data one bit at a time. As a system-level interface, SCSI is very different from a device-level interface such as ESDI (enhanced small device interface). SCSI is an independent and intelligent local I/O bus through which a variety of different devices and one or more controllers can communicate and exchange information independent of what the rest of the system is doing. ESDI, on the other hand, is limited to two devices, both of which can only be ESDI drives, and communication can only exist with participation of the rest of the system.

However, although SCSI was a groundbreaking standard, early SCSI devices weren't easy to work with. The primary drawback to using SCSI was that very few devices coexisted happily on the bus, making installation and configuration of a SCSI system very difficult.

SCSI-1 devices were also limited to a peak throughput of five megabytes per second (5 MB/sec), which was comparable to the transfer rate of ESDI. And ESDI doesn't have all the compatibility headaches that SCSI-1 did. But ESDI has a significant problem: a lack of flexibility. While ESDI is fast, ESDI drives only work with ESDI controllers, which brings us back to the one controller-one device problem. So while SCSI had the advantage of flexibility over ESDI, and had comparable speed, something had to be done to solve the integration problem in order to make SCSI a more attractive solution.

Even before SCSI-1 had been made an official standard, improvements to it were already in the works. SCSI-1 had some shortcomings: it wasn't as general-purpose as it needed to be, and, although it was fast, some felt that its speed could be improved. In January 1994, ANSI approved the X3T9.2 committee's updated draft standard, SCSI-2. The standard was designated X3.131-1994 to indicate that it replaced SCSI-1.

Everyone had been calling this new standard SCSI-2 as early as 1986, when it was proposed. In fact, just as there are a variety of unofficial SCSI-3 devices on the market today (with the SCSI-3 standard still in the development process), there had been a number of SCSI-2 devices on the market prior to the adoption of the SCSI-2 standard.

NOTE *Because SCSI-2 devices were on the market before the adoption of a SCSI-2 standard, there were some compatibility problems between SCSI-2 devices. You may still encounter these problems if you have SCSI-2 hardware developed prior to approval of the standard. But, if your SCSI-2 devices were purchased within the last year or so, you probably won't encounter any compatibility problems because they should have been developed to adhere to the official ANSI SCSI-2 standard.*

The following is a list of the improvements provided in the SCSI-2 specification, together with a brief description of what makes these advances important. We'll explore them in more detail in Chapter 2.

- DB-50 Type-1 connectors were replaced by high-density connectors, which shrank the size of the connector and made for more efficient and trouble-free connections.

- The speed of data transfer along the SCSI bus was increased by allowing for synchronous transfers, now standard with optional fast synchronous data transfer mode (Fast SCSI-2).

- The speed of data transfer was also increased by widening the size of the bus. Both 16-bit and 32-bit buses were defined (Wide SCSI-2).

- To increase the reliability of device-to-device communication, synchronous negotiation must be invoked whenever the initiator or target device detects a change. Previously, many target devices refrained from starting such negotiations because some early host adapters locked up.

- Signal integrity was improved with the addition of mandatory SCSI bus parity checking.

Fast SCSI Doubles the Data Transfer Rate

The SCSI bus allows for both asynchronous and synchronous data transfer modes (see Chapter 2 for a detailed discussion of these transfer modes). Synchronous transfer tends to be considerably faster than asynchronous. SCSI-1 allowed asynchronous transfer rates of 1.5 MB/sec and synchronous transfer rates at a maximum of 5 MB/sec. In order to improve on this, Fast SCSI was introduced as an optional SCSI-2 operating mode.

Fast SCSI squeezed some of the timing margins so that faster handshaking (connections) could occur, doubling the synchronous transfer rates of SCSI. The maximum SCSI-1 synchronous transfer rate doubled, from 5 MB/sec to 10 MB/sec.

The term "fast" is generally used to describe SCSI devices that can support synchronous transfers at this improved rate of 10MB/sec. Fast SCSI may only be used when describing SCSI-2, since SCSI-1 did not support this faster synchronous transfer mode.

But this increase in speed did not come without added costs and demands. Sending data twice as fast means that devices need better electronics to ensure error-free data transfers. Similarly, faster data transfer also means that the cables used for the SCSI bus must be of higher quality than those used for SCSI-1 or regular SCSI-2. (We'll talk more about cables in Chapters 2 and 3.) This is the typical path for SCSI and any advancing technology—faster and better always means that all supporting technology needs to advance too.

NOTE *In order to use Fast SCSI, both your SCSI interface and SCSI devices must have Fast SCSI capability. Be sure to check the device's specifications if you're interested in using Fast SCSI, because not all SCSI-2 devices support it. Remember, Fast SCSI is an option with SCSI-2; you don't need to use Fast SCSI in order to use SCSI-2-compatible devices.*

Wide SCSI Allows More Data to Be Transferred over the SCSI Bus

Besides doubling the rate at which data can be transferred over the SCSI bus or pathway, SCSI-2 also provides the option to double or quadruple the width of the SCSI bus with Wide SCSI.

The width of the bus is a measure of its number of data lines. By increasing the width of the bus from 8 bits to either 16 or 32 bits, the Wide SCSI bus can transfer two to four times more data in the same amount of time than regular SCSI-2. Of course, this also means that the size of the cables must be increased, because more bits require more wires.

NOTE *As with Fast SCSI, both the SCSI interface and SCSI devices have to support Wide SCSI in order to take advantage of the Wide capability. If your SCSI controller supports Wide SCSI but your device does not, or vice versa, communication between the controller and device will take place at regular 8-bit SCSI-2—you won't be able to take advantage of Wide SCSI. But, although your system won't use Wide SCSI, communication will still take place without a hitch; it will simply be slower.*

Fast Wide SCSI Is the Best of Both Worlds

While Fast and Wide SCSI can certainly operate independently, a combination of the two provides even greater improvement in the rate of data transfer. The faster transfer rate of Fast SCSI and the wider bus of Wide SCSI can be combined to create what is called Fast Wide SCSI, which can send data at 40 MB/sec.

Data on a SCSI-2 bus won't travel any faster than the 40 MB/sec achieved with Fast Wide SCSI, and this speed is probably more than most people need on their desktop. However, you'll really appreciate this rapid transfer rate when you get into tasks such as full-motion digital video (for editing movies) and large-scale computer networks. In fact, in such demanding SCSI applications, you're likely to find that even Fast Wide SCSI isn't enough and you'll need even more speed. Don't worry—help is on the way with SCSI-3 (though it's a bit delayed in traffic).

SCSI-3 Is on Its Way from the ANSI Committee

Throughout the short history of SCSI, there has always been a new SCSI standard on the way, and today is no different. Proposals are currently before the X3T10 committee for the next generation of SCSI, called SCSI-3. For several reasons, including size and flexibility, SCSI-3 is being partitioned into a family of 16 standards. These standards will be used as building blocks, much like communications standards, to create various combinations of SCSI-3, including serial versions. And, although the SCSI-3 standards have yet to be officially approved, you may even notice a bunch of devices claiming to include SCSI-3 features cropping up on store shelves.

Fast-20 SCSI, also marketed as Ultra SCSI or DoubleSpeed SCSI, may be the feature most commonly found with SCSI-3 devices. Fast-20 SCSI is basically an extension of the Fast SCSI found in the SCSI-2 specification, except that Fast-20 SCSI promises even higher data rates. Fast-20 SCSI will provide 20 MB/sec over the 8-bit bus or 40 MB/sec over the 16-bit Wide SCSI bus. This new draft standard is referred to as Fast-20.

NOTE *Unfortunately, as with everything in real life, speed has its price. The high data transfer rates promised by Fast-20 SCSI will limit the SCSI bus length to 1.5 meters for 8 devices or 3.0 meters for 4 devices, and will require even higher quality cables.*

Another hot topic on the SCSI-3 table is SCAM (SCSI configured "automagically"). SCAM, along with Intel/Microsoft's Plug-and-Play, will allow users to plug in SCSI interface cards and attach SCSI devices without worrying about jumpers, switches, wheels, or any other kind of configuration option. All configuration options will be handled by the computer—no more headaches.

Perhaps SCSI-3's most notable addition to SCSI is its introduction of support for a new breed of very high-speed serial devices. The existing standards for serial communication, such as RS-232, are much too slow for hard disks and other SCSI devices. In general, parallel data transfer is faster than serial, but not in the case of SCSI-3. SCSI-3 defines both serial and parallel communication, and its serial mode is so fast that it's even faster than SCSI's parallel mode. Today's silicon electronics can operate at speeds approaching 300 MHz (megahertz, or cycles per second), and SCSI-3 will make use of every bit of it. In fact, expensive gallium arsenide chips offer speeds in excess of 1 GHz (1,000 MHz). That's blazing speed compared with the 5 MHz clock rate of SCSI-1.

But the way in which SCSI-3 will allow for this high-speed serial communication is still up in the air. Three interfaces are competing to provide the link between the new high-speed SCSI-3 serial devices: Fibre Channel, P1394 (Apple's FireWire), and IBM's SSA. All of these interfaces offer from 100 to 200 Mb/sec (megabit per second) transfer rate (as opposed to the 5 MB/sec parallel transfer rate of SCSI-2), and each promises quick and easy cabling between devices and the SCSI interface card via small, keyed connectors. (For those of you who struggle with SCSI device connections, this is sure to be a welcome improvement.)

Going serial also means that cables will have fewer wires (or fibers, as the case may be). Rather than the monstrous 50- and 68-wire cables required by parallel SCSI implementations, serial SCSI will only need 6 (or fewer).

For the latest information about SCSI developments, for SCSI standards, and for the latest on SCSI-3, you can call the X3T10 committee's BBS at 719-574-0424, or write to Global Engineering Documents, 15 Inverness Way, Englewood, Colorado 80112 (800-854-7179).

TABLE 1.1 SCSI Versus IDE and EIDE

	SCSI	IDE/Enhanced IDE
Computers available	PC, Macintosh, Sun, etc.	PC only
Devices available	Hard disk, CD-ROM, scanner, printer, tape backup, optical, WORM, etc.	Hard disk, CD-ROM (enhanced IDE only)
Maximum number of devices	7 (regular SCSI) 15 (16-bit Wide SCSI) 31 (32-bit Wide SCSI)	2 (IDE) 4 (enhanced IDE or special drivers)
External device support	Yes	No
Data transfer rate	5 MB/sec (SCSI-1) 10 MB/sec (Fast SCSI) 40 MB/sec (Fast Wide SCSI)	3 MB/sec (IDE) 3.3 MB/sec (enhanced IDE)
Multitasking support	Yes	No
Error checking	Yes	No

THERE ARE MANY REASONS TO CHOOSE SCSI OVER COMPETING INTERFACES

If you're reading this book, you've probably either already purchased SCSI hardware, you're thinking about it, or you're just wondering what SCSI is. But have you thought about why you should use SCSI and not some other standard, such as the mass-market IDE or EIDE? Well, take a look at the benefits SCSI brings, as well as the pitfalls, as shown in Table 1.1.

SCSI Is Truly a Multiplatform Interface

As you can see in the first row of Table 1.1, SCSI is a cross-platform interface. As such, it is a highly flexible interface. In most cases, a SCSI device taken from one type of computer system (like a Mac or a PC) will work on a completely different one without your having to modify it in any way. As long as your computer has a SCSI controller card, you simply buy a SCSI drive, as opposed to a Mac or a PC drive. In contrast, this is definitely not the case with IDE and many other kinds of drives. PC IDE drives will not work with your Mac. When buying a drive for an IDE system, you must buy an IDE drive for PCs or compatibles.

NOTE *SCSI's ability to swap peripherals between platforms comes in particularly handy if you've got both a Mac and a PC at home or in the office. As long as the PC is SCSI-based, you'll be able to share SCSI devices—whether hard drive, CD-ROM, or the like—between both systems. Of course, while you can interchange the drives, you won't necessarily be able to read the data on the drive, since Macs and PCs format the drive differently and their file structure is different.*

SCSI is widely supported by many operating systems and platforms, including Macintosh, UNIX, DOS, Windows, Windows NT, OS/2, and a variety of other operating systems. Most of these operating systems even have built-in support for SCSI, which makes it even easier to use, install, and swap SCSI devices between all operating systems.

SCSI Supports More Devices Than IDE

The second row of Table 1.1 compares the devices supported by SCSI with devices supported by IDE. You'll notice that the list for SCSI is considerably longer than the list for IDE. In fact, IDE and EIDE support only hard drives and CD-ROM drives. SCSI can basically support any device you throw at it.

SCSI Is Much More Expandable Than IDE

SCSI offers efficient expandability. As you can see in the third row of Table 1.1, if you have a SCSI-based system, you'll be able to connect up to seven devices to one interface card, as opposed to a maximum of four if you have EIDE. These seven devices could be any combination of hardware, such as hard disks, CD-ROMs, tape drives, image scanners, or even printers. If seven devices aren't enough, just add a second SCSI adapter, and you're ready for the next seven devices. Or, with SCSI-2, you can connect 15 devices (with 16-bit Wide SCSI) or 31 (with 32-bit Wide SCSI). Imagine the daisy chaining! We're talking about a real system of devices here.

NOTE *In fact, as of this writing there are almost no 32-bit SCSI host adapters, and it's doubtful that 32 devices will work electrically on single-ended buses. We'd probably need differential to make this work.*

SCSI Is Fast and Getting Faster

Although SCSI isn't always as fast as simpler interfaces (like IDE or EIDE) when using one hard disk, it leaves them behind when attaching several drives. (That's the reason network servers use SCSI drives—they provide the flaming speeds required by heavy network use.) Also, since SCSI supports multitasking environments, multitasking operating systems such as UNIX, Windows, and OS/2 can realize better performance with SCSI than with IDE or EIDE. Only SCSI devices will multitask in multitasking operating systems. IDE and EIDE devices are single-tasking, so although they'll work fine in a multitasking environment, they won't multitask. (See Appendix B, "The All-Platform Technical Reference," for more detailed comparisons of IDE, EIDE, and SCSI.)

SCSI Supports External Devices

Unlike IDE or EIDE, SCSI supports devices connected to your computer externally. With IDE or EIDE, all drives that you connect must fit inside your computer. This presents some limitations. If you're using IDE or EIDE and you've maxed out your computer case's expandability with something like two floppy drives, a CD-ROM, tape backup, and a hard disk, you won't have room to add anything else. On the other hand, with SCSI you can buy devices that are housed in their own cases and simply connect them to the back of your computer with a SCSI cable, so you won't need a refrigerator-sized computer case and you're system's expandability is much greater.

SCSI Offers Built-In Error Checking

Unlike IDE or EIDE, SCSI offers built-in error checking. This capability ensures that data transferred through your system from card to device and back will be error-free. (We'll talk more about SCSI's error-checking ability in Chapter 2.)

SCSI Is Easy to Use

And finally, believe it or not, SCSI is easy to use. (It must be if it's used on Macs, right?) For example, when you connect a new SCSI hard disk, you don't have to worry about all the things that plague many IDE hard disk installations, such as the number of heads, cylinders, and sectors per track in your hard drive. Even the computer doesn't worry about such details. The SCSI interface takes care of all that. In essence, all you have to do is plug it in. And Windows 95 and OS/2 *Warp* make this installation even easier with their built-in detection of SCSI cards and devices.

BUT SCSI ISN'T A PANACEA

While SCSI has a tremendous amount to offer its users, it's not without its drawbacks. You should be aware of these drawbacks before going out to buy a SCSI system.

For one, SCSI interface cards aren't all that easy to install. If you've ever had problems installing interface cards before, SCSI is no less a challenge. While we'll help you through as much of the installation as possible in this book, the best way to minimize the installation problems is to look for Plug-and-Play SCSI interface cards that configure themselves. (Or, have your dealer do the installation.) If you have Microsoft's Windows 95 you should look to its built-in tools for step-by-step help with the installation of your SCSI card. Similarly, IBM's OS/2 *Warp*'s installation program scans for the most popular SCSI host adapters and installs them automatically.

Another drawback to SCSI is the cost of the interface card. Although you can pick up interface cards for less than $50, the performance you'll get out of them often isn't worth the trouble. To really take advantage of SCSI you need a "real" SCSI card, and it's going to cost upwards of $100, depending on its capabilities. At a minimum, we consider a real SCSI card to be one with built-in BIOS, which has the ability to boot the system from a SCSI hard disk. Cheap cards do not have built-in BIOS, which means you'll have to boot your system from a floppy disk or non-SCSI hard disk.

As of this writing, SCSI devices also cost more than IDE or EIDE devices. In order to be flexible, fast, and easy to use, SCSI devices need more built-in intelligence than simple IDE devices. However, the difference in prices is shrinking because of the competition posed by EIDE. When you consider the benefits of SCSI (speed, flexibility, and expandability), the slightly higher cost of SCSI is easily justifiable.

NOTE *SCSI is for you if, like us, you struggle to have a useful computer without upgrading every six months. SCSI devices tend to be used longer than any others. Since the interface isn't changing so often, a lot of SCSI disks from as far back as 1988 are still in use, whereas other early standards for drives from the same period in time were generally replaced with SCSI or IDE disks. And, unlike IDE- or EIDE-based systems, you're not likely to run out of bus slots with a SCSI system. This means that you can easily add a second or even a third hard disk to your system and still have room to add more devices to the SCSI bus.*

Finally, in order to use SCSI effectively, you'll need some basic knowledge of SCSI technology. You need to know how to install and configure the interface card (if it isn't Plug-and-Play), how to set device IDs, how to terminate the SCSI bus, how to use drivers, and how to optimize your system and keep it healthy. We'll show you how to handle all of these issues in later chapters.

THERE ARE A VARIETY OF SCSI DEVICES

One of the great advantages of using SCSI is that it gives you the flexibility of connecting a variety of devices, not just hard disks. (Appendix A, "SCSI Sources," is a directory of manufacturers that produce SCSI hardware and where you can get more information about specific models of devices.) Following are descriptions of the many devices you can connect to a SCSI system.

Hard Disks

Of all the types of hardware you can connect via SCSI, hard disks are by far the most common. Until recently, hard disks were generally mounted inside the computer, enclosed in a sealed case. Because the platters or media inside the drive were fixed to it, they were called fixed disks. Widely available removable media drives, such as those from SyQuest, allow you to not only take them with you but also lock them up for safekeeping.

The benefit of using SCSI hard disks is that they are available in larger capacities than the IDE hard disks used in most PCs today. Although recent developments have made one gigabyte (1 GB) hard disks available for IDE, SCSI hard disks are now available with capacities of up to 9 GB, and even bigger disks are on the way. (One GB is equivalent to 1,024 MB.)

Tape Backups

Tape backups can easily be attached to the SCSI bus. Tape backups come in various types and are used to store large amounts of data, in case something happens to the computer's hard disks. The low cost and large storage capability of tape cartridges makes them ideal for backup and archiving purposes.

Quarter-Inch Cartridge (QIC)

Quarter-inch cartridges are the most common type of tape backup used on PCs. They are so named because the tape used in the first cartridges was one quarter of an inch wide. QIC tapes can hold from 40 MB to as much as 1.3 GB. QIC-150 and QIC-525 are common QIC drives. Tape drives that adhere to these standards are available with SCSI interfaces and can be used with other SCSI devices.

NOTE *The minicartridge family recently received some new high-capacity standards such as QIC-555. These new standards for 3.5-inch drives, with capacities of up to 3 GB, should greatly increase the use of minicartridge systems.*

Digital Audio Tape (DAT)

Digital audio tape is well known in the music industry for recording digital audio. In the PC world, the DAT system provides huge data storage capacity in a small form. For example, 4mm DDS (digital data storage) standard DAT tapes hold from 1.3 GB to 2 GB and cost one-third the price of QIC tapes per megabyte. The newer DDS-2 tapes store up to 4 GB on one tape.

8mm Tape

The 8mm tape, similar to the tape used in camcorders, is now used for recording data. It provides slightly more storage capability than DAT, coming in at a whopping capacity of 2 GB to 5 GB per cartridge!

Optical Drives

Optical drives are so named because they use light (optics) in the form of a laser to read and write data. Optical drives can store more data than magnetic drives such as hard disks. Several different types of optical drives may be attached to a SCSI bus.

CD-ROM Drive

CD-ROM (compact disk read-only memory) made its mark in the industry with the birth of multimedia, due to the large amounts of storage required for audio and video data. CD-ROMs are manufactured in the same way as audio CDs and are designed to be read-only. As a result, they are used to distribute programs and data files, not to back up your hard disk. CD-ROMs can store up to 650 MB of data.

CD-ROM Writer

CD-ROM writers take the read-only out of CD-ROM. By using a special kind of CD called a CD-R (compact disk recordable), the CD-ROM writer makes a CD-ROM by burning the data onto the disk using a high-powered laser. CD-ROM writers are also referred to as CD-ROM burners or CD-ROM mastering drives. The data can only be burned on once. You can't erase or overwrite data on CD-R, but data can be written to it in multiple "sessions." The best-known example for this is Kodak's PhotoCD system.

Magneto-Optical (MO) Drive

Magneto-optical drives are a cross between an optical drive and a hard disk. MO drives read data just like a CD-ROM drive, and some are as fast as hard drives. While the fastest MO drive access time—around 30 ms (milliseconds)—is slower than the average hard disk access times (around 15 ms or less), the transfer rates of MOs are comparable to hard disks.

Magneto-opticals use a high-powered laser to write to the disk. The laser heats up the surface of the disk and, once the disk material is hot enough, a magnetic field changes the heated material so it either absorbs or reflects light.

Magneto-optical disks have several advantages over hard disks: their storage space is nearly limitless and expandable for relatively little money; the disks themselves last for a very long time (about 30 years, or nearly 100,000 rewrites); and data stored on magneto-opticals lasts for several decades.

Write-Once Read-Many (WORM) Drives

WORM drives are similar to CD-ROM writers. They burn data onto the disks and cannot be erased or overwritten. WORM drives are slightly cheaper than MO drives, but because the disks can't be reused, they are more expensive in the end and used only for specific archival purposes.

Printers and Scanners

Storage devices aren't the only devices that work with SCSI. Even printers and scanners are available with SCSI interfaces.

Printers

Printers with SCSI interfaces aren't commonly used now, but SCSI should get a bigger market share in the high-end market segment. The amount of data transferred to the printer increases with color images, so a bi-directional high-speed interface, like SCSI's, is very desirable. High-end PostScript printers tend to have a SCSI interface for attaching hard disks as font, macro, or cache memory that is used by the printer when printing large files with a variety of typefaces.

Image Scanners

Some of the most common SCSI devices are image scanners. The amount of image data increases dramatically with color depth (the number of colors in the image), so SCSI is the device of choice for most scanner manufacturers, compared to standard parallel and serial interfaces. In fact, it's difficult to find non-SCSI full-page scanners. Although some are around, they're generally too slow for professional scanning.

CONNECTING DEVICES

Now that you know a little bit about the history of SCSI, the benefits of SCSI, and the kinds of hardware you can connect to your computer with SCSI, it's time to get this adventure rolling. In the next two chapters, you'll get your hands dirty as you learn more about the SCSI bus and how to connect SCSI devices to it.

2

S C S I   A N A T O M Y

Before venturing deep into the heart of connecting and configuring SCSI devices, you should know some of the basics of SCSI technology. Once we've cut through the morass of techno-babble, we hope you'll find that the principles behind the way SCSI works are actually quite easy to understand.

SCSI Devices Can Be Initiators or Targets

Although there are a number of different kinds of SCSI devices—such as interface cards, hard disks, CD-ROMs, and scanners—all of them fall into two fundamental categories: initiators and targets. The initiator device is also called the host, and it starts or initiates device-to-device communication. The target device receives the communication from the initiator and responds. For example, when reading a file from a SCSI hard disk, the SCSI interface card (the initiator) requests data from the SCSI hard disk, and the hard disk (the target) responds to the request by sending the data. This is the most common initiator-target interaction in a SCSI system.

In general, the SCSI interface card will be the initiator on the bus. Your other devices may be either targets or initiators, depending upon whether they're sending or receiving signals.

SCSI peripherals can act both as initiators and as targets. For example, when you copy data from one SCSI hard disk to another, the disk that holds the data to be copied (the source disk) acts as the initiator, and the hard disk that receives the file is the target.

SCSI systems can have up to eight devices connected in a daisy chain (16-bit Wide SCSI can have up to sixteen devices). While these devices can be any combination of initiators and targets, at least one must be an initiator and one a target in order to have a working system. Typically, a system will have one interface card and one or more peripheral devices, such as hard disks and CD-ROM drives.

SCSI IDs and LUNs Identify Individual SCSI Devices

If you have a system with only one initiator and one target, you have a pretty simple system—no confusion here. But what happens if you have one initiator and more than one target? How do you tell one target from another? For example, if you've hooked three hard disks—E, F, and G—onto the bus and you want to talk to F, how do you send the command to F, bypassing E and stopping before G?

This is a challenging problem but not one without a resolution. SCSI's answer is to give each device on the SCSI bus, including the SCSI interface, some kind of unique identification called a SCSI ID. These IDs, or addresses, are a lot like postal or E-mail addresses, which identify each of us or each destination uniquely so that the mail (whether snail-mail or electronic) gets to the right place. Without this identification, there would be no way to know where to send commands and data along the bus and no way to direct signals to a specific device.

Every SCSI device is assigned its own unique SCSI ID number. For example, in our example above, hard disk E might get ID 2, hard disk F might have ID 3, and hard disk G could get ID 4. Since SCSI-1 and SCSI-2 allow you to attach up to 8 SCSI devices on the bus, you can have 8 possible SCSI IDs. These SCSI IDs range from 0 to 7, counting 0 as the first number. Note that 16-bit Wide SCSI allows a maximum of 16 devices, ranging from 0 to 15 and 32-bit Wide SCSI allows for 32 devices, ranging from 0 to 31.

Ah, the Mysteries of LUNs

If you've been working with SCSI, then you've probably already encountered LUNs (logical unit numbers). LUNs can really make some people freak out, but don't fret. They're similar to SCSI IDs in that they identify SCSI devices. The difference between LUNs and SCSI IDs, though, is that LUNs represent devices within devices; they're divisions within IDs. The way this works in practice is that every device ID, from 0 to 7, can have up to 8 LUNs, also numbered 0 to 7, for a total of 8 subdevices or partitions within the IDs. LUNs give SCSI a certain added flexibility.

If you want to have more than eight devices on a SCSI bus, you might consider using Wide SCSI, which allows up to 16 devices (since it uses a 16-bit bus instead of regular SCSI's 8-bit bus). But that's not your only alternative. You could also have several devices respond to a single device ID but have each device respond to a different LUN for that ID. So, for example, three hard drives, labeled E, F, and G, could be put together into one drive case and assigned SCSI ID 2, but each drive would have a different LUN number: drive E might be LUN 0, drive F might be LUN 1, and drive G might be LUN 2.

THE SCSI BUS ALLOWS COMMUNICATION BETWEEN YOUR COMPUTER AND YOUR SCSI DEVICES

Once you have an initiator and a target settled, you have to provide a means for communicating between them—to send commands and data. Cables are the answer here, and when you connect a cable between the two devices you provide a bus or pathway between them. This pathway is the SCSI bus, and it is the communication channel between all SCSI devices. The SCSI bus begins at the first device on one end of the bus and ends at the last device on the bus, usually the SCSI interface card. We'll go into more detail about using connectors and cabling in Chapter 3.

A SCSI bus with one initiator and one target might look like this:

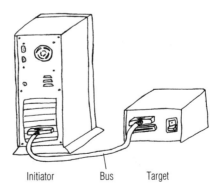

Initiator   Bus   Target

FIGURE 2.1   *A typical SCSI bus.*

Types of SCSI Buses

SCSI buses come in two physical types: single-ended and differential. The basic difference between the two is that on a single-ended bus the devices communicate over one set of wires while on a differential SCSI bus the devices communicate over two sets of wires. When compared with differential SCSI, single-ended communication is relatively inexpensive and it's fast over short distances. Differential SCSI is more expensive than single-ended SCSI, but it allows your system to communicate over longer distances.

Single-Ended SCSI Is Cheap and Fast over Short Distances

Most SCSI systems use a single-ended bus, which is a bus with only one set of wires. Single-ended buses are the most economical way to communicate between devices, because the electronics used to send and receive the signals are relatively inexpensive. Single-ended buses provide high-speed communication for short distances, ranging from up to six meters for regular SCSI (5 MHz) or three meters for Fast SCSI (10 MHz). The length of the single-ended bus cable for Fast SCSI is shorter than that for regular SCSI, because Fast SCSI is more error-prone than regular SCSI. The longer the cable, the more chance of introducing errors into the signal, so the Fast SCSI bus cable is kept short.

Differential SCSI Allows Communication over Longer Distances

When you want to go beyond the six-meter maximum distance of single-ended SCSI, you risk encountering signal loss and noise problems due to the extended length of the cable. Differential SCSI offers an alternative to single-ended SCSI, when you want a system to communicate over greater distances. The differential SCSI bus carries commands and data over two sets of wires, taking the difference between each set of signals (see the box that follows for more information on this process). Differential SCSI extends the maximum bus cable length to 25 meters.

NOTE *Single-ended SCSI is based on sending a single signal, while differential SCSI takes the difference between two signals. As a result, the two cannot coexist. You must have single-ended SCSI devices on a single-ended SCSI bus and differential SCSI devices on a differential SCSI bus. You cannot have single-ended SCSI devices connected to differential SCSI devices.*

NOTE *Regardless of whether you use a single-ended or differential bus, make sure that you maintain a minimum of 10 cm between devices in order to prevent signal degradation.*

The Differences Between Single-Ended and Differential SCSI

Table 2.1 illustrates the differences between single-ended and differential SCSI by comparing a 50-pin cable for each. In the single-ended configuration, wires 26 through 50 carry signals between devices. Wires 1 through 25 are unused or ground. Since signals are present on only one set of wires, information is interpreted by the voltage (the strength of the signal) on the wire. Unfortunately, electrical noise from the outside world can cause the voltage to fluctuate, resulting in corrupted data.

In the differential configuration, information is sent simultaneously through two sets of wires. The information is interpreted by the *difference* in voltage between the wires, not the voltage of the signal on a single wire. When noise interferes with the signal in this bus configuration, both wires are disturbed equally. Since the noise on one wire is the same as the noise on the other wire and both are affected equally, the difference in voltage is zero. The result is that the device receives the information free of noise.

Don't worry about the details in Table 2-1, but notice that the wires in a single-ended bus are used for a different purpose than the wires in a differential bus. Remember, the two cannot coexist. You must have single-ended SCSI devices on a single-ended SCSI bus and differential SCSI devices on a differential SCSI bus. You cannot have single-ended SCSI devices connected to differential SCSI devices.

TABLE 2.1   Single-Ended Versus Differential SCSI 50-Pin Cables

Single-Ended				Differential			
1	GND	26	D0–	1	GND	26	GND
2	GND	27	D1–	2	D0+	27	D0–
3	GND	28	D2–	3	D1+	28	D1–
4	GND	29	D3–	4	D2+	29	D2–
5	GND	30	D4–	5	D3+	30	D3–
6	GND	31	D5–	6	D4+	31	D4–
7	GND	32	D6–	7	D5+	32	D5–
8	GND	33	D7–	8	D6+	33	D6–
9	GND	34	DPAR–	9	D7+	34	D7–
10	GND	35	GND	10	DPAR+	35	DPAR–
11	GND	36	GND	11	DIFFSENS	36	GND
12	RESERVED	37	RESERVED	12	RESERVED	37	RESERVED
13	OPEN	38	TERMPWR	13	TERMPWR	38	TERMPWR
14	RESERVED	39	RESERVED	14	RESERVED	39	RESERVED
15	GND	40	ATN–	15	ATN+	40	ATN–
16	GND	41	ATN–	16	GND	41	GND
17	GND	42	GND	17	BSY+	42	BSY–
18	GND	43	BSY–	18	ACK+	43	ACK–
19	GND	44	ACK–	19	RST+	44	RST–
20	GND	45	RST–	20	MSG+	45	MSG–
21	GND	46	MSG–	21	SEL+	46	SEL–
22	GND	47	SEL–	22	C/D+	47	C/D–
23	GND	48	C/D–	23	REQ+	48	REQ–
24	GND	49	REQ–	24	I/O+	49	I/O–
25	GND	50	I/O–	25	GND	50	GND

CABLE SPECIFICATIONS

The most common internal cable is the 50-conductor (which means it has 50 wires) flat-ribbon cable, which typically uses 28 AWG (the wire's gauge or diameter) wires, with 0.050 inches between the centers of each wire. Typical free-air characteristic impedances for this type of cable run about 105 ohms.

Externally shielded 8-bit SCSI cables typically contain 25 twisted pairs (50-conductor) with an overall foil/braid composite shield. Typical free-air characteristic impedances for this type of cable have run about 65 to 80 ohms. Higher, single-ended, round-shielded cable impedances of 90 to 100 ohms are becoming available and should be strongly considered.

The SCSI-2 specification requires that systems with the fast synchronous data transfer option use cables consisting of 26 AWG or 28 AWG conductors. Characteristic impedance is measured between 90 and 132 ohms. In addition, signal attenuation should be 0.095 dB maximum per meter at 5 MHz. The pair-to-pair propagation delay delta should not exceed 0.2 ns per meter. Finally, the DC resistance is specified as 0.23 ohms maximum per meter at 20 degrees C.

SCSI CABLES AND CONNECTORS

Cables are the physical makeup of the SCSI bus. As a result, they become the lifeline of the entire system. To ensure that the correct cables are used to build the bus, SCSI-2 and SCSI-3 define minimum requirements for the number of wires needed as well as the electrical properties of the cable. SCSI systems can utilize cabling both inside and outside the device cabinet (or case). Internal cables are typically flat, unshielded ribbon cables, while external cables are generally round and shielded.

Tables 2.2 and 2.3 summarize the number of wires, maximum transfer rate, maximum length, and type of cables for the different SCSI standards.

Table 2.2 gives a list of the SCSI standards in the first column, the bus width or the number of bits transferred simultaneously on the bus in the second column, the maximum transfer rate through the bus in

TABLE 2.2 SCSI Cable Reference Table

Standard	Bus Width	Maximum Transfer Rate (MB/sec)	Cable Type	Number of Conductors
SCSI-1	8-bit	4	Not specified	Not specified
SCSI-2	8-bit	5	A	50
	16-bit	10	B	68
SCSI-3	16-bit	10	P	68
	32-bit	20	P and Q	68 and 68

TABLE 2.3 **SCSI Bus Length Specifications**

Bus Type	Property	Single-Ended	Differential
SCSI-1	Maximum bus length	6 meters	25 meters
SCSI-2	Maximum bus length	6 meters	25 meters
Fast SCSI-2	Maximum bus length	3 meters	25 meters
All	Maximum stub length	0.1 meters	0.2 meters
	Minimum stub spacing	0.3 meters	n/a

the third column, the type of cable in the fourth column (the letters are the names for the cable type), and finally, in the last column, the number of wires (also referred to as conductors) in each cable. Note that for SCSI-3 32-bit, you need to use two cables, P and Q, each with 68 wires.

Table 2.3 lists the maximum and minimum lengths for different parts of the bus for each SCSI standard. The table is fairly straightforward. We didn't include SCSI-3 here since it's not an official standard and we don't know what its maximum length will be. The stub is a section of cable that runs between the device and the bus.

TERMINATING THE SCSI BUS

If there's one aspect of SCSI that always raises the hair on even the wisest of technicians, that honor must go, unequivocally, to properly terminating the SCSI bus. This section covers the types of termination. How to terminate the bus will be discussed further in Chapter 3.

Since the SCSI bus is a chain of devices rather than a loop, the two ends of the bus must be capped off or terminated. Every wire has a specific impedance or, in English, resistance to the passing of electrical signals. The SCSI bus, too, has a specific impedance; but when the signals reach the end of the cables that make up the bus, they encounter the air, which has very high impedance and acts as a wall of infinite resistance. (That's why the electricity doesn't jump out of your wall outlet—the air keeps it in.) The only problem with the high impedance at the end of the bus for electrical signals is that any signal coming down the bus is reflected back in the other direction once it hits this barrier. (While this is good in racquetball, it's bad in SCSI.) That's where termination comes in.

Termination is an electrical requirement that must be met in order to prevent the reflection of signals when they reach the ends of the bus. You terminate the bus by attaching a circuit, the terminator, to the physical ends of the SCSI bus. The terminator provides an impedance that matches the cable's, thereby preventing the signal from bouncing back. The terminators use power, and the power to operate them comes from the SCSI interface card by way of the termination power (TERMPWR) wire on the bus. (You'll see this wire in the Cabling and Connector Pin Out diagrams in Appendix B.)

There are three methods for terminating the bus: passive, active, and forced perfect termination.

Passive Termination

Passive termination is the oldest method of termination, defined in the specs for SCSI-1. Basically, a passive terminator sits on the bus to minimize reflections at the end of the cable.

The terminator doesn't really do any work to regulate power for termination; it relies on the interface card to provide steady power. A passive terminator simply provides an impedance that's close to the impedance of the cable.

Active Termination

Active termination works to control the impedance at the end of the SCSI bus by using a voltage regulator, not just the power supplied by the interface card. Because it is active, regulating the power that it gets from the interface card, active termination is more stable than passive termination.

Forced Perfect Termination (FPT)

Forced perfect termination (FPT) is the most complex of the terminators, going beyond merely stabilizing the power applied to the termina-

ACTIVE TERMINATION IN DETAIL

In order to overcome any fluctuations in the TERMPWR supplied by the host adapter, the preferred termination for 10 MHz Fast SCSI buses is active termination. This type of termination is known as Alternative-2 in SCSI-2 and uses only a 110-ohm resistor on each signal line connected to a voltage regulator. This regulator actively adjusts its output to maintain 2.85 V, thereby offering partial immunity to voltage drops on the TERMPWR line.

By using 110-ohm resistors, the terminator's impedance is a much closer match to the impedance of the cable (105 to 108 ohms) than passive termination (132 ohms). A closer impedance match between termi-nators and cables minimizes reflections at the ends of the bus to reduce data errors.

The lower resistor values in the terminator also result in higher pull-down currents. As a result, actively terminated buses don't suffer from rising "staircase" waveforms commonly seen on weakly driven transmission lines.

Studies by Kurt Chan and Gordon Matheson, both of Hewlett-Packard, have shown that mixing termination types will yield better performance than using passive termination alone. Wherever possible, use SCSI devices that employ active termination.

tor. It can actually alter its impedance to compensate for variations in impedance among many different cables, devices, and terminators. It is usually used in high-speed SCSI systems that have many different devices, cables, and terminator types. The complexity of such a system can introduce many impedance mismatches that degrade the signals sent through the bus. FPT actively compensates for these impedance variations by means of diode switching and biasing to force the impedance of the cable to match each device.

PARITY CHECKING IS A SIMPLE FORM OF ERROR CHECKING, BUT YOU CAN ONLY USE IT IF ALL OF YOUR DEVICES SUPPORT IT

When working with SCSI systems, you'll probably encounter the term *parity checking*. Parity checking is built into all SCSI-2 devices and it will be part of all future SCSI devices. It's not always present in older, SCSI-1 devices, because parity checking was an option in the SCSI-1 specification. So, if you have a SCSI-1 device, be sure to check your manual to see whether your device supports parity checking.

In short, parity checking is a simple and fast way of detecting errors in the data sent through the SCSI bus by checking the number of 1's carried in a byte (eight bits) of data along with a reference bit called the parity bit. The parity bit is set so that you always have either an even or odd number of 1's. There are two types of parity, even and odd. In even parity, there is always an even number of bits set to 1, including the

When a device receives a byte of data, it can check the data for errors by counting the number of bits that are set to 1. Since SCSI uses odd parity, the number of bits set to 1, including the parity bit, must always be odd. For example, the decimal value 35 in binary format is 00100011. Looking at this byte, you see a total of three 1's—an odd number of 1's. Therefore, the parity bit for this byte is 0 so that the total number of 1's is still odd. The data actually sent is then 001000110. The trailing 0 is the parity bit. When the receiving device gets this data, it counts the number of 1's in the nine data bits, sees that the total is odd, and accepts it as correct.

If the number of 1's received isn't odd, the device knows that an error has occurred in the data transmission, and it asks to have the data sent again. However, parity checking is not foolproof. As you can see in the last rows of Table 2.4 and Table 2.5, as long as there is an odd number of 1's, it doesn't matter if one, three, five, seven, or nine 1's are received—an error is not generated. This is definitely a limitation of parity checking. But because it's fast and inexpensive to implement, it provides a satisfactory level of security. IDE and EIDE don't offer any error checking of the data that's transmitted over the cable.

TABLE 2.4 Odd Parity Checking (Odd Number of 1's)

Data Value (8 bits)	Number of 1's Sent	Odd Parity Bit	Data Received (9 bits, includes parity bit)	Number of 1's Received	Error?
00100011	3 (odd)	0	001000110	3 (odd)	No
00100011	3 (odd)	0	001001110	4 (even)	Yes
00100011	3 (odd)	0	001011110	5 (odd)	No

TABLE 2.5 Even Parity Checking (Even Number of 1's)

Data Value (8 bits)	Number of 1's Sent	Even Parity Bit	Data Received (9 bits, includes parity bit)	Number of 1's Received	Error?
00100001	2 (even)	0	001000010	2 (even)	No
00100001	2 (even)	0	001001010	3 (odd)	Yes
00100001	2 (even)	0	001011010	4 (even)	No

parity bit. In odd parity, there is always an odd number of bits set to 1, including the parity bit.

When you send eight bits of data, you count how many ones there are, and you set the parity bit to either 0 or 1, depending on the type of parity being used. See the box "How Parity Checking Works" for a detailed explanation of setting the parity bit. When the target receives the data, it counts the number of bits that are set to 1. If the number of 1's is odd when it should be even or vice versa, the target knows that there's been a data error, and it can request that the device send the signal again.

SCSI uses odd parity, which means that the byte of data always contains an odd number of bits set to 1. If there is an even number of 1's, then something went wrong with the data transfer. The parity bit is included with each byte of data that is transferred. Thus, rather than sending eight bits of data with each byte, nine bits are sent. The ninth bit is the parity bit.

While parity checking is simple and effective, whether you'll be able to use it depends on the capabilities of all of your SCSI devices. All devices on the bus must be able to perform parity checking in order for you to enable it. In fact, if even only one device lacks support for parity checking, you must turn parity checking off for all of the others. Otherwise, the one device that doesn't know how to do the check won't understand the extra data, and your system won't work properly.

NOTE *Parity checking was optional under the old SCSI-1 standard but is required of all SCSI-2 devices. If you're unsure if all your devices support parity checking, check the manual that came with each device. Only old SCSI-1 devices may lack this feature.*

YOUR SCSI DEVICES CAN COMMUNICATE EITHER SYNCHRONOUSLY OR ASYNCHRONOUSLY

SCSI devices have two basic methods of sending and receiving data between devices. These methods are called asynchronous and synchronous, and their names are a clue to their methods of operation. When communicating asynchronously, every byte of data sent from initiator to target must be acknowledged by the target with a kind of return receipt. While this is a safer way to communicate, it's also slower because the target needs to send a receipt and the initiator needs to receive it before another byte of data is sent, resulting in a delay in communication.

Synchronous communication, while also requiring acknowledgment, allows the initiator to send many bytes without having to wait first for an "acknowledge" from the target. So the initiator can send a whole stream of data and it doesn't matter when the stream of receipts comes back. Thus, synchronous communication is much faster than asynchronous, because instead of a delay between each byte sent, a flood of data is sent, followed by a delay until a flood of receipts comes back. So, in effect, you have one delay rather than a whole bunch of delays.

Asynchronous Communication Is
Slower but Safer Than Synchronous

SCSI devices communicate with the host adapter asynchronously by default. Asynchronous "handshaking" ensures that the data reaches the target. Because devices wait for a return receipt before sending another byte of data, communication between devices sending and receiving at different speeds is possible.

For example, let's say that your SCSI hard disk and SCSI floppy drive need to communicate with each other, but they send and receive data at very different speeds: your hard disk receives data much faster than your floppy drive can send it. If your floppy drive were to keep sending data to your hard disk, you shouldn't have a problem because there is no need for one device to catch up with the other. But reverse the situation, and you have a bottleneck. The hard disk dumps out data faster than the floppy disk can receive it, and the transfer falls apart.

Asynchronous transfer mode provides the solution for the latter case. With asynchronous transfers in place, the hard drive will wait for the floppy drive to send acknowledgment that it has received the data. Once the hard disk receives this acknowledgment, it will send its next byte of data, and so on. Thus, asynchronous negotiation allows for compatibility between devices despite variations in communication speed.

Because asynchronous transfer mode has this built-in "receipt requested" feature, it's also a great method for protecting the integrity of data, since data is only sent after the previous data has been received successfully. But due to the overhead of the return receipt process, the maximum speed over the SCSI bus is reduced when using asynchronous transfer.

Synchronous Communication
Is Faster Than Asynchronous

To speed up the communication process over the bus, synchronous transfer mode was included in the SCSI specification. Synchronous means that the initiator can issue multiple requests without waiting for the target to acknowledge each one. As a result, the overhead of transferring data is greatly reduced.

However, we have a new problem in the case of our hard disk sending data faster than the floppy disk can receive it. Since the acknowledgments don't have to be returned after every byte, how would the hard disk know that it's sending data too quickly for the floppy drive? Simple. Before a synchronous transfer is going to take place, both devices must agree on the maximum data transfer speed between them—a process called synchronous transfer negotiation. For example, a synchronous transfer from hard disk to floppy disk would be negotiated at the maximum speed of the floppy drive, since it's the slower device. Problem solved.

How do you know if your devices can communicate synchronously or only asynchronously? Choosing the wrong method could lead to trouble with devices that don't support synchronous transfers. Synchronous transfer negotiation takes care of this problem as well. Before a synchronous transfer is attempted, the devices negotiate whether to use synchronous or asynchronous transfer modes. If the target device can handle synchronous transfers, then synchronous transfer mode is used. Otherwise, asynchronous mode is used for maximum compatibility between the devices.

DISCONNECT/RECONNECT

Even though SCSI provides features such as synchronous transfer mode, Fast SCSI, and Wide SCSI to increase the performance of data transfers, all of its attempts to speed up communication are for naught if you have to wait for the device to be ready to send or receive the data. To overcome this problem of having to wait for devices to respond, SCSI offers an important feature referred to as disconnect/reconnect.

SCSI transfers data so fast that, compared to the speed with which signals can move across the bus, almost any device can become a time-waster. The simple fact is that operations such as positioning hard disk heads, fast-forwarding or rewinding tape cartridges, or changing CDs in a CD-ROM jukebox all become time-wasters. In cases such as these, where the hardware itself becomes the time-waster, the time-wasting device can remove itself from the bus and get out of the way of other SCSI devices that need to communicate. It basically gets off the bus to go about its work and stops holding up the train.

In the meantime, with the time-wasting device booted off the bus, other SCSI devices can go about their business performing various operations, like sending and receiving data, and so on. When the time-wasting device is ready, it is reconnected to the bus to perform its data transfer. Of course, at some point all of your devices will be time-wasters, depending on the operations that they're performing at any given moment.

NOTE *If one device gets booted off the bus because it's "busy," and you end up communicating with another device that also becomes busy (so that now it's wasting time), this new busy device will get booted off the bus, ad nauseum. This process will continue as devices bounce on and off the bus in different order. As the devices finish their "busy" operations, they get to transmit or receive their data, in a first-come, first-served fashion.*

Consider the case in which you request a file from your tape backup. Since the tape in the cartridge is very long, a considerable amount of time can be spent fast-forwarding or rewinding the tape to a specific position in order to read a file. Rather than tie up the SCSI bus while the tape drive whirrs away, the device can be disconnected from the bus so that you can still access hard drives and any other SCSI devices attached to the bus, thus preventing devices from hogging the communication channel. When the tape drive has found the file and is ready to send, it is reconnected to the bus and allowed to send the file. Whew—what a relief!

Disconnect/reconnect is particularly important in multitasking environments, where more than one program can send and request data at the same time. Since devices can disconnect during slow operations, other programs that are running concurrently within the multitasking environment don't have to wait to access other devices on the bus while one device is busy. When using disconnect/reconnect in a multitasking environment, the bus can multitask the use of devices for greater efficiency and ensure that the bus is not tied up waiting for a device to be ready.

NOTE   *While SCSI's disconnect/reconnect feature allows you to multitask the use of devices in multitasking environments (like Windows, OS/2, and UNIX), IDE and EIDE only support single-tasking because they lack any similar feature.*

How to Connect Your SCSI Hardware

Once you've amassed a bunch of SCSI hardware, you'll probably want to connect it to your computer (unless you're a collector). This chapter focuses on attaching SCSI devices to the computer. The discussion is general to all SCSI devices, regardless of the type of computer you own. If you own a PC and you have a SCSI controller you need to install, then to Chapter 4, which addresses PC-specific issues about plugging in and configuring a SCSI interface.

High-Quality Cables and Connectors Are Critical to the Health of Your SCSI System

Before you even begin to connect anything together, you should know a bit about cables. Cables carry the commands and data between SCSI devices and the computer. If you don't have good quality cables specifically meant for SCSI, you're liable to mess up the lifeline.

There is a direct relationship between the quality of your SCSI cables and the performance of your whole SCSI system. Cheap cables can cause data errors as well as performance loss. There is also a direct relationship between cable quality and price—high-quality cables often command a high price. Here is the best rule of thumb for buying cables:

If it seems like too good a deal, it is.

When setting out to buy SCSI cables, do a little shopping and compare prices. For example, companies such as Amphenol and Adaptec sell their own brand of high-quality SCSI cables. The "hole in the wall" clone shops and warehouse superstores carry low- to midgrade cables. These midgrade cables will probably be just fine if you're using SCSI-1 or SCSI-2. On the other hand, Fast SCSI-2 is extremely sensitive to cable quality and will not perform well at all if you're using low- to midgrade cables. If you're using Fast SCSI, Wide SCSI, or SCSI-3, be sure that you buy only cables certified for SCSI-2 or SCSI-3. You should find some note of that certification on the cable's packaging. If you don't find it, don't buy it.

The Shorter the Cable, the Better the Performance

Cable quality is not the only factor that will affect system performance. Because cables carry signals, cable length also impacts performance. Contrary to what you might think, in the case of SCSI cables, shorter is better. The reason is that signals weaken as they travel longer distances. Signals have energy and, as the signals pass through the wires in your system, they progressively lose some of that energy to the wires themselves. The farther the signals have to travel, the weaker they get. As signals weaken, your devices and your host adapter start to have problems interpreting them.

If you're having trouble imagining how signals lose their strength over greater distances, think of water rushing through a water pipe. As the water rushes through, it loses energy to the walls of the pipe and slows down. Eventually, if nothing pushes the water (thus adding energy to it), the water will slow down further until it stops. The strength of the signals that travel through your SCSI system is finite—the signals are created once and then they are sent or broadcast through the system.

How Long Can Your Cables Be?

According to the SCSI standards for SCSI-1 and SCSI-2 hardware, SCSI signals are good for a total bus length of only six meters (about 19 feet) when traveling through SCSI-compliant cables. If you're using Fast SCSI, the maximum cable length is cut in half to only three meters. Of course, if you're using poorer-quality cables, your signals will be even weaker and will break up much sooner. The bottom line is this: Whenever connecting a SCSI device, use the shortest possible cable for the situation; don't exceed a total of six meters for regular SCSI hard-

FINDING THE RIGHT CABLE

To ensure the best performance and data integrity of the SCSI bus, AMP Incorporated recommends the following specification in selecting cables. See Appendix A, "SCSI Sources," for a listing of cable manufacturers.

External SCSI cables should be made up of twisted pairs of 28 AWG wire encased in a shielded jacket. A-type cables consist of 25 twisted pairs; B, P, and Q consist of 34 twisted pairs. The single-ended impedance of the cable should be 80 ohms.

There are also four requirements, listed below, for the arrangement of conductors in the external cable. These requirements are compatible with all single-ended and differential SCSI implementations.

1. The conductors assigned to the single-ended REQ signal and its associated ground are a twisted pair located in the cable core. The conductors assigned to the single-ended ACK signal and its associated ground are a twisted pair located in the cable core. If there are more than three twisted pairs in the cable core, the REQ and ACK pairs should not be adjacent to each other.

2. All conductors assigned to single-ended data and parity signals and their associated grounds are twisted pairs located in the outer layer of the cable closest to the external shield.

3. The conductors assigned to +SIGNAL and −SIGNAL in a differential configuration are associated as twisted pairs.

4. Conductors are not to be connected together anywhere along the cable or within any connectors except in the case of P-to-A transition cables.

Internal SCSI cables can be either unshielded flat-ribbon or unshielded twisted-pair flat. Single-ended systems generally use flat-ribbon cable; this cable is available in 28 AWG with 0.050 inches between the centers of each wire or 30 AWG with 0.025 inches between centers. Normally, stranded wire is used for flexibility, but solid conductors can also be used for slightly higher impedance.

The SCSI standard recommends unshielded twisted-pair flat cables for use as internal cables in differential systems. The twisted-pair configuration helps to reduce cross talk between wires. Twisted-pair flat cables come in the same size/spacing as flat-ribbon cables and have flat sections spaced at intervals, such as every 12 inches, for attaching connectors.

ware and three meters for Fast SCSI. Remember, this is the total length of the bus, including all internal and external cables.

TIP   *As cables get longer, the signals weaken and are more susceptible to noise. Buying a longer cable than you need to do the job, because it seemed like a good value, is false economy. Use the shortest possible cable for the job.*

Going Farther Requires Repeaters
If you must extend the length of your SCSI bus, you will need to use repeaters. A repeater is placed at the end of the cable once the maximum bus length is reached. Then, another cable is attached to the repeater to extend the bus. The repeater picks up the signal from the host adapter and reproduces it on the next section of cable, thereby producing a clean, strong signal to the devices further down the bus.

Cables Come in Internal and External Flavors

When you shop for SCSI cables, you'll find two main types: internal and external. They're used just as you'd expect—the internal for internal connections; external for external hookups.

Internal Cables Look Like Ribbons

Internal SCSI cables look a lot like the cables used for any other internal computer storage device. They're also called ribbon cables because they look like ribbons. If you haven't seen an internal ribbon cable (because you haven't dared to open your computer), here's what a typical one might look like:

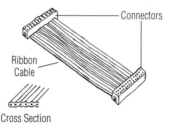

FIGURE 3.1   **A Typical Internal or Flat-Ribbon Cable, with a Cutaway View of a Cross Section**

As you can see, flat-ribbon cables consist of a flat bunch of wires all strung together and packaged in plastic like a ribbon. One edge of the cable has a colored stripe, most commonly red but sometimes some other color. This colored stripe indicates the first wire of the group, which becomes very important when you need to know how to orient the cable.

Differential SCSI systems use twisted-pair flat cables instead of the more common flat-ribbon cables to reduce interference between the wires. A twisted-pair flat cable looks similar to a flat-ribbon cable, except that each pair of wires is twisted together along the length of the cable. As a result, it looks more like a bunch of twisted wires than a bunch of straight wires. The ends of the cable aren't twisted so that the connectors can be attached to them, as you can see here:

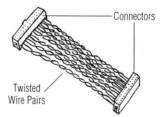

FIGURE 3.2   **Twisted-Pair Flat Cable**

External Cables Are Round and Thick

An external SCSI cable looks like the cables you probably have hanging from the back of your computer. They are long, round, and rather thick. You'll often find similar cables attached to your printer, looking something like this:

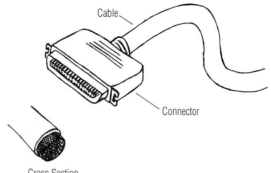

Cable

Connector

Cross Section

FIGURE 3.3 A Typical External SCSI Cable with a Cutaway View of a Cross Section

TIP *Since external SCSI cables are thick and heavy, they have screws or clips on their connectors to keep them firmly attached to your computer. Always make sure that the screws or clips are properly fastened. If they fall off while you're saving an important file, you won't be a happy camper.*

There are four common types of external cables, though they differ only by the number of wires that they contain. The four types are

- A cables (with 50 wires for regular and Fast SCSI)
- B cables (with 68 wires for 16- and 32-bit Wide and Fast Wide SCSI-2, used in conjunction with A cables)
- P and Q cables (with 68 wires for 16- and 32-bit Wide and Fast Wide SCSI-3, P used alone for 16-bit, P and Q used together for 32-bit)

You don't need to worry about the number of wires in the cables, though. When buying SCSI cables, you'll need to know the type of SCSI bus you're using (e.g., regular 8-bit, 16-bit Wide, 32-bit Wide) and the type of connector, not the wire count. At least you hope that the cable manufacturer used the correct cables for the connectors. Just kidding.

How to Tell Your Cable Connectors Apart

Connectors attach the cables to SCSI devices and to the computer. The connector is the plastic or metal end of the cable and it may have screws or clips. External and internal SCSI cables have different types of connectors, and it's important to recognize the basic differences so that you'll fit the right cable to the task. Here's how to identify the different types of connectors.

Internal Cables Usually Have Rectangular Connectors with Holes

Internal SCSI-1 and SCSI-2 cables usually have a rectangular plastic connector with 50 holes in it. The connectors typically look like this:

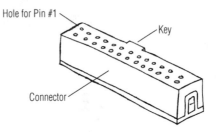

FIGURE 3.4 A Typical Internal SCSI Cable Connector

Wide SCSI cable connectors have 68 holes in them, otherwise they look similar to the connectors on internal SCSI-1 or SCSI-2 cables.

There Are Four Common Types of External SCSI Connectors and Some Not-So-Common Ones

There are four main types of external SCSI connectors: the 25-pin D-sub, the Centronics 50-pin, the high-density 50-pin, and the high-density 68-pin. The 25-pin connectors are used on Apple computers and low-end SCSI adapters; they can only support 8-bit SCSI. The 50-pin connectors are used with regular and Fast 8-bit SCSI. Most SCSI-1 devices have the Centronics version, while SCSI-2 devices have the high-density-style connectors. The 68-pin connectors are used with 16- and 32-bit Wide and Fast Wide SCSI in order to handle the additional signals for 16- and 32-bit data. You can use the connector outlines in Appendix B to see which kind you have or which kind you need.

Following are a few special connectors that were specifically made for a particular manufacturer's computer.

IBM created its own version for the PS/2 models by adding ten pins, which they marked as "reserved" but never actually used. If you have an IBM PS/2 with an IBM SCSI host adapter, you'll need a special IBM-to-SCSI adapter cable between your computer and the cable to the first device.

Apple created a new, smaller connector for their PowerBook notebooks to save space. There isn't anything particularly special about it. It's just optimized for space reduction. You can find these cables in better-equipped shops, but they're more expensive than standard cables, of course.

SCSI devices are connected together with cables to form a chain known as a daisy chain. It begins at one end of the cable and continues from device to device until it reaches the last device, usually the SCSI interface inside the computer. The entire chain is called the SCSI bus, and it carries commands and data between the host computer and the devices.

A typical SCSI daisy chain might look like this:

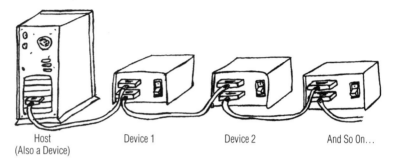

Host
(Also a Device)   Device 1   Device 2   And So On…

FIGURE 3.5 **A Typical Daisy Chain of SCSI Devices**

In a simple SCSI configuration, consisting of the computer and one other device (a hard disk, for example), the bus connects the computer to the hard disk so that the two can communicate.

In order to make the function of the SCSI bus a bit more tangible (so that you'll know what to do with it), try thinking of it again as a kind of water pipe with water flowing through it. Imagine that a section of pipe represents a cable, all the sections of pipe connected together represent the bus, and the water flowing through the pipe is the signal that would pass through the SCSI bus. The pipe might look like this:

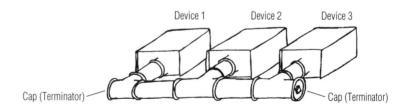

Device 1   Device 2   Device 3

Cap (Terminator)   Cap (Terminator)

FIGURE 3.6 **SCSI Plumbing**

If only one device (let's take the hard disk again) is connected to the SCSI bus, your installation should be simple. You basically have a direct pipeline between the computer and the hard disk, in the same way that you might have a pipe running directly from your main water line to your kitchen faucet, with no other branches or other faucets drawing water from that pipe.

Whenever you connect the cable to a device, you must orient it correctly. External cables have connectors that are shaped so that you can only connect them one way. There is no need to worry that you'll connect them upside down. Internal cables, however, don't always have such a safeguard. As a result you should always be aware of the colored stripe on internal cables. The stripe on one of the edges of the cable indicates wire number one and hence pin number one on the connector.

SCSI devices also have pin number one on one side or the other of their connector. It's usually indicated by a small △ printed on or near the connector. If you can't find it, check the manual that came with the device to see which side of the connector is pin one. Once you've established the orientation of the device's connector, match the orientation of the internal cable's connector to it—pin one to pin one—and plug it in, as shown here:

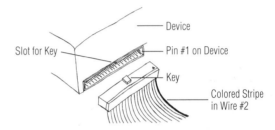

Device

Pin #1 on Device

Slot for Key

Key

Colored Stripe
in Wire #2

FIGURE 3.7   **Properly Oriented Internal Cables**

If you want to add another device to this connection, say another hard disk to your SCSI installation, you need to extend the bus to that device to make it part of the system too. In the case of our analogy, imagine that you want to have that main water line in your house feed not only your kitchen faucet but your bathroom faucet too. In that case, you need to add another pipe that will allow the signal to go to both the original and the new destinations.

In order to add this second hard disk to your system, you simply add a pipe (actually, a cable) between the first hard disk and the second one—not between the second hard disk and your computer. That system might look like this:

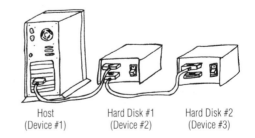

Host
(Device #1)

Hard Disk #1
(Device #2)

Hard Disk #2
(Device #3)

FIGURE 3.8   **Two Devices on the Bus**

You now have three SCSI devices connected on your SCSI bus: the computer, the first hard disk, and the second hard disk. You've started the daisy chain—connecting the first device to another device, to another device, and so on. An elaborate daisy chain, with a couple of hard disks, a CD-ROM, and an optical drive, might look like this:

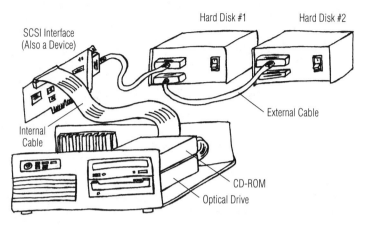

FIGURE 3.9   **Example of a Daisy-Chained SCSI System**

This is one of SCSI's greatest features—the ability to connect many devices to one slot on your motherboard, all coming off the same SCSI bus.

If you wanted to max out this daisy-chained system with other SCSI devices, you'd simply repeat the process of connecting device to device until the number of devices totaled the maximum for the type of SCSI you're using (8 for 8-bit SCSI, 16 for 16-bit SCSI, and 32 for 32-bit SCSI). A maxed-out system would look like this:

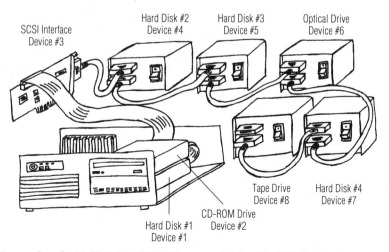

FIGURE 3.10   **Example of a Full 8-Bit SCSI System (a Total of Eight Devices)**
Note that the device numbers do not refer to their SCSI IDs.

So that's all there is to making the basic connections for the SCSI bus. But there is one more thing you have to do to have a fully operational SCSI bus. As with water pipes, you have to cap off the ends of your SCSI pipeline (the cables running between devices), or all the water (the signal) runs out.

ALERT! *Before you panic about your SCSI signals running out of the cables, let me assure you that this won't happen. In our water pipe analogy, the water would run out of the end of a pipe. But don't worry—your data won't dribble out from a nonterminated SCSI bus.*

SCSI caps are called terminators, and you only use two terminators —one on each end of the chain. For a more detailed discussion on the types of terminators, refer to Chapter 2. You want your signal to flow freely up and down the chain. Just as you wouldn't put a cap in the middle of a series of water pipes, you don't want to terminate a device in the middle of the SCSI bus. If you break the chain in the middle, all the devices connected to the bus are affected, possibly resulting in any number of problems accessing your SCSI devices. Here's an example of what not to do:

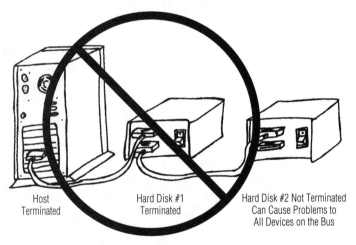

Host
Terminated

Hard Disk #1
Terminated

Hard Disk #2 Not Terminated
Can Cause Problems to
All Devices on the Bus

FIGURE 3.11 **SCSI Bus Terminated in the Middle**
Note that the second hard disk, which is connected past the terminator, is lost to your system.

NOTE *Correctly placing these terminators is critical for proper operation. Always terminate only the first and last devices on the SCSI bus.*

The most common mistake made when connecting devices to the bus is incorrect termination. All SCSI devices can be terminated (not killed). Some devices have built-in terminators, and if you attach a device to the middle of the bus but forget to remove the terminator, you'll have the configuration shown in the preceding illustration. Make sure you check each device so that all devices in the middle of the bus are not terminated. The only devices that must be terminated are the ones on the ends.

Here's what a properly terminated SCSI system would look like:

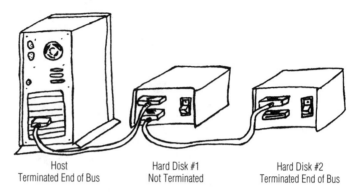

Host
Terminated End of Bus

Hard Disk #1
Not Terminated

Hard Disk #2
Terminated End of Bus

FIGURE 3.12 **Example of a Properly Terminated SCSI System**

One more thing to keep in mind is that the computer is also a device on the bus. As a result, if the computer is on one end of the bus, it must be terminated. However, if you have both internal and external SCSI devices, the computer is in the middle of the bus and must not be terminated.

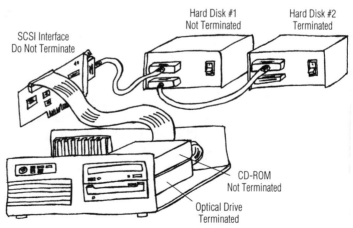

SCSI Interface
Do Not Terminate

Hard Disk #1
Not Terminated

Hard Disk #2
Terminated

CD-ROM
Not Terminated

Optical Drive
Terminated

FIGURE 3.13 **A Correctly Terminated SCSI Bus with the Host in the Middle**

Mix and Match: Combining Regular and Wide SCSI

Until now, we've only discussed methods of connecting devices of the same bus width: 8-bit devices on an 8-bit bus, 16-bit devices on a 16-bit bus, and 32-bit devices on a 32-bit bus. However, these devices can coexist to a certain extent.

When mixing devices, you must be aware of three important requirements.

1. The bus you use must be as wide as the widest device used on the bus. For example, you can connect an 8-bit device to a 16-bit bus, but not vice versa.

2. You must terminate the entire width of the bus, independent of the width of the last device. Just because the last device on your 32-bit bus is 8-bit doesn't mean you can simply use an 8-bit terminator. The full 32-bit bus must be terminated; otherwise, only the 8-bit devices will communicate properly.

3. All 8-bit devices will have IDs from 0 to 7, 16-bit devices will have IDs from 0 to 15, and 32-bit devices will have IDs from 0 to 31. As a result, the ID range for 8-, 16-, and 32-bit devices overlaps

from 0 to 7, and 16- and 32-bit devices overlap from 0 to 15. You have to make sure that you don't have any devices with the same ID, regardless of their width.

In a 16-bit Wide SCSI-2 system, an A cable and a B cable are used to form the bus. Since 8-bit SCSI also uses A cables, 8-bit devices can coexist with these 16-bit devices if you connect the 8-bit devices to the A cables. In a 16-bit Wide SCSI-3 system, a P cable is used. The P cable does not require an accompanying A cable, so 8-bit devices cannot be connected as easily as in the SCSI-2 case. In order to attach 8-bit devices to this bus, you will need a P-to-A transition cable.

There are two configurations for 32-bit Wide SCSI. SCSI-2 uses an A and a B cable, so connecting 16-bit devices isn't any different since they use both cables as well. Connecting 8-bit devices to the 32-bit bus is the same as in the 16-bit Wide SCSI-2 scenario. SCSI-3 uses a P and a Q cable for 32-bit. To attach 16-bit SCSI-3 devices, you simply connect them to the P cables. If you're also attaching 8-bit SCSI devices, you'll also need P-to-A transition cables.

So How Do You Terminate Your Particular Device?

There is more than one way to terminate a SCSI device. Most SCSI devices have an internal terminator that can be turned on or off with a switch. The switch is either a jumper or toggle on SCSI devices, or it may be software controlled on some interface cards. The manual for your particular device will tell you whether it's terminated by a switch and, if so, by what kind. Some older devices have physical terminators that must be pulled off or plugged in to turn termination off or on, respectively. Here's what a typical physical terminator might look like, just in case you can't find either your device's manual or your manufacturer to tell you whether you have one:

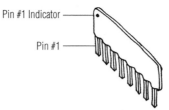

Pin #1 Indicator

Pin #1

FIGURE 3.14   **A Typical Physical Terminator Found on Internal SCSI Devices**

External SCSI devices can also have a large physical terminator on the outside of the device, which might look like the following illustration:

FIGURE 3.15   **A Typical Physical Terminator on an External SCSI Device**
This particular type of external terminator looks like a cable connector without the cable.

If you've determined that you need to terminate a device (because it's either at the beginning or end of the chain), you'll do so by either turning on its terminator switch or inserting the physical terminator. To turn off termination, turn off the switch or remove the physical terminator. Remember to be sure that none of the devices in the middle of the SCSI bus have their terminators switched on, or you'll break the chain. If you break the chain, you'll end up with some unrecognized and inaccessible devices on the daisy chain, and you'll be very upset.

SCSI IDs IDENTIFY INDIVIDUAL DEVICES IN THE SCSI CHAIN

Since all devices on a SCSI daisy chain are hooked together in one continuous string, each device on the bus, including the computer itself, must have a unique SCSI device ID. The number of available IDs is directly related to the width of the bus, like so:

- Regular SCSI-1 and SCSI-2 have eight possible SCSI IDs, one for each of the eight SCSI devices that can be attached to the bus. These SCSI IDs range from zero to seven, counting zero as the first number.

- With a wider, 16-bit bus, 16-bit Wide SCSI has 16 IDs, ranging from 0 to 15.

- Likewise, 32-bit Wide SCSI has 32 SCSI IDs, ranging from 0 to 31.

SCSI IDs Must Be Set by Hand

SCSI IDs are set by changing a numbered wheel, a group of switches, or a set of jumpers on each device. The settings for a particular device will differ. Check your user manual for each device to see exactly how to set them. There will be a table of SCSI IDs showing the jumper or switch configuration that corresponds to each ID. If your device has a numbered wheel, just turn the wheel to the desired ID.

When choosing SCSI IDs, you can use any number you like, as long as it's not in use by another device on the bus and as long as it's within the range for the type of bus you're using.

NOTE *SCSI-3 will introduce new bus designs that will allow more devices on a single bus.*

Here's an example of how you might assign IDs to your SCSI devices. Let's say that you have one hard disk attached to your computer and you want to add a second SCSI hard disk and a SCSI CD-ROM drive. Assigning the IDs is simple. First of all, call the SCSI interface card on your computer ID 7, just so it's the last device. Now, give the first hard disk ID 0, the second hard disk ID 1, and your CD-ROM ID 2.

NOTE *Again, you'll set these IDs with some sort of wheel, switch, or a jumper. Check your manual.*

In the case of the above system, the devices and their ID numbers would look like this:

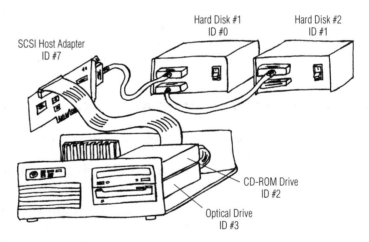

FIGURE 3.16 SCSI System Described Above with ID Numbers Assigned

PARITY CHECKING IS A SIMPLE FORM OF ERROR CHECKING, BUT YOU CAN ONLY USE IT IF ALL OF YOUR DEVICES SUPPORT IT

When configuring your SCSI system, you'll probably encounter an option for parity checking. Parity checking is a simple and fast method of error checking that is discussed in more detail in Chapter 2. You should turn parity checking on if your devices support it. Parity checking is turned on or off by either hardware or software, using a switch, jumper, or configuration program. (Check your manual to see which method your device uses.) Parity checking is mandatory for all SCSI-2 and future SCSI devices, but it's optional on SCSI-1 devices and may not always be present.

Whether you'll be able to use parity checking will depend on the capabilities of all of your SCSI devices. All devices on the bus must be able to perform parity checking in order for you to enable it. In fact, if only one device lacks support for parity checking, you must turn parity checking off for all of the others. Otherwise, the one device that doesn't know how to do the check won't understand the extra data, and your system won't work properly.

NOTE *Parity was optional under the old SCSI-1 standard but is required of all SCSI-2 devices. If you're unsure if all your devices support parity checking, check the manual that came with each device. Only old SCSI-1 devices may lack this feature.*

4

ADDING SCSI TO YOUR PC

You've decided to add SCSI to your PC. Your reason may be one of several: you want the flexibility of SCSI; you got your hands on a cheap SCSI hard drive; or maybe you need to install a device that works only with a SCSI interface. Whatever the reason, the first thing you'll need to do is select and install a SCSI controller card. So what are you going to get? Caching or noncached? Bus mastering or not? ISA? PCI? VLB? And then, of course, once you've bought the controller, you still have to install it and get it working. Do you know what interrupt to use? DMA channel? Port address? Because none of these questions have a single answer that's right for all installations, it's important to understand the concepts behind the terminology so that you can figure out what's right for your system.

TYPES OF SCSI INTERFACES FOR THE PC

Once upon a time, you could be pretty well assured that you could buy any card for your PC and it would work in any open slot inside your machine. Those days are gone. Nowadays, PCs have different types of slots, and not all adapter cards will work in all types of slots.

A Bus by Any Other Name...ISA, EISA, MCA, VESA, PCI

You undoubtedly have heard of one or more of the following bus architectures: ISA, EISA, MCA, VESA, and PCI. Whereas SCSI is a bus for transferring data between the computer and a device such as a hard disk, the above-mentioned buses provide the means for sending data between the computer and interface cards.

ISA, or industry-standard architecture, is the bus used on the original IBM PC. It is an 8-bit bus running at a maximum data rate of 8 MHz, or 8 MB/sec—very slow by today's standards. Upon introduction of the IBM AT and the 16-bit Intel 80286, the ISA bus was extended to support 16-bit data transfers and 16-bit cards. However, the data rate stayed the same. This proved to be a performance bottleneck once 32-bit (386, 486, and Pentium) computers came on the scene, since their higher performance demanded more data, faster than the bus could send it.

IBM decided the only way to increase the data rate performance between the computer and plug-in cards was to totally redesign the bus. (IBM also wanted to eliminate the plethora of PC clones.) The micro-channel architecture (MCA) was developed to provide 32-bit data transfers at up to 33 MHz. But, since it wasn't compatible with existing ISA cards, the standard fell by the wayside.

In order to continue using existing ISA cards, an extension to the ISA standard was developed. The enhanced industry-standard architecture (EISA, pronounced EE-sa) provides 32-bit data transfers at up to 33 MHz, but it can also accept older ISA cards. The cost of EISA was high, thus reserving its use to expensive network servers and those with large pocketbooks.

The Video Electronics Standards Association (VESA, pronounced VEE-sa) stepped in and proposed an inexpensive 32-bit bus that could be used in conjunction with ISA. The VESA Local Bus (VL-Bus, or VLB) allows data to be transferred at up to 40 MHz between the computer and VL-Bus–compatible cards. (A 50 MHz version is out but is still problematic.) Although VL-Bus is limited to two or three slots for interface cards, it is the most commonly used 32-bit bus on 386 and 486 computers because of its speed, low cost, and compatibility with existing ISA cards.

Most recently, Intel introduced PCI to solve the bottleneck between the computer and peripheral cards. This new bus offers 32-bit or 64-bit data transfers at 33 MHz, and it supports more slots than VL-Bus. The maximum number of card slots depends on the manufacturer's design. But beware: PCI is not compatible with existing ISA or EISA cards, so you'll need to buy new cards for a PCI machine.

During the transition period from ISA and VL-Bus to PCI, you can find many machines with both ISA/VL-Bus and PCI slots, so you won't have to throw away your old cards just yet. PCI is the bus of choice if you're running a Pentium or faster machine, because the speed of the computer won't be bogged down waiting for data to come over a sluggish bus.

Many PCI motherboard manufacturers are beginning to include SCSI controller chips on the motherboard. If you buy a PCI motherboard with built-in SCSI, you won't need to buy a separate SCSI controller card. If you're considering one of these motherboards, be sure to ask around and check out the hardware forums online if you can, to see which combinations from which manufacturers are working well for people. Much of the technology is very new, and its newness brings problems with it.

As with most things in the world of PCs, there is a trade-off between price and performance when it comes to SCSI host adapters (controller cards). You can expect to pay more for a high-speed VLB or a PCI host adapter than you would for a slower ISA one. However, it doesn't do any good to install an adapter card that supports DMA rates faster than the bus allows. For example, the Adaptec 1542 supports DMA bus mastering speeds of up to 10 MB/sec, which is fast enough for Fast SCSI; but since the ISA architecture supports only 5 MB/sec DMA throughput, there would be a bottleneck at the bus, and your system wouldn't be able to take advantage of the higher transfer rate.

CACHING CONTROLLER CARDS CAN INCREASE PERFORMANCE

Caching SCSI controller cards can increase the performance of your system by increasing the disk I/O performance. Caching works by keeping a copy of certain data segments in memory so that they are immediately handy if the CPU asks for them. Because it's faster for the system to retrieve a block of data from memory than to read it off the disk, caching results in faster data transfer. Caching data read from a device is called read caching.

A cache can also be used to increase performance by postponing the writing of changed blocks of data to disk. This process is known as write caching. While write caching doesn't usually significantly decrease the number of disk accesses, it can allow the accesses to take place when the system isn't busy doing something else. When the system is idle (waiting for you to figure out where your mouse cursor just went, for example) the blocks in the cache that are marked as changed, or *dirty*, are written, or *flushed*, out to disk.

Because these changed blocks of data are written to disk only when the CPU is idle, the CPU is free to finish other processing tasks, and idle time is minimized.

Software Caching Is Flexible

Caching can be maintained either through software or hardware. The advantage of software caching is that, unlike a hardware cache, it doesn't require dedicated memory on the controller card. A software cache uses a portion of the system memory to cache data, and you can adjust the size of the cache to suit your needs. Most operating systems use software caching to increase disk performance, and many caching controllers simply duplicate the caching algorithms of the operating system software. For example, UNIX and Novell are already heavily software cached, and DOS comes with a software caching program called Smart-Drive (smartdrv.exe), which provides both read and write caching capabilities. The fact is that adding a disk cache to your system can dramatically increase its performance and minimize "thrashing" your hard disk with repetitive reads and writes of the same data.

Hardware Caching Can Duplicate Software Caching

Hardware caching is another form of caching. It uses the controller as the location of the cache. However, since the memory exists on the controller card itself, you cannot use that memory for any purpose other than the cache. Also, if you need more cache memory, you have to buy more memory specifically for that purpose. The benefit of a hardware cache, though, is that the cache management and maintenance is performed by the controller card, not the CPU. As a result, there's no overhead when using a hardware cache.

So, a software cache is good and a hardware cache is good. Why not use both? Well, using software-caching environments like UNIX, Novell, or DOS with smartdrv.exe with a hardware cache duplicates the caching algorithms in CPU, as well as the disk controller. This double-caching of the same data adds extra overhead, and it usually slows down the system.

Which Caching Is Right for You?

Should you switch to a caching controller card if you're already using software caching? Not if yours is a single-user system. Single-user systems running DOS and Windows and already using software caching won't see much improvement in disk performance with the extra cost of a hardware cache. The zero cost (it's included!) and flexibility of a software cache is the best solution. Also, single-user systems generally have plenty of available idle time to write data to disk, so you'd probably want to avoid write caching on your PC. There is a danger to using write caching too: if you lose power while there are dirty blocks in the cache or your system crashes, you'll lose any changes that you made to your data and you probably won't be able to recover them. To prevent this problem, you can invest in a battery backup for your computer so it has time to flush its cache when the power goes out.

On the other hand, a caching SCSI controller can give a big performance boost if you're building a multiuser system like a Novell fileserver. The reason is that with such a heavily loaded system, there may not be enough idle time for the software cache to keep up with all the requests for disk access. This causes two bad things to happen. First, as the system becomes more heavily loaded, the software cache begins to fill up with dirty sectors waiting to be written to disk. These sectors take up space in the software cache that could otherwise be used for read caching—an operation at which the software cache is much more effective. Second, the software cache flushing operations can begin to interfere with other system activity as more users are added to the system and less idle time results. In fact, when the system is under heavy loads with no idle time, the benefit of software write caching completely disappears, and hardware caching is an excellent option.

Some caching controllers are specifically designed to work cooperatively in software-caching environments like UNIX or Novell. These controllers are engineered to make the process of writing changed data blocks more efficient. Installing one of these specially designed hardware caching controllers in a software caching system doesn't eliminate the need for the operating system's cache buffers to flush the dirty blocks from cache to disk, but it improves the efficiency and speed of this operation. The hardware cache receives the flushed data in a fraction of the time it would take without hardware caching, and it then proceeds to copy the data back to disk concurrently without interfering with other system activity.

Adding SCSI with a Sound Card

A popular way to add SCSI to PCs today is with a sound card. Many companies now manufacture cards that contain both a SCSI interface and sound capabilities so that you can get both capabilities while taking up only one slot in your PC. For example, the SCSI Audio Machine AMM 1570 from Adaptec combines a bootable SCSI interface with sound capabilities. Creative Labs also makes a combination sound and SCSI card called the Sound Blaster 16 SCSI-2. The Sound Blaster card isn't bootable, since it doesn't have a BIOS, but it will allow you to attach SCSI devices and it supports the SCSI-2 standard. If you're purchasing a combination SCSI and sound card, make sure it's SCSI-2–compatible.

If you've chosen to add SCSI to your PC by way of a sound card, you can purchase a cable that will allow you to attach external SCSI devices to your sound card. The cable comes with a connector mounted on a face plate that fits into an unused slot on the back of your PC. Call Connect Group Inc. in Severna Park, Maryland or TTS Multimedia Systems in Santa Clara, California for more information. (Detailed contact information for each is in Appendix A, "SCSI Sources.")

BIOS ON THE CONTROLLER LETS YOU BOOT FROM SCSI DEVICES

Unfortunately, the BIOS in most PCs doesn't know how to control a SCSI drive. Therefore, if you want to boot up your system from a SCSI hard drive, you must have a SCSI controller with a built-in BIOS. During the boot process, the BIOS on the computer's motherboard first checks the setup for a bootable disk. If it doesn't find one, it scans for another BIOS either on the motherboard or on a peripheral card. When it finds the BIOS on a SCSI controller, it allows the SCSI BIOS to handle the boot process. If you don't have a BIOS on your SCSI card, you'll have no choice but to boot from another type of hard disk (such as IDE or EIDE) or via floppy disk, as the system's BIOS will recognize all of these.

How About Mixing SCSI and Non-SCSI Controllers in One System?

If you already have non-SCSI types of hard drives like IDE, MFM, or RLL in your system, you can still add a SCSI hard drive. The only catch is that the computer will boot from the non-SCSI drive rather than the SCSI drive. The reason is that during the boot process, the motherboard BIOS first looks for bootable drives that have been set up in its BIOS configuration.

SCSI host adapters will, in general, coexist with other disk controllers (though you need to make sure there are no IRQ or port conflicts between the controllers). And mixed systems have their advantages, including faster booting and easier setup. Bootup in mixed systems is faster than in pure SCSI systems, because the system can boot from the non-SCSI drive. Rather than spend the time hunting for the SCSI BIOS and then running the boot code in it, the computer will just boot the drive it already knows about, the non-SCSI one.

Another beneficial side effect of mixing drive types is that it's easier to set up your system with two different operating systems. For example, you could have an IDE drive with DOS installed and a SCSI drive with Windows NT. In such a configuration, you could (from your setup screen) define the DOS IDE drive as drive C, in which case the PC will boot to DOS. Then, with Windows NT loaded on the SCSI drive, when you want to boot with Windows NT, you could simply enter the setup program again and change it so that drive C is not installed. The system will see that there are no drives installed in its setup and will look for the SCSI BIOS to boot from, into Windows NT.

The one downside to this scenario is that when you boot up from the SCSI hard disk, you won't have access to the IDE drive anymore, since you removed it from the BIOS configuration. This is not the case with the reverse—booting up from the IDE drive—because SCSI drives are added to the system after all non-SCSI drives.

NOTE *When choosing a SCSI host adapter, it's important to consider what other features the BIOS offers. Many SCSI cards offer additional features, such as the ability to format a drive, extra diagnostics, and the ability to configure IRQ, DMA settings, and the SCSI ID through software instead of with jumpers. These built-in features, as well as available software configuration of hardware settings, are becoming common in SCSI adapters. So, before buying a SCSI card, evaluate its performance and ease of use before you get excited about the built-in software.*

INSTALLING THE SCSI INTERFACE CARD

The SCSI interface card is the link between your computer and all the SCSI devices you connect to it. Once you purchase the SCSI interface card, you have to configure and install it before you can start adding SCSI devices. If you have Intel/Microsoft's Plug-and-Play SCSI interface, the configuration is handled for you after plugging the card in and powering up the computer.

For those of you who don't have a Plug-and-Play card, you will need to set the SCSI ID, I/O port, interrupt and, on some cards, the DMA channel. We'll go over each of these settings, what they do, and what happens if you set them incorrectly.

Setting the Port Address—the Front Door to the Interface

Every interface card has a port address, also known as the input/output (I/O) port. The I/O port is the communication channel through which all commands are passed. Incorrectly setting the port address will render the interface card useless, because the computer won't know where the card is. Setting the port address incorrectly is the same as writing the wrong mailing address on a letter. The message won't go where you want it to.

There's more than one way to select the port address, but the general procedure is that you change a set of switches or jumpers. More and more SCSI cards allow you to configure the port address through their configuration software, so you don't have to actually change any physical settings on the card. The only way to find out how to change the port address on your card is to read the manual that came with the card.

Regardless of how you set the port address on your card, you will have several three-digit addresses to choose from. Common addresses include numbers like 130, 134, 230, 234, 330, and 340, but your particular SCSI card may have other addresses. The particular address you select depends on one thing—it cannot be the same as an address already being used by another interface in your PC, like your printer or mouse, for example.

To avoid choosing a conflicting port address, you need to know what ports are already being used by other devices. To help you to determine which ports are already being used in the PC, see Appendix C, which lists all the common I/O port addresses. In addition, check the manuals for the other interface cards in your computer to see what ports they're set to.

A variety of diagnostic programs, such as Microsoft Diagnostic (msd.exe), come with DOS 6.x and Windows 3.1, but they cannot always identify all the devices in your computer. The only way to know for sure what you have in there and what I/O ports your drives use is to open the computer and take a look. Pull out those old manuals and compare the jumpers or switches on the interface cards in your system with the information in the manual. Once you determine the settings for the card, write them down so you won't have to go through this entire process next time you add a card.

It's very important to know what you have in your system and what I/O ports are in use. When two ports are set to the same address, your system ends up with a hardware conflict or, more specifically, an I/O port conflict. You'll know when you have a hardware conflict, because either your SCSI card or the other interface card, or both, will not function properly, if at all. This doesn't mean that the cards are broken. The solution is to simply change the port address on either the SCSI card or the other conflicting card and try again. As long as there isn't a conflict, and assuming no other problems exist with your card or your system, your SCSI card should begin to work properly.

Setting Interrupts

Without the ability to be interrupted while running a program, your CPU would be oblivious to any hardware or software around it, including interface cards (unless the program were specifically programmed to check up on devices periodically to see if they were in need of attention). Your computer is a complex system, with different devices placing demands on the CPU at different times, regardless of whether the

CPU is doing something else at the time. What happens when your interface card wants to send data to the CPU but it doesn't want to wait around until a program asks when it wants to send data? The device uses a hardware interrupt to request CPU time.

Hardware interrupts are the way that your computer manages different devices requesting attention from the CPU. Your computer has a number of interrupt lines that carry these requests to interrupt the task the CPU is working on. When you set hardware interrupts, also called IRQs or interrupt requests, you're selecting the interrupt line (your CPU has several interrupt lines built in as pieces of hardware) in your system that will be used by a particular device when it wants to request attention from the CPU. Once IRQs have been set, your devices will use their assigned interrupt line to request the CPU's attention. The device, like your interface card or your modem, will put a signal on the bus via this interrupt line to signal to the CPU that the device needs servicing—it wants to send data, for example. Setting the hardware interrupt is simply selecting which interrupt line the device will use to tell the CPU that it needs servicing.

NOTE *On systems where interrupts are not used, polling is required. Polling is a process whereby the CPU goes out at regular intervals to see if a device needs attention. The biggest problem with polling is that it wastes a lot of time in your system. Each time a device needs attention from the CPU, it has to wait for the CPU to poll it. It can't interrupt the CPU with a request for attention as it can when using IRQs.*

Like the port address on your computer, you set the interrupts on your card by changing a switch or jumper on the card. Interrupts can also be set on some cards by using the manufacturer's configuration software. See your card's manual for specifics on how to change or select your card's IRQ setting if the factory default setting won't work.

Your PC has 16 possible interrupts, ranging from 0 to 15. The interrupt you select should be free, meaning that it's not being used by anything else. Use Appendix C, which lists the interrupts commonly used in most computers, as an aid to setting your interrupts, but be sure to check the other interface cards in your system to see exactly which interrupts are used and which ones are free.

One way to see which interrupts are in use in your system is to run Microsoft Diagnostics, msd.exe, from the DOS command prompt. This program comes bundled in DOS 6.*x*. A selection in the program will give you a list of all of the interrupts and their status (free or in use) in your system. Be sure to run the program from the DOS prompt, not from within Windows, for the most accurate picture of your system. Although this is a useful tool, remember that it isn't foolproof. The only way to know for sure is to open your system and log the settings

A Note About Interrupts

Although there are 16 interrupts on 286 and higher-class computers, IRQ 2 is not specifically used. These machines use two interrupt controller chips, in a master and slave configuration, with each chip providing 8 interrupts. However, the 8 interrupts from the slave are channeled into the master via IRQ 2. As a result, IRQs 8 to 15 will trigger through IRQ 2. However, IRQ 2 is not completely lost. A device that is set to IRQ 2 will be relocated to IRQ 9.

for all the cards in your computer. Appendix C also lists IRQs used by the motherboard. This is important so that you don't run into an IRQ conflict with a built-in device such as the real-time clock.

When you assign the same interrupt to each of two or more cards, you create the potential for a hardware conflict commonly called an IRQ conflict. An IRQ conflict is like having two houses with the same doorbell. When you push the button, the people in both houses hear the ring and come running to the door. Funny thing is, you're probably at only one of the doors.

This is not to say that it's not possible to share one IRQ setting between two devices. In fact, interrupts can be shared between devices, but only if the devices sharing the IRQs have some other way of identifying themselves to the host, or they never need to request CPU attention at the same time. The printer port is an example of such a device. For example, if you have a sound card at IRQ 7, it will share its interrupt with the printer port at IRQ 7. As long as you don't use both devices simultaneously, a conflict doesn't occur. (One way to ensure that there won't be a conflict is to make sure that any software running knows what interrupt to expect from each device.) Not all devices are good about sharing IRQs, and the risk you run when your devices share IRQs is that your computer will lock up when it encounters a conflict between the devices at the IRQ. The best rule of thumb is to give each device its very own IRQ.

Using DMA for High-Speed Data Transfer

When your system accesses a peripheral device, like a disk or tape drive, large amounts of data are moved back and forth between the device and the computer's RAM (random access memory). One of the most efficient methods of moving this data is called direct memory access, or DMA. DMA is a method by which a plug-in card that controls a peripheral (also called a peripheral controller, or simply a controller)

Data Transfer Methods:
DMA, Bus Mastering, Programmed I/O

Some controller cards, including many SCSI host adapters, use a process called bus mastering DMA (commonly referred to as bus mastering) to attain the maximum throughput when reading from or writing to RAM. Bus mastering accomplishes this by taking control of the system bus away from the CPU and sending data from its own buffer directly into RAM. By so doing, bus mastering allows the data transfer to and from RAM to occur at the maximum rate that the bus will support, while at the same time freeing up the CPU to process other commands while the data transfer is taking place. While DMA improves the performance of the SCSI adapter, controller cards that use bus mastering, rather than regular DMA, will generally have the highest performance.

In cases where you don't have a bus mastering controller card or a controller card that supports regular DMA transfers, your system uses a data transfer method called programmed input/output, or PIO. PIO was used by the hard disk controller on the first PC/AT. PIO uses the CPU to move data between a controller card and the computer's memory, with data transfer speeds reaching about 2.5 MB/sec. In comparison, data transfer rates on even a slow ISA machine with a bus mastering SCSI card can achieve more than 5 MB/sec, quite a significant increase in performance.

PIO's relatively slow data transfer is its primary drawback. Its performance is hampered by the fact that it needs the CPU to read or write each block of data. As a result, transfer speed is slow and the CPU is unavailable for other tasks, thus slowing down the entire system. PIO's drawbacks make it unsuitable for multiuser environments like Windows, UNIX, or Novell fileservers. DMA, by contrast, is a much more sophisticated and effective method of data transfer.

Two primary types of DMA are used in PCs: third-party DMA and first-party (or bus-mastering) DMA. Third-party DMA, used on floppy disk controllers in PC/AT ISA and EISA computers, is the slower and less expensive of the two types of DMA. It relies on an independent DMA controller, typically built into the PC motherboard, to move data between a peripheral card (the first party) and system RAM (the second party). Since it can be shared by multiple peripheral cards, the DMA controller is considered the third party.

Bus-mastering SCSI controllers can take advantage of the faster DMA, called first-party or bus-mastering DMA. These controllers can move data to and from system RAM much faster than either PIO or third-party DMA, because they control the DMA transfer themselves. They don't need the help of the CPU or a third-party DMA controller in order to transfer data. While transferring the data using first-party DMA, the DMA hardware on the peripheral controller suspends CPU operation and takes control of the system bus. The hardware then automatically moves the data between system RAM and a buffer on the controller, resulting in much faster data transfer, because the CPU is not being used—the controller takes care of the data transfer.

can read or write directly to RAM. In contrast, when DMA is not being used, the CPU, rather than the controller, reads or writes to RAM, thus taking time away from the CPU that could be used for other sorts of data crunching. Controllers that support DMA free up the CPU and, as a consequence, speed up the rest of your system.

If your SCSI card supports DMA, you will have to set its DMA channel. As with I/O ports and IRQs, make sure when selecting the DMA channel that you select one that is unused by any other card in your system. Not to belabor the point, but the only way to really know what DMA channels are in use is to log the settings of all the cards currently in your system. Also check Appendix C for common DMA usage in the PC. That's the last time we'll say that. Promise.

In addition to setting its DMA channel, you may also have the option to set the DMA transfer speed on your SCSI card. Your choice of DMA transfer speed will depend on the type of bus slots in your PC. Relatively speaking, ISA is slow, supporting DMA transfer rates of up to 5 MB/sec. In most machines, it has been replaced by newer and much faster bus alternatives, namely EISA, VLB, and PCI. In contrast to ISA's top speed of 5 MB/sec, the EISA bus supports DMA transfer speeds of up to 33 MB/sec. VESA local bus, also called VL-Bus or simply VLB, supports DMA burst speeds (transfers of small blocks of data) of up to 130 MB/sec, though the sustained rate (continuous data transfer) is closer to 32 MB/sec. PCI local bus has a sustained rate of 132 MB/sec, which beats even the highest measured burst speeds of VLB. In a continuing attempt to improve on bus transfer rates, a forthcoming PCI standard will support DMA rates of 264 MB/sec, twice the current sustained rate for PCI.

It's important that when you set the DMA transfer speed you set it no higher than the highest transfer speed that the bus slot holding your card can handle. For example, since most ISA slots can handle data transfer rates no higher than 5 MB/sec, setting an ISA SCSI card higher than 5 MB/sec could introduce intermittent data corruption into your system resulting from the incompatible transfer rates. (This data corruption can be very hard to track down, too.) When setting the DMA transfer speed, your best option is to use the card's factory-set default transfer rate. Don't experiment with faster DMA transfer speeds unless you know that your computer can support them.

Setting the DMA is similar to setting the I/O port and IRQ. There will be a set of jumpers, a switch, or a configuration program to make the changes. The installation section of your SCSI card's manual will show you which method to use.

Set the SCSI ID on Your Interface Card

As with any SCSI device, when you install a SCSI interface card you have to assign it a SCSI ID. The interface card's SCSI ID is also called its host ID, because the card acts as host to all the devices on the SCSI bus. You set the host ID by changing a set of switches or jumpers on the card or by using the manufacturer's configuration software. See the manual that came with your SCSI card for specifics on how to set its host ID.

The host ID is normally set to 7, the last device ID on the SCSI bus—and you're probably safest setting it to 7, since almost all manufacturers of SCSI hardware or software assume a setting of 7. By using this default, you'll help to prevent possible conflicts. However, you can select any ID from 0 to 7 as the host ID, as long as the ID is not in use by another SCSI device. If your interface card is a 16-bit or 32-bit Wide SCSI interface, you'll have more than the 0 to 7 IDs to choose from. 16-bit Wide SCSI offers IDs from 0 to 15, while 32-bit offers IDs from 0 to 31.

Things to Keep in Mind When Setting SCSI Host IDs

If you're combining regular and Wide SCSI devices on the same bus, set the host adapter's ID to an ID between 0 and 7; otherwise, the 8-bit SCSI devices won't be able to find the host adapter.

If you have more than one computer on the same SCSI bus to share SCSI devices, make sure that the SCSI ID for the host adapter in each computer is unique. For example, if you're connecting two computers and two hard drives onto the SCSI bus, you could set the ID for hard disk number one to ID 0, hard disk number two to ID 1, the host adapter in computer number one to ID 2, and the host adapter in computer number two to ID 3.

INSTALL THE RIGHT DRIVERS

Drivers are programs that allow the operating system and your applications to communicate with peripheral devices. When you load a driver, you're actually loading a program in memory that the computer can use when it needs to access a device. Some devices, like floppy disk drives for example, have their driver built into the computer's BIOS, so you probably won't have to load a driver for them. Also, you may not need to load any driver for your interface card if it has a built-in BIOS and you're only using it to access hard disk drives—its BIOS probably has all of the software that you'll need to access your hard disk.

Still, there are many types of SCSI devices on the market besides hard disk drives, and each requires its own special driver. But it's not the case that each type of SCSI adapter needs a different driver for each type of SCSI device. If this were the case, SCSI systems would end up with a multiplicity of drivers and a lot of confused users. People asking questions like "Where can I get a driver so my Adaptec AHA-1540CF can talk to my Toshiba XM-3301T CD-ROM?" would probably drive manufacturers crazy.

To avoid this potentially unpleasant situation, SCSI card manufacturers have developed standards for drivers that allow most SCSI devices to talk to their particular interface card. These special drivers are called layered drivers, because they're built up of layers of different drivers.

The bottom, or adapter-specific, layer is a driver that communicates with the hardware on the SCSI adapter. This is also called the low-level driver. You load drivers for your specific SCSI devices on top of this adapter-specific, low-level layer. Instead of communicating directly with the SCSI adapter card itself, these layered device drivers communicate only with the bottom layer adapter driver, so that only this bottom-layer driver needs to be able to communicate with the SCSI device. The use of layered drivers really simplifies the problems of driver writing and compatibility, since manufacturers need to focus only on the bottom layer of the driver, rather than what may be several layers of drivers on top.

Of course, the world of drivers isn't quite that simple. There are several competing standards for SCSI device drivers. The most widely used device driver standard right now is ASPI. ASPI, which stands for Advanced SCSI Programming Interface, was developed by Adaptec and has since been adopted by most other card manufacturers. ASPI exists for DOS, Windows, OS/2, and NetWare. (See Appendix D, contributed by Adaptec, for a look at programming ASPI. You'll appreciate the complexity of writing good device drivers and, if you're a programmer, you'll get a good feel for the potential to program the SCSI interface.)

Another widely used driver standard is CAM. CAM, or Common Access Method, is the proposed ANSI software interface for SCSI devices and is a part of the forthcoming SCSI-3 standard. At this writing, CAM isn't as widely implemented as ASPI, though CAM drivers are available for most popular devices. For example, NCR calls its CAM drivers NCR SCSI Device Management System or SDMS, and it embeds the drivers in its SCSI BIOS so you don't have to load a CAM driver into memory. Appendix E, contributed by Future Domain Corporation, offers an overview of CAM programming.

Get the Latest SCSI Drivers

Probably the most important thing to keep in mind when dealing with SCSI device drivers is that hardware manufacturers are constantly updating them. Always make sure you have the latest drivers for your hardware. You can usually download the drivers from the manufacturer's BBS or from the support conferences on online services like CompuServe or America Online (see Appendix A for a list of SCSI vendors and their BBS and phone numbers). At the same time that you're making sure you've got the latest device drivers, you should also make sure that the latest drivers aren't buggy. Keep up with the latest information about device drivers by checking out the appropriate conference on your favorite online service or read the SCSI newsgroup on Usenet (see Appendix L for a list of these online resources). A little knowledge about what's happening in the world of drivers can save you a lot of headache and frustration.

Software That Will Simplify Your Driver Installation

The major SCSI host adapter manufacturers all have SCSI driver installation tools. For example, Adaptec's program is called EZSCSI, Future Domain's is PowerSCSI!, and NCR has SDMS. When you run these programs on your system, they analyze your hardware and software, load the appropriate drivers, and then add the necessary driver installation commands to your config.sys and autoexec.bat files. In addition to the installation tool, the packages often include some extra utilities, like a disk formatter or a tape backup program.

One of the best third-party programs available is CorelSCSI! from Corel Corporation, which probably has all the drivers you'll need to install in your system. CorelSCSI! takes a device-independent approach by communicating with the ASPI drivers of your SCSI devices. If you don't have ASPI drivers for your interface card, you don't need to worry, because CorelSCSI! supplies ASPI drivers for many devices, including some for devices that don't come with them from the manufacturer. For more information on CorelSCSI!, call the Corel Corporation directly at 800-836-7274 (more detailed contact information is in "SCSI Sources," Appendix A). They're based in Ontario, Canada.

DOS Drivers

Although the major SCSI host adapter manufacturers supply an easy-to-use installation program to install and configure your drivers, there may come a time when you have to change the configuration manually. To become familiar with the drivers that are commonly installed into a DOS SCSI system, let's take a look at the two standard types of SCSI drivers, ASPI and CAM, and what each driver does.

NOTE *The following examples give you a general idea of which DOS drivers might have been loaded by your adapter's installation program. You should check the manual for your SCSI interface to see exactly what drivers it uses and what drivers it comes with for the devices you want to attach. If you have a SCSI device that doesn't have drivers supplied by the host adapter manufacturer, the driver may have been included with the device. Check the documentation to see if it has its own SCSI drivers.*

ASPI

The main ASPI driver is the low-level or adapter-specific driver. It's the driver that talks directly to your SCSI adapter. Each manufacturer's SCSI card has its own version of the low-level driver so that programs don't have to worry about the brand of host adapter you're using. Although the exact name of the low-level driver changes from company to company and host adapter model to host adapter model, they usually have ASPI as a part of the filename, like aspi*xx*.sys. Some drivers also have DOS in the filename so that you know it's a DOS driver. For example, Adaptec's 1542 SCSI host adapter's low-level driver is called aspi4dos.sys. The ASPI at the beginning indicates that it's an ASPI-compliant driver. The 4 stands for the 4*x* model of the 15*xx* series of cards, and DOS indicates that it's a DOS driver. If you have a different brand of SCSI card, your driver won't have exactly the same name, but it will be similar.

All the drivers following the low-level driver are device-specific drivers. These drivers provide support for a certain type of device—a hard disk, for example. Once again, ASPI device-specific drivers will usually have ASPI in the filename as well as the type of device it supports. For example, Adaptec's aspidisk.sys provides support for hard disks and aspicd.sys supports CD-ROM drives. Some drivers may only use the device name to identify the driver, such as cdrom.sys.

The DOS ASPI drivers are loaded by the config.sys file. This is a sample config.sys file:

```
device=c:\aspi\aspi4dos.sys
dos=high
files=30
buffers=20
device=c:\dos\himem.sys
device=c:\aspi\aspicd.sys /d:mscd001
```

This file contains entries that load a low-level ASPI driver (device= c:\aspi\aspi4dos.sys), as well as device-specific drivers for hard disks (device= c:\aspi\aspidisk.sys) and CD-ROMs (device=c:\aspi\aspicd. sys/d:mscd001—where /d:mscd001 is an identifying label for the drive). Your installation may have additional options after the name of each driver, depending on the particular driver you're using. Refer to your host adapter's device driver manual for the use of any additional options.

If you're using DOS 5.0 or higher and EMM386 or a third-party memory manager such as QEMM or 386Max, you can load the ASPI driver into upper memory by using the devicehigh command instead of the device command, as shown by the series of devicehigh statements in the config.sys below (check your DOS manual for more information about upper memory and loading drivers into upper memory):

```
device=c:\dos\himem.sys
device=c:\dos\emm386.exe ram
```

```
dos=high,umb
file=30
buffers=20
devicehigh=c:\aspi\aspi4dos.sys
devicehigh=c:\aspi\aspidisk.sys
devicehigh=c:\aspi\aspicd.sys /d:mscd001
```

CAM

Like ASPI, CAM also has a low-level or adapter-specific driver that talks directly to the SCSI adapter. As in the case of ASPI drivers, each manufacturer has its own version of the low-level driver. CAM drivers usually have CAM as a part of the filename, and some also have DOS in the filename so that you know it's a DOS driver. For example, NCR's low-level CAM driver is called doscam.sys. The "dos" indicates that it's a DOS driver and CAM indicates that it supports CAM functions. If you have a different brand of SCSI card, your driver will have a similar name.

Device-specific CAM drivers follow a naming convention similar to that used with ASPI device-specific drivers. They may have CAM in the filename and also the type of device supported. For example, NCR's scsidisk.sys provides support for hard disks and cdrom.sys supports CD-ROM drives.

CAM drivers are loaded by entries in the config.sys file such as this sample file:

```
device=c:\cam\doscam.sys
dos=high
files=30
buffers=20
device=c:\dos\himem.sys
device=c:\cam\scsidisk.sys
device=c:\aspi\cdrom.sys /d:mscd001
```

This sample config.sys file contains entries that load CAM drivers for an NCR SCSI adapter (device=c:\cam\doscam.sys), as well as device-specific drivers for hard disks (device=c:\cam\scsidisk.sys) and CD-ROMs (device=c:\aspi\cdrom.sys /d:mscd001). Again, /d:mscd001 in this example is simply an identifying number for the CD-ROM. Your installation may look different depending on your system configuration. (Refer to your host adapter's device driver manual for more information on the use of your host adapter's drivers.)

If you're using DOS 5.0 or higher and EMM386 or other memory manager, you can load the CAM drivers into upper memory with the devicehigh command, as shown by the series of devicehigh statements in this config.sys file (check your DOS manual for more information about upper memory and loading drivers into upper memory):

```
device=c:\dos\himem.sys
device=c:\dos\emm386.exe ram
dos=high,umb
file=30
buffers=20
devicehigh=c:\cam\doscam.sys
devicehigh=c:\cam\scsidisk.sys
devicehigh=c:\cam\cdrom.sys /d:mscd001
```

If you have a SCSI card that uses CAM drivers, you may also have an ASPI-to-CAM translation driver. This driver is used to translate commands from programs that only support ASPI to ones that your CAM driver can understand. It's only needed if you're using ASPI-specific programs and drivers that don't talk CAM, such as CorelSCSI! and Central Point Tape Backup. This translation driver is called aspicam.sys, aspi2cam.sys, or something close to that.

NOTE *The ASPI-to-CAM driver should be loaded after the CAM low-level driver and before any ASPI-specific drivers.*

Windows 3.1 Drivers

DOS SCSI drivers are compatible with Windows 3.1, so once you finish installing them, Windows will be able to access all your wonderful SCSI devices. Some manufacturers also include Windows-specific drivers to squeeze out an extra bit of performance or to support additional features used by their own utility programs, such as tape backup software, music CD players, or diagnostic tools. For example, Adaptec's software installs two files for Windows ASPI support: winaspi.dll and vaspid.386. Your particular SCSI card may not use Windows-specific drivers. If it doesn't, don't worry unless you can't access your SCSI devices from Windows. If your card does use a Windows driver, make sure that it's been copied into the Windows System directory (usually c:\windows\system) and that the correct entry exists in the 386Enh section of your system.ini file. The example below shows a section of a typical system.ini file, including the Adaptec Windows ASPI driver vaspid.386:

```
[386Enh]
device=vaspid.386
```

```
device=dva.386
keyboard=*vkd
device=*int13
```

And so on.

Windows 95 Drivers

Windows 95 will include drivers for SCSI cards from the leading manufacturers. In most cases, Windows 95 will know when you install a
SCSI card into your system, and you will be sent straight to the Add
Hardware Wizard (in which case you should skip to step 5 below). If
your card wasn't detected, you'll need to run the Add Hardware Wizard yourself as follows.

1. Click the Start button on the Windows 95 desktop tray.
2. Click on the Settings menu option.
3. Click on Control Panel.
4. In the Control Panel window, double-click the Add Hardware
   Wizard icon.
5. At the Add Hardware Wizard opening screen, click the Next button.
6. You can now install hardware by autodetection or you can install it
   yourself. Autodetection isn't foolproof and can lock up your system
   in some cases. However, it is the simplest way to add new drivers,
   so try it first. To autodetect, click on the button next to Autodetect.
   To choose the type of hardware driver yourself, click on the button
   next to Install Specific and skip to step 1 under the "Install
   Specific" section below.
7. Now click the Next button to run Autodetect.

Autodetect Installation

1. Windows will begin autodetection. This may take a while. If the
   progress meter at the bottom of the window stops for a long period
   of time, the computer has probably locked up, and you'll have to
   restart your system.
2. After all devices have been properly detected, a new window will
   come up. If you want to see what devices were detected, click the
   Details button. Otherwise, click the Finish button to install the
   new drivers.
3. If the required drivers aren't already on your system, Windows will
   ask you for the appropriate disk. Follow the instructions from
   Windows for any drivers it needs.

4. After all the drivers are installed, you will need to restart the system for the changes to take effect. Click the Restart button to restart Windows.

Install Specific

1. To use Install Specific, first scroll down the list of hardware devices until you get to SCSI Controllers and then double-click on SCSI Controllers.
2. Select the manufacturer of your SCSI controller from the list on the left by clicking on it. If the manufacturer is not listed, click on the Have Disk button.
3. Select the model of SCSI card that you installed from the list on the right by clicking on it.
4. If you have updated drivers on a disk that came with your SCSI card, you can install the newer version by clicking on the Have Disk button.
5. Click the Next button to install the driver(s).
6. A window will come up showing you the current settings for your SCSI card. Write this down for future reference so that you can avoid an I/O, IRQ, or DMA conflict with the SCSI card when installing an interface card into your system. Click the Next button after you write down the settings.
7. Click the Finish button to finish installing the driver(s).
8. After all the drivers are installed, you will need to restart the system for the changes to take effect. Click the Restart button to restart Windows.

Windows NT Drivers

Windows NT includes drivers for many SCSI interfaces. After installing your SCSI card, start Windows NT and see if you can access your SCSI devices. If not, you have to install the NT drivers for your SCSI interface as follows.

1. Open Program Manager if it isn't already opened.
2. Open the Main group window and start the Windows NT Setup program.
3. Select Add/Remove SCSI Adapters from the Options menu.
4. Click the Add button and select the type of SCSI adapter you've installed.

5. If Windows tells you that the driver already exists on the system, you can click Current to use the existing driver or New to install a new copy.

6. If you choose to use the current driver, it will be installed and you will return to the main window where the new SCSI card will be listed.

7. If you choose to install a new driver, Windows will ask you for the full path to the location of the driver. Type in **A:** or **B:**, depending on which drive you inserted the driver disk in, and click OK.

8. After the driver is installed, you will see it listed in the Main Setup window. Click the OK button to close the setup program.

9. Restart Windows NT for the changes to take effect.

OS/2 Drivers

OS/2 has its own set of standards and conventions for SCSI device drivers. Beginning with version 2.0, OS/2 includes drivers that allow for direct SCSI access. OS/2 includes drivers for SCSI disks, CD-ROM drives, and optical disks, as well as an ASPI driver for communicating with other devices.

The basic concept behind OS/2's drivers isn't that different from that of ASPI in DOS. If you're running OS/2 and adding a new SCSI device, you have to load a hardware-specific driver for your host adapter card. Either you'll find this driver on a disk that came with your card or you'll need to get it directly from the card's manufacturer or its BBS (see Appendix A for a listing of manufacturers, including their BBS numbers). This hardware-specific device driver will probably have a filename with an .add extension.

To load these device drivers, choose Device Driver Install from System Setup. Follow the directions on your screen, and you should be on your way. Once you've loaded your hardware-specific .add driver, you may be asked to load OS/2's device type specific drivers, which usually have a .dmd extension. Again, either you'll find this driver on a disk that came with your card or you'll need to get it from the manufacturer.

Finally, some devices running under OS/2 may require that you load drivers to change or enhance their operation. These drivers will have an .flt extension.

NOTE *Before direct SCSI support was implemented in version 2.0 of OS/2, Microsoft and IBM developed a standard driver interface called LADDR. LADDR, which is short for Layered Device Driver, was used in OS/2 versions 1.2 and 1.3, but it is not needed in later versions of OS/2.*

- Before you remove the SCSI interface card from the package, be sure to ground yourself. Touch a static discharge plate or your computer's case to make sure you aren't carrying a static charge. If you do zap your card with a static discharge, you're liable to fry it with as much as 10,000+ volts!

- Before getting started, print out the BIOS setup for your system. You can usually do this by going into the setup program (usually pressing the DEL key at boot up) and then pressing the PRINT SCRN key. If that doesn't work, jot down the values that you see on your screen. You should also print out your autoexec.bat and config.sys files before you start changing them, so that you can return to where it was if something goes wrong. (Actually, this is good advice any time you install anything.) You can also copy the files to another directory to save a lot of typing in case you have to return your system to its original state.

- Be sure you have a bootable floppy disk handy before fiddling with the BIOS setups so that you can boot your machine if you really screw it up.

Remember, when you load the drivers for your SCSI devices, you have to specify some of the same parameters, like the I/O port, which you determined when you set up your hardware. If you select an I/O port for the driver that's different from the one you set on your controller card, for example, you'll have to change the port on your controller card too.

SCSI CD-ROM Drives

If you're installing a SCSI CD-ROM drive for use with DOS and Windows, be sure that you install the DOS CD extensions driver, mscdex.exe. And, if you use smartdrv.exe for disk caching, be sure to load mscdex.exe first in your autoexec.bat so that the caching program will recognize the CD drive.

SCSI Hard Drives

Once you've installed a SCSI hard drive, the controller's BIOS will assign it a drive letter when you boot the PC. If you're using DOS or Windows version 3.11 or earlier, you will have to run fdisk, or a similar disk partitioning utility that came with your SCSI interface, to create a DOS partition. Then, run the DOS format command on the disk. Be sure to use the /s of format to transfer system files for booting.

TABLE 4.1 The Relationship Between Partition and Cluster Size

Partition Size (MB)	Cluster Size (Bytes)
< 32	512
33–64	1024
65–128	2048
129–256	4096
257–512	8192
513–1024	16384

TABLE 4.2 DOS-Assigned Device Drive Letters

Device	Drive Letter
5-1/4-inch floppy drive	A:
3-1/2-inch floppy drive	B:
IDE primary partition (partition 1)	C:
SCSI primary partition (partition 1)	D:
IDE first logical partition (partition 2)	E:
SCSI first logical partition (partition 2)	F:
SCSI second logical partition (partition 3)	G:

When creating a DOS partition with fdisk or the partitioning utility supplied by the SCSI interface manufacturer, don't create a partition that is larger than what you need even if you have a large hard disk. Larger partitions use larger clusters to store data. Since the size of most files aren't an even multiple of the cluster size, more space is wasted with larger clusters. Table 4.1, above, illustrates how the cluster size increases with larger partitions.

DOS assigns drive letters to the primary partitions on drives before any logical (second, third, fourth, and so on) partitions. As a result, partitioning SCSI drives will result in some pretty interesting arrangements of drive letters. For example, let's say you have a setup that consists of a PC with two floppy drives, one IDE drive (the boot drive) with two partitions, and one SCSI drive with three partitions. Table 4.2, above, lists the devices along with the drive letters as they are assigned by DOS.

For more tips and hints on perfecting your SCSI installation, see Chapter 5.

5

TROUBLESHOOTING YOUR SCSI INSTALLATION

by Stefan Groll and Gerhard Islinger

Everyone hopes that troubleshooting will never need to be done—and then trouble strikes. Although some vendors seem to make a company secret of it, troubleshooting a SCSI system is like all other troubleshooting jobs. You need to know a few basic rules, and then it's just a logical process. Before beginning your troubleshooting, run through the following short checklist of a few basics. In many cases, you'll be able to solve your problem by resolving one of these issues:

✓ Does the host adapter have any resource conflicts (namely I/O port, IRQ, or DMA)?

✓ Does each device have its own unique SCSI ID?

✓ Does termination appear only at the bus ends?

✓ Are cabling rules obeyed?

✓ Is the device connected properly? Shrouded header connectors have a plastic guard around their perimeter with a notch on one side. To prevent you from incorrectly inserting connectors, these shrouded headers use a mechanical key (a slot or tab in the connector), which requires that the cable be inserted only one way into the shroud. Some cheaper devices use only simple connectors, mostly for cost reasons, though some high-end host adapters also use these cheap connectors. These cheap connectors aren't keyed and have no way of preventing incorrect connections.

Usually, you will need to test the system with whatever parts you already have; but when looking for particularly pesky problems, you may find the following parts useful:

- At least one known good internal and external cable.
- Active and passive terminators.
- A diagnostic cable (one with an unused connector) for measuring purposes.
- A multimeter (for voltage and resistance measurements).
- If your host adapter's BIOS doesn't have a format utility or similar modules, you'll need one or more software tools that show all the devices attached to the bus (note that all such tools need an installed ASPI or CAM driver).
- For DOS users, a bootable floppy disk with DOS and your adapter's ASPI or CAM driver. If possible, have a newer DOS variant (DOS 6.0 or above) on this floppy with multiple boot configurations, which will allow you to decide which drivers to load at startup.
- If you troubleshoot frequently, it's a good idea to also have a spare host adapter and a small hard disk with a bootable partition on it.
- An oscilloscope or transient recorder is necessary for some very tricky things, like measuring RF distortion or noise on static signals like TERMPWR. There is no way around buying these tools if you want to take measurements like these.

COMMON PROBLEMS

Now that you know what tools you should have (and which, of course, you don't have handy when you need them most), here is a list of some of the most basic system problems and possible cures for them.

Problem: Host adapter not recognized by the system

Symptom:
The host adapter isn't recognized on startup, or you get a message like "Couldn't initialize host adapter."

Possible causes:
The SCSI adapter isn't seated correctly in the computer's bus connector.

Your system's hardware is using conflicting system resources, like an I/O address, interrupt (IRQ), or DMA channel.

An illegal system resource is set on the host adapter.

The host adapter is plugged into the wrong type of bus slot.

A device on the bus is locking up the SCSI controller, due to a conflict in SCSI settings such as parity checking.

Explanations and possible remedies:
Check to see that the host adapter is seated properly in the system's card slot. Make sure that it's not installed at an angle so that, although some functions seem to work, a few conductors are not making contact.

The host adapter could have a resource conflict. (If you encounter a resource conflict when installing a new SCSI host adapter, see the installation guidelines in Chapter 4, "Adding SCSI to Your PC.") Many systems worked fine before the SCSI card was installed. You'll usually encounter resource conflicts in your system immediately after you add a new adapter card to your computer. (Sound cards are especially notorious for causing resource conflicts, because many sound cards use the same I/O ports, interrupts, or DMA channels as SCSI host adapters.)

Some adapters have a set of jumpers or DIP switches but allow you to set only a few specific combinations. If you set an undefined combination, you can create all sorts of problems in your system. Verify your adapter's jumper and switch settings with its user manual.

Some adapters restrict the combination of resources that they can use. For example, the older Adaptec 1540A and B models could set different I/O addresses, but the BIOS could work only with I/O address 330 hex.

EISA, VLB, and PCI systems have both busmaster-capable and non-busmaster-capable slots available. Since nearly all SCSI host adapters for these bus systems use bus mastering, ensure that you select the correct slot type when you install the adapter.

In some cases, where the SCSI device offers a data transfer option, like parity, that option has been set but it is incompatible with the host adapter's setting (not all host adapters will support parity checking, for example). This incompatibility might lock up the SCSI controller chip on the host adapter, thus causing the BIOS or driver to think the adapter is defective.

Finally, in the worst case, the host adapter may be defective.

Hints:
After ensuring that the board is seated properly and that there are no resource conflicts, disconnect the bus cables from the host adapter to see if the adapter is recognized. If it is, your problem is caused by something related to the SCSI bus.

If you inserted a new board, or you changed the setup of another board, the affected board may now have a resource conflict. For example, some sound boards' MIDI addresses conflict with those of SCSI host adapters.

When you encounter errors like those listed above, always remember that the BIOS and the SCSI controller are independent components on the board. Just because one of them works doesn't necessarily mean that the other one also works.

Problem: One device not found

Symptom:
A device isn't found on startup.

Possible causes:
There is a power failure in this component or its power connector.

There are conflicting SCSI ID settings.

Termination is incorrect.

Cabling is incorrect. A connector plugged in the wrong way may be very dangerous! Incorrect connections can cause short circuits.

The cables are too long.

There is a bad cable(s).

An external device was turned on after the SCSI bus scan.

Explanations and possible remedies:
Check to see that the device powers on. Make sure that the connector is seated correctly, that the device spins up, or that the device accepts a tape or CD-ROM, and so on. If not, attach another power cable and check the voltage on the device's connector to ensure that power is available at the device.

If a new or external device is connected to the bus, its SCSI ID may conflict with that of a device already on the bus. This conflict may cause the device(s) sharing this ID to malfunction and may even cause the entire bus to fail.

Make sure that the bus is terminated properly. Make sure that you didn't add a terminated device in the middle of the bus or an unterminated device at the end of the bus. Be sure that you correctly enabled or disabled the host adapter's termination.

It sometimes happens (usually only with cheap host adapters or devices with nonkeyed connectors) that an internal connector is plugged in the wrong way. The shrouded (keyed) connectors, found on better host adapters and devices, prevent you from plugging a connector in the wrong way. Incorrectly inserted connectors may be hazardous to the SCSI bus itself because termination power may be connected to ground, thereby causing a short circuit.

Your cables may be too long. External devices, especially scanners, sometimes come with a cable two or three meters long, which results in an overall bus length that exceeds the SCSI limitation.

With external devices, you may have a cheap cable that doesn't meet the SCSI specifications. It is especially important to use high-quality cables when using Fast SCSI.

If the device is external, was it powered on too late to be recognized by the SCSI bus scan? Some drivers don't recognize devices that are turned on after they have scanned the bus for devices. If you turn on your system and then turn on your external device—a CD-ROM drive, for example—the external device may take too long to react to inquiry commands from the SCSI bus, such that the host adapter thinks it isn't present. As a result, the device's driver fails to install. To see whether this is your problem, try a warm reboot.

Hint:

If you have a working setup and suddenly a device isn't recognized, then a power failure or a termination problem are the most likely causes. However, incorrect setups can continue working for some time and then fail without an obvious reason, so it's best to check all possible causes.

Problem: No device found

Symptom:

The host adapter seems to work, but it can't find any device on the bus.

Possible causes:

The bus cable may have lost its connection.

Termination power may have failed.

Termination is incorrect.

Cabling is incorrect or bad.

Cables are too long. While very seldom a reason for a complete bus failure, it's worth checking to see that the length of your cables doesn't exceed the maximum.

There's a bad cable on the bus.

Explanations and possible remedies:

If the SCSI cable was under tension, it may have lost contact with the host adapter's connector. Make sure that the cable is still connected.

Check the termination. You should have terminators only on the ends of the bus and no terminators on any other devices.

If a new or external device is connected to the bus, its SCSI ID may conflict with that of a device already on the bus. Such a conflict will cause the device(s) with this ID to malfunction and may cause the entire bus to fail.

If you have internal devices, a connector may have been plugged in the wrong way, which may either blow the termination power fuse or simply draw most signals to ground. Either way, the bus won't work. The recommended shrouded header connectors prevent this by a mechanical key, a slot in the connector that requires that the cable be inserted only one way. There are some devices that use only simple connectors, mostly for cost reasons, but there are also some high-end host adapters with these cheap connectors.

A bad cable could be somewhere in the external chain. Try disconnecting a device or two and swap cables to see if there's a bad one.

Hints:

If you have a working setup, and suddenly a device isn't recognized, then a power failure is the most likely cause. However, some setups may continue working for some time before failing for no apparent reason.

If you have a new setup and the devices aren't recognized, turn the system off immediately and double-check the complete setup. The fault may involve terminators on the host adapter and/or devices.

Problem: System can't boot from SCSI hard disk

Symptom:

While the host adapter seems to work and recognizes all devices, the system won't boot from a SCSI hard disk or it locks up when booting.

Possible causes:

There is a non-SCSI (IDE, ESDI, etc.) hard disk in the system.

The hard disk has an ID higher than that supported for booting. Some adapters only boot from a particular ID or range of IDs.

There is no active partition on the SCSI disk.

A DOS memory manager overwrites the SCSI BIOS.

Your SCSI host adapter has no BIOS or its BIOS is disabled.

Your SCSI adapter may need an entry for the disk in the computer's setup.

Explanations and possible remedies:

If a non-SCSI hard disk (IDE, EIDE, ESDI, or ST506) is in the system, it has boot priority in the system BIOS. So, if you have a non-SCSI disk, booting from SCSI won't work until you disable the non-SCSI hard disk. Many host adapters will only boot from devices with an ID of 0 or 1. So, if your disk is set on ID 6, booting either isn't possible or you need to set a parameter in the SCSI host adapter's settings or a jumper. It's best to set the hard disks to lower IDs to prevent this sort of problem.

As with any other disk drive, you need a bootable and active primary partition to boot from a SCSI hard disk drive. Use FDISK to set the primary partition to bootable.

If your system boots from the SCSI hard disk, but then locks up, the DOS memory manager may be overwriting the SCSI BIOS when it is started in CONFIG.SYS. To see if this is the problem, make a backup copy of your CONFIG.SYS file and then remove the line for the memory manager. Now try booting the system again to see if it boots from the SCSI hard disk.

If you get "no boot device" or similar messages, see if your SCSI BIOS is enabled. Sometimes people try to run a hard disk from a sound card's SCSI port. While this usually works, the hard disk isn't bootable if the sound card's embedded SCSI host adapter doesn't have a SCSI BIOS, which most do not.

Some older SCSI host adapters (older DPT models, for example) emulate a WD1003 hard disk interface and need a CMOS entry for the bootable hard disk. (This is so unusual for SCSI, that it's easy to forget—so check your manual.)

Problem: Intermittent lockups and communication errors

Symptom:
The SCSI system usually works but shows intermittent lockups.

Possible causes:
Termination is incorrect.

Termination power is too low and/or noisy.

You may have folded your internal cable into a tight, neat package, and as a result, created an R-C (resistor-capacitor) network that has unforeseeable side effects under dynamic load.

Cables are too long. This often happens with external devices, especially scanners, which sometimes come with a cable two or three meters long.

One of your cables is bad.

Explanations and possible remedies:
Check the termination thoroughly. Did you obey all the rules? Remember, termination occurs only at both ends of the bus.

When using internal devices with resistor SIPs (single inline package), are they inserted in the right direction? Pin 1 is usually marked with a colored spot or line. An incorrectly inserted passive terminator (for example, TERMPWR and ground on the opposite ends, signals on the middle pins) shifts the working point of the terminator. The bus may continue to work but will be unreliable.

Passive termination is particularly vulnerable to low termination power voltage. If you follow the specs, TERMPWR should be between 4.25 and 5.25 volts. However, most manufacturers start with the +5 volts DC (VDC) from the PC's power supply and connect a silicone rectifier for protection. Now, if the +5VDC is really only 4.85 volts and we lose about 0.6 to 0.7 volts across the rectifier, we're below spec. If you add the loss on the SCSI cable, we're clearly under spec. Active termination is far less vulnerable here, since it works with a voltage regulator, and a good voltage regulator needs just about 0.5 to 1 volt over the needed 2.85 volts.

The same applies for noisy TERMPWR. The basic voltage supply for the termination power isn't very clean, which may cause some systems to hiccup. Noise might get through the termination network to the signal lines. As stated above, active termination is less vulnerable because the voltage regulator suppresses the noise to some degree. If noisy TERMPWR is your problem, you will need an oscilloscope or transient recorder to find it—and then you'll need even more good ideas to get rid of it.

Sometimes, people fold all their internal cables in neat packages, securing them with cable fasteners or plastic belts. This may or may not work. When you fold the cables, you create a very complex R-C network, which may cause the bus to fail at certain dynamic situations under load. So, even if you're an order fanatic or neat-nick, resist this temptation! Let the cables flow freely in the case.

Keep the bus length inside the computer at a minimum. The maximum bus lengths are defined for an ideal setup, and a real-world setup is never an ideal one. Also, each connector, each cable change, and each device introduces impedance changes; so, if possible, keep the cables shorter than the specified maximum length as a security margin.

If you get a bad cable, replace it. When you identify a cable that gives you trouble, you may find a cable sequence that works, but it will always be a suspicious point. So, if possible, replace it right away. If you buy a cable, especially an external one, don't get the cheapest, get one that adheres to the specs.

NOTE *SCSI vendors with a good reputation tend to have good quality cables, so their cables are usually a good choice.*

How to Check Typical Issues

Two Devices with the Same ID

If two or more installed devices do not work, but one of them is recognized by a tool like SHOWSCSI or the host adapter is not able to detect one of them during the boot phase, then it's likely that you have two devices at the same ID. Let's create a scenario for this situation: You have a setup with hard disk drives at IDs 0 and 1, a tape drive at ID 2, and a CD-ROM drive at ID 3. Now you add an external device, say, a Bernoulli-Box, configured also for ID 3.

This change in your setup could cause various error situations: the two devices at ID 3 simply don't work, but the system works with the remaining devices; the CD-ROM driver locks up on initializing its device; or the host adapter hangs at the bus scan.

Whatever happens, check all IDs carefully. If you don't know your IDs or aren't able to find out easily, use this quick-and-dirty approach.

1. Power up the system and note what devices are found on what IDs during bootup.

2. Turn off the system and disconnect the devices that were recognized—the ones that the system knows about.

3. Turn the system on again and watch, during bootup, for devices to show up that weren't present before you disconnected the recognized or known devices.

4. Add these devices to the list of known devices.

5. Repeat these steps until no device is left on your system.

After following these steps, you may be surprised to discover even three devices at the same ID, and you'll have a list of all attached devices and their IDs. Now, armed with your list, change the conflicting device ID(s) so that it no longer conflicts, and everything should be OK.

Remember, ID 0 and ID 1 are usually used for hard disks, and ID 7 should remain reserved for the host adapter. Do not try to attach more devices than the host adapter is able to handle. A special case of this problem is if you set a peripheral device to the host adapter's ID. Usually, on a bus scan, this device shows up on all IDs except the host adapter's ID (because the host's ID isn't checked). The problematic part of this situation is that a single-device configuration usually works, but if you connect a second peripheral device, you won't get it to show up during the bootup of your system.

NOTE   *Some devices have incomplete implementations of the SCSI interface, and some older devices have fixed IDs (though a device with an ID fixed at 7 is unheard of). See "Tricky Devices" later in this chapter for more information on how to handle these devices.*

Dead Devices

Electronic devices have many ways of dying, and heaven only knows which path your device will choose. Usually, if the SCSI electronics are OK, the system finds the device, it reacts to inquiry commands, but on accesses or tests you get a "device not ready" or similar message. This is very common for defective disk drives or tape devices. If the device is "electronically dead," it won't react at all. This is the easy symptom to detect.

Termination

If the termination rules are violated, the violation may not show up at once. A one-sided termination (only one terminator on the bus) usually won't work with multiple devices or a longer bus cable. Some companies (for example, Apple in some older systems and NEC with some of their OEM CD-ROMs) claim that the SCSI bus in their configuration will work even with only one terminator. Although this may be true under some circumstances, it isn't generally true and is definitely not recommended. Incorrect termination has essentially one result: the system won't work correctly. "Not correctly" can range from "sometimes works, sometimes doesn't" to "definitely dead."

There are two possible ways to estimate the number of passive terminators installed. First, count them. This can be a time-consuming job, especially if you have to open your computer, remove the drives to look at them, and so on. But if you do, you can check to see that all terminators are installed correctly. Pay attention to the correct orientation of internal terminators also.

Second, use your multimeter. Take appropriate diagrams of the connector layouts (see Appendix B) and note the position of the following signals:

- Termination power (TERMPWR)
- Ground (GND)
- One of the data lines

Then power down your computer and all devices attached to it. You can now either replace one of the SCSI cables with your diagnostic cable or you can remove one of the SCSI devices, preferably an external one. If you remove a device, don't forget to see whether it's terminated or not.

Detecting passive terminators is fairly easy. With your multimeter, you only have to measure three resistances. If the termination is correct, your measurement will match those listed in Table 5.1.

All resistances may differ in a range of approximately 5 percent.

Measuring active terminators is difficult and unpredictable. Active terminators may respond like the example in the table above (our specific model didn't show up when not powered on), but they don't necessarily react this way. Some of them can be identified by yielding different readings when the multimeter probes are interchanged.

Since an active terminator's output resistors are clamped directly to the signal, without the simple pull-up and pull-down resistors, active

TABLE 5.1 Termination Measurements

	Any Signal to GND	Any Signal to TERMPWR	TERMPWR to GND
No terminator	—	—	—
1 passive terminator *	143.0 ohms	136.8 ohms	30.5 ohms
2 passive terminators	71.5 ohms	68.4 ohms	15.25 ohms
3 passive terminators	47.6 ohms	45.6 ohms	10.2 ohms
More than 2 passive terminators	< 71.5 ohms	< 136.8 ohms	< 30.5 ohms
1 passive and 1 active terminator *	71.5 ohms	68.4 ohms	30.5 ohms

* The active terminator we used in our example (we measured it) didn't show up when not powered. Other active terminators may behave differently, depending on their internal circuits.

terminators affect only the signal-to-TERMPWR reading, if at all, not the signal-to-ground and TERMPWR-to-ground measurings.

If you find out that there are too many terminators in the bus, you have no other choice but to remove the additional terminators.

Termination Power

Passive termination is especially vulnerable to low or noisy termination power voltage. The SCSI specification states very clearly that TERMPWR should be between 4.25 and 5.25 volts. In their board designs, most manufacturers start with the +5VDC level from the PC's power supply and have a silicone diode in the line as a protection diode. Now, if the +5VDC is just 4.85 volts and we lose about 0.6 to 0.7 volts across the diode, it's below spec. If you add the loss on the SCSI cable, it's clearly under spec.

If this low voltage appears in your system, you might want to adjust the voltage of your power supply. ***Do not try this if you don't know exactly what you are doing!*** Since this can be done only if the computer is powered on and is open, it can be very dangerous if you touch the wrong parts. Computers from vendors with their own power supply design sometimes have test pins and adjusting elements that can be reached without opening the computer, or at least without opening the power supply; but most clone manufacturers' power supplies are the sealed-box type. ***If you open it, you not only lose your warranty, but also might lose your life by touching the wrong part! We don't recommend that you play with it unless you really know what to do with it.***

Active termination is far less vulnerable to low or noisy termination power voltage because it uses a voltage regulator, and a good voltage regulator needs just about 0.5 to 1 volt over the needed 2.85 volts.

Noise at the TERMPWR line, especially noise in the frequency range used by SCSI data, can be even more of a nightmare. It can lead to all sorts of unpredictable behavior. The supply voltage for termination power isn't always clean, and its noise might get through the termination network to the signal lines. If you encounter strange lockups, you've sorted out the basics, and have access to an oscilloscope, it might be a good idea to use the oscilloscope to check the signal condition on the TERMPWR line.

Situating the computer near a high-voltage wire may also cause strange behavior. If you encounter this sort of noise, it can sometimes help to change the computer's orientation relative to the wire.

If noisy TERMPWR is your problem, you will need an oscilloscope or a transient recorder to find it. If you find noise in the terminator power, look at the +5V pins from the power supply and see if they show the same noise. If they do, replace the power supply with a better quality model. Also, a good surge suppressor might work wonders for this problem.

Tricky Devices

Some devices can cause some grief because of their particular SCSI implementation. For example, most parallel-to-SCSI adapters draw their supply power from the TERMPWR line. So, if your external device(s) doesn't supply termination power to the SCSI bus, these adapters won't work. Also, some older devices can create strange situations, because their SCSI implementations can be limited to some extent.

For example, the old NEC CDR-35 and CDR-36 portable CD-ROM drives don't have termination, and they have only one SCSI connector. Thus, they can only be used on the end of the chain, and they must be connected via a pass-through terminator. In addition, the CDR-35 is fixed to SCSI ID 1 and can't be changed.

On some older devices, you may not see a switch to change the ID. This may be for two reasons: either the device really is fixed to a specific ID (the Siemens HighScan 800 scanner, for example), or the switch is hidden somewhere inside the device. The second case occurs primarily on devices that have SCSI as an option only, like some older EPSON scanners. They came by default with special serial and parallel interfaces only, and the SCSI interface card was an option, with the ID switch on the PCB deep inside the scanner.

If you encounter some strange problems and can't find a logical explanation, it's probably time to give the manuals a look. Most of the time these kinds of things are stated somewhere inside the manual.

Driver Problems

Sometimes, the SCSI device drivers for DOS can be real troublemakers. They may have problems with memory managers, incompatibilities with each other, bugs, or all sorts of other nasty things. However, when installed correctly, and with the few hints that follow, you'll usually be able to avoid this trouble.

Let's look at a sample configuration, taken from a real support case, that shows the problems you, or the install program, might run into.

Sample 1: ASPI

The first erroneous sample configuration is for an ISA PC with an Adaptec 1540 host adapter:

```
device=c:\dos\himem.sys
devicehigh=c:\dos\scsi\aspicd.sys /d:aspicd    - The ASPI CDROM driver
device=c:\dos\emm386.exe ram
devicehigh=c:\dos\scsi\aspi4dos.sys /d         - The 1540's ASPI driver
shell=c:\dos\command.com c:\dos\ /e:256 /p
dos=high,umb
lastdrive =f
devicehigh=c:\dos\scsi\aspidisk.sys            - The ASPI disk driver for
                                                 non-BIOS disks
```

This configuration has one error and two points for possible problems:

1. The first error is that the device driver, ASPICD.SYS, is started before the low-level driver, ASPI4DOS.SYS; so at the device driver's loading time, no ASPI interface is present. The driver refuses to load and the CD-ROM won't work.

2. Second, EMM386.EXE is loaded with the RAM parameter without excluding the SCSI BIOS area. This may or may not work, depending on the memory manager and its version; but it's usually the case that on loading the EMM386.EXE driver, the SCSI BIOS address range is overwritten with RAM to gain upper memory blocks (UMBs) for drivers and resident programs.

3. Third, many SCSI device drivers cannot (or should not) be loaded high. In general, the basic ASPI or CAM shell drivers for SCSI adapters should be placed before all memory manager commands, as virtually all those drivers do more than just the ASPI layer. They either provide additional services and/or they provide bug fixes for the BIOS and other things.

A working configuration would look like this:

```
device=c:\dos\scsi\aspi4dos.sys /d
device=c:\dos\himem.sys
device=c:\dos\emm386.exe ram x=dc00-dfff
dos=high,umb
devicehigh=c:\dos\scsi\aspicd.sys /d:aspicd
```

```
devicehigh=c:\dos\scsi\aspidisk.sys
shell=c:\dos\command.com c:\dos\ /e:256 /p
lastdrive=f
```

Of course, there are possibilities for further optimizations, but the basic changes to the configuration are fairly straightforward.

In this working configuration, the following are true:

- The ASPI driver is loaded before the memory manager, so as not to interfere with it.
- EMM386.EXE excludes the BIOS address range, in this case DC00 to DFFF, the 1540's default.
- All ASPI-dependent drivers are loaded after the ASPI low-level driver so that they will be able to communicate with the ASPI driver.

Sample 2: CAM

CAM drivers may cause problems similar to ASPI.

NCR's CAM drivers also have a potential performance trap. NCR supplies two CAM base drivers, MINICAM.SYS and DOSCAM.SYS. MINICAM.SYS is very attractive for a DOS system at first glance, because it works and needs much less memory than does DOSCAM.SYS. The drawback is that the MiniCAM drivers only support basic asynchronous transfers. If you need synchronous negotiation (Fast SCSI), Wide SCSI negotiation, disconnect/reconnect, or a few of the other advanced SCSI possibilities, you need DOSCAM.SYS. In other words, if you want anything over 3 MB/sec bus throughput, MINICAM.SYS is not enough, and you'll need to use DOSCAM.SYS.

 Ironically, the safety precaution for the ASPI drivers brings problems. NCR states that emm386.exe must be loaded before the CAM drivers.

A working CONFIG.SYS file for NCR's CAM drivers might look like the following:

```
device=c:\dos\himem.sys
device=c:\dos\emm386.exe ram x=dc00-dfff
dos=high,umb
device=c:\doscam.sys               - The CAM shell driver
device=c:\aspicam.sys              - ASPI translation layer
device=c:\cdrom.sys /d:aspicd      - Generic CD-ROM driver
device=c:\scsidisk.sys             - Multi-purpose disk driver
shell=c:\dos\command.com c:\dos\ /e:256 /p
lastdrive =f
```

Future Domain Corporation also supports CAM with its own implementation and slightly different driver names. (See Appendix E for an overview of CAM, contributed by Future Domain Corporation.) Interestingly, Future Domain also has a full-featured CAM driver, called DCAM*xxxx*.EXE, and a smaller MiniCAM driver MCAM*xxxx*.SYS ("*xxxx*" stands for the SCSI controller chip, 950 or 1800, depending on the model). The main difference here is that the single-tasking version (MCAM950.SYS) provides all the CAM functionality except that disconnect/reconnect and command queuing are not supported (all CAM commands are processed serially).

The above driver order holds here too, though the driver names differ. The ASPI-over-CAM layer is called ASPIFCAM.SYS, and there are other minor differences, but the principles remain the same.

General Rules

■ If you suspect driver problems, or the system locks up when initializing the SCSI drivers, try a clean boot with only the SCSI drivers to see if you have a memory conflict or similar problem. Then add in the other drivers one by one.

■ If one or multiple devices are found by the bus scan, but won't operate later, check the order of the drivers in CONFIG.SYS.

■ Avoid loading the SCSI drivers in upper memory unless you've tested it thoroughly.

■ Check memory manager address ranges for proper exclusions.

Driver Combinations

Combinations of different ASPI drivers may cause big trouble. By definition, ASPI drivers should be cascadable. One manufacturer's ASPI extensions should work on another's low-level driver, but this is in theory only. Virtually every manufacturer makes his own (read incompatible) extensions to the drivers. As an example, Adaptec and Buslogic ASPI drivers don't cooperate. Either the Buslogic driver kicks the Adaptec driver out, or the Adaptec driver refuses to load after the Buslogic driver. Ironically, both adapters (in this case, a 1740A and a Buslogic BT-742) work together at BIOS level without any hassles, but only one ASPI driver can be used. No possible combination gives you both adapters with full ASPI support, and nearly the same applies for all other combinations we tried.

Different drivers from the same vendor usually don't share this problem. The manufacturers are definitely interested in their own adapters working together, but don't count on it before you've tried it.

HOW THE BUS WORKS

by David A. Deming, Founder, Solution Technology

As we all know, by now, SCSI is an acronym for the small computer system interface. That is all fine and dandy, but what *is* SCSI? This chapter goes beyond where the rest of the book has been to look at the way the SCSI bus really works.

AN INTELLIGENT INTERFACE

SCSI is an intelligent interface that hides a device's physical format. Each SCSI device attaches to the SCSI bus in the same manner, and the host computer's only concern is what type of device is attached (e.g., disk, tape, and so on). Information is retrieved from a SCSI device via logical block addressing, a scheme that hides the device's physical configuration. This is beneficial, because the host is not required to know the head, cylinder, sector, etc. of where information is stored. If a host needs a file from a device, it requests the file in the form of an address that is logical from zero to the maximum address available on the device.

SCSI Is an Interface That Supports Generic Software

SCSI uses device-generic commands, which, in standardized system software, support many devices. In most systems, the host computer requires special software to properly format the command for each specified device type. This software is known as a device driver. There is usually a separate device driver for each device type attached to the SCSI bus, though some system architectures use one driver for all device types.

SCSI Is a True Peripheral Interface

SCSI is a true peripheral interface that allows up to eight devices (SCSI-2) or 16 devices (SCSI-3) to be attached to a single bus/cable. These devices can be any combination of peripherals or hosts, but there must be at least one host. In SCSI, there is a standard protocol, which is device-independent. The host computer can attach disk drives, tape drives, optical disks (WORM, CD-ROM, erasable), and other devices (printers, scanners, etc.) to the same port.

In addition, SCSI is a buffered interface where all activities can "shake hands," so that slow or fast devices operate properly with slow or fast hosts. SCSI's handshaking allows devices of various communication speeds to coexist on the same cable. (We talk more about handshaking later in this chapter, in the section titled "Handshaking of Information.")

SCSI is also a peer-to-peer interface, where communication can take place from one host to another, one peripheral device to another, or, most commonly, a host to a peripheral device.

Initiators, Targets, and Logical Units

To understand how SCSI works, you must first know some definitions. For each communication (I/O process) that occurs between two devices, each device involved assumes a particular role. One device assumes the role of an initiator and is responsible for starting or initiating the I/O process. The other device is the initiator's target, and it is responsible for managing or controlling the I/O process. Logical units are physical peripheral devices that are addressable through a target or peripheral controller (i.e., subaddress of the target). This basic operational diagram (Figure 6.1) shows a host-to-peripheral device connection.

What Is an I/O Process?

In SCSI, the term *I/O process* defines a particular method of doing something with an input/output device. The I/O process generally involves numerous steps. Figure 6.2 shows what an I/O process might look like if we were to model it.

FIGURE 6.1 Basic Diagram of the Host-to-Peripheral Device Connection

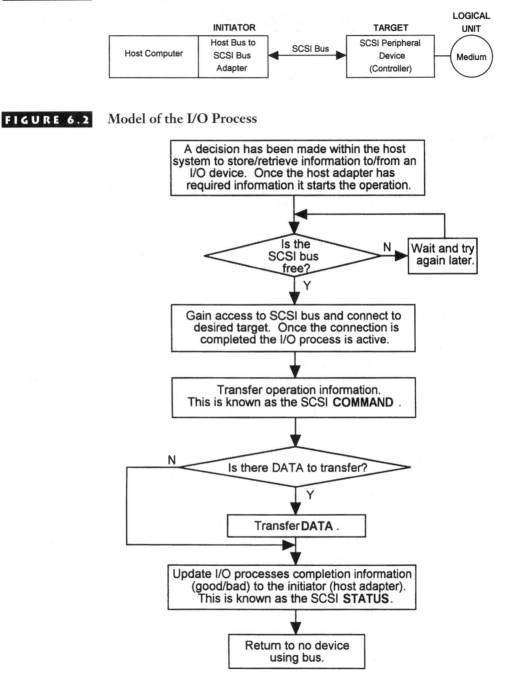

FIGURE 6.2 Model of the I/O Process

FIGURE 6.3 **A Look at a SCSI Transfer at Its Simplest**

Bus Connection	COMMAND	DATA	STATUS	Bus Disconnection

The illustration in Figure 6.3 is an example of a SCSI transfer at its simplest. We'll discuss SCSI protocol in detail later in this chapter.

SCSI CONFIGURATIONS

A SCSI system can have many different configurations, including a single initiator and single target, single initiator and multiple targets, and multiple initiators and multiple targets. The diagrams in Figure 6.4 show how the SCSI standard defines each of these different bus configurations. Note that the "Single Initiator and Single Target" diagram has been modified from the SCSI-2 standard to show more information about the host adapter and peripheral device.

BUS AND DEVICE CHARACTERISTICS

A SCSI device can be a host adapter or target controller attached to the SCSI bus. Each device usually has a fixed role as an initiator or target, but some may assume either role. The host adapter is a device that connects the host system to the SCSI bus and performs the lower layers of protocol when accessing the SCSI bus. Host adapters usually act as initiators.

NOTE *SCSI is an "interlocked interface," which means that only two devices can communicate at any given time. When these two devices are communicating, all other devices must wait for the bus to free up before they can access the bus.*

When two devices are talking to one another, they are performing an I/O process. The I/O process involves an initiator and a target connecting to one another and transferring information, with the responsibilities of each device in the I/O process as follows.

Initiators

When a device is acting as an initiator, it does the following:

- Originates operations.
- Determines what task needs to be executed and which target will perform the desired task.

FIGURE 6.4 **Various SCSI Configurations**

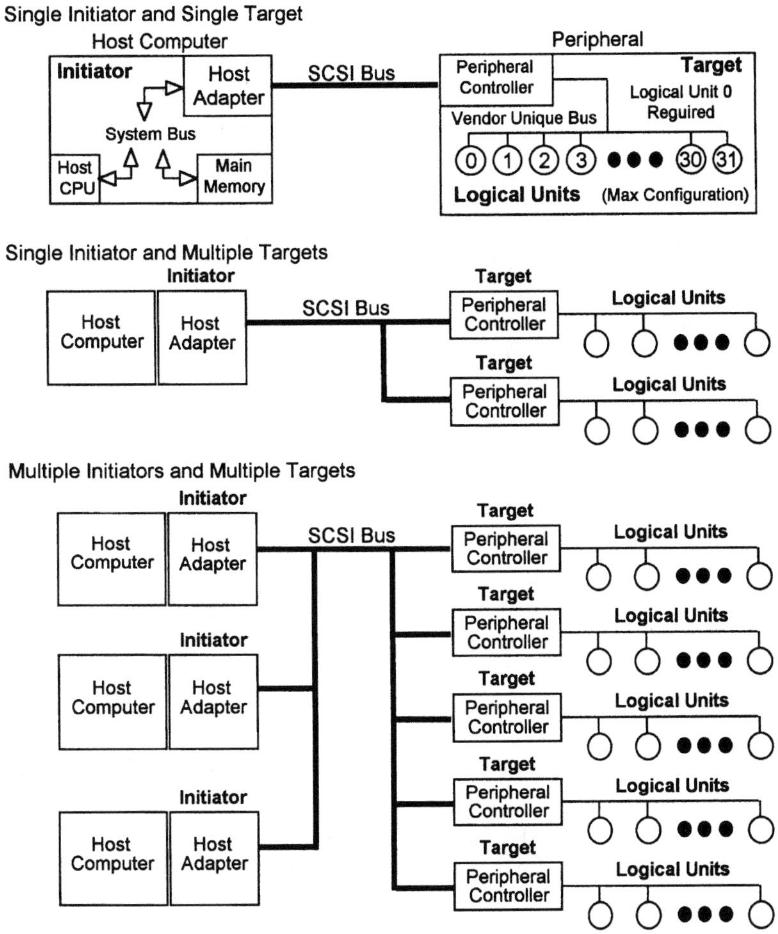

- Delegates authority to the target device to control the I/O process.
- Is responsible for certain bus functions like arbitrating and target selection.
- Confirms that the target performed the task assigned to it.

Targets

When a device is acting as a target, it does the following:

- Controls the entire data transfer process after being successfully selected by an initiator.

- Requests that the transfer of COMMAND, DATA, STATUS, or MESSAGE information be sent across the data bus.

- May arbitrate and reselect an initiator for the purpose of continuing an operation that was previously suspended because the device disconnected.

- May be physically housed within or on the peripheral device. When housed internally, the target device is referred to as an embedded SCSI device.

SCSI IDs

Each device has a SCSI ID that relates to the data bus bits. Priority on the data bus is determined by the bit numbers 0 through 7, with 7 the highest priority and 0 the lowest. The priority on the bus is only used when multiple devices are trying to access the bus simultaneously. In this instance, the device with the higher SCSI ID will take over the bus and the other device will sit back and wait until the bus is free for communication.

A device's address is determined by a jumper, as seen in Table 6.1. Most enclosed SCSI devices come with a switch mounted on the rear of the peripheral, and newer host adapters allow you to set the ID via software configuration utilities. If the standard SCSI-1 or -2 A-cable is used, then jumpers A0, A1, and A2 are required to set the SCSI ID jumper settings, because only eight devices may be attached to the A-cable.

If the SCSI-3 P-cable is used, an additional eight devices may be attached to the bus. When using the SCSI-3 P-cable, priority for the lower bits will stay the same and the remaining bits will be as seen in Table 6.1. The additional addressing of 16 devices is easily achieved by just adding a single jumper A3. If the Q-cable is implemented, then 32 devices can be attached to a single bus and a jumper A4 will have to be added.

SCSI CABLES

The cables used to connect SCSI devices are all basically the same, though the number of conductors or the cable quality vary. In order to understand how SCSI protocol works, you'll need to know what's inside the physical cable. In this section, we'll go inside the SCSI bus, where you'll learn about the bus's data and control signals. You will also learn which devices drive which signals, and how these signals control the protocol.

But first, let's look at the evolution of the different cables from SCSI-1 through SCSI-3. The A-cable is associated with both SCSI-1 and SCSI-2, B-cable with SCSI-2 only, and the P- and Q-cables with SCSI-3.

TABLE 6.1 **SCSI IDs as They Relate to Their Priority on the Bus and Jumper Settings**

SCSI ID	Priority*	Jumper A4	Jumper A3	Jumper A2	Jumper A1	Jumper A0
7	1	0	0	1	1	1
6	2	0	0	1	1	0
5	3	0	0	1	0	1
4	4	0	0	1	0	0
3	5	0	0	0	1	1
2	6	0	0	0	1	0
1	7	0	0	0	0	1
0	8	0	0	0	0	0
15	9	0	1	1	1	1
14	10	0	1	1	1	0
13	11	0	1	1	0	1
12	12	0	1	1	0	0
11	13	0	1	0	1	1
10	14	0	1	0	1	0
9	15	0	1	0	0	1
8	16	0	1	0	0	0
23	17	1	0	1	1	1
22	18	1	0	1	1	0
21	19	1	0	1	0	1
20	20	1	0	1	0	0
19	21	1	0	0	1	1
18	22	1	0	0	1	0
17	23	1	0	0	0	1
16	24	1	0	0	0	0
31	25	1	1	1	1	1
30	26	1	1	1	1	0
29	27	1	1	1	0	1
28	28	1	1	1	0	0
27	29	1	1	0	1	1
26	30	1	1	0	1	0
25	31	1	1	0	0	1
24	32	1	1	0	0	0

*Where 1 is the highest priority and 32 is the lowest

The A-cable (Figure 6.5) is a 50-conductor cable that consists of 8 data signals (i.e., physical transmission lines), parity, and 9 control signals.

The B-cable (Figure 6.6) is a 68-conductor wide bus option that would add 24 data lines, 3 parity lines, and 2 control signals (REQB and ACKB) to the A-cable.

NOTE *The A-cable must be used in conjunction with this alternative, as seen in the diagram on the following page. The B-cable is obsolete and has been replaced by the P-cable, the half-wide SCSI-3 cable alternative. This bus was never used commercially, and the SCSI-3 alternative offers a better wide bus solution with only 1 cable and up to 16 devices.*

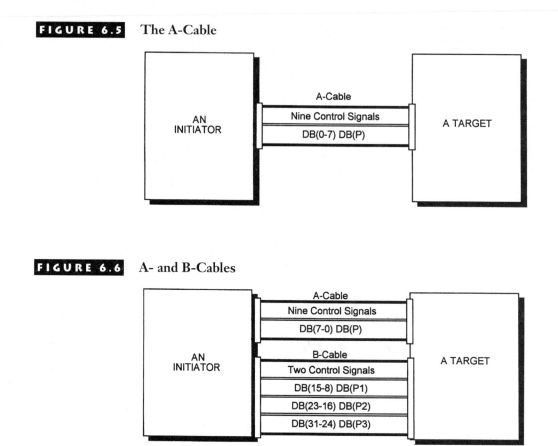

FIGURE 6.5 The A-Cable

A-Cable
Nine Control Signals
DB(0-7) DB(P)

AN INITIATOR

A TARGET

FIGURE 6.6 A- and B-Cables

A-Cable
Nine Control Signals
DB(7-0) DB(P)
B-Cable
Two Control Signals
DB(15-8) DB(P1)
DB(23-16) DB(P2)
DB(31-24) DB(P3)

AN INITIATOR

A TARGET

The half-wide P-cable (Figure 6.7) is a 68-conductor bus option that has 9 control signals (just like the A-cable) and 16 data and 2 parity signals. In equation form, we can look at the P-cable as

P-cable = (A-cable) + (8 data lines and a parity bit)

The Q-cable option (Figure 6.8) adds full wide capability to the P-cable and must be used in conjunction with the P-cable. This option adds 2 control signals (REQQ and ACKQ), 16 data lines, 2 additional parity bits, and 68 conductors.

NOTE *SCSI-3 replaces the A-cable and B-cable with the P-cable and Q-cable.*

SCSI-1, SCSI-2, and SCSI-3 Cabling Diagram

The diagram in Figure 6.9 shows all the different cabling and bus options and what is transferred across them.

FIGURE 6.7 The P-Cable

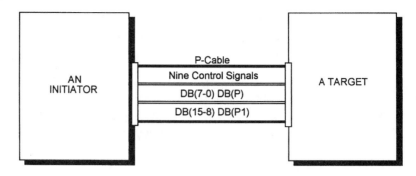

FIGURE 6.8 The P- and Q-Cables

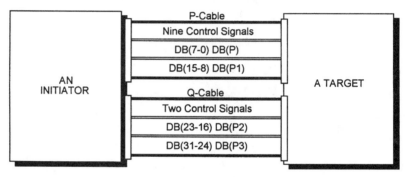

FIGURE 6.9 SCSI-1, SCSI-2, and SCSI-3 Cabling Diagram

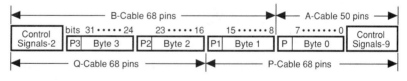

Legend:

Control signals—9	BSY, SEL, C/D, I/O, MSG, ATN, RST, REQ, ACK
Control signals—2	B-cable—REQB/ACKB or Q-cable—REQQ/ACKQ
P, P1, P2, and P3	The parity bits and byte (0 to 3) are data bus bytes.

This section describes each bus signal's definition and characteristics. This information will give you a detailed description of what each transmission line is and what it does. Bus signals are either data bus or control signals. We'll address data bus signals first, since they're relatively straightforward.

NOTE *The device driving the signals depends upon whether the device is initiator or target. Also, note that the minus sign in front of each signal name denotes active low signals, meaning that when a device drives the signal, it goes to a zero voltage level. Since the device no longer wants to drive the signal line, it releases the signal. Now, the question is, where does the signal go to when it is released? It goes to termination—this is one reason why the SCSI bus must be terminated.*

Data Bus Signals

Data bus signals are relatively straightforward. The only thing to keep in mind is your data bus width. The data bus signals are DB(31-0, P, P1, P2, and P3), and data bus signals have these five characteristics:

- Up to 32 data bus signals plus their respective parity bits (usually only 8-bit or 16-bit).
- DB7 is MSB and has highest priority during ARBITRATION; DB0 is LSB.
- Data bit is defined as 1 when signal is true.
- Data bit is defined as 0 when signal is false.
- Parity is odd.

Control Signals

There are nine control signals, which can be split into three categories:

- **Basic Control** signals, which are used to determine if the bus is in use, to select another device, to get the target's attention, and to reset the bus.
- **Information Transfer Control** signals, which are used by the target to control the information transfer phases. Information transfer phases are used to transmit COMMAND, MESSAGE, DATA, and STATUS information across the bus.
- **Data Clock** signals, which are used to latch and validate the data at the receiving device.

TABLE 6.2 ## SCSI Bus Control Signals

Signal	Definition	Category	Initiator	Target	Description
−BSY	Busy	Basic	1	1	Indicates that the bus is being used.
−SEL	Select	Basic	1	1	Indicates that a SCSI device is trying to select or reselect another SCSI device. The initiator uses this signal to select a target, and the target uses it to reselect the initiator.
−ATN	Attention	Basic	1	0	Used by the initiator to indicate an Attention condition, marking a moment when the initiator needs to get the target's attention.
−RST	Reset	Basic	1	0	Indicates the Reset condition and gets everyone's attention. (Targets typically do not drive this signal, even though the SCSI standard says they could.)
−C/D	Control/data	Information transfer	0	1	Indicates whether control or data information is on the bus. False indicates data information and true indicates control (COMMAND, MESSAGE, or STATUS) information is on the bus.
−I/O	Input/output	Information transfer control	0	1	Indicates which device is responsible for driving the data bus and controls the direction of data movement on the data bus with respect to the initiator. False indicates the direction of data is out of the initiator and true indicates the direction of data is into the initiator. This signal is also used to distinguish between SELECTION and RESELECTION phases.
−MSG	Message	Information transfer control	0	1	Indicates that a SCSI device has a message to transfer to another SCSI device. This signal is driven during a MESSAGE phase.
−REQ	Request	Data clock	0	1	Target indicates a request for an information transfer handshake. When the target is driving the data bus, this signal is used to latch the data bus into the initiator's buffer.
−ACK	Acknowledge	Data clock	1	0	This signal indicates the initiator's acknowledgment of an information transfer handshake. When the initiator is driving the data bus, this signal is used to latch the data bus into the target's buffer.

Legend:

1 Drives signal
0 Doesn't drive signal

FIGURE 6.10 Diagram of SCSI Signal Sources

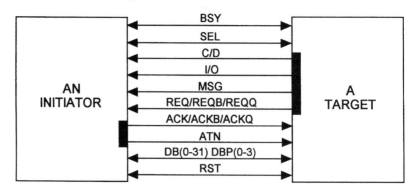

The diagram in Figure 6.10 shows all the signal names and which device can drive which signals. Notice that some signals are only driven by initiators and others only by targets. Conversely, there are signals that can be driven by both initiators and targets. The control signals are used to achieve certain protocol phases, which are, in turn, used to transmit all information (including DATA) across the data bus. We'll talk about the protocol in detail later in the next section.

Table 6.2 shows you the actual signal name, the signal definition, whether the signal is driven by an initiator or target, and a brief description of the signal's function.

THE SCSI PROTOCOL

SCSI utilizes a protocol method to transfer data between devices on the bus, in a circular process that starts and ends in the same layer. From the first layer, additional layers of protocol must be executed before any data is transferred to or from another device, and layers of protocol must be completed after the data has been transferred to end the process.

NOTE *The diagram in Figure 6.11 assumes no disconnection occurs (disconnection is covered later in this chapter).*

The protocol layers are referred to as SCSI bus phases. Protocol layers and their SCSI bus phase equivalents can be seen in Table 6.3.

NOTE *In Table 6.3, when the term In or Out is used, the point of reference is the initiator. The numbers next to the bus phase refer to the illustration in Figure 6.11.*

FIGURE 6.11 SCSI Protocol

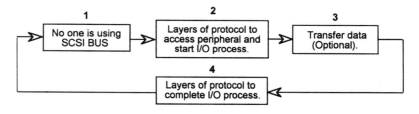

TABLE 6.3 Protocol Layers and Their SCSI Bus Phases

Protocol Layer Characteristics	SCSI Bus Phase
1. This protocol layer indicates no bus activity. 2. Devices use this layer to recognize that the bus is available. 3. Any time a device is not ready to transfer information, protocol reverts to this phase. 4. This phase can happen many times for each I/O process.	BUS FREE 1
1. This protocol layer is used to gain control of the bus. 2. Initiators or targets use this layer to resolve bus contention. 3. This phase can occur many times for each I/O process.	ARBITRATION 2
1. This is the protocol layer that an initiating device uses to choose another device (a target). 2. Initiators use this layer to select targets to start an I/O process. 3. This phase occurs only once for each I/O process.	SELECTION 2
1. This protocol layer provides interface management to an I/O process. 2. Initiators use this layer to ask targets to transmit a message. 3. This phase can occur many times for each I/O process.	MESSAGE OUT 2
1. This protocol layer transfers the I/O process operation information. 2. This phase tells the target which operation to perform. 3. This phase occurs only once, at the beginning of each I/O process.	COMMAND OUT 2
1. This protocol layer transfers data to or from the device. 2. This phase can occur many times for each I/O process.	DATA OUT/IN 3
1. This protocol layer gives an update of the status of an operation. 2. This phase occurs only once, at the end of each I/O process.	STATUS IN 4
1. This protocol layer provides interface management to an I/O process. 2. Targets use this layer to tell initiators to transmit a message. 3. This phase may occur many times for each I/O process.	MESSAGE IN 4
1. This protocol layer is used by a target to choose an initiator. 2. Targets use this layer to continue a previously disconnected I/O process. 3. This phase can occur many times for each I/O process.	RESELECTION

FIGURE 6.12 Phase Sequence Diagram

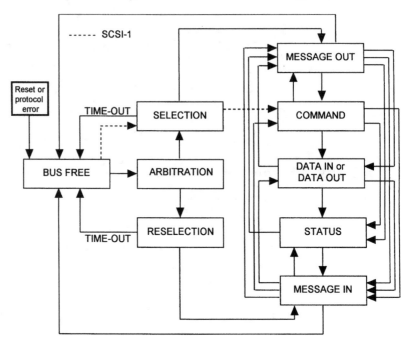

The SCSI bus can be in only one bus phase at any given time. Each phase has a predetermined set of rules, or protocol, that apply when changing from one bus phase to another. The rules are part of device code, or firmware, that resides on all devices attached to the SCSI bus. This device code makes the device "intelligent" and moves peripheral operations onto the peripheral device.

Phase Sequence Diagram

The sequence diagram in Figure 6.12 is taken from the SCSI-2 standard. It was developed by the "SCSI gods." Firmware developers, IC manufacturers, and basically anyone who has anything to do with SCSI use this chart as the bible for SCSI protocol.

Following the diagram in Figure 6.12, the normal progression of bus phase sequencing is as follows:

1. BUS FREE to ARBITRATION,

2. ARBITRATION to SELECTION or RESELECTION,

3. SELECTION or RESELECTION to one or more of the information transfer phases (MESSAGE, COMMAND, DATA, or STATUS).

FIGURE 6.13 Bus Phase Sequence Diagram

*	Timing s.mmm_μμμ_nnn	Protocol Layer or Bus Phase That Transpired	Data Bus (Single values represent SCSI IDs. Otherwise values are in hex bytes.)		Event
1	00.000_000_000	Bus Free Detected			0000
2	26.032_853_700	Arbitration Start	7		0001
2	26.032_856_100	Arb_win	7		0002
2	26.033_514_100		(Atn Assertion)	ATN	0003
2	26.033_521_700	Selection Start	7 4	ATN	0004
2	26.033_522_600	Selection Complete		ATN	0005
2	26.034_161_850		(Atn Negation)	ATN	0006
2	26.034_833_950	Message Out	C0		0007
2	26.039_035_750	Command Out	08 00 01 00 01 00		0008
3	26.055_860_800	Data In	00 00 00 00 00 00		0009
3	26.055_862_300		00 00 00 00 00 00		0010
3	26.056_494_450		00 00 00 00 00 00		0011
4	26.056_894_350	Status In	00		0012
4	26.057_852_350	Message In	00		0013
1	26.058_426_300	Bus Free Detected			0014

Legend:
*1 No one using bus
*2 Protocol to access peripheral and start process
*3 Transfer data
*4 Protocol to complete process

Figure 6.13 is an actual bus phase sequence trace taken from a popular SCSI bus analyzer, which translates the bus signals into protocol phases and data information. This information is very detailed, but if you read carefully you will get a real understanding of how SCSI protocol works.

Table 6.4 provides a detailed description of the bus phase sequence in Figure 6.13, event by event.

Bus Phases

Now, we bet that last section made perfect sense. If not, this section dives a little deeper into the phases of the bus and provides further examples and descriptions. Not counting the INs and OUTs, there are eight distinct bus phases, which can be divided into three categories, namely the waiting phase, bus control phases, and information transfer phases, as shown in Figure 6.14.

TABLE 6.4 Analysis of SCSI Bus Phase Sequence Diagram

Event	What Happened
0000	The SCSI bus is in a BUS FREE phase.
0001	A device (initiator) with a SCSI ID=7 starts the ARBITRATION phase to gain bus access.
0002	The initiator was granted access to the bus and the ARBITRATION phase ends.
0003	The initiator asserted the ATN signal to notify the peripheral that it will have a message to transfer after the SELECTION phase is completed (Attention condition).
0004	The initiator starts the SELECTION phase and is attempting to select a peripheral (target) with a SCSI ID=4. The initiator's ID can also be seen.
0005	The SELECTION phase has ended successfully. At this point the target is in control of the bus and will continue controlling the protocol until the I/O process is complete.
0006	The initiating device drops the attention signal.
0007	The peripheral goes into the MESSAGE OUT phase and accepts the "C0" message. This is because the initiator had the ATN signal asserted during the SELECTION phase.
0008	The target enters into the COMMAND phase and requests that the command bytes be sent.
0009	The target deciphers the command code (READ command) and knows to enter the DATA IN phase. The requested data is transferred to the initiator that started the I/O process. Even though only 18 bytes of data are shown, one block (512 bytes) had been transferred. The analyzer used in the above display has a data byte filter.
0012	When the target completes the DATA phase it enters into the STATUS phase and transfers a "00" status to inform the initiating device that all went well.
0013	When the target completes the STATUS phase, it enters into the MESSAGE IN phase and transfers a "00" message to inform the initiating device that the I/O process is complete.
0014	The target disconnects from the bus and the SCSI bus returns to the BUS FREE phase.

FIGURE 6.14 Bus Phases

Waiting Phase	Bus Control Phases	Information Transfer Phases
BUS FREE	ARBITRATION	MESSAGE IN/OUT
	SELECTION	COMMAND
	RESELECTION	DATA IN/OUT
		STATUS

Two basic phase sequences occur when an I/O process begins, namely the phase sequence with no disconnection and the phase sequence with disconnection, as shown in Figures 6.15 and 6.16.

NOTE *The ATN signal has been purposely omitted in the phase diagrams in Figures 6.15 and 6.16.*

FIGURE 6.15 **Phase Sequence with No Disconnection**

PHASE	BSY	SEL	C/D	I/O	MSG	DATA BUS
Bus Free	0	0	X	X	X	X
Arbitration Start	1	X	X	X	X	Init SCSI ID
Arb_win	1	X	X	X	X	Init SCSI ID
Selection Start	0	1	X	0	X	Both SCSI IDs
Selection Complete	1	1	X	0	X	Both SCSI IDs
Message Out	1	0	1	0	1	Message Byte(s)
Command Out	1	0	1	0	0	Command Bytes
Data In	1	0	0	1	0	Data Byte(s)
or (Optional-data is not required for some commands.)						
Data Out	1	0	0	0	0	Data Byte(s)
Status In	1	0	1	1	0	Status Byte
Message In	1	0	1	1	1	Message Byte(s)
Bus Free	0	0	X	X	X	X

FIGURE 6.16 **Phase Sequence with Disconnection**

PHASE	BSY	SEL	C/D	I/O	MSG	DATA BUS
Bus Free	0	0	X	X	X	X
Arbitration Start	1	X	X	X	X	Init SCSI ID
Arb_win	1	X	X	X	X	Init SCSI ID
Selection Start	0	1	X	0	X	Both SCSI IDs
Selection Complete	1	1	X	0	X	Both SCSI IDs
Message Out	1	0	1	0	1	Message Byte(s)
Command Out	1	0	1	0	0	Command Bytes
Message In	1	0	1	1	1	Message Byte(s)
Bus Free	0	0	X	X	X	X
Arbitration Start	1	X	X	X	X	Targ SCSI ID
Arb_win	1	X	X	X	X	Targ SCSI ID
Reselection Start	0	1	X	1	X	Both SCSI IDs
Reselection Complete	1	1	X	1	X	Both SCSI IDs
Message In	1	0	1	1	1	Message Byte(s)
Data xxx	1	0	0	1 or 0	0	Data Byte(s)
Status In	1	0	1	1	0	Status Byte
Message In	1	0	1	1	1	Message Byte(s)
Bus Free	0	0	X	X	X	X

Legend:
1 True
0 False (doesn't necessarily mean driven false)
X Not driven

Init Initiator
Targ Target
xxx In or Out

FIGURE 6.17 Examples of SCSI IDs and How They Are Used to Form a Nexus

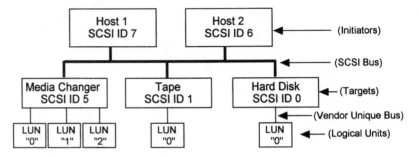

CONNECT, DISCONNECT, AND RECONNECT CONCEPTS

The processes that underlie connect, disconnect, and reconnect are what make SCSI capable of multitasking. The basic idea behind the connect, disconnect, and reconnect process is that when a device experiences some type of delay, mechanical or otherwise, it gets off the bus and lets another device on.

Connect

The SCSI objective underlying connect is to establish a nexus. A nexus is simply a link between initiator, target, and logical unit. The most basic SCSI nexus is called an I_T_L (initiator, target, logical unit) nexus. The nexus is used by both initiators and targets to identify an I/O process. Initiators use the nexus to ensure that the SCSI pointers in the host adapter associated with an I/O process are correctly updated when a previously disconnected I/O process resumes. That was a mouthful, but here is a translation. The nexus allows a host adapter (initiator) to keep track of multiple operations. The initiator makes sure that for every I/O process it starts, a unique I_T_L nexus is established. If an initiator is going to send multiple I/O processes to the same target and logical unit, then the initiator needs to extend the nexus to an I_T_L_Q nexus. The Q provides a command queue value that allows an initiator to queue up to 256 commands to the same target and logical unit.

Targets use the nexus to differentiate I/O processes of one initiator from that of another. They also use the nexus to differentiate multiple processes from the same initiator, as in tagged command queuing (i.e., I_T_L_Q nexus).

The diagram in Figure 6.17 shows some examples of nexus.

Here are a couple of nexus scenarios, following the diagram in Figure 6.17.

1. Host 1 wants to send data to the hard disk. Because the hard disk has only one LUN, the process is directed to LUN 0. Therefore the I_T_L nexus would be 7_0_0.

2. Host 2 wants to get data from the media changer. The desired library file is on LUN 2. Therefore the I_T_L nexus will be 6_5_2.

If the bus phase sequence in Figure 6.18 occurs, a nexus between the initiator, target, and logical unit will be established.

NOTE *In the phase sequence shown in Figure 6.18, we have listed what the control signals are doing during the protocol phases. This is how an analyzer can tell the difference between one bus phase and another. For example, when the BSY is asserted (true) and all other control signals are not driven (false), the bus phase is ARBITRATION.*

Here's a detailed description of the phase sequence shown in Figure 6.18, following it step by step:

1. Bus is free, as indicated by the simultaneously false (not driven) BSY and SEL signals.

2. A device, in this instance an initiator, arbitrates for the bus by asserting the BSY signal and its SCSI ID via a data bus bit. The initiator wins the ARBITRATION phase and proceeds onto the SELECTION phase. The SELECTION phase is used to transfer control of the I/O process from the initiator to the target. (It is interesting to note that with respect to SCSI devices, targets control all I/O processes.) Once a target allows itself to be selected, it controls the I/O process until its completion.

3. The initiator starts the SELECTION phase by driving SEL and its SCSI ID as well as that of the target it wants to talk to. Next, the initiator waits a little while (maybe a couple of hundred nanoseconds) for the signals to propagate down the cable and settle. Then the initiator releases the BSY signal. By the initiator driving the SCSI IDs on the data bus, the target can retrieve the initiator's ID

FIGURE 6.18 **Bus Phase Sequence Showing Establishment of the I_T_L Nexus**

	PHASE	BSY	SEL	C/D	I/O	MSG	DATA BUS
(1)	Bus Free	0	0	X	X	X	X
(2)	Arbitration Start	1	0	0	0	0	Initiator ID on bus
	Arb_win	1	0	0	0	0	I nexus
(3)	Selection Start	0	1	X	0	X	Both SCSI IDs on bus
(4)	Selection Complete	1	1	X	0	X	I_T nexus
(5)	Message Out	1	0	1	0	1	Identify: I_T_L nexus

from the setting of the data bus bits. The initiator will now wait for the target to drive the BSY signal or for a time-out condition to occur (i.e., the target doesn't drive BSY).

4. The target drives the BSY signal. This notifies the initiator that the selection process has completed successfully. Once the initiator detects that the target is driving the BSY signal, the initiator releases the SEL signal, thereby ending the SELECTION phase.

5. The target switches to the MESSAGE OUT phase for no particular reason except that it's following one of the rules of protocol. The target must know the logical unit number that tells it where to direct the I/O process, and it gets this LUN from the Identify message sent by the initiator to the target. Not only does the Identify message contain the LUN, but it also carries an important data bit known as the Disconnect Privilege bit. If the initiator sets this bit in the Identify message, then the target can disconnect.

Disconnect

The SCSI objective underlying disconnect is to temporarily terminate the link between devices so that other devices can access the bus. The reasons for terminating the link are

- To increase the number of I/Os per second
- To allow a device to disconnect if it is not ready, whether because of mechanical latency or a full or empty buffer, so that another device can access the bus

NOTE *Targets cannot disconnect unless the initiator has granted disconnect privilege in the Identify message during the original connection process.*

Disconnect can have two possible protocol sequences, depending on the type of operation, how much information is to be transferred, and buffer sizes. For example, if the initiator asks the target to store a file (WRITE), or to retrieve a file (READ), a different sequencing of protocol may occur. Also, if an initiator issues a command that writes more data than the target can store in its buffer, a disconnection will be required. The target disconnects from the initiator when its buffer is full and it writes the data to the medium. Once the target has written the data to the medium, it will reconnect to the initiator and ask for more data, and so on, and so on, until all the data has been transferred.

An actual SCSI phase disconnection sequence can be seen in the phase sequence in Figure 6.19. The target can cause a disconnection by simply switching to the MESSAGE IN phase and sending a Disconnect message to the initiator. As soon as the initiator decodes a Disconnect message from the target, it will expect the target to go to the BUS FREE phase.

FIGURE 6.19 An Actual SCSI Phase Disconnection Sequence

PHASE			BSY	SEL	C/D	I/O	MSG	DATA BUS
(1)		Message In	1	0	1	1	1	04h-disconnect
(2)	Bus Free		0	0	0	0	0	

FIGURE 6.20 Message Sequence Involving the Save Data Pointer

PHASE			BSY	SEL	C/D	I/O	MSG	DATA BUS
(1)		Message In	1	0	1	1	1	02h-save data pointer
(2)		Message In	1	0	1	1	1	04h-disconnect
(3)	Bus Free		0	0	0	0	0	

Another disconnection sequence, involving the Save Data Pointer message, can take place if only some of the data has been transferred and a target wants to disconnect. SCSI pointers point to an absolute or relative location in the memory of a host computer. Pointers can be either indirect or indexed and are located on the host adapter or are internal to the actual SCSI chip. The objectives of SCSI pointers are to break up large data transfers into smaller bursts and to facilitate error retry and recovery.

This Save Data Pointer message sequence acts as a placeholder to ensure that the initiator remembers where it left the data transfer if a disconnection occurs before all the data has been transferred. The Save Data Pointer message tells the initiator to copy its current SCSI pointers to a saved pointer value. A message sequence involving the Save Data Pointer is shown in the phase sequence in Figure 6.20.

Reconnect

The SCSI objective underlying reconnect is to reestablish the I_T_L nexus. When speaking of reconnection in regard to SCSI, we're talking about a target relinking (reconnecting) to an initiator, in one of the following scenarios:

- A target reselects an initiator to continue a previously disconnected I/O process.
- The target determines when it's ready to reconnect to an initiator.
- The target and initiator resume their roles when a reconnection occurs.
- Reconnect is a series of bus phases.

FIGURE 6.21 **An Actual SCSI Phase Reconnection Sequence**

	PHASE	BSY	SEL	C/D	I/O	MSG	DATA BUS
(1)	Bus Free	0	0	X	X	X	X
(2)	Arbitration Start	1	0	0	0	0	Targ SCSI ID
	Arb_win	1	0	0	0	0	T portion of nexus
(3)	Reselection Start	0	1	X	1	X	Both SCSI IDs
(4)	Reselection Complete	1	1	X	1	X	I_T nexus
(5)	Message In	1	0	1	1	1	80h: I_T_L nexus

Figure 6.21 shows an actual SCSI phase reconnection sequence. At the end of the sequence, the I_T_L nexus is reestablished. This is a detailed description of the above phase sequence:

1. Bus is free, indicated by the BSY and SEL signals simultaneously being not driven (i.e., false).

2. A device, in this instance a target, arbitrates for the bus by asserting the BSY signal and its SCSI ID via a data bus bit. The target wins the ARBITRATION phase and proceeds onto the RESELECTION phase. The RESELECTION phase is used by the target to reconnect to a previously disconnected initiator.

3. The target starts the RESELECTION phase by driving the SEL, I/O, and SCSI IDs of itself and the initiator it wants to talk to. Next the target waits a little while for the signals to propagate down the cable and settle (maybe a couple hundred nanoseconds). Then the target releases the BSY signal. By the target driving the SCSI IDs on the data bus, the initiator can retrieve the target's ID from the setting of the data bus bits. The target now waits for the initiator to drive the BSY signal or for a time-out condition to occur (i.e., the initiator doesn't drive BSY).

4. Once the target detects that the initiator has driven BSY, it drives the BSY signal. Once the initiator detects the target's release of the SEL signal, it releases the BSY signal. As a result, the target drives the BSY signal, as it should, because targets are responsible for controlling the I/O process.

5. The target switches to the MESSAGE IN phase, because the SCSI gods say so (this is just one of those rules of protocol). The Identify message sent from target to initiator tells the initiator the logical unit number of the I/O process. Once the initiator knows the logical unit number, it deduces the I_T_L nexus and then restores its SCSI pointers. Once the SCSI pointers are restored, the I/O process picks up where it left off.

Tagged Command Queuing

Tagged command queuing is used when an initiator wants to send multiple I/O processes to the same target and logical unit. When tagged command queuing is used in a connection sequence, its protocol is like that found in Figure 6.22. Here, a two-byte message follows the Identify message. The message consists of the Queue Tag Message (6) with a code that designates either Ordered, Simple, or Head of Queue command queue type followed by the Q_Tag value. The Q_Tag (7) value allows up to 256 commands to be queued to the same target-logical unit combination from the same initiator. As mentioned earlier, the nexus is extended to an I_T_L_Q nexus when tagged command queuing is used.

When tagged command queuing is used in a reconnection sequence, its protocol is like that found in Figure 6.23. In the example, the two queue messages are used to reestablish the I_T_L_Q nexus upon reconnection.

FIGURE 6.22 **Tagged Command Queuing Protocol as Used in a Connection Sequence**

	PHASE	BSY	SEL	C/D	I/O	MSG	DATA BUS
(1)	Bus Free 0	0	X	X	X	X	
(2)	Arbitration Start	1	0	0	0	0	Initiator ID on bus
	Arb_win	1	0	0	0	0	I nexus
(3)	Selection Start	0	1	X	0	X	Both SCSI IDs on bus
(4)	Selection Complete	1	1	X	0	X	I_T nexus
(5)	Message Out	1	0	1	0	1	Identify: I_T_L nexus
(6)	Message Out	1	0	1	0	1	Queue Tag Message
(7)	Message Out	1	0	1	0	1	Q_Tag: I_T_L_Q nexus

FIGURE 6.23 **Tagged Command Queuing Protocol as Used in a Reconnection Sequence**

	PHASE	BSY	SEL	C/D	I/O	MSG	DATA BUS
(1)	Bus Free	0	0	X	X	X	X
(2)	Arbitration Start	1	0	0	0	0	Targ SCSI ID
	Arb_win	1	0	0	0	0	T portion of nexus
(3)	Reselection Start	0	1	X	1	X	Both SCSI IDs
(4)	Reselection Complete	1	1	X	1	X	I_T nexus
(5)	Message In	1	0	1	1	1	80h: I_T_L nexus
(6)	Message In	1	0	1	0	1	Queue Tag Message
(7)	Message In	1	0	1	0	1	Q_Tag: I_T_L_Q nexus

How Disconnects and Reconnects Work

The sequence diagrams in Figure 6.24 demonstrate how disconnection and reconnection can help increase the number of I/Os per second on the SCSI bus when a target is not ready for an I/O process.

With regard to disconnections and reconnections in general, note that

- Any time the bus is disconnected, any device can start an I/O process, or the same device can start another I/O process (as in tagged command queuing).

- There is no limit on how many disconnections and reconnections may occur for each I/O process.

- The COMMAND phase occurs only once at the beginning of the I/O process. and the STATUS phase occurs only once at the end of the I/O process.

FIGURE 6.24 **Two Sequence Diagrams Showing How Disconnection and Reconnection Can Help to Increase the Number of I/Os per Second on the SCSI Bus When a Target Is Not Ready for an I/O Process**

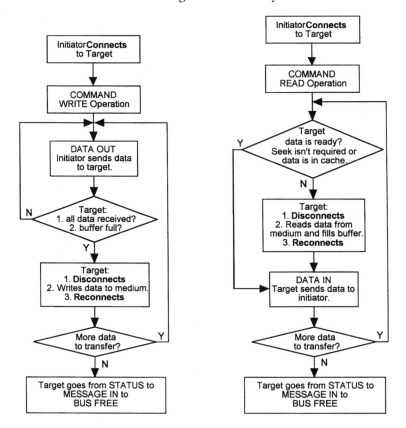

INFORMATION TRANSFER PHASES

Now that you know about BUS FREE, ARBITRATION, SELECTION, and RESELECTION phases, it's time to learn about the other protocol phases. This section lists all of the information transfer phases that are controlled by the target and are used to transfer real information across the data bus. Before we get into any detail about the information transfer phases though, note that all phase directions are referenced from the initiator's point of view, as shown in Figure 6.25.

The following are descriptions of each of the information transfer phases shown in the diagram in Figure 6.25 (following the phase order shown in the diagram from top to bottom):

COMMAND Phase

- Allows the target to request command information from the initiator.
- Target asserts C/D, negates I/O and MSG during the REQ/ACK handshake.

STATUS Phase

- Allows the target to request that status information be sent to the initiator.
- Target asserts C/D, I/O, and negates MSG during the REQ/ACK handshake.

MESSAGE IN Phase

- Allows the target to request that it send message(s) to the initiator.
- Target asserts C/D, I/O, and MSG during the REQ/ACK handshake.

MESSAGE OUT Phase

- Allows the target to request that the initiator send it message(s).
- Target invokes this phase in response to the Attention condition from the initiator.
- Target asserts C/D, MSG, and negates I/O during the REQ/ACK handshake.

FIGURE 6.25   **Information Transfer Phases**

TABLE 6.6	**Contents of the Data Bus and What Is Responsible for Determining the Information**		
Information Transfer Phase	**Contents of data bus**	**Device That Determines Information**	
COMMAND	CDB bytes	Initiator	
DATA IN	Data in byte(s)	Target	
DATA OUT	Data out byte(s)	Initiator	
STATUS	Status byte	Target	
MESSAGE IN	Message in byte(s)	Target	
MESSAGE OUT	Message out byte(s)	Initiator	

DATA IN Phase

■ Allows the target to request that it send data to the initiator.

■ Target asserts I/O, negates C/D and MSG during the REQ/ACK handshake.

DATA OUT Phase

■ Allows the target to request that the initiator send it data.

■ Target negates I/O, C/D, and MSG during the REQ/ACK handshake.

Table 6.6 lists the contents of the data bus and what is responsible for determining the information.

Characteristics of the Information Transfer Phases

NOTE *The information contained in Figure 6.26 comes directly from the SCSI standard, so it may seem a bit deep.*

The characteristics of the information transfer phases shown in Figure 6.26 are the following:

1. As seen in Figure 6.26, three bus signals are used to distinguish the different information transfer phases, as follows:

    ■ **MSG**   When negated, this signal says that the bus is not in a MESSAGE phase. When asserted, the bus is in a MESSAGE phase.

    ■ **C/D**   When negated, this signal says that the bus is in a DATA phase. When asserted, the bus is in a COMMAND, STATUS, or MESSAGE phase.

    ■ **I/O**   When negated, this signal says that the direction of transfer is from the initiator to the target. When asserted, the direction of transfer is to the initiator.

FIGURE 6.26 Information Transfer Phases

Phase Name	MSG	C/D	I/O	Direction of Transfer	Comment
DATA OUT	0	0	0	Initiator to target	DATA phase
DATA IN	0	0	1	Target to initiator	DATA phase
COMMAND	0	1	0	Initiator to target	
STATUS	0	1	1	Target to initiator	
Reserved for future	1	0	0		
Reserved for future	1	0	1		
MESSAGE OUT	1	1	0	Initiator to target	MESSAGE phase
MESSAGE IN	1	1	1	Target to initiator	MESSAGE phase

FIGURE 6.27 **Diagram Showing How the Target Continuously Envelopes the REQ/ACK Handshake(s) with the C/D, I/O, and MSG Signals Until the Negation of the ACK Signal at the End of the Handshake**

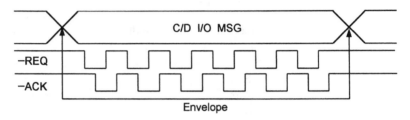

2. The target drives all of these signals, and therefore controls all changes from one information transfer phase to another. Once the target is selected it is in control of the bus.

3. The initiator can request a MESSAGE OUT phase by asserting ATN.

4. The target can cause BUS FREE by releasing MSG, I/O, C/D, and BSY.

5. During information transfer phases, BSY remains true and SEL remains false.

6. Information transfer phases use one or more REQ/ACK handshakes to control the transfer of information.

7. Each REQ/ACK handshake transfers one byte of information (except for wide DATA phase transfers).

8. The target continuously envelopes the REQ/ACK handshake(s) with the C/D, I/O, and MSG signals so that these signals are valid for a bus settle delay (400 ns) before the assertion of REQ, and they remain valid until the negation of the ACK signal at the end of the handshake of the last transfer of the phase, as shown in Figure 6.27.

MESSAGE Phase and Code Descriptions

Certain interface functions must be managed in order for SCSI to work properly. These functions include error recovery, synchronous negotiations, and the Identify message, which we discussed earlier in this chapter.

Messages are used to manage the SCSI interface. Some messages are used exclusively by initiators to abort processes, reset devices, clear a target's command queue, or recover from SCSI parity errors. In order for the initiator to get the target to take a message, it must assert the ATN (Attention) signal. (Remember that the target is in control of the I/O process and that the initiator must get the target's attention before it can send a message.) Once the target detects the Attention condition, it switches to the MESSAGE OUT phase and requests the message from the initiator.

Other messages are used exclusively by targets to tell the initiator that the I/O process is completed, ignore invalid data bytes, initiate a recovery procedure, or instruct host adapter to save, restore, or modify its data pointers. Because the target is in control of the I/O process, it simply switches to the MESSAGE IN phase and requests that the initiator take the message. The initiator can tell the bus is in the MESSAGE IN phase by the state of the C/D, I/O, and MSG signals.

Though most messages are a single byte long, some messages are two bytes long and require two consecutive message bytes. Single-byte messages require the transfer of a single message code from one device to another in order to perform one of the functions described above.

SCSI-land is also populated with messages known as extended messages. Extended messages are used to negotiate for synchronous and wide data transfers. Once power-on has completed, the SCSI interface defaults to asynchronous, non-wide (1 byte) data transfers. If a device wants to transfer data using either synchronous or wide data transfer, it must negotiate with the receiving device with an extended message before it can do so.

Probably one of the most important message functions in the SCSI interface is to recover from data bus parity errors. The message system allows two devices to recover and retry the operation without having to involve an upper-level protocol, namely the device driver. Thus, the recovery can be handled by the firmware on each device. Table 6.7 is a complete, alphabetical listing of all message codes.

Protocol Example of a Synchronous Negotiation

Figure 6.28 is a logic analyzer display of how messages are used to negotiate for a synchronous data transfer request (SDTR) between an initiator and target. The SDTR is established between devices via extended messages. Figure 6.28 lists the extended message codes and their descriptions.

TABLE 6.7 Complete Alphabetical List of All Message Codes

Code	Support Init	Support Targ	Message Name	Direction	Negate ATN Before Last ACK
06h	O	M	ABORT	Out	Yes
0Dh●	O	O	ABORT TAG (Note 1)	Out	Yes
24h□	M	M	ACA TAG	Out	No
0Ch	O	M	BUS DEVICE RESET	Out	Yes
14h□	O	M	BUS DEVICE RESET OTHER PORT	Out	No
16h□	M	M	CLEAR ACA	Out	No
0Eh●	O	O	CLEAR QUEUE (Note 1)	Out	Yes
00h	M	M	COMMAND COMPLETE	In	—
12h□	O	O	CONTINUE I/O PROCESS	Out	Yes
04h	O	O	DISCONNECT	In	—
04h	O	O	DISCONNECT	Out	Yes
01h	O	O	EXTENDED MESSAGE	In Out	Yes
80h+	M	O	IDENTIFY	In	—
80h+	M	M	IDENTIFY	Out	No
23h●	O	O	IGNORE WIDE RESIDUE (Two Bytes)	In	—
0Fh●	O	O	INITIATE RECOVERY	In	—
0Fh●	O	O	INITIATE RECOVERY (Note 2)	Out	Yes
05h	M	M	INITIATOR DETECTED ERROR	Out	Yes
0Ah	O	O	LINKED COMMAND COMPLETE	In	—
0Bh	O	O	LINKED COMMAND COMPLETE (WITH FLAG)	In	—
09h	M	M	MESSAGE PARITY ERROR	Out	Yes
07h	M	M	MESSAGE REJECT	In Out	Yes
***	O	O	MODIFY DATA POINTER	In	—
08h	M	M	NO OPERATION	Out	Yes
			Queue Tag Messages (Two Bytes)		
21h●	O	O	HEAD OF QUEUE TAG	Out	No
22h●	O	O	ORDERED QUEUE TAG	Out	No
20h●	O	O	SIMPLE QUEUE TAG	In Out	No
10h●	O	O	RELEASE RECOVERY	Out	Yes
03h	O	O	RESTORE POINTERS	In	—
02h	O	O	SAVE DATA POINTER	In	—
***	O	O	SYNCHRONOUS DATA TRANSFER REQUEST	In Out	Yes
*** ●	O	O	WIDE DATA TRANSFER REQUEST	In Out	Yes
13h□	O	O	TARGET TRANSFER DISABLE	Out	Yes
11h●	O	O	TERMINATE I/O PROCESS	Out	Yes
15h			Reserved		
17h-1Fh			Reserved		
24h-2Fh			Reserved for two-byte messages		
30h-7Fh			Reserved		

Legend:

M	Mandatory support	O	Optional support
In	Target to initiator	Out	Initiator to target
—	Not applicable	***	Extended message
Yes	Initiator shall negate ATN before last ACK of message	No	Initiator may or may not negate ATN before last ACK of message
●	Messages added in SCSI-2; these messages are reserved in SCSI-1	□	Messages added in SCSI-3; these messages are reserved in SCSI-2
80h+	Codes 80h through FFh are used for Identify message		

FIGURE 6.28 Protocol Example of a Synchronous Negotiation

Timing/Description	Phase	Data Bus						Event #
00.000_000_000	Bus Free Detected							0000
26.032_853_700	Arbitration Start	7						0001
26.032_856_100	Arb_win	7						0002
26.033_514_100		(Atn Assertion)					ATN	0003
26.033_521_700	Selection Start	7	4				ATN	0004
26.033_522_600	Selection Complete						ATN	0005
26.034_161_850	Message Out	C0					ATN	0006
Extended Message	Message Out	01					ATN	0007
Ext. Msg. Length	Message Out	03	**INITIATOR**				ATN	0008
Sync Data Transfer Request	Message Out	01	**MESSAGES**				ATN	0009
Transfer Period 200ns	Message Out	32					ATN	0010
		(Atn Negate)						0011
REQ/ACK Offset	Message Out	07						0012
Extended Message	Message In	01						0013
Ext. Msg. Length	Message In	03	**TARGET**					0014
Sync Data Transfer Request	Message In	01	**MESSAGES**					0015
Transfer Period 248ns	Message In	3E						0016
REQ/ACK Offset	Message In	07						0017
26.039_035_750	Command Out	08	00	01	00	01	00	0018
26.055_860_800	Data In	00	00	00	00	00	00	0019
26.055_862_300		00	00	00	00	00	00	0020
26.056_494_450		00	00	00	00			0021
26.056_894_350	Status In	00						0022
26.057_852_350	Message In	00						0023
26.058_426_300	Bus Free Detected							0024

We don't expect you to fully comprehend the extended message above; this display simply demonstrates what an extended message exchange would look like. Having provided a protocol sequence of how synchronous negotiations are handled, here are the characteristics of synchronous data transfers.

1. The synchronous negotiation is done only once, usually during initialization, because both devices have the ability to remember if an agreement had been previously established.

2. Either initiator or target can start the negotiation process. Once the negotiation process is completed successfully, all DATA IN and DATA OUT phases will be synchronous.

3. An initiator usually starts the negotiation process if the host adapter has a jumper installed or a software switch set that directs the host adapter to initiate the process.

4. A target usually starts the negotiation process if a jumper is installed or a software switch is set that directs the target to initiate the process.

5. Once an agreement is established, it can only be cleared by the following events:

   ■ Reset, power-on reset, or a Bus Device Reset message

   ■ A renegotiation between the same initiator and target

   ■ A Wide Data Transfer Request message sequence

COMMAND Phase and Code Descriptions

A command is executed when an initiator sends a command descriptor block (CDB) to the target during the COMMAND phase. Commands are used to tell the target what operation to perform. The following are true for each CDB:

■ The first byte of the CDB is always known as the operation code.

■ The last byte of the CDB is the control byte.

■ The format of the operation code and control byte are identical for every SCSI command in the SCSI universe.

Table 6.8 shows an example of the basic format of a six-byte command, although by no means is it the case that all six-byte SCSI commands look like this.

Here's what's happening in Table 6.8:

Operation Code. This field tells the target how long the CDB will be and what operation the initiator wants the target to perform.

Logical Unit Number field. Although used in SCSI-1, this field is almost never used today, because the LUN is determined in the Identify message.

TABLE 6.8   **Basic Six-Byte CDB**

	bit 7	bit 6	bit 5	bit 4	bit 3	bit 2	bit 1	bit 0
byte 0	Operation code							
byte 1	Logical unit number*			(MSB)				
byte 2	Logical block address (if required)							
byte 3								(LSB)
byte 4	Transfer length (if required)							
byte 5	Control byte							

*Reserved in SCSI-3

TABLE 6.9 **Basic Ten-Byte CDB**

	bit 7	bit 6	bit 5	bit 4	bit 3	bit 2	bit 1	bit 0
byte 0	Operation code							
byte 1	Logical unit number*			Reserved				
byte 2	(MSB)							
byte 3	Logical block address (if required)							
byte 4								
byte 5								(LSB)
byte 6	Reserved							
byte 7	(MSB)	Transfer length (if required)						
byte 8								(LSB)
byte 9	Control byte							

*Reserved in SCSI-3

Logical Block Address. This field tells the target where the information is located on the physical medium. Logical blocks start at zero and are contiguous to the last block location on the device's medium. Blocks, measured in bytes, are the smallest unit of measurement on a device, with a typical block size measuring 512 bytes.

Transfer Length. This field tells the target how much data to transfer, usually as an amount of blocks, with 512 bytes to each block of data. Some devices, like tape, may be able to store any number of bytes, from one to the maximum size of the file.

Control Byte. This field is used for special operations like command linking (chaining), and it also has some bits that can be used for vendor-unique operations.

Sometimes all the information required to perform an operation cannot be squeezed into a six-byte command, and SCSI has a cure for this. Its solution is to allow commands to also come in 10-, 12-, and 16-byte formats. (The 16-byte format was added in SCSI-3.) As you can see in Table 6.9 and Table 6.10, the 10-byte and 12-byte CDBs allow the initiator to address a higher logical block and transfer more blocks with a single CDB.

Some devices support different CDB sizes and others may only support six-byte CDBs. This information must be known by the device driver before it can properly format the CDBs it sends to the target. SCSI has specific commands to find out this information, which can determine the block size of the device, the maximum logical block address available, the type of device (e.g., disk, tape), and all other operational parameters that the device driver requires.

TABLE 6.10　Basic Twelve-Byte CDB

	bit 7	bit 6	bit 5	bit 4	bit 3	bit 2	bit 1	bit 0
byte 0	Operation code							
byte 1	Logical unit number*			Reserved				
byte 2	(MSB)							
byte 3	Logical block address (if required)							
byte 4								
byte 5								(LSB)
byte 6	(MSB)							
byte 7	Transfer length (if required)							
byte 8								
byte 9								(LSB)
byte 10	Reserved							
byte 11	Control byte							

*Reserved in SCSI-3

Table 6.11 lists all the operation codes for the device type know as direct access (disk), which should give you an idea of the type of operations that a disk can perform. We have only shown the operation code (the first byte) of the CDB. Each command will have a specific format of all remaining bytes.

Status

This section explains when a status is sent and describes the status byte's format and codes. A single status byte is sent from the target to the initiator during the STATUS phase at the completion of each command, unless the command is terminated by one of the following events:

- An Abort message
- An Abort Tag message
- A Bus Device Reset message
- A Clear Queue message
- A hard reset condition
- An unexpected disconnect

The STATUS phase normally occurs at the end of an I/O process, but in some cases may occur prior to transferring the command descriptor block (the COMMAND phase).

TABLE 6.11 **Direct-Access Devices Commands (Numerical)**

Operation Code	Command Name	Type
00h	TEST UNIT READY	M
01h	REZERO UNIT	O
03h	REQUEST SENSE	M
04h	FORMAT UNIT	M
07h	REASSIGN BLOCKS	O
08h	READ(6)	M
0Ah	WRITE(6)	M
0Bh	SEEK(6)	O
12h	INQUIRY	M
15h	MODE SELECT(6)	O
16h	RESERVE	M
17h	RELEASE	M
18h	COPY	O
1Ah	MODE SENSE(6)	O
1Bh	START STOP UNIT	O
1Ch	RECEIVE DIAGNOSTIC RESULTS	O
1Dh	SEND DIAGNOSTIC	M
1Eh	PREVENT-ALLOW MEDIUM REMOVAL	O
25h	READ CAPACITY	M
28h	READ(10)	M
2Ah	WRITE(10)	M
2Bh	SEEK(10)	O
2Eh	WRITE AND VERIFY	O
2Fh	VERIFY	O
30h	SEARCH DATA HIGH	O
31h	SEARCH DATA EQUAL	O
32h	SEARCH DATA LOW	O
33h	SET LIMITS	O
34h	PRE-FETCH	O
35h	SYNCHRONIZE CACHE	O
36h	LOCK-UNLOCK CACHE	O
37h	READ DEFECT DATA	O
39h	COMPARE	O
3Ah	COPY AND VERIFY	O
3Bh	WRITE BUFFER	O
3Ch	READ BUFFER	O
3Eh	READ LONG	O
3Fh	WRITE LONG	O
40h	CHANGE DEFINITION	O
41h	WRITE SAME	O
4Ch	LOG SELECT	O
4Dh	LOG SENSE	O
55h	MODE SELECT(10)	O
5Ah	MODE SENSE(10)	O

Legend:

M   Command implementation is mandatory.
O   Command implementation is optional.

TABLE 6.12 **Status Byte Format**

bit 7	bit 6	bit 5	bit 4	bit 3	bit 2	bit 1	bit 0
Reserved		Status byte code					Reserved

TABLE 6.13 **Status Byte Codes**

Status	Hex	Description
GOOD	00	Target has successfully completed the command.
CHECK CONDITION	02	Indicates a contingent allegiance condition has occurred.
CONDITION MET	04	Requested operation is satisfied (SEARCH DATA or PREFETCH commands).
BUSY	08	Indicates the target is busy. Returned whenever a target is unable to accept a command from an otherwise acceptable initiator.
INTERMEDIATE	10	Is returned for every successfully completed command in a series of linked commands (except for the last command).
INTERMEDIATE-CONDITION MET	14	Combination of CONDITION MET and INTERMEDIATE status.
RESERVATION CONFLICT	18	The logical unit or an extent (a portion) within the logical unit is reserved for another device.
COMMAND TERMINATED*	22	Target terminates current I/O process. This also indicates that a contingent allegiance condition has occurred.
QUEUE FULL* TASK SET FULL **	28	Is implemented if tagged command queuing is supported. Indicates that the target's command queue is full.
ACA ACTIVE ***	30	Indicates that an auto contingent allegiance condition exists.
All other codes		Reserved

Legend:

* New in SCSI-2
** New name in SCSI-3 (SAM)
*** New in SCSI-3 (SAM)

Some status codes, like 00 = good, are easy to comprehend, while others, like the 02 code—which says that a contingent allegiance condition has occurred—are more difficult. (A contingent allegiance condition is basically equal to an error condition.) The status byte format and status byte code are shown in Tables 6.12 and 6.13, respectively.

HANDSHAKING OF INFORMATION

In the previous section, we talked about how to determine which phase the bus is in. Now we'll explain how information is transferred. Handshaking is the term SCSI gods use when they speak of transferring

FIGURE 6.29 **The Four Steps of Asynchronous Transfer**

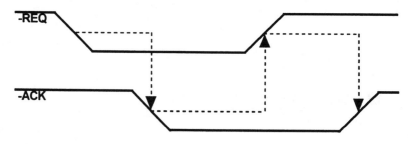

information across the data bus. Handshaking the information ensures that data on the bus is properly latched into the receiving device.

Earlier in this book, in Chapter 2, we told you a bit about asynchronous and synchronous transfer. These are the two methods of handshaking information. We'll take you beyond a basic understanding of these concepts in the paragraphs that follow.

> **NOTE** *COMMAND, MESSAGE, and STATUS information can only be transferred via the asynchronous handshake method, while the DATA phase is the only phase that can transfer information with both asynchronous and synchronous handshake methods.*

Asynchronous Handshake Method

Asynchronous transfer is characterized by the transfer of one byte of data via the following four-step process:

1. The target asserts the REQ signal.
2. The initiator asserts the ACK signal.
3. The target negates the REQ signal.
4. The initiator negates the ACK signal.

Asynchronous handshaking is shown in the diagram in Figure 6.29.

> **NOTE** *During asynchronous transfer, the following rules apply: The ACK signal can't assert until the REQ asserts; the REQ signal can't negate until the ACK signal asserts; the ACK signal can't negate until the REQ negates.*

The name asynchronous transfer stems from the fact that this transfer method is not dependent upon any uniform timing. Asynchronous transfer rates range from 2 MB to 6 MB transfers/sec, because asynchronous data transfer is subject to a number of delays, including cable propagation delays; internal device delays between receiving a signal and responding to that signal; deskew delays; and cable skew delays. These delays occur because the REQ and ACK pulses must interlock with one another and because handshake must occur for each byte of data transferred.

Synchronous Handshake Method

Synchronous transfers allow devices to transfer data more quickly. This is accomplished by allowing the target to request that the initiator either send or receive data before the initiator has to acknowledge the target's request. It is all done in hardware (thank goodness!), so don't worry about it.

That's the simple explanation. Now for the more technical, detailed explanation, which sometimes takes half an hour to explain to a roomful of people during a training session.

The synchronous handshake method is optional and must be negotiated for between a target and an initiator. Synchronous transfer depends on uniform, or synchronous, timing, hence its name. The objective behind synchronous transfers is to minimize the effect of cable and device delays. Although these delays cannot be eliminated entirely, their effects can be minimized.

Synchronous handshaking can support transfers of up to 10 MB transfers/sec when the Fast SCSI option is implemented. Synchronous minimizes the effects of cable and device delays, because the REQ and ACK pulses do not have a one-to-one interlock. Synchronous transfer is commonly referred to as offset interlock.

In order to transfer one byte of data, or up to four bytes if a wide transfer, via synchronous handshaking, the process is the following:

1. A REQ/ACK offset is used to establish a pacing mechanism. During the synchronous data transfer, the REQ and ACK signals are issued independent of one another, offset from one another to minimize the effects of delays and to provide an elasticity buffer for pacing the transfer, and checked by each device at the end of the DATA phase to assure that the number of REQ (or ACK) pulses sent is equal to the number of ACK (or REQ) pulses received.

2. The initiator and target form a transfer period from the leading edge of a REQ/ACK signal to the leading edge of the next REQ/ACK signal. During the data transfer, the REQ and ACK signals are clock pulses used to latch the information on the data bus into the receiving device; are a string, or chain, of pulses that are asserted and negated for a uniform amount of time; and form a transfer period from the leading edge of one pulse to the leading edge of the next in the clock train. The width of this period dictates the speed at which data can be transferred across the bus.

If any of the foregoing makes sense to you, you're doing great. The timing diagram that follows in Figure 6.30 may help you understand the technical side of synchronous transfers.

FIGURE 6.30 **Synchronous Offset Timing Diagram**

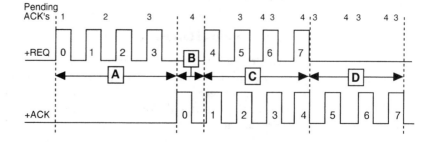

NOTE *It takes special hardware to achieve Fast synchronous transfer rates, including ICs and cables. Other restrictions on cable length may also impact your configuration. Fast synchronous transfers are usually implemented on higher-end systems and workstations. You should be careful if you are going to use the single-ended cable option and Fast transfers, because the signal quality decreases as the cable length increases. When using the Fast SCSI and single-end alternative, make sure that the cable length does not exceed three meters.*

Synchronous Offset Timing Diagram

Figure 6.30 demonstrates how the synchronous offset works. The "Pending ACKs" represent the number of acknowledgments that an initiator must send to the target to complete the synchronous transfer successfully.

Here's what's happening in the diagram in Figure 6.30, following along step by step, letter by letter:

A A target issues four REQ pulses, because an offset count of four was agreed upon between the initiator and target. Now the offset state machine puts a hold on further data transfers until an ACK pulse is received from the initiator.

B The initiator issues an ACK pulse, thereby allowing the REQ generator on the target to issue a REQ pulse. After this occurs, the REQ and ACK generators are free to issue REQ and ACK pulses independent of one another unless the data FIFOs are full, empty, or the offset count is exceeded.

C This represents the data transfer area. The REQ and ACK pulses form a transfer period that both the initiator and target agreed upon long before data was transferred.

D Eventually the ACK pulses sent by the initiator must equal the REQ pulses sent by the target. Because the first ACK pulse was received at the beginning of the transfer, three more must be sent to "clean house" and complete the transfer.

7

A Look at SCSI-3

by John Lohmeyer, Senior Consulting Engineer, Symbios Logic Inc.

As Chair of the X3T10 Technical Committee (the committee that is responsible for the SCSI standards), I am often asked about SCSI-3. SCSI-3 departs from SCSI-1 and SCSI-2 in that it is not a single standard. SCSI-3 is a collection of over a dozen standards that are arranged in a building-block fashion. This gives a great degree of flexibility: SCSI-3 supports the traditional parallel bus plus three serial interfaces. Also, the building-block approach permits the various pieces of SCSI-3 to be published when they are ready rather than waiting for all of the pieces to be ready at the same time (which is nearly impossible).

In developing a SCSI-3 product, all designers must first conform to two of the above standards, namely SCSI-3 Architecture Model and SCSI-3 Primary Commands. Then they must pick a physical interface (a pair of associated standards) and a command set (one of the standards shown on the top line of Figure 7.1). In sum, each SCSI-3 peripheral product must conform to five standards. While this may be a bit confusing at first, don't forget that this is a powerful architecture. And a bit of confusion will be well worth it—there is no need to rewrite SCSI-3 driver software when moving from one physical interface to another!

If you are already familiar with communications standards, then you probably recognize that SCSI-3 has essentially adopted the layered

FIGURE 7.1   SCSI-3 Organization Chart

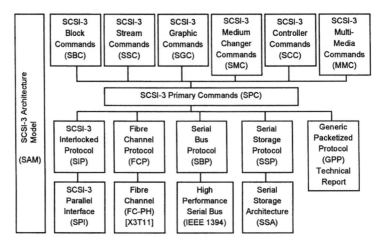

standards architecture promoted in the ISO Reference Model, with one key difference: SCSI-3 is optimized for storage and local I/O applications and is not designed to operate over the long distances typically associated with communications.

SPI (SCSI-3 Parallel Interface)

The SCSI-3 Parallel Interface (SPI, pronounced "spy") is the furthest along in the development and approval phases. Barring any snags, SPI may be an approved ANSI standard by the time you read this. In fact, many current SCSI products include features defined in SPI, such as 16-bit single-cable (P cable), more than eight SCSI IDs, and single-ended Fast SCSI. In addition, the X3T10 committee is working on bringing a low-power version of SCSI to notebook computers, possibly by as early as 1996.

Fast-20

Another SCSI-3 concept much talked about is Fast-20, which you may also hear referred to by its marketing terms "UltraSCSI" and "Double-Speed SCSI." Don't despair—they're all referring to the same thing. Fast-20 defines how to move data at 20 MB/sec over an 8-bit bus. When combined with 16-bit Wide SCSI, it is still called Fast-20 but you get a 40 MB/sec transfer rate.

Fast-20 doesn't even appear on the SCSI-3 organization chart (Figure 7.1). You can think of it as a wart on the SPI standard. While the Fast-20 concepts are within the scope of SPI, no one wanted to delay SPI while the committee finished developing Fast-20, so it is left as a separate standard. X3T10 is now investigating doubling SCSI speeds again with, what else? Fast-40. Stay tuned.

SERIAL SCSI

Serial SCSI means different things to different people. I think of serial SCSI as a generic term used to describe the process of transporting SCSI commands over any serial interface. X3T10 has defined SCSI mappings for three serial interfaces, namely Fibre Channel (FC), Serial Storage Architecture (SSA), and High Performance Serial Bus (IEEE 1394). While all three interfaces have attractive features, it's still a three-horse race for which one, if any, will becomes an important PC interface, and it takes years for new I/O interfaces to catch on. Also, since the price of the traditional parallel SCSI bus is getting fairly inexpensive, new vendors face slim profit margins in the race. There is a particularly vigorous fight between the FC and SSA camps over getting into the disk drive market.

Fibre Channel

Fibre Channel is being positioned as the high-end "universal pipe." It is capable of connecting almost anything to anything else at speeds up to 1000 MB/sec (1 GB/sec) using either coaxial cable or fiber optics. FC devices are connected through networks that are called "fabrics." Most of these fabrics are actually made up of circuit switches.

The only trouble with Fibre Channel is that its flexibility and speed are expensive, and the challenge for its proponents is to get the costs of its fabric down to a competitive level. One approach to Fibre Channel is called the Fibre Channel Arbitrated Loop (FC-AL). FC-AL simplifies connections by eliminating the separate and expensive fabric, by including a piece of the fabric in each FC-AL device. A number of FC-AL devices can be connected in a loop or ring, referred to as an arbitrated loop. The loop is called "arbitrated" because, like parallel SCSI, FC-AL devices arbitrate or compete for exclusive use of the loop. The winning device gets access to the loop and, once finished, the winning device gives up control of the loop so that another device may arbitrate.

Serial Storage Architecture

Serial Storage Architecture (SSA) is less of a general standard than FC, since it was principally designed by IBM as a storage interface. While SSA *could* be used for many of the same applications as FC, it does not extend as far or connect as many devices as FC. Still, SSA is a powerful interface that can connect more devices than any PC system is ever likely to need.

While SSA transfer rates are somewhat lower than FC (20 MB/sec today, with 40 MB/sec planned), SSA loops work differently from FC-AL loops. SSA loops are full-duplex, allowing for simultaneous two-way conversations, thus permitting more than one conversation at a time. SSA proponents call this two-way conversation spacial reuse (and FC-AL proponents call it hogwash). In the best case, spacial reuse could give SSA an effective quadrupling of bandwidth. However, the reality is this: because many of today's operating systems (particularly DOS and Windows) are not multithreaded, they cannot exploit spacial reuse, although multithreaded 32-bit operating systems, like Windows 95 and OS/2, could exploit it.

IEEE 1394

The third contender for the title of serial SCSI is IEEE 1394, which you may have heard called *Firewire*, Apple Computer's name for their version. 1394 was designed to be a serial replacement for parallel SCSI, and it solves almost every problem that Apple's engineers perceived was wrong with SCSI. It uses simple flexible cables that can be plugged into almost any empty socket, there are no terminators to worry about, no IDs to set, and it logically appears to be a bus, just like parallel SCSI. Furthermore, 1394 supports isochronous services. Isochronous is a rather big word that means it has guaranteed timely delivery of certain data. It's a great way to deliver voice and video data.

Early 1394 chips support 100 MB/sec data rates, clearly a transfer rate that is not competitive with FC and SSA. To remedy this problem, chips are under development to support 200 MB/sec, and a 400 MB/sec version is planned.

1394 is not really a true serial interface, though it carries three types of signals, including a data signal and a strobe signal. While this approach simplifies the interface logic, it limits the ultimate data rates. A third power signal keeps the low-level interface logic alive even in powered-down devices, thus keeping the bus intact even when a device is unplugged. Since 1394 has these three types of signals, its cables have three twisted pairs.

Largely due to marketing rather than technical reasons, 1394 has not been a serious contender as a disk drive interface. The interface is starting to show up as a consumer electronics interface for such things as video cameras and VCRs. If it catches on in the consumer electronics market, its sales volume will probably drive down the electronics costs to the point where 1394 may become very interesting as a PC I/O interface.

Fiber SCSI

If you hear anyone talking about using Fiber SCSI, they probably haven't priced fiber optic components or they need to go *real* far. Fiber optic components and connectors—except for plastic fiber, which has a rather low bandwidth—are too expensive for most I/O applications.

NOTE *There is a ray of hope for a shortwave laser method of connecting fiber optic components with some versions of Fibre Channel. These lasers have become fairly inexpensive due to their usage in CD-ROMs.*

Fibre Channel defines both fiber and copper versions; SSA has focused on copper, but could use fiber optics; and 1394 is strictly copper (I certainly wouldn't want to look into the power fiber!).

GPP (GENERIC PACKETIZED PROTOCOL)

You may have noticed that the SCSI-3 organization chart in Figure 7.1 includes a Generic Packetized Protocol (GPP) called a technical report, not a standard. GPP does not have an associated interface—it can run over any interface that delivers data packets. While GPP has a lot of powerful features, it has not caught on in the industry, probably because as a generic interface it does not exploit many of the features of whichever physical interface is used. The proponents of the competing physical interfaces all opted to design protocols that make better use of the physical interface features. Then, to avoid market confusion, they voted to make GPP a technical report instead of a standard. Most people reading this book will have no need for GPP; but if you have a specialized need to operate SCSI over very long distances (say, cross-country), GPP is the most efficient long-distance protocol available.

SCSI-2's GREATEST VALUE IS ITS COMMAND SETS

The part of SCSI-2 that has the most value is its command sets. Because the computer industry has made a huge investment in SCSI driver software, all of the serial interfaces need SCSI command set mappings to leverage the command set investment and get to market quicker. Even IDE proponents have leveraged the SCSI command sets: the ATAPI protocol maps the SCSI CD-ROM command set onto the IDE interface to permit internal IDE CD-ROMs.

The command sets that were in SCSI-2 are partitioned across five of the six SCSI-3 command set documents on the top line of the organization chart. While enhancements are being made, most of the changes are evolutionary. The SCSI-3 Controller Commands (SCC) is a new command set for RAID controllers. It mostly provides a standardized method of reporting and configuring SCSI RAID controllers. The individual disk drives in the array would most likely be SCSI disks, but they could have any interface.

WHEN WILL WE SEE SCSI-3?

So when will SCSI-3 be done? Of course, there is not one date; each document goes through the standards approval process individually. Several documents, including SCC, SAM, FCP, SBP, GPP, SPI, and Fast-20, are in the approval process as I write this. Others are nearing completion of their development phase.

The fact is that manufacturers rarely wait for final ANSI approval before starting product development, and you may have already seen products advertised as offering SCSI-3 capabilities. Will products that are early adopters of SCSI-3 have compatibility problems? Occasionally, but usually not.

And the final question: How soon will serial SCSI devices be available? Well, we'd all love to know the answer to this one. Some prototypes already exist, but it will probably be several years before serial SCSI devices are available in significant volumes. New physical interfaces take a long time to mature, and old physical interfaces take an even longer time to die.

SCSI Sources

How to Use This Directory

This is a directory of vendors that manufacture or publish SCSI-related hardware or software. It's not a comprehensive listing. All of the names, addresses, phone or fax numbers, and product information were verified at the time of publication but are subject to change.

You should use this directory to reach manufacturers that interest you. When first setting out to reach a manufacturer, try the toll-free numbers first (because they're free). If you can't get through on the toll-free number, try the main number or another relevant phone number, like one for sales or technical support. Many companies have special tech support phone numbers or fax lines, which are listed here.

If you're after the latest drivers for your hardware, check out the manufacturer's BBS first. These BBSs will also often contain lists of commonly asked questions and answers about particular products, as well as more general information about SCSI. Rather than spend your long-distance time searching the BBS, look for a downloadable index of the files on the BBS first and download it so that you can search offline. If you can't find an index, look for file directories that are appropriate to your interests, like collections of software or drivers or the latest technical support bulletins. You may also be able to use the BBSs as a way to reach the manufacturer with technical support questions when other means fail or are less attractive. Look for a way to post a message to the SYSOP and then post your question. Most times you'll get an answer, though you may have to wait a while for a response.

You should use this directory to not only track down manufacturers and their BBSs or help hotlines but also to search for various SCSI-based products. This directory also has product listings for each manufacturer. We hope that this will make your shopping a bit easier. Scan these product listings for hard-to-find products or simply use them for comparison shopping. We've left out the prices because prices will vary from store to store and from month to month. Of course, product listings will also change, so if a manufacturer strikes your fancy, your best bet is to call their sales information line or main number for their latest catalog. We suggest that you use the product listings not as a definitive list of all of a company's products but more as a clue to what they produce.

Faxback services can be a terrific resource for getting answers to your tech support questions. They're almost always available for free, 24 hours a day. The best way to use a faxback service is to request an index of publications first and then to "shop" the service using this index as your guide. Of course, you'll need to have access to a fax machine in order to use the faxback services.

Finally, some manufacturers offer E-mail addresses. If you've got an E-mail connection, you might wish to try E-mailing your questions to the manufacturer. The only downside to this method is that your message is liable to fall into a great black hole. One way you can combat this is to use a very clear subject in the message's heading, like "My darn QRS123 controller caught fire yesterday and melted my machine, can you help?" That's sure to get someone's attention.

The matrix that follows lists every vendor in the directory and crosses each with their product categories. Use this matrix as a way to find vendors in the directory who make products that interest you. In Appendix L you will find a listing of online SCSI resources. We hope that these resources will provide you with still more venues for future SCSI adventures.

Company	Cables	CD-ROM Drives	Connectors	Developer Kits	Drivers	Hard Disk Drives	Host Adapters	Magneto-Optical Drives	Printers	RAID Products	Repeaters	Scanners	Software	Sound Cards	Switches	Tape Drives	Terminators	Tools	WORM Drives	Miscellaneous
Acculogic Inc.							•													
Adaptec Inc.				•	•		•						•							
Advanced Integration Research (AIR)							•													
Advanced Storage Concepts					•		•						•							
Advanced System Products Inc. (AdvanSys)							•													
Aeronics Inc.																	•			
Always Technology Corporation							•													
American Digital Systems									•		•						•			
American Megatrends Inc.							•			•										
Ameriquest Technologies							•	•									•			
Amp Incorporated	•		•															•		
Analogic Corporation							•													
Ancot Corporation							•											•		
Antex Electronics Corporation														•						
Apex Data Inc.							•													
Apple Computer								•					•				•			
Applied Concepts Inc.											•				•					
APS Technologies								•		•										
Ariel Corporation							•													
AST Research Inc.							•						•							
AT&T Global Information Solutions							•													
ATTO Technology Inc.	•			•	•		•			•			•							•
Automated System Methodologies Inc.																•				
Award Software International Inc.													•							•
Aztech Labs Inc.														•						
Belkin Components	•						•											•		
Bi-Tech Enterprises Inc.							•													
Buffalo Inc.	•																			
BusLogic Inc.							•			•			•							
Canon USA Inc.												•								
CD ROM Inc.			•																	
CD (Custom Design) Technology Inc.			•																	
Ciprico Inc.							•			•										
CMD Technology Inc.							•													
CoComp Inc.	•																	•		
Compaq Computer Corp.							•			•						•				
CompuADD Corp.							•													
Computer Connections																•				
Computer Modules Inc.																				•

Company	Cables	CD-ROM Drives	Connectors	Developer Kits	Drivers	Hard Disk Drives	Host Adapters	Magneto-Optical Drives	Printers	RAID Products	Repeaters	Scanners	Software	Sound Cards	Switches	Tape Drives	Terminators	Tools	WORM Drives	Miscellaneous
Connect Group, Inc.	•							•										•		
Conner Peripherals Inc.							•										•			
Conner Storage Systems Group										•					•		•			
Contemporary Cybernetics Group								•									•			
Control Concepts Inc.								•												
Core International						•		•		•							•			
Corel Corp.					•			•					•							
Corporate Systems Center								•												
Creative Labs, Inc.		•												•						
Cristie Electronics Ltd																	•			
Curtis Inc.							•													
Data General Corporation										•							•			
Dataquest																				•
Data Technology Corporation (DTC)								•												
DBM Associates																	•			
Dekka Technologies Inc.										•										
Digi-Data Corporation										•							•			
Disk Emulation Systems							•													
Distributed Processing Technology (DPT)								•					•							
ECCS Inc.									•	•							•			
Everex Systems Inc.																	•			
Exabyte Corporation																	•			
Fintec Peripheral Solutions								•									•			•
FOREX Computer Corporation								•												
Future Domain Corporation				•				•												
FWB Inc.		•						•									•			
Genoa Systems Corporation																•	•			
GoldStar USA Inc.		•																		
Greystone Peripherals Inc.													•							
Industrial Computer Source								•		•										•
Interface Data Inc.																	•			
Interphase Corporation								•												
Iomega Corporation							•		•					•			•			
I-TECH Corporation								•											•	
Jets Cybernetics							•	•												
Kingston Technology Corporation							•		•	•							•			
Kres Engineering											•									•
Landmark Research International Corporation																		•		
Laura Technologies Inc.								•									•			

Company	Cables	CD-ROM Drives	Connectors	Developer Kits	Drivers	Hard Disk Drives	Host Adapters	Magneto-Optical Drives	Printers	RAID Products	Repeaters	Scanners	Software	Sound Cards	Switches	Tape Drives	Terminators	WORM Drives	Tools	Miscellaneous
Legacy Storage Systems Inc.		•								•							•			
Linksys																				•
Logitech Inc.												•								
Lomas Data Corporation							•													
Longshine Microsystems							•													
Loviél Computer Corporation		•					•		•								•			
MacProducts USA		•					•													•
MagicRAM Inc.							•													
Maxtor Corporation						•														
Media Integration Inc.							•		•	•							•			
Megabit Communications Inc.							•													
MemTech																				•
Micro Design International Inc.		•							•	•							•		•	
MicroNet Technology Inc.		•				•	•			•							•			
Micropolis Corporation						•				•										
Morton Management Inc.		•				•				•										•
Mountain Network Solutions Inc.																•	•			
Mustek Inc.												•								
Mylex Corporation							•			•										
NEC Technologies Inc.		•					•							•						
NextStor							•													
New Media Corporation							•													
Optima Technology Corporation									•	•							•			
Pacific Electro Data																		•		
Parity Systems Inc.						•											•			
Perceptive Solutions Inc.							•													
Perifitech Inc.						•	•													
Peripheral Interface Ltd.									•											
Peripheral Land Inc. (PLI)						•	•	•		•							•			
Philips Consumer Electronics		•																		
Plexstor Coporation		•																		
Prima Storage Solutions							•										•			
Procomp USA Inc.							•											•		
Procom Technology Inc.		•					•	•												
QLogic Corporation							•													
Quantum						•														
Quatech Inc.							•													
Raidtec Corporation										•										
Rancho Technology Inc.							•													

Company	CD-ROM Drives	Cables	Connectors	Developer Kits	Hard Disk Drives	Host Adapters	Magneto-Optical Drives	Printers	RAID Products	Repeaters	Scanners	Software	Sound Cards	Switches	Tape Drives	Terminators	Tools	WORM Drives	Miscellaneous
Relax Technologies Inc.		•				•	•												
Relisys Corporation											•								
SC&T International, Inc.																			•
Seagate Technology Inc.					•														
Shaffstall Corporation												•							
Silicon Composers Inc.						•													
Sony Electronics Inc., Computer Peripherals Products	•						•		•						•			•	
Spectrum Engineering Inc.						•													
Storage Dimensions Inc.									•			•			•			•	
Sun Microsystems, Inc.						•			•										
Symbios Logic Incorporated						•						•							
Targa Electronics Systems Inc.						•													
Teac America Inc.	•				•										•				
Tecmar Inc.												•			•				
Teknor Microsystems Inc.						•													
Tekram Technology						•													
TTS Multimedia Systems				•															
Tulin Technology						•	•								•				
TWD Electronics Inc.						•													
UltraStor Corporation						•			•										
Wangtek Inc.															•				
Western Automation Labs Inc.														•		•			
Western Digital Corporation					•	•						•							
Western Systems						•													
Winchester Systems Inc.						•			•						•				
Xirlink Inc.						•													•

Acculogic Inc.

Part of ACC Technology Group.

Address: 7 Whatney
     Irvine, CA 92718

Main Phone: 800-234-7811 or 714-454-2441

Fax: 714-454-8527

BBS: 714-470-1759

SCSI Products: Host adapters

EISAPPORT-20 supports Fast and Wide SCSI

EISAPPORT-40 Fast and Wide SCSI with CorelSCSI!

ISAPPORT-20

ISAPPORT-40 with CorelSCSI!

ISAPPORT/95

PCIPPORT-20 Fast and Wide SCSI

PCIPPORT-40 Fast and Wide SCSI with CorelSCSI!

PCIPPORT/Wide Differential SCSI

PCMCIAPPORT

VESAPPORT-20 Fast and Wide SCSI
VESAPPORT-40 Fast and Wide SCSI with CorelSCSI!

Adaptec Inc.

Address:	691 South Milpitas Blvd. Milpitas, CA 95035
Main Phone:	408-945-8600
Fax:	408-262-2533
Tech Support:	800-959-7274 or 408-934-7274
Faxback:	408-957-7150 (you can get over 100 items from this service)
BBS:	408-945-7727
Pre-Sales:	800-934-2766 (call for information on most Adaptec products)
Ordering:	800-442-7274

International

Sales Office: 011-81-3-5276-9882

(Call for sales information, compatibility information, to purchase a cable, or for the names and addresses of international dealers.)

United Kingdom

Phone:	44252811200
Fax:	44252811212
BBS:	44252811956

Germany

Phone:	49894564060
Fax:	498945640615
BBS:	498945640618

France

Phone:	33130649874
Fax:	33130649872
BBS:	33130609539

Belgium

Address:	Avenue Tedesco 5 B-1160 Brussels
Phone:	3226781911
Fax:	3226602836
BBS:	3226757036

SCSI Products: Developer Kits, Drivers, Host Adapters, Software

AHA-1510 SCSI host adapter board

AHA-1520/1522 SCSI host adapter with floptical support

AHA-1540/1542 Bus Master ISA SCSI host adapter board

AHA-1640 16-bit MCA SCSI host adapter board

AHA-1740 series of 32-bit EISA bus SCSI host adapter boards

AHA-2740 series of 32-bit EISA bus SCSI host adapter boards

AHA-2840A family of VL-bus SCSI-2 host adapter boards

AHA-2842VL VL-bus SCSI host adapter board

AHA-2940 PCI Fast SCSI (SCSI adapter board for PCI bus)

AIC-6060 mass storage controller board

AIC-6070 mass storage controller board

AIC-6110 mass storage controller board

AIC-6160 mass storage controller board

AIC-6190 mass storage controller board

AIC-7110 mass storage controller board

AIC-7160 mass storage controller board

AIC-7165 mass storage controller board

AIC-7870 PCI bus SCSI host adapter board

AIC-8010 mass storage controller board

AIC-8060 mass storage controller board

AIC-8110 mass storage controller board

AIC-8160 mass storage controller board

AIC-9110 mass storage controller board

AME-1570 16-bit ISA bus sound card with SCSI-2 adapter

AMM-1572 16-bit ISA bus sound card with SCSI-2 adapter

APA-460 SlimSCSI Adapter (PCMCIA SCSI adapter board)

ASW-1240 SCSI Manager software

ASW-1250 SCSI Manager software

ASW-1420 SCSI Manager software

ASW-1440 SCSI Manager software

ASW-1450 SCSI Manager software

EISA SCSI Master, The (SCSI host adapter kit)

EZ-SCSI (SCSI installation software)

Floptical Connection, The (SCSI interface and driver software)

MultiMedia Connection, The (SCSI host adapter for CD-ROMs)

SCSI Backup, The (SCSI interface and backup software for DAT tape)

SCSI Channel, The (interface package for Micro Channel)

SCSI Direction Plus, The (SCSI host adapter kit)

SCSI Direction, The (SCSI host adapter kit)

SCSI Master Plus, The (SCSI host adapter kit)

SCSI Master, The (ISA SCSI host adapter kit)

SCSI Software Developer's Kit

SlimSCSI (PCMCIA SCSI interface adapter)

T338 Mini SCSI (parallel port SCSI interface adapter)

T348 Mini SCSI Plus (parallel port SCSI interface adapter)

T358 Mini SCSI EPP (parallel port SCSI interface adapter)

TotalCD (CD-ROM drive interface hardware/software package)

TotalConnect (CD-ROM drive interface hardware/software package)

VL SCSI Master Kit, The (AHA-2842 adapter and software)

Advanced Integration Research (AIR)

Address:	2188 Del Franco Street San Jose, CA 95131
Main Phone:	800-866-1945 or 408-428-0800
Fax:	408-428-0950
Tech Support:	408-428-1547 (phone) 408-428-2845 (fax)
BBS:	408-428-1735

International

(Call the Main Phone number for information.)

SCSI Products: Host Adapters

EISA Bus Master SCSI adapters

SCSI-2V EISA Bus Master SCSI controller card

SCSI-2V VL-Bus SCSI controller card

Advanced Storage Concepts

Address:	10713 Ranch Road 620 N. Suite 305 Austin, TX 78726
Main Phone:	512-335-1077
Fax:	512-335-1078
BBS:	512-335-3499
E-mail:	asc@eden.com

Internet

WWW:	http://www.eden.com/~asc/

SCSI Products: Drivers, Host Adapters, Software

ASC-PCI (PCI SCSI host adapter)

ASC-86 (16-bit ISA SCSI host adapter)

ASC-88 (8-bit host adapter)

ASC-PS2 (Microchannel host adapter)

Advanced System Products Inc. (AdvanSys)

Address:	1150 Ringwood Court San Jose, CA 95131
Main Phone:	800-525-7443 or 408-383-9400
Fax:	408-383-9612
Tech Support:	800-525-7440 (24 hours)
Faxback:	408-383-9753
BBS:	408-383-9540

International

UK:	Thame Systems, 0844261919
Italy:	PC Plus, 39226140346
Germany:	Krystal-Tech, 49712194610
Singapore:	Ocean Radio, 653394133

SCSI Products: Host Adapters

ABP94O PCI Bus Master

ABP95O PCI Dual Channel Bus Master

ABP842 VL Bus Master

ABP75O/752 VL Dual Channel Bus Master

ABP542 ISA Bus Master

ABP742 EISA Bus Master

ABP752 EISA Dual Channel Bus Master

AdvanSys

See Advanced System Products Inc.

Aeronics Inc.

Address:	12741 Research Blvd., Suite 500 Austin, TX 78759
Main Phone:	512-258-2303
Fax:	512-258-8441
Sales:	512-258-8040

SCSI Products: Terminators

Forced Perfect Termination (FPT) active SCSI bus terminators and contract assembly

Always Technology Corporation

Address:	31336 Via Colinas, Suite 101 Westlake Village, CA 91362
Main Phone:	818-597-1400
Fax:	818-597-1496
BBS:	818-597-0275

SCSI Products: Host Adapters

AL-1000 high-speed SCSI adapter board

AL-2010 16-bit extended performance SCSI host adapter with floppy

AL-4000 EISA 32-bit SCSI host adapter board

AL-6200 Bus Master EISA bus SCSI host adapter board

AL-7048 VL-bus SCSI host adapter board

IN-2000 16-bit PC/AT SCSI host adapter board

American Digital Systems

Address:	490 Boston Post Road Sudbury, MA 01776
Main Phone:	800-767-7712 or 508-443-7711
Fax:	508-443-4332

SCSI Products: Magneto-Optical Drives, RAID Products, Tape Drives

MasterDisk Optical (magneto-optical disk drive)

MasterTape 4 (SCSI interface 12GB DDS-2 tape drive)

American Megatrends Inc.

Address:	6145-F Northbelt Parkway Norcross, GA 30071
Main Phone:	404-263-8181
Fax:	404-263-9381
Tech Support:	404-246-8645
Faxback:	404-246-8787
BBS:	404-246-8782
Sales:	800-828-9264

SCSI Products: Host Adapters, RAID Products

EISA SCSI adapter

PCI SCSI caching RAID controller

PCI SCSI cache controller

Ameriquest Technologies

Includes the CMS Enhancements product line.

Address:	2722 Michelson Drive. Irvine, CA 92715
Main Phone:	714-222-6000
Fax:	714-222-6303
Tech Support and Sales:	800-237-2707
Tech Support Fax:	714-222-6081
BBS for Apple:	714-222-6601
BBS for IBM:	714/222-6318
Sales Fax:	714-222-1446

SCSI Products: Host Adapters, Magneto-Optical Drives, Tape Drives

BA-ESPRV2F Bus Master 32-bit EISA bus SCSI host adapters

HBA-ISPRV2F Bus Master ISA bus SCSI host adapters

HBA-LSPRV2F Bus Master 32-bit VL-bus SCSI host adapters

HBA-MSPRV2F Bus Master 32-bit MCA bus SCSI host adapters

HBA-SA0 Bus Master 16-bit ISA bus SCSI host adapter

Platinum 8mm 10GB 8ɲm DAT tape drive, SCSI-2 interface

PMO128/D-E magneto-optical disk drive

TapeMaster and Tapestack series of backup tape drives

Amp Incorporated

Address:	P.O. Box 3608 Product Information Center Mail Stop 38-03 Harrisburg, PA 17105
Main Phone:	800-522-6752 (Amp FAX button #1, customer support #2, product information #3)
Fax:	717-986-7575
Faxback:	800-522-6752
SCSI Products:	Cables, Connectors, Terminators

Analogic Corporation

Address:	8 Centennial Drive Peabody, MA 01960
Main Phone:	800-446-8936 (ask to be transferred to the Peabody offices) or 508-977-3000
Fax:	508-532-6097
SCSI Products:	Host Adapters

Ancot Corporation

Address:	115 Constitution Drive Menlo Park, CA 94025
Main Phone:	415-322-5322
Fax:	415-322-0455

Internet

Information:	info@ancot.com
Tech Support:	help@ancot.com
Sales:	sales@ancot.com

SCSI Products: Host Adapters, Tools

ASA-400 XT/AT SCSI adapter board

ASA-682 I/O Adapter Board (serial/parallel/mouse/FDD/HDD)

ASA-700 XT/AT SCSI adapter board with buffering

AST-156 SCSI emulation tester

ASW-110, ASW-116 and ASW-210 SCSI Disk Drive Testers

SMA-924 SMART Switch (automatic SCSI switch)

Antex Electronics Corporation

Address:	16100 South Figueroa Street Gardena, CA 90248
Main Phone:	800-338-4231 or 310-532-3092
Fax:	310-532-8509
Tech Support:	310-532-3092
BBS:	310-768-3947
SCSI Products:	Sound Cards

Series 3/Model Z1 MPC sound board with SCSI and MIDI interfaces

Apex Data Inc.

Address:	6624 Owens Drive Pleasanton, CA 94588
Main Phone:	800-841-2739 or 510-416-5656
Fax:	510-416-0909
BBS:	510-416-0809
SCSI Products:	Host Adapters

PCMCIA SCSI Adapters

Apple Computer

Address:	1 Infinite Loop Cupertino, CA 95014
Main Phone:	408-996-1010

Fax:	408-996-0275	
Tech Support:	800-767-2775	
Faxback:	800-505-0171	
E-mail:	@applelink.apple.com	
Product Information:		
	800-776-2333	

Internet

WWW:	http://www. apple.com
Tech Support:	www.info.apple.com
Product Information:	
	www.info.apple.com
Software Updates:	
	www.support. apple.com
FTP:	ftp.support.apple.com
	ftp.info.apple.com (software updates and product information)
SCSI Products:	Hard Disk Drives, Software, Tape Drives

Applied Concepts Inc.

Address:	9130 S.W. Pioneer Court Wilsonville, OR 97070
Main Phone:	800-624-6808 or 503-685-9300
Fax:	503-685-9099
SCSI Products:	Repeaters, Switches

SCSI Plus Bus Repeater

SCSI Switch (switches locally or remotely between SCSI devices)

APS Technologies

Address:	6131 Deramus P.O. Box 4987 Kansas City, MO 64120-0087
Main Phone:	800-235-8935

Internet

WWW:	http: //www.apstech.com
Sales:	sales@apstech.com
International sales:	
	intlsales@apstech.com
Tech Support:	support@apstech.com
Repair:	service@apstech.com

SCSI Products:	Hard Disk Drives, RAID Products

SR 2000

SCSI StacKit

SCSI StacKit II

Ariel Corporation

Address:	433 River Road Highland Park, NJ 08904
Main Phone:	908-249-2900
Fax:	908-249-2123
E-mail:	ariel@ariel.com
BBS:	908-249-2124
SCSI Products:	Host Adapters

DAT-Link (intelligent SCSI interface for DAT/CD control)

AST Research Inc.

Address:	16215 Alton Parkway Irvine, CA 92619
Main Phone:	800-876-4278 or 714-727-4141
Fax:	714-727-9355
Faxback:	800-926-1278
BBS:	714-727-4723

Germany

Address:	AST Research Deutschland GmbH Schiess-Str. 58 D-W4000 Dusseldorf 11
BBS:	905-512-8558
Phone:	0211-59570
Fax:	0211-591028
SCSI Products:	Host Adapters, Software

AT&T Global Information Solutions

Address:	1700 South Patterson Blvd. Dayton, OH 45479
Main Phone:	513-445-5000
Fax:	513-445-4732
Tech Support:	800-531-2222

BBS:	800-692-8872
Sales:	800-637-2600
SCSI Products:	Host Adapters

ATTO Technology Inc.

Address:	40 Hazelwood Drive, Suite 106 Amherst, NY 14228
Main Phone:	716-691-1999
Fax:	716-691-9353
BBS:	716-691-9403
E-mail:	AOL: atto1@aol.com Compuserve: 76570,1510 AppleLink: ATTO Internet: atto@localnet.com
SCSI Products:	Host Adapters, Solid State Disk, Solid State Cache, RAID Products, Cables, Drivers, Software, Developer Kits

VantagePCI series of SCSI host adapter boards for PCI (PC)

ExpressPCI series of SCSI host adapter boards for PCI (Macintosh)

SiliconExpress series of SCSI host adapter boards for Nubus

SCSI Expander (SCSI Device Expansion Unit)

Automated System Methodologies Inc.

Address:	16100 Fairchild, Boatyard #105 Clearwater, FL 34622
Main Phone:	800-992-0120 or 813-535-7272
Fax:	813-531-7510
SCSI Products:	Tape Drives

Gator-1G 1.5GB streaming cartridge tape drive

Jackal series of DDS SCSI interface tape drives

Award Software International Inc.

Address:	777 Middlefield Road Mountain View, CA 94043
Main Phone:	415-968-4433

Fax:	415-968-0274
BBS:	415-568-0249

Taiwan

Address:	Award Taiwan 9F No.17 Sec 1 Cheng Te Road Taipei
Phone:	88625550880
Fax:	88625554420

Germany

Address:	Award Europe Elsenheimerstr. 50 80687 Munchen
Phone:	4989575750
Fax:	4989575998
SCSI Products:	Miscellaneous Hardware, Software

NCR SCSI Device Management System (SDMS)

Aztech Labs Inc.

Address:	47811 Warm Springs Blvd. Fremont, CA 94539
Main Phone:	800-886-8859 or 510-623-8988 (8:00 A.M. to 5:00 P.M.)
Fax:	510-623-8989
Tech Support:	800-886-8879
BBS:	510-623-8933

Singapore

Address:	Aztech Systems Pte. Ltd. 31 Ubi Road 1, AVS Building Singapore 1440
Phone:	657417211
Fax:	657418678

Germany

Address:	Aztech Systems GmbH Birkenstrasse 15 2800 Bremen 1
Phone:	04211690843
Fax:	04211690845
SCSI Products:	Sound Cards

Sound Galaxy Orion 16 (16-bit sound card with FM tuner and SCSI)

Belkin Components

Address:	1303 Walnut Parkway Compton, CA 90220
Main Phone:	800-2-BELKIN or 310-898-1100
Fax:	310-898-1111
SCSI Products:	Cables, Host Adapters, Terminators

Bi-Tech Enterprises Inc.

Address:	10 Carlough Road Bohemia, NY 11716
Main Phone:	516-567-8155
Fax:	516-567-8266
BBS:	516-567-8267
SCSI Products:	Host Adapters

Buffalo Inc.

Address:	2805 19th St S.E. Salem, OR 97302-1520
Main Phone:	800-345-2356 or 503-585-3414
Fax:	503-585-4505
BBS:	503-585-5797
E-mail:	7230.2252@compuserve.com
SCSI Products:	Cables

BusLogic Inc.

Formerly BusTek Corp.

Address:	4151 Burton Dr. Santa Clara, CA 95054
Main Phone:	800-707-SCSI or 408-492-9090
Fax:	408-492-1542
Tech Support:	408-970-1414
BBS:	408-492-1984
Sales:	800-707-7274

Internet

General Inquiries:	
	info@buslogic.com
WWW:	http://www.buslogic.com
Tech Support:	techsup@buslogic.com

FTP Site:	ftp://ftp.buslogic.com
SCSI Products:	Host Adapters, RAID Products, Software

BT-445S VESA local bus SCSI host adapter board

BT-542 family of 16-bit PC/AT SCSI host adapter boards

BT-545S SCSI-2 host adapter board

BT-640 32-bit MCA SCSI host adapter board

BT-646 32-bit MCA Fast SCSI host adapter board

BT-742 32-bit EISA SCSI host adapter board

BT-747 32-bit EISA Fast SCSI host adapter board

BT-757 EISA bus master Wide SCSI adapter boards

BT-946C intelligent PCI local bus SCSI host adapter board

DA-2788 and DA-2988 dual channel SCSI disk array controller

DA-4988 four-channel SCSI disk array controller

Paragon (disk array software for NetWare)

Canon USA Inc.

Address:	Canon Computer Systems Inc. 123 East Paularino Avenue Costa Mesa, CA 92628
Main Phone:	800-848-4123 (call this number first to find out where to call within Canon for answers to your questions) or 714-438-3000
Fax:	714-438-3099
Tech Support:	800-423-2366
Tech Support Fax:	
	800-922-9068 (Fax in questions with your name and phone number.)
Faxback:	800-526-4345
BBS:	714-438-3325
SCSI Products:	Scanners

IX-30F scanner with SCSI interface, 256 gray levels

CD ROM Inc.

Address:	603 Park Point Drive, Suite 110 Golden, CO 80401
Main Phone:	303-526-7600
Fax:	303-526-7395
SCSI Products:	CD-ROM Drives

CD-ROM drives with SCSI interface

CD (Custom Design) Technology Inc.

Address:	764 San Aleso Avenue Sunnyvale, CA 94086
Main Phone:	408-752-8500
Fax:	408-752-8501
SCSI Products:	CD-ROM Drives

Porta-Drive CD-ROM drive with SCSI interface

Ciprico Inc.

Address:	2800 Campus Drive, Suite. 60 Plymouth, MN 55441
Main Phone:	800-727-4669 or 612-551-4000
Fax:	612-551-4002
SCSI Products:	Host Adapters, RAID Products

RAID disk arrays

SCSI host bus adapter boards

CMD Technology Inc.

Address:	1 Vanderbilt Irvine, CA 92718
Main Phone:	800-426-3832 or 714-454-0800
Fax:	714-455-1656
BBS:	714-454-0795
SCSI Products:	Host Adapters

CSA-6300 VL-bus SCSI caching disk controller

CMS Enhancements Inc.

See Ameriquest Technologies.

CoComp Inc.

Address:	2330 S. McClintock Drive Tempe, AZ 85282
Main Phone:	800-658-5981
Tech Support:	602-784-4801
E-mail:	scsitech@cocomp.com
SCSI Products:	Cables, Tools

SCSI Tool Set Professional

SCSICable Plus (a parallel port to SCSI adapter cable)

Compaq Computer Corp.

Address:	20555 State Highway 249 Houston, TX 77070-2698
Tech Support:	800-652-6672
Tech Support Fax:	800-888-5329
Customer Service and Faxback:	800-345-1518
Information:	800-888-5858
BBS:	713-378-1418
SCSI Products:	Host Adapters, RAID Products, Tape Drives

Smart SCSI Array Controller (full-featured SCSI-2)

Compaq 6260 SCSI-2 Controller for ISA and EISA systems

Compaq 32-Bit Fast-SCSI-2 controller

Compaq 5GB DAT Drive (DDS-1 tape drive with SCSI interface)

CompuADD Corp.

Address:	12337 Technology Blvd. Austin, TX 78727
Main Phone:	512-219-2800
Tech Support:	800-999-9901 (phone) 800-766-9711 (fax)
Faxback:	800-933-9002
Customer Service:	800-753-5766

BBS: 512-250-3226

Sales: 800-333-2429 (phone)
512-250-3494 (fax)

SCSI Products: Host Adapters
HardCache/SCSI Controller Card

Computer Connections

Address: 19A Crosby Drive
Bedford, MA 01730

Main Phone: 800-438-5336 or 617-271-0444

Fax: 617-271-0873

SCSI Products: Tape Drives
Data Shuttle (portable tape backup using
parallel or SCSI)

Computer Modules Inc.

Address: 2350 Walsh Avenue
Santa Clara, CA 95051

Main Phone: 408-496-1881

Fax: 408-496-1886

SCSI Products: Expansion Hardware
Dynamic Drive (SCSI interface solid-state
RAM drives)

Connect Group, Inc.

Address: 836 Ritchie Highway, Unit 6
Severna Park, MD, 21146

Main Phone: 800-296-3374 or 410-315-8500

Fax: 410-315-8502

SCSI Products: Cables, Host Adapters,
Terminators

Conner Peripherals Inc.

Address: 3081 Zanker Road
San Jose, CA 95134

Main Phone: 800-426-6637 or 408-456-4500

Fax: 408-456-4501

Faxback: 408-456-4903

BBS: 408-456-4415

SCSI Products: Hard Disk Drives, Tape Drives

Anaconda series of SCSI streamer tape drives

Chinook series of 3.5-inch low profile SCSI
hard disk drives

Python series of DAT tape drives

Conner Storage Systems Group

Formerly Maynard Electronics.

Address: 450 Technology Park Drive
Lake Mary, FL 32746

Main Phone: 407-263-3500

Fax: 407-263-3442

Customer Service:
800-537-2248

BBS: 407-263-3502 or 407-263-3662

Accessory Sales: 800-531-0968

General Sales: 800-626-6637

SCSI Products: RAID Products, Software, Tape
Drives

ArchiveST (SCSI tape drive kits)

Conner Optical Jukebox Model 16L-MO

CR6-RAID system (external 6-disk drive
RAID solution)

Irwin 7000 series of quarter-inch data cartridge tape drives

Irwin 9000 series of DAT tape drives

Irwin Accutrak series of cartridge tape
backup subsystems

Irwin EzArc server-based tape backup software

Irwin EzPort transportable tape backup
system

Irwin EzTape (tape backup software for
DOS and Windows)

Irwin EzTape Plus (tape backup software)

MaynStream CS series of cassette tape
backup systems

MaynStream DAT series of 4mm DAT tape
backup systems

MaynStream HS series of helical scan 8mm
tape backup systems

MaynStream Q series of cartridge tape
backup systems

Tape-Stor 4000 (GB SCSI-2 minicartridge tape drive)

Tape-Stor 700 (700MB minicartridge tape drive)

Contemporary Cybernetics Group

Address:	11846 Rock Landing Newport News, VA 23606
Main Phone:	804-873-9000
Fax:	804-873-8836
SCSI Products:	Magneto-Optical Drives, Tape Drives

CY-10CHS (8mm drive and 10 tape cartridge handling subsystem)

CY-10LT (20.8GB optical disk library, 16 platter autoloader)

CY-12CHS (4-drive/120-tape cartridge handling subsystem)

CY-2000 1GB SCSI optical disk drive

CY-3300 multifunction optical drive

CY-3600 9QIC streaming cartridge tape drive, 250MB capacity

CY-3800 QIC 320/525 525MB cartridge tape drive

CY-4000 1GB streaming QIC cartridge tape drive

CY-4200 2GB streaming QIC cartridge tape drive

CY-8200 2.5GB 8mm helical scan tape drive

CY-8500 5GB 8mm helical scan tape drive

Model 100T Optical Disk Library (4 drives, 144 platters)

Model 10T Optical Disk Library (1 drive, 16 platters)

Model 20T Optical Disk Library (2 drives, 32 platters)

Model 60T Optical Disk Library (4 drives, 88 platters)

Control Concepts Inc.

Address:	8500 Executive Park Avenue Fairfax, VA 22031

Main Phone:	800-922-9259 or 703-876-6444
Fax:	703-876-6416
Tech Support:	800-922-9259
SCSI Products:	Host Adapters SCSI ISA/VLB cards

Core International

Address:	7171 North Federal Highway Boca Raton, FL 33487
Main Phone:	407-997-6044
Fax:	407-997-6009
Tech Support:	407-997-6033
BBS:	407-241-2929
Sales:	800-688-9910

United Kingdom

Address:	Core International UK Ltd. John Scott House Bracknell, Berkshire RG12 1JB United Kingdom
Phone:	0344861776
Fax:	0344861604
SCSI Products:	Hard Disk Drives, Host Adapters, RAID Products, Tape Drives

COREarray family of scaleable RAID disk array subsystems

COREdisk family of high-capacity SCSI hard disk drives

COREfast (backup software)

Coretape Gigafile (tape backup)

Coretape Light (Novell-compatible tape backup unit)

CT series of tape backup systems

HC series of SCSI hard disk drives

LANArray fault-tolerant RAID disk subsystem

MicroArray fault-tolerant RAID disk subsystem

SLAN Fast family of RAID disk subsystems

Corel Corporation

Address:	1600 Carling Avenue Ottawa, Ontario K12 8R7 Canada
Main Phone:	800-836-7274 or 613-728-8200
Fax:	613-728-9790
Tech Support for CorelSCSI!: 	613-728-1010
Faxback:	613-728-0826, x3080
E-mail:	GO COREL on CompuServe
BBS:	613-728-4752
SCSI Products:	Drivers, Host Adapters, Software

CorelRAID

CorelSCSI! (SCSI host adapter and drivers with videotape guide)

CorelSCSI! Network Manager (drivers for NetWare fileserver)

CorelSCSI! Pro (SCSI host adapter and drivers)

LS 2000 SCSI host adapter board

Corporate Systems Center

Address:	1294 Hammerwood Avenue Sunnyvale, CA 94089
Main Phone:	408-734-3475
Fax:	408-745-1816
SCSI Products:	Host Adapters

FastCache-32 high-speed caching SCSI controller board

Creative Labs, Inc.

Subsidiary of Creative Technology, Ltd.

Address:	1901 McCarthy Blvd. Milpitas, CA 95035
Main Phone:	800-998-5227 or 408-428-6600
Fax:	408-428-6611
Tech Support:	405-742-6622 (automated phone support); 405-742-6633 (fax)
BBS:	405-742-6660

SCSI Products: CD-ROM Drives, Sound Cards

CD-ROM drive

Sound Blaster 16 sound board with SCSI-2 interface

Cristie Electronics Ltd.

Address:	Bonds Mill, Stonehouse Gloucestershire GL10 3RG United Kingdom
Main Phone:	453823611
Fax:	453825768
SCSI Products:	Tape Drives

TS5450 DAT tape drive with parallel port and SCSI interfaces

Curtis Inc.

Address:	418 West County Road D St. Paul, MN 55112
Main Phone:	612-631-9512
Fax:	612-631-9508
SCSI Products:	Hard Disk Drives

Clipper (5.25-inch solid-state SCSI-2 disk drive with battery)

PCE FERO low-cost disk emulator using EPROMS or Flash

ROMDisk (solid-state disk and drive emulators)

Data General Corporation

Address:	4400 Computer Drive Westboro, MA 01580
Main Phone:	508-898-5000
Fax:	508-366-1319
Tech Support:	800-344-3577
Product Information: 	800-328-2436
SCSI Products:	RAID Products, Tape Drives

CLARiiON Series 2000 disk array (RAID disk subsystems)

CLARiiON Series 4000 tape array (SCSI 4mm DAT tape drives)

Dataquest

Address:	1290 Ridder Park Drive San Jose, CA 95131
Main Phone:	408-437-8000
Fax:	408-437-0292
SCSI Products:	Publications

Data Technology Corporation (DTC)

Address:	1515 Center Point Drive Milpitas, CA 95035
Main Phone:	408-942-4000
Fax:	408-942-4052
Tech Support:	408-262-7700
Faxback:	408-942-4005
BBS:	408-942-4010
SCSI Products:	Host Adapters

DTC3180 16-bit SCSI host adapter board

DTC3280 16-bit SCSI host adapter board

DTC3292 EISA SCSI host adapter board

DBM Associates

Address:	One Salem Square, Suite 104W Whitehouse Station, NJ 08889
Main Phone:	908-534-1665
SCSI Products:	Tape Drives

SCSI 8mm tape drives for AT&T systems

Dekka Technologies Inc.

Address:	611 Main Street Winchester, MA 01890
Main Phone:	617-721-0077
Fax:	617-729-7946
SCSI Products:	RAID Products

ZERODOWN T-005 Series open-platform SCSI/RAID enclosure and subsystems

Digi-Data Corporation

Address:	8580 Dorsey Run Road. Jessup, MD 20794-9487
Main Phone:	301-498-0200
Fax:	301-498-0771
SCSI Products:	RAID Products, Tape Drives

2000 Series tape backup systems

Digi-Data Model Z SCSI-to-SCSI disk array controller (RAID)

Gigastore VHS tape backup system

Disk Emulation Systems

Address:	3080 Oak Mead Village Drive Santa Clara, CA 95051
Main Phone:	408-727-5497
Fax:	408-727-5496
E-mail:	info@diskmsys.com
SCSI Products:	Hard Disk Drives

DES Model 800R/SCSI solid-state SCSI-2 disk drive

Distributed Processing Technology (DPT)

Address:	140 Candace Drive Maitland, FL 32751
Main Phone:	800-322-4378 or 407-830-5522
Fax:	407-260-5366
BBS:	407-831-6432 or 830-1070
Sales Fax:	407-260-6690
SCSI Products:	Host Adapters, Software

DM3011 SmartCache mirroring module

MM3011 SmartCache memory modules

PM2001 SmartConnex ISA bus SCSI controller

PM2012 (no-cache smart-connect EISA SCSI controller)

PM2022 EISA bus SCSI controller

PM2122 EISA bus SCSI controller

PM3011 SmartCache caching disk controller

SmartCache III SCSI host adapters

SmartCache Plus cache-convertible SCSI controller

SmartRAID Controller (RAID SCSI disk controller)

DPT

See Distributed Processing Technology

ECCS Inc.

Address: One Sheila Drive, Building 6A
Tinton Falls, NJ 07724

Main Phone: 800-322-7462 or 908-747-6995

Fax: 908-747-6542

Tech Support: 800-2GETHLP

SCSI Products: Magneto-Optical Drives, RAID
Products, Tape Drives

Backup Module (integrated 8mm DAT tape
drive and changer)

DFT-1 RAID Module (disk fault-tolerant
storage system)

Exa Module Turbo-5200 DAT tape drive

FFT-1 RAID Module (disk fault-tolerant
storage system)

FFT-1035 fault-tolerant RAID disk array
subsystem

Optical Module 600 and 1000 (optical disk
drives)

Space Maker (SCSI hard disk data compression daughtercard)

Space Module Turbo (SCSI hard disk data
compression card)

Everex Systems Inc.

Address: 5020 Brandin Court
Fremont, CA 94538

Main Phone: 800-821-0806 or 510-498-1111

Tech Support: 510-498-4411 (phone)
510-683-2062 (fax)

Faxback: 510-683-2800

BBS: 510-226-9694

Sales Fax: 510-683-2186

SCSI Products: Tape Drives

Excel 560 (SCSI interface 560MB tape
backup system)

Excel series of tape backup systems

Exabyte Corporation

Address: 1685 38th Street
Boulder, CO 80301

Main Phone: 800-EXABYTE or
303-442-4333

Fax: 303-447-7170

Tech Support: 800-445-7736

E-mail: support@exabyte.com

BBS: 303-447-7100

SCSI Products: Tape Drives

8mm, 4mm, and quarter-inch minicartridge
tape drives

Recording media

Tape libraries

Fintec Peripheral Solutions

Address: 15520 Rockfield Blvd., Suite I
Irvine, CA 92718

Main Phone: 714-768-8219

Fax: 714-768-2986

SCSI Products: Converters, Host Adapters, Tape
Drives

Bus and Tag to SCSI

Emulator controllers

Pertec to SCSI Converters

SCSI to STC

Tape backup solutions for quarter-inch,
half-inch, 4 mm, 8 mm, DLT, 3480/3490

FOREX Computer Corporation

Address: 1999 Concourse Drive
San Jose, CA 95131

Main Phone: 408-955-9280

Fax: 408-955-9611

BBS: 408-955-0938

SCSI Products: Host Adapters

FR600A VL BusMaster VESA SCSI host
adapter board

Future Domain Corporation

Address:	2801 McGaw Avenue
	Irvine, CA 92714
Main Phone:	714-253-0400
Fax:	714-253-0913
Tech Support:	714-253-0440
BBS:	714-253-0432
Order Line:	800-879-7599
SCSI Products:	Drivers, Host Adapters

FPU-OS/2 fixed disk device driver for SCSI host board

Future/CAM for Windows (SCSI multitasking for Windows)

MCS-350 8-bit MCA SCSI host adapter board

MCS-600 ISA and MCA SCSI host adapter boards

MCS-700 MCA SCSI host adapter board

SCSI2GO PCMCIA SCSI interface card

TMC-1600 series of 16-bit ISA SCSI host adapter boards

TMC-1760 16-bit EISA SCSI bus host adapter board

TMC-1790 16-bit EISA SCSI bus host adapter with 16-bit BIOS

TMC-3260 PCI bus SCSI-2 adapter board with boot ROM

TMC-3260MEX economical PCI bus SCSI-2 adapter board

TMC-7000EX Bus Master EISA SCSI host adapter board

TMC-800 series of 8-bit PC/AT SCSI host adapter board

FWB Inc.

Address:	2040 Polk Street, Suite 215
	San Francisco, CA 94109
Main Phone:	415-474-8055
Fax:	415-775-2125
SCSI Products:	CD-ROM Drives, Magneto-Optical Drives, Tape Drives

AT-to-SCSI 16-bit ISA SCSI host adapter board

EISA-to-SCSI SCSI host adapter board

HammerCD external CD-ROM Drive

HammerDAT 16G 8GB DAT tape drive

HammerDAT 2000 2GB DAT tape drive

HammerDAT 5000 5GB DAT tape drive

HammerDisk PE250 (SyQuest-based 256MB hard disk)

HammerDisk1000/4 (magneto-optical storage system)

HammerDisk1300FMF (magneto-optical storage system)

HammerDisk600S (magneto-optical storage system)

MCA-to-SCSI (SCSI host adapter board)

Genoa Systems Corporation

Address:	75 East Trimble Road
	San Jose, CA 95131
Main Phone:	800-934-3662 or 408-432-9090
Fax:	408-434-0997
Tech Support:	408-432-8324
BBS:	408-943-1231
SCSI Products:	Sound Card, Tape Drives

AudioBahn multimedia audio board with SCSI interface

Galaxy series of tape backup systems

GoldStar USA Inc.

For Product Information:

	1000 Sylvan Avenue
	Englewood Cliffs, NJ 07632
Main Phone:	201-816-2000
Customer Support:	
	201 James Record Road
	Huntsville, AL 35824
Tech Support:	800-777-1192
Customer Access Line:	
	800-222-6457
SCSI Products:	CD-ROM Drives

GCD-R320B/SCSI-II CD-ROM drive

Greystone Peripherals Inc.

Address: 130-A Knowles Drive
Los Gatos, CA 95030

Main Phone: 800-600-5710 or 408-866-4739

Fax: 408-866-8328

BBS: 408-866-6938

SCSI Products: Software

GigaBlaster family of software duplication systems for SCSI HDD

Industrial Computer Source

A division of Dynatech Corporation.

Address: 9950 Barnes Canyon Road
San Diego, CA 92121

Main Phone: 800-523-2320 or 619-271-9340

Tech Support Fax:
619-677-0898

SCSI Products: Hardware, Host Adapters, Publications, RAID Products

MAI series of self-contained RAID hard disk arrays

PCE2 ROMDISK (solid-state disk emulator boards)

PCF1 series of flash disk boards

PCSSD-0 solid-state disk drive

PM2000 series of ISA and EISA SCSI-2 controllers with cache optimization

Intellistor Inc.

See NextStor

Interface Data Inc.

Address: 600 West Cummings Park,
Suite 3100
Woburn, MA 01801

Main Phone: 800-370-DATA or 617-938-6333

Fax: 617-938-0626

SCSI Products: Tape Drives

9-track tape subsystems for mainframe data exchange

DX-SCSI 16GB 4mm DAT tape drive

ID2000 2GB DAT tape drive

Interphase Corporation

Address: 13800 Senlac
Dallas, TX 75234

Main Phone: 800-327-8638 or 214-919-9000

Fax: 214-919-9200

E-mail: fastnet@phase.com

WWW Page: http://www.iphase.com

Japan
Address: 1-22-2 Midori-Ku, Hakusan Park
Yokohama City 226

Phone: 81459357780

Fax: 81459357781

United Kingdom
Address: Astral House, Granville Way
Bicester, Oxon OX6 0JT

Phone: 44869321222

Fax: 44869247720

SCSI Products: Host Adapters

V/SCSI 4220 Version 1 Fast SCSI Narrow (8 bit)

V/SCSI 4220 Version 2 Fast SCSI Wide (16 bit)

Iomega Corporation

Address: 1821 West 4000 South
Roy, UT 84067

Main Phone: 800-777-4045 or 801-778-1000

Fax: 801-778-3450

BBS: 801-392-9819

Faxback: 801-778-5763

Germany
Address: IOMega
Botzinger, Strasse 48
79111 Freiburg

Main Phone: 4976145040

Fax: 497614504423

United Kingdom

Address: IOmega
             Keeley House, 22-30 Keeley Rd.
             Croydon, Surrey CR0 1TE

Phone: 0816867171

Fax: 0816805895

SCSI Products: Hard Disk Drives, Magneto-
               Optical Drives, Software, Tape
               Drives

Bernoulli Box (removable mass storage)

Bernoulli Dual MultiDisk 150 removable disk drive

Bernoulli Insider 150 IDE removable 150MB disk drive

Bernoulli Insider 90 PRO removable 90MB disk drive

Bernoulli Insider MultiDisk 150 removable disk drive

Bernoulli MultiDisk 150 removable 150MB disk drive

Bernoulli MultiDisk 35 removable 35MB disk drive

Bernoulli MultiDisk 65 removable 65MB disk drive

Bernoulli Transporter 90 PRO (90MG removable disk drive)

Bernoulli Transporter MultiDisk 150 (removable 150MB disk)

Floptical Drive (21MB SCSI floppy drive)

Iomega Backup for OS/2 (backup/restore software for tape drives)

LaserSafe Plus (1.3GB magneto-optical disk drive)

LaserSafe PRO (1GB erasable magneto-optical disk drive)

Tape250 (250MB cartridge tape drive)

Tape250 Parallel Port II Drive (250MB cartridge tape drive)

Tape510 (5100MB QIC tape drive)

Transportable 90 (removable-cartridge disk drive)

I-TECH Corporation

Address: 6975 Washington Avenue,
             Suite 220
             Edina, MN 55439

Main Phone: 612-941-5905

Fax: 612-941-2386

BBS: 612-941-9610

SCSI Products: Host Adapters, Tools

IPC-2000 PassPort portable test chassis (SCSI testing hardware)

IPC-5010 SCSI-2 bus tester (full-length IC I/O board with software)

IPC-6020 16-bit SCSI bus test board

IPC-6500 16-bit SCSI bus analyzer board

SCSI-2 Fast Testers (PC-based SCSI-2 testers)

Jets Cybernetics

Address: 535 Ramona St., The Penthouse
             Palo Alto, CA 94301

Main Phone: 415-322-7070

Fax: 415-327-5387

SCSI Products: Hard Disk Drives, Host Adapters

FileSurfer 1-2GB large-capacity hard disk drives

SurfBoard XPe 32-bit MCA and EISA SCSI host adapter boards

Kingston Technology Corporation

Address: 17600 Newhope Street
             Fountain Valley, CA 92708

Main Phone: 800-435-0642 (for workstations
             and storage) or 714-435-2600

Fax: 714-435-2699

Tech Support: 800-435-0640 or 714-435-2639

E-mail: tech-support@kingston.com

BBS: 714-435-2636

SCSI Products: Hard Disk Drives, Magneto-
               Optical Drives, RAID Products,
               Tape Drives

Removable Data Express and storage boxes

Kres Engineering

Address: P.O. Box 1268
               La Canada, CA 91011

Main Phone: 818-957-6322

SCSI Products: Extenders, Repeaters

    Portable external backup subsystems

    SCSI bus extenders

Landmark Research International Corporation

Address: 703 Grand Central Street
               Clearwater, FL 34616

Main Phone: 800-683-6696 or 813-443-1331

Fax: 813-443-6603

Tech Support: 800-683-0854

BBS: 813-442-6726

SCSI Products: Tools

    Kickstart (system diagnostics card)

    Landmark DOS (Windows shell)

    Landmark SysInfo (system analysis software)

    Landmark System Speed Test (system performance test software)

    PC Certify (diagnostic software package for end users)

    PC Probe (system diagnostics and benchmarks)

    SCSI Troubleshooter Toolbox, The (diagnostic software)

    WinProbe (system diagnostics and benchmarks)

Laura Technologies Inc.

Formerly Ten Time Technologies.

Address: 106 South 54th Street
               Chandler, AZ 85226-3203

Main Phone: 602-940-9800

Fax: 602-940-0222

BBS: 602-940-1050

SCSI Products: Host Adapters, Tape Drives

    High-performance caching SCSI host adapters

VDAT SCSI data storage system

TNT-6000 32-bit caching SCSI controller

Legacy Storage Systems Inc.

Address: 138 River Road
               Andover, MA 01810

Main Phone: 800-966-6442

Fax: 508-689-9004

Tech Support: 800-361-5685

E-mail: user@lss-chq.mhs.compuserve.com

BBS: 905-475-5793 (based in Canada)

SCSI Products: CD-ROM Drives, RAID Products, Tape Drives

    Legacy 1000s 4mm DAT backup subsystem

    Legacy 1100Q 2GB QIC cartridge tape drive

    Legacy 150*x* 60MB cartridge tape backup system

    Legacy 2200D high-performance DAT backup subsystem

    Legacy 2200s 8mm DAT backup subsystem

    Legacy 4000D high-performance DAT backup subsystem

    Legacy 5000H 8mm helical scan 5GB tape drive

    Legacy 500s 525MB QIC cartridge tape drive

    Legacy 8000D 8GB 4mm DAT tape drive

    Legacy CD-ROM 2*x* (stand-alone single CD-ROM drive)

    Legacy DATA AutoLoader (32GB capacity with four DAT tapes)

    Legacy M.A.S.S. HFD (Hot Fix Device) SCSI-based storage system

    Legacy M.A.S.S. NetSpan (RAID disk subsystem for NetWare)

    Legacy M.A.S.S. SL CD-ROM (full-featured CD-ROM subsystem)

    Legacy M.A.S.S. SL entry-level SCSI-based storage system

    Legacy M.A.S.S. XE integrated SCSI-based storage system

    Legacy SmartArray (RAID hard disk array subsystem)

Linksys

Address:	16811-A Millikan Avenue
	Irvine, CA 92714
Main Phone:	714-261-1288
Fax:	714-261-8868
Sales:	800-546-5797
SCSI Products:	Converters

ParaSCSI (parallel port to SCSI external converter)

Logitech Inc.

Address:	6505 Kaiser Drive
	Fremont, CA 94555
Main Phone:	510-795-8500
Fax:	510-792-8901
Tech Support:	510-795-8100
Faxback:	800-245-0000
BBS:	510-795-0408
Sales:	800-231-7717
Factory Outlet:	510-713-5200

Germany

Address:	Logitech GmbH
	Gabriele Munter Strasse 3
	D-82110, Germering
Phone:	4989894670
Fax:	498989467200

United Kingdom

Address:	Logitech UK
	Hawes Hill Court, Drift Road
	Windsor SL4 4QQ
Phone:	0344894300
Fax:	0344894303

Switzerland

Address:	Logitech International SA
	Moulin du Choc 1
	Romanel-sur-Morges
Phone:	218635111
Fax:	218635311
SCSI Products:	Sound Cards

SoundMan soundcards with SCSI interface

Lomas Data Corporation

Address:	420 Maple Street, Suite 2
	Marlboro, MA 01752
Main Phone:	508-460-0333
Fax:	508-460-0616
SCSI Products:	Host Adapters

SCSI disk caching controller boards

Longshine Microsystems

Address:	10400-9 Pioneer Blvd.
	Santa Fe Springs, CA 90670
Main Phone:	310-903-0899
Fax:	310-944-2201
SCSI Products:	Host Adapters

Pocket-sized external parallel port to SCSI adapter

SCSI-caching adapter

SCSI/IDE combined controller

Loviél Computer Corporation

Address:	5599 W. 78th Street
	Minneapolis, MN 55439
Main Phone:	800-688-3696
Fax:	612-828-6881
E-Mail:	info@loviel.com
	tech@loviel.com
	lovielmpls@aol.com
	D4382 (AppleLink)

Internet

WWW:	http://www.loviel.com/
SCSI Products:	CD-ROM Drives, Hard Disk
	Drives, Magneto-Optical Drives,
	Tape Drives

MacProducts USA

A division of Bottomline Distribution.

Address:	4544 South Lamar Blvd.,
	Suite D100
	Austin, TX 78745
Main Phone:	512-892-4070

Fax:	512-892-4455
Tech Support:	512-892-4090
Sales:	800-622-8721
SCSI Products:	CD-ROM Drives, Magneto-Optical Drives, SyQuest Drives

MagicRAM Inc.

Address:	1850 Beverly Blvd. Los Angeles, CA 90057
Main Phone:	213-413-9999
Fax:	213-413-0828
Sales:	800-272-6242
SCSI Products:	Host Adapters

MagicRAM PCMCIA SCSI II adapter

Maxtor Corporation

General Information:

Address:	211 River Oaks Parkway San Jose, CA 95134
Main Phone:	800-356-5333 or 408-432-1700
Fax:	408-432-4698

Tech Support:

Address:	2191 Miller Drive Longmont, CO 80501
Tech Support:	800-262-9867 or 303-651-6000
Fax:	303-678-2618
Faxback:	303-678-2618
BBS:	303-678-2222
SCSI Products:	Hard Disk Drives

Panther series of high-capacity SCSI hard disk drives

Media Integration Inc.

Address:	3949 Research Park Court, Suite 190 Soquel, CA 95073
Main Phone:	800-824-7385 or 408-475-9400
Fax:	408-475-0110
E-mail:	sales@mediaint.uucp.netcom.com

SCSI Products:	Hard Disk Drives, Magneto-Optical Drives, RAID Products, Tape Drives

DAT Manager 5 (3.5-inch 4mm DAT tape drive)

DAT Manager 60 (external 4mm DAT autochanger)

Disk Manager series of external hard disk subsystems

EXA Manager 5 (5.25-inch 5GB SCSI 8mm tape drive)

EXA Manager 50 (8mm tape autochanger)

Opti Manager 1 (5.25-inch 650/940MB optical disk drives)

Opti Manager 10/20 (5.25-inch 10/20GB optical disk jukebox)

Opti Manager 128/256 (3.5-inch 128/256MB optical disks)

Opti Manager 50 (5.25-inch 50GB optical disk jukebox)

Opti Manager 60/100 (5.25-inch 57/94GB optical disk jukebox)

QIC Manager 2 (5.25-inch 2GB cartridge tape drive)

RAIDstor Rack (RAID fault-tolerant disk subsystem)

RAIDstor Server (RAID fault-tolerant disk subsystem)

RAIDstor Tower (RAID fault-tolerant disk subsystem)

SMARTstor Rack (intelligent fault-tolerant disk subsystem)

SMARTstor Server (intelligent fault-tolerant disk subsystem)

SMARTstor Tower (intelligent fault-tolerant disk subsystem)

Megabit Communications Inc.

Address:	90 West County Road C St. Paul, MN 55117
Main Phone:	800-886-6778 or 612-481-0921
Fax:	612-481-1538
SCSI Products:	Host Adapters

Ultima SCSI (fiber-optic SCSI)

MemTech

Address:	1257-A Tasman Drive Sunnyvale, CA 94089
Main Phone:	800-445-5511 or 408-745-1600
SCSI Products:	Miscellaneous Hardware

SSD924 CMOS/Flash solid-state disk drive using SCSI-II

Micro Design International Inc.

Address:	6985 University Blvd. Winter Park, FL 32792
Main Phone:	800-228-0891 or 407-677-8333
Fax:	407-677-8365
BBS:	407-677-4854
SCSI Products:	CD-ROM Drives, Magneto-Optical Drives, RAID Products, Tape Drives, WORM Drives

Laserbank 1300D and 2000D 2GB DAT tape drives

Laserbank 600 R (600MB rewritable optical disk system)

LaserBank 600CI/CE CD-ROM drives

LaserBank Library 5-16DX optical disk jukebox

SCSI Express 1300MX 1.3GB R/W optical WORM disk

SCSI Express 300R (256MB rewritable magneto-optical disk)

SCSI Express 600CDX (single and dual CD-ROM drive units)

SCSI Express 940W (940MB WORM optical disk drive)

SCSI Express Library (optical disk jukebox)

MicroNet Technology Inc.

Address:	80 Technology Irvine, CA 92718
Main Phone:	714-453-6100
Fax:	714-453-6101

Tech Support:	714-453-6060
E-mail:	CompuServe: 76004,1611; AppleLink: MICRONET.SLS
SCSI Products:	CD-ROM Drives, Hard Disk Drives, Host Adapters, RAID Products, Tape Drives

D16000 DDS-2 4mm DAT tape drive

D2000 20GB 8mm DAT tape drive

D8000 DDS-1 8GB 4mm DAT tape drive

HA-01/PC ISA SCSI host adapter board

HA-05/PC MCA SCSI host adapter board

HA-06/PC EISA SCSI host adapter board

Micro/CD-ROM (325msec access CD-ROM drive)

Micro/DataShuttle series of removable drive systems

Micro/LAN series of network-compatible hard disk subsystems

Micro/Optical PC series of magneto-optical storage systems

Micro/PC External Systems (external SCSI hard drives)

Micro/PC Internal Systems (internal hard drive systems)

Micro/PC Removable series of removable-cartridge disk drives

Micro/PC Tape and DAT backup systems

Performance Plus Protection Series (network storage subsystem)

RAIDbank (RAID hard disk subsystem)

Rapid Access Series (SCSI host adapter and hard disk drives)

Micropolis Corporation

Address:	21211 Nordhoff Street Chatsworth, CA 91311
Main Phone:	800-395-3748 or 818-709-3300
Fax for Sales:	818-701-2809
Tech Support or Customer Service:	818-709-3325
BBS:	818-709-3310

Germany

Address: Micropolis GmbH
Behringstrabe 10
D-W8033 Planegg

Phone: 0898595091

Fax: 0898597018

SCSI Products: Hard Disk Drives, RAID Products
A/V drives
Hardware-based disk arrays
SCSI hard drives

Morton Management Inc.

Address: 12079 Tech Road
Silver Spring, MD 20904

Main Phone: 301-622-5600

Fax: 301-622-5438

SCSI Products: CD-ROM Drives, Hard Disk
Drives, Miscellaneous, RAID
Products

GigaBox (high-performance, large-capacity
external disks)

GigaBox CD (7-drive CD-ROM subsystem)

GigaRaid disk subsystems (fault-tolerant
SCSI disk subsystem)

Mountain Network Solutions Inc.

Address: 360 El Pueblo Road
Scotts Valley, CA 95066

Main Phone: 800-458-0300 or 408-438-6650

Fax: 408-438-7623

BBS: 408-438-2665

BBS for Software Downloads or End Users:
900-555-3333 (call to check on
current fees)

United Kingdom

Address: Mountain UK Ltd.
Dolphin House
Unit G, Albany Park
Camberley, Surrey GU15 2PL

Phone: 44276686454

Fax: 44276686574

SCSI Products: Software, Tape Drives

Assorted tape backup systems and software

FileSafe 1200 1.3-2.6GB 4mm DAT tape
backup system

FileSafe 1200Plus 2GB 4mm DAT tape
backup system

FileSafe 1400 family of DDS/2 DAT tape
backup systems

FileSafe 2100 2.2GB 8mm DAT tape
backup system

FileSafe 4000 Series 40-120MB tape backup
systems

FileSafe 5000 5GB 8mm helical scan tape
subsystem

FileSafe 7060 Series 60MB tape backup
systems

FileSafe 71000 1GB DC9000 cartridge tape
drive

FileSafe 72000 2GB quarter-inch cartridge
tape drive

FileSafe 7250 Series 250MB SCSI tape
backup systems

FileSafe 7300 Series 300MB tape backup
systems

FileSafe 7500 Series 525MB-1GB SCSI
tape backup systems

FileSafe 8000Plus Series 80-340MB tape
backup systems

FileSafe TD-250 250MB minicartridge tape
drive

Mustek Inc.

Formerly Marstek.

Address: 1702 McGaw Avenue
Irvine, CA 92714

Main Phone: 714-250-8855

Fax: 714-250-3372

Tech Support: 714-250-4880

BBS: 714-250-4263

SCSI Products: Scanners

Paragon 1200 flatbed scanner with buffered
SCSI interface

Mylex Corporation

Address:	34551 Ardenwood Blvd. Fremont, CA 94555
	P.O. Box 5035 Fremont, CA 94537
Main Phone:	800-77-MYLEX or 510-796-6100
Tech Support Fax:	
	510-745-7715
BBS:	510-793-3491
Sales Fax:	510-745-8016
SCSI Products:	Host Adapters, RAID Products

DAC/1 EISA Bus Master SCSI host adapter board

DAC960 fault-tolerant RAID hard disk storage system

DC376 and DCE376 32-bit caching SCSI disk controller boards

DNE 960 EISA bus SCSI host adapter board

NCR Microelectronics

See Symbios Logic Incorporated

NEC Technologies Inc.

Formerly NEC Home Electronics (USA) Inc.

Address:	1414 Massachusetts Avenue Boxborough, MA 01719-2298
Main Phone:	800-632-4636 or 508-264-8000
Fax:	508-264-8673
BBS:	508-635-4706
Tech Support:	800-388-8888
Faxback:	800-366-0476
SCSI Products:	CD-ROM Drives, Host Adapters, Software

CD Express (CD-ROM hardware and software bundle)

CD Gallery (bundled CD-ROM drive and software)

Intersect CDR-35 portable CD-ROM player

Intersect CDR-36 portable CD-ROM drive

Intersect CDR-70 and CDR-80 full-size CD-ROM drives

Intersect CDR-73 and CDR-83 full-size CD-ROM drives

MultiSpin 38 portable CD-ROM drive

MultiSpin 3X series of internal/external/personal CD-ROM drives

MultiSpin 4X Pro quad-speed external CD-ROM drive

MultiSpin 74 external CD-ROM drive

MultiSpin 84 internal CD-ROM drive

NextStor

Formerly Intellistor Inc.

Address:	631 S. Milpitas Blvd. Milpitas, CA 95035
Main Phone:	408-262-1074
Fax:	408-262-1082
BBS:	408-946-6932
SCSI Products:	Host Adapters

Drive controllers, SCSI host adapters, and add-in boards

Newer Technology

See Spectrum Engineering Inc.

New Media Corporation

Address:	One Technology, Bldg. A Irvine, CA 92718
Main Phone:	800-453-0550 or 714-453-0100
Fax:	714-453-0114
Tech Support:	714-453-0314
Faxback:	714-789-5212
BBS:	714-453-0214
Sales:	800-453-0550
SCSI Products:	Host Adapters

Bus Toaster (PCMCIA SCSI adapter card)

Visual Media PCMCIA SCSI Card

Optima Technology Corporation

Address: 17526 Von Karman
                    Irvine, CA 92714

Main Phone: 714-476-0515

Fax: 714-476-0613

BBS: 714-476-0626

SCSI Products: Magneto-Optical Drives, RAID
                    Products, Tape Drives

Concorde 18000 Array (RAID hard disk subsystem)

Concorde 5000T 5GB DAT tape drive

DisKovery 128MO magneto-optical disk drive

DisKovery 250 tape drive

DisKovery 45R and 88R removable-cartridge disk drives

DisKovery 525T tape drive

DisKovery 8200 Array (RAID hard disk subsystem)

MiniPak 2000DAT 2GB DAT tape drive

MiniPak 2100 2.1GB SCSI hard disk drive

MiniPak 8000DAT 8GB DAT tape drive

MiniPak F8000DAT 16GB DAT tape drive

Optima Concorde 600MO (magneto-optical storage system)

Pacific Electro Data

Address: 14 Hughes, Suite B205
                    Irvine, CA 92718

Main Phone: 800-676-2468 or 714-770-3244

Fax: 714-770-7281

SCSI Products: Tools

SCSI bus analysis and emulation systems

Palindrome Corporation

See Seagate Technology Inc.

Parity Systems Inc.

Address: 110 Knowles Drive
                    Los Gatos, CA 95030

Main Phone: 800-514-4080 or 408-378-1000

Fax: 408-378-1022

SCSI Products: Hard Disk Drives, Tape Drives

SCSI subsystems—a variety of hard disk and tape subsystems

Perceptive Solutions Inc.

Address: 2700 Flora Street
                    Dallas, TX 75201

Main Phone: 800-486-3278 or 214-954-1774

Fax: 214-953-1774

BBS: 214-954-1856

SCSI Products: Host Adapters

easyCACHE (caching IDE/SCSI disk controllers)

easyCACHE Pro (caching IDE/SCSI/EDSI disk controllers)

hyperSTORE 1600 high-performance caching disk controller

Perifitech Inc.

Address: 1265 Ridge Road
                    Hinckley, OH 44233-9601

Main Phone: 216-278-2070

Fax: 216-278-2309

SCSI Products: Hard Disk Drives, Host
                    Adapters

4mm DAT backup

Fast, Wide, and Wide Differential SCSI

SCSI CD and CD server products

SCSI enhancement kit

SCSI removable hot-swap disks

Peripheral Interface Ltd.

Address: 15-32 Higashicho, Isogo-ku
                    Yokohama 235 Japan

Main Phone: 0457550208

SCSI Products: Printers

Full-color sublimation thermal printer with SCSI I/O

Peripheral Land Inc. (PLI)

Address: 47421 Bayside Parkway
Fremont, CA 94538

Main Phone: 800-288-8754 (outside California only); 800-788-9440 (within California); 510-657-2211

Fax: 510-683-9713

BBS: 510-651-5948

SCSI Products: Hard Disk Drives, Host Adapters, Magneto-Optical Drives, RAID Products, Tape Drives

Infinity Floptical (21MB floptical disk drive)

Infinity Optical (600MB magneto-optical removable drive)

Infinity Turbo series of removable Winchester hard drives

Mac-to-DOS for Windows (Macintosh disk access tool)

MachOne (high-performance drive technology device)

Parallel to SCSI (parallel port adapter)

PL Turbo Drives (fixed hard disk drives)

PLI CD-ROM Drive 10305

PLI DAT 10GB (DDS-2 16GB DAT tape drive)

PLI DAT 5GB (DDS-1 8GB DAT tape drive)

QuickArray-R RAID hard disk subsystem

SCSI host bus adapters

Philips Consumer Electronics

Address for CD-ROM Products:

Philips LMS
4425 Arrowswest Drive
Colorado Springs, CO 80907

Information: 800-531-0039

Main Phone: 800-777-5674 or 719-593-7900

Fax: 719-593-4597

BBS: 719-593-4081

Repair and Accessory Center:

Address: 5164 Blazer Parkway
Dublin, OH 43017

Phone: 614-792-1495

SCSI Products: CD-ROM Drives

Plexstor Coporation

Formerly Texel America Inc.

Address: 4255 Burton Drive
Santa Clara, CA 95054

Main Phone: 800-886-3935 or 408-980-1838

Fax: 408-980-1010

BBS: 408-986-1569

SCSI Products: CD-ROM Drives

DM-3024 and DM-5024 half-height SCSI-2 CD-ROM drives

DM-3028 and DM-5028 CD-ROM drives

DM-5020 series of external CD-ROM drives

DM-5120 ruggedized external CD-ROM drive

DoubleSpeed PLUS family of CD-ROM drives

Plus Development Corporation

See Quantum.

Prima Storage Solutions

Subsidiary of Prima International.

Address: 3350 Scott Blvd., Building 7
Santa Clara, CA 95054

Main Phone: 800-73-PRIMA or 408-727-2600

Fax: 408-727-2435

SCSI Products: Host Adapters, Tape Drives

Identica-brand Parallel, QIC, DAT, and helical scan tape drives

Priam PDQ Parallel, AT, SCSI, ESDI, IDE, RLL, MFM interfaces

Priam PDQ removable Winchester drive

Procomp USA Inc.

Address: 6777 Engle Road
Cleveland, OH 44130-7907

Main Phone: 216-234-6387

Fax: 216-234-2233

BBS: 216-234-6581

SCSI Products: Host Adapters, Tools

F-DCB family of asynchronous 16-bit SCSI-2 host adapters

M-DCB family of high-performance 16-bit SCSI-2 host adapters

PRO-MASTER BusMastering 32-bit EISA SCSI controller

PRO-VAL 16-bit SCSI-2 controller

S-DCB family of high-performance SCSI-2 host adapters

SCSI analyzer board

Procom Technology Inc.

Address: 2181 Dupont Drive
Irvine, CA 92715

Main Phone: 800-800-8600 or 714-852-1000

Fax: 714-852-1221

BBS: 714-852-1305

SCSI Products: CD-ROM Drives, Host Adapters, Magneto-Optical Drives

CD Tower4-DS and Tower7-DS double-speed CD-ROM towers

Enabler series of SCSI host adapter boards

Floptika 20/M (external 20MB floptical disk drive)

GigaTower II line of high-capacity hard disk drives

IDAT/MDAT 2000 series of 2GB DAT tape drives

IDAT/MDAT 8000 series of 4GB DAT tape drives

ISA SCSI Xelerator (SCSI host adapter board)

LANForce5 (external disk array subsystem)

MCD-ROM 650/E CD-ROM drive

MCDN-3X external CD-ROM drive

MEOD128 (128MB magneto-optical storage system)

MEOD1300 1.3GB magneto-optical disk drive

MEOD650 (594MB magneto-optical storage system)

MRD270 half-height 256MB removable cartridge disk drive

MRD40 (44MB removable cartridge disk drive)

MRD80 (88MB removable cartridge disk drive)

Multimedia CD Station (hardware/software upgrade kit)

Multimedia Station Pro (hardware/software upgrade kit)

PCDS-DS double-speed AT/Bus interface CD-ROM drive

PF20i (internal 20MB floptical disk drive)

PICDL internal CD-ROM drive

Prolink SCSI host adapter board

PXCDL CD-ROM drive

PXCDL external CD-ROM drive

SICDS-C8 internal CD-ROM drive

SXCDS-C8 external CD-ROM drive

QLogic Corporation

Address: 3545 Harbor Blvd.
Costa Mesa, CA 92626

Main Phone: 800-867-7274 or 714-438-2200

Fax: 714-668-6950

BBS: 714-708-3170

SCSI Products: Host Adapters

Quantum

Quantum has merged with Plus Development Corporation.

Address: 500 McCarthy Blvd.
Milpitas, CA 95035

Main Phone:	408-894-4000
Fax:	408-894-3218
Tech Support:	800-826-8022
Faxback:	800-434-7532
Customer Service:	
	800-345-3377
BBS:	408-894-3214
Presales:	800-624-5545
SCSI Products:	Hard Disk Drives

Plus Impulse (AT and SCSI interface hard disk drives)

Plus Passport (removable Winchester disk drives)

Quatech Inc.

Address:	662 Wolf Ledges Parkway Akron, OH 44311
Main Phone:	800-553-1170 or 216-434-3154
Fax:	216-434-1409
BBS:	216-434-2481
SCSI Products:	Host Adapters

Ultra-100 Plus multiport adapter board (1P/2S/IDE/FDD/SCSI)

Raidtec Corporation

Address:	105-C Hembree Park Drive Roswell, GA 30076
Main Phone:	404-664-6066
Fax:	404-664-6166
SCSI Products:	RAID Products

FlexArray series of fault-tolerant SCSI disk arrays '

RUAC MX RAID Controller (3-channel entry-level controller)

Rancho Technology Inc.

Address:	10783 Bell Court Rancho Cucamonga, CA 91730
Main Phone:	909-987-3966
Fax:	909-989-2365
SCSI Products:	Host Adapters

Relax Technologies Inc.

Address:	3101 Whipple Road Union City, CA 94587
Main Phone:	510-471-6112
Fax:	510-471-6267
SCSI Products:	CD-ROM Drives, Host Adapters, Magneto-Optical Drives

Relax Jukebox (680MB magneto-optical disk drive)

Relax Mesa 680MB CD-ROM Drive

Relax Optical 600 Plus (magneto-optical storage system)

Relax Sierra Optical 128 (128MB magneto-optical storage system)

Relax Vista Optical (620MB magneto-optical disk drive)

T-100 8-bit PC/XT/AT SCSI host adapter board

T-128 8-bit PC/XT/AT SCSI host adapter board using NCR 5380

T-200 8-bit PS/2 SCSI host adapter board

Relisys Corporation

Parent company is TECO Information Systems Co, Taiwan.

Address:	320 South Milpitas Blvd. Milpitas, CA 95035
Main Phone:	800-783-2333 or 408-945-9000
Fax:	408-945-0587
Tech Support:	800-835-7354 (for all scanners)
BBS:	408-946-7027
SCSI Products:	Scanners

VM6520 1200-dpi SCSI interface color scanner

SC&T International, Inc.

Address:	3837 East LaSalle St Phoenix, AZ 85040
Main Phone:	800-760-9004 or 602-470-1334
Fax:	602-470-1507

SCSI Products: SCSI Kit for Logitech Sound Cards

Internal SCSI Kit for Sound Cards (Internal CD-Audio cable, 24-inch internal SCSI ribbon cable)

External SCSI Kit for Logitech sound cards CD-Audio cable (SCSI extension port, internal CD-Audio cable, 7-inch internal SCSI ribbon cable, drivers)

Seagate Technology Inc.

Also known as Palindrome Corporation.

Address:	920 Disc Drive
	Scotts Valley, CA 95066
Main Phone:	800-468-DISC or 408-438-6550
Fax:	408-429-6356
BBS:	408-438-8771

Italy

Address:	Seagate Technology
	Via Degli Artaria No. 15
	20161 Milan
Phone:	34266201515
Fax:	34266202530

United Kingdom

Address:	Seagate Technology
	Fieldhouse Lane, Globe Park
	Marlow, Bucks SL7 1LW
Phone:	44628890366
Fax:	44628890660
BBS:	44628478011

Sweden

Address:	Seagate Technology
	Osterogatan 3, Box 46
	164 93 Kista
Phone:	4687522560
Fax:	4687520565

Ireland

Address:	Seagate Technology
	67 Mount Anville Wood
	LR Kilmacud Rd., Dublin 14
Phone:	35312887758
Fax:	35312889920

Europe, Middle East, Africa Headquarters

Address:	Seagate Technology
	14 Rue Pergolese
	75116 Paris France
Phone:	33140671300
Fax:	33140671037

Asian/Pacific Headquarters

Address:	Seagate Technology
	International
	202 Kallang Bahru
	Singapore 1233 Singapore
Phone:	65-292-6266
Fax:	65-292-2082
BBS:	65-292-6973

Canada

Address:	Seagate Technology
	3800 Steeles Avenue West
	Woodbridge, Ontario L4L 4G9
Phone:	905-856-9333
Fax:	905-856-9331

Germany

Address:	Seagate Technology GmbH
	Messerschmittstr. 4
	D-W8000 Munchen 50
Phone:	0891498910
Fax:	0891407617
BBS:	49891409331

SCSI Products: Hard Disk Drives

Barracuda series of high-capacity hard disk drives

Elite family 5.25-inch, high-capacity hard disks

Hawk series of high-capacity hard disk drives

ST01 and ST02 (SCSI interface hard disk interface)

Swift family 3.5-inch half-height form factor hard disks

Wren family 5.25-inch full-height, high-capacity hard disks

Shaffstall Corporation

Address:	7901 East 88th Street
	Indianapolis, IN 46256
Main Phone:	317-842-2077
Fax:	317-842-8294
Sales:	800-248-3475

Canada

Address:	Shaffstall Canada Inc.
	250 Don Park Road
	Unit 15
	Markham, Ontario L3R 2V1
Phone:	905-477-4610
Fax:	905-477-9723

SCSI Products: Software

SCSI tape data transfer software

Silicon Composers Inc.

Address:	655 West Evelyn Avenue, Suite 7
	Mountain View, CA 94041
Main Phone or Fax:	
	415-961-8778

SCSI Products: Host Adapters

Sony Electronics Inc., Computer Peripherals Products

Address:	3300 Zanker Road
	San Jose, CA 95134
Main Phone:	408-432-0190
Fax:	408-432-0253
Tech Support:	408-894-0555
Faxback:	408-955-5505
BBS:	408-955-5107
Presales:	800-352-7669
Address:	Sony Computer Peripheral
	Products
	3300 Zanker Road
	San Jose, CA 95134
Tech Support:	408-894-0225
Fax:	408-955-5171

SCSI Products: CD-ROM Drives, Magneto-Optical Drives, RAID Products, Tape Drives, WORM Drives

CDU-541 internal CD-ROM drive, SCSI I/O

CDU-6211 external CD-ROM drive, SCSI I/O

CDU-7811 SCSI interface CD-ROM drive

CDW-900E double-speed CD write-once subsystem

OSL-2000 5.25-inch rewritable and WORM magneto-optical jukebox

RMO-S350 128MB 3.5-inch optical disk drive

RMO-S550 5.25-inch 650MB magneto-optical disk drive

RVP-4010QA multiscan 40-inch read projection system

SDT-1020 5.25-inch 4mm DDS tape drive

SDT-2000 3.5-inch 4mm DDS tape drive

SDT-4000 4GB DAT tape drive

SDT-5000 8GB DAT tape drive

SDT-5200 4GB DAT tape drive

SDU-7811 double-speed external CD-ROM drive

SMO-E301F 3.5-inch 128MB rewriteable optical disk drive

SMO-E511 multifunction magneto-optical disk drive

SMO-F521 rewriteable optical drive

SMO-S350 half-height 3.5-inch 128MB optical disk drive

SMO-S550 5.25-inch 650MB optical disk drive

WDA-330 write-once mini autochanger (WORM disk drive)

WDA-610 write-once autochanger (WORM disk drive)

WDA-930 large write-once autochanger (WORM disk drive)

WDA-931 write-once stand-alone drive

WDD-931 write-once optical disk drive

Spectrum Engineering Inc.

Products are Newer Technology.

Address:	7803 East Osie, Suite 105 Wichita, KS 67207
Main Phone:	800-678-3726 or 316-685-4904
Fax:	316-685-9368
SCSI Products:	Hard Disk Drives

SCSI Dart and SCSI DartCard (solid-state hard disks)

Storage Dimensions Inc.

Address:	1656 McCarthy Blvd. Milpitas, CA 95035
Main Phone:	408-954-0710
Tech Support:	408-894-1325
Tech Support Fax:	408-944-1203
Customer Service Fax:	408-944-1206
BBS:	408-944-1220
Sales Fax:	408-944-1200
Sales:	408-894-1331
SCSI Products:	RAID Products, Software, Tape Drives, WORM Drives

LANstor Continua (fault-tolerant RAID hard disk storage system)

LANStor Optical (optical/WORM storage subsystems)

LANStor RAIDMaster disk array software for NetWare

LANStor ReFlex (flexible disk/tape storage system)

LANStor Tape 2000 (2GB DAT tape drive)

LANStor Tape Array (48GB DDS-2 DAT tape autoloader)

LANStore RedAlert (network management utility for NetWare)

SpeedCache (disk caching software)

SpeedStor PC (hard disk management and partitioning software)

SpeedStore (hard drive subsystems)

Sun Microsystems, Inc.

Address:	2550 Garcia Avenue Mountain View, CA 94043-1100
Tech Support (SunService):	800-USA-4SUN
Canada:	800-722-4SUN
Australia:	008-02-4417
Japan:	044-819-3121
UK:	44-1276-691974

Internet

WWW:	http://www.sun.com
SCSI Products:	Hard Disk Drives, RAID Products

SPARCstorage Array Models 100 and 200 (Up to 300GB, RAID levels 0, 1, 0+1 and 5)

Sun 2.1-GB 5.25-inch Fast Differential SCSI-2 drive

Sun Differential SCSI Drive Tray (up to 12.6-GB of SCSI disk storage capacity)

SCSI Expansion Pedestal (total disk capacity of 17 GB)

4.2 and 8.4-GB Multi-Disk Packs (small footprint subsystems for desktop SPARC-servers and SPARCstations)

Symbios Logic Incorporated

Formerly NCR Microelectronics.

Address:	1635 Aero Plaza Drive Colorado Springs, CO 80916
Main Phone:	719-596-5795
Information:	800-334-5454 (phone)
Fax:	719-573-3289
BBS for device drivers and chip support:	719-573-3562
BBS for SCSI standards (not for product support):	719-574-0424
Tech Support:	719-573-3016
Tech Support E-mail:	ncr.chips@hmpd.com
FTP site for updated drivers and SCSI information:	ftp.hmpd.com

SCSI Products: Host Adapters, Software

    53C90 SCSI-1 and SCSI-2

    53C400 ISA

    53C406A SCSI-2

    53C416 Plug and Play ISA, Fast SCSI-2

    53C500 PCMCIA to Fast SCSI controller

    53C700 Fast Wide SCSI-2 Bus Mastering Host Adapter (Bus specific)

    53C800 PCI with Fast Wide SCSI-2

    SDMS (SCSI Device Management System) software

Targa Electronics Systems Inc.

Address:	1 Annabel Lane
	San Ramon, CA 94583
Phone:	510-277-0188
Fax:	510-277-0196

SCSI Products: Hard Disk Drives

    SCSI-SB solid-state disk drive

Teac America Inc.

Address:	7733 Telegraph Road
	Montebello, CA 90640
Main Phone:	213-726-0303
Fax:	213-727-7672
Faxback:	213-272-7629

Japan

Address:	Teac Corporation
	3-7-3 Naka-cho
	Musashino, Tokyo 180
Phone:	0422525041
Fax:	0422552554

United Kingdom

Address:	Teak UK Ltd.
	5 Marlin House, Croxley Centre
	Watford, Herts WD1 8YA
Phone:	0923225235
Fax:	0923236290

Germany

Address:	Teac Deutschland GmbH
	Arzbergerstr. 10
	D-W8036 Herrsching
Phone:	08152370820
Fax:	08152370826

SCSI Products: CD-ROM Drives, Hard Disk Drives, Tape Drives

    CD-50 Internal SCSI interface CD-ROM drive

    FD-505 quarter-height 3.5-inch floppy disk drive

    OD-3000 3.5-inch multifunction optical disk drive

    SD-340, SD-380, and SD-3105 3.5-inch hard disk drives

    Super Quad (quad-speed CD-ROM drive)

    Teac-Stor series of removable 3.5-inch hard disk drives

    TurboTape family of cassette tape backup systems

Tecmar Inc.

A division of Rexon Inc.

Address:	6225 Cochran Road
	Solon, OH 44139-3377
Main Phone:	800-422-2587 or 216-349-0600
Fax:	216-349-0851
Tech Support:	800-344-4463
Faxback:	216-349-2997
BBS:	216-349-0853

United Kingdom

Address:	Tecmar Inc.
	#1, Apollo House, Calleva Park
	Aldermaston RG7 4QW
Phone:	025627890
Fax:	0256479461

SCSI Products: Software, Tape Drives

    Tape backup systems and software

Teknor Microsystems Inc.

Address: 616 Cure Boivin
Boisbriand
Sainte-Therese, PQ J7G 2A7
Canada

Main Phone: 800-387-4222 or 514-437-5682

Fax: 514-437-8053

SCSI Products: Host Adapters

TEK760 flat panel/CRT controller with optional SCSI interface

VIPer803 486DX2-66 single-board computer with SCSI

TenTime Controllers L.T.I.

See Laura Technologies Inc.

Tekram Technology (Alpha Research Corporation)

Address: P. O. Box 27140
Austin, TX 78755-2140

Main Phone: 512-418-0220

Fax: 512-418-0720

Tech Support: 512-418-1520 (8:30 A.M. to 6:00 P.M. Monday–Friday CST)

BBS: 512-418-0821

Sales: 800-556-6218

SCSI Products: Host Adapters

Texel America Inc.

See Plexstor Coporation.

Trantor Systems Ltd.

See Adaptec Inc.

TTS Multimedia Systems

Address: 2045 San Elijo Avenue
Cardiff, CA 92007

Main Phone: 800-887-4968

Fax: 619-632-9957

Tech Support: 619-942-3766

SCSI Products: Connectors

ES\1 (allows the internal SCSI controller from any sound card to be used externally)

Tulin Technology

Address: 2156H O'Toole Avenue
San Jose, CA 95131

Main Phone: 408-432-9057

Fax: 408-943-0782

E-mail: 74264.3710@compuserve.com

SCSI Products: Hard Disk Drives, Magneto-Optical Drives, Tape Drives

A-Hive enclosure for SCSI drives with power supply

A-Hive Jr. optical drive (3.5-inch rewritable 128MB drive)

A-Hive optical drive (1.3GB rewritable optical rive)

Hermit Crab (small portable hard drive)

SCSI disk and tape storage subsystems

TWD Electronics Inc.

Address: 1800 Constellation Drive
Colorado Springs, CO 80906

Mailing Address:

P.O. Box 38384
Colorado Springs, CO 80937

Main Phone: 719-634-1800

Fax: 719-634-8187

SCSI Products: Host Adapters

Model 2001 SCSI interface PCMCIA card

UltraStor Corporation

Address: 13766 Alton Parkway, Suite 144
Irvine, CA 92718

Main Phone: 714-581-4100

Fax: 714-581-4102

Tech Support: 714-581-4016

Faxback: 714-581-4541

E-mail: ultrastor@primenet.com

BBS: 714-581-4125

SCSI Products: Host Adapters, RAID Products

Ultra 124F EISA SCSI disk array controller, RAID level 0, 1, 4, 5

Ultra 14C and 14F 16-bit PC/AT SCSI host adapter boards

Ultra 24C and 24F 32-bit EISA SCSI host adapter boards

Ultra 34F VESA local bus-compatible SCSI bus masterboard

Wangtek Inc.

A division of Rexon.

Address: 6225 Cochran Road
           Solon, Ohio 44139

Main Phone: 800-422-2587 or 216-349-0600

Fax: 216-349-0851

Tech Support: 216-349-3130

Faxback: 216-349-2997

BBS: 216-349-0853

SCSI Products: Tape Drives

9200 streaming tape cartridge drive

WangDAT Model 3300DX 4GB DAT tape drive

WangDAT Model 3400DX 8GB DDS-2 DAT tape drive

Wangtek 5100 (1-2GB SCSI cartridge tape drives)

Wangtek 5150 (250-500MB SCSI cartridge tape drives)

Wangtek 9500 5GB QIC cartridge tape drive

Western Automation Labs Inc.

Address: 1700 North 55th Street
           Boulder, CO 80301

Main Phone: 800-833-1132 or 303-449-6400

Tech Support Fax:
           303-939-8844

SCSI Products: Software, Tape Drives

Ramstor (SCSI solid-state RAM disks)

Software and hardware for data backup on SCSI systems

Western Digital Corporation

Address: 8105 Irvine Center Drive
           Irvine, CA 92718

Phone: 800-832-4778 or 714-932-5000

Tech Support: 714-932-4900

Fax: 714-932-6498

Faxback: 714-932-4300

BBS: 714-753-1068 or 714-753-1234

Tech Support Fax:
           714-932-4012

Canadian Tech Support:
           800-448-8470

Sales: 714-932-4900

Internet

WWW: http://www.wdc.com

SCSI Products: Hard Disk Drives, Host Adapters, Software

WD7000-FASST2 series (SCSI adapters and software)

WD7193A 8-bit, Fast SCSI host bus adapter board for PCI systems

WD7197A 16-bit Fast SCSI host adapter board for PCI systems. Supports Plug and Play

WD7296A Fast and Wide PCI/SCSI host adapter

WDAT-140R integrated drive interface for 2 drives

WDAT-240R integrated drive interface for 2 drives and floppies

WDAT-440R integrated drive interface with serial and parallel I/O

WD33C95A SCSI-2 Fast and Wide bus controller, single-ended or differential, 8- or 16-bit

WD33C96A single-ended SCSI controller, 8- or 16-bit

WD33C197A 8/16-bit Fast and Wide SCSI bus controller for PCI-based PCs, workstations, and RAID controllers. 32-bit bus master DMA PCI interface

WD33C296A same features as above but adds expansion memory port to support 256 or more active commands, scatter/gather lists, and RISC code

Flexware (suite of software drivers, firmware, BIOS, and development tools to provide application flexibility and to speed system integration.

Western Systems

Address: Ruislip, Middlesex
                United Kingdom
Main Phone: 44818458383
SCSI Products: Host Adapters

SCSI Cache (SCSI bus to ISA bus host adapter)

Winchester Systems Inc.

Address: 400 West Cummings Park
                Woburn, MA 01801
Main Phone: 617-933-8500
Tech Support: 800-325-3700
Tech Support Fax:
                617-933-6174
SCSI Products: Hard Disk Drives, RAID Products, Tape Drives

FlashDAT 6GB DAT tape drive

FlashRAID 3/5 arrays (RAID hard disk system)

FlashServer (SCSI RAID hard disk controller and subsystems)

Xirlink Inc.

Address: 4118 Clipper Court
                Fremont, CA 94538
Main Phone: 510-770-5188
Fax: 510-770-5189
BBS: 510-770-5186
SCSI Products: Host Adapters, Miscellaneous Hardware

ShareWork (share printers and SCSI devices with up to 32 PCs and SCSI controllers)

PCMCIA SCSI-2 controllers

B

A L L - P L A T F O R M
T E C H N I C A L   R E F E R E N C E

by Gerhard Islinger

ELECTRICAL SPECS

In order to differentiate between "single-ended" and "differential" SCSI interfaces, the type of interface is identified by logos, as shown in Figure B.1. If you have a newer system or external device, it may have one of these logos, near the SCSI port to differentiate between the visually identical connectors. The icons are used on devices, cables, terminators, and connectors. The symbols may be used with or without the labeling SE (single-ended) or DIFF (differential).

FIGURE B.1 **Single-Ended and Differential SCSI Symbols**

TABLE B.1 Single-Ended SCSI Signal Levels

Signal State	Electrical Level	Voltage
High	Low	0.0 to 0.5 volts DC
Low	High	2.5 to 5.25 volts DC

Single-Ended SCSI Interface

The standard electrical interface for SCSI is single-ended. Single-ended basically means an interface with one signal line and one corresponding ground line for each SCSI signal. All signals are active low, which means when the voltage is high the signal is low, and when the voltage is low the signal is high. The official SCSI term for the high signal state is "signal assertion."

To define it more technically, the single-ended SCSI interface consists of an open-collector or tri-state driver for each signal, capable of sinking up to 48 milliamps of current on signal assertion. The signal levels are listed in Table B.1.

The single-ended SCSI interface can have a bus length of up to 6 meters, when using standard 5 MB/sec SCSI-2 timing. Using higher signal frequencies makes it necessary to shorten the bus accordingly. Therefore, if you use Fast SCSI, your maximum bus length drops to 3 meters. Because Fast-20 SCSI is twice as fast as Fast SCSI, it requires a halving of the bus length again, resulting in a maximum bus length of 1.5 meters.

Differential SCSI Interface

The differential SCSI interface was defined to overcome the maximum bus length limitation of single-ended SCSI. Two-wire differential signaling is an old and well-proven way to achieve reliable signal transmission in noisy environments and over long distances. The industry standard for differential SCSI interfaces is EIA-RS-485.

Differential SCSI's greatest advantage is its ability to use bus lengths of up to 25 meters, regardless of the signal timing used. Also, differential SCSI is the only SCSI-2 interface that officially supports Fast SCSI timing. It's interesting to note the elegant way the SCSI-2 specification says this: "Use of single-ended drivers and receivers with the fast synchronous data transfer option is not recommended."

In differential SCSI, each signal consists of two lines called "–Signal" and "+Signal." A signal is high if the +Signal is higher than the –Signal, and low if the –Signal is higher than the +Signal. This setup, along with twisted-pair cables, yields very good noise immunity. Also, the resultant higher voltage levels of the differential configuration makes it possible to achieve a 25-meter bus.

To avoid the risk of burning up a SCSI bus by accidentally connecting a single-ended device to a differential bus, the SCSI specification defines a protection scheme. The differential line drivers are enabled by a signal called DIFFSENS (differential sense) on the SCSI bus. If you connect a single-ended device to the bus, the DIFFSENS line is grounded and the drivers are disabled. However, some (fortunately only a few) older devices didn't use the DIFFSENS line, so if you have some older differential SCSI disks, be sure to find out if they are single-ended or differential *before* connecting them to your system. Single-ended and differential devices can't coexist on the same bus.

CABLE SPECS

It's important to know SCSI's very tight cable specifications in order to get the best performance from your SCSI system. Let's look at the cables for internal devices first. The SCSI specification defines 50 and 68 conductor flat ribbon cables to have an impedance between 90 and 140 ohms, and a minimum conductor size of 0.080 inches (28 AWG). Also specified is a 25- or 34- signal twisted-pair cable. The twisted-pair cable is better for two reasons. First, a signal line twisted with its ground wire is less sensitive to RF (radio frequency) noise than a flat ribbon cable. Second, twisted-pair cables have loose cable pairs between the connectors, making them more flexible and easier to handle than a rather stiff 50 or 68 conductor ribbon cable.

The electrical specifications for external cables are identical to internal cables. External cables are, in virtually all cases, round shielded cables with a SCSI connector on both ends. There is even a defined layout for an external cable, where the signals are distributed in three layers of wire pairs with REQ and ACK, the most sensitive signals, in the center. For cables that have a third pair of wires in the center, the SCSI specification defines the third pair as ground.

Figure B.2 shows a cross section of an external SCSI cable with some of the wire pairs drawn in to indicate the layers. The REQ and ACK signals are in the very center, control signals in the middle layer, and data lines and termination power in the outer layer.

> **NOTE** *The largest hurdle to overcome with external SCSI cabling is the numerous connections between the round external cables and ribbon cables. The junction of every connector causes impedance mismatches and signal losses. As a result, a SCSI system with many external devices is more susceptible to data errors than one with many internal devices.*

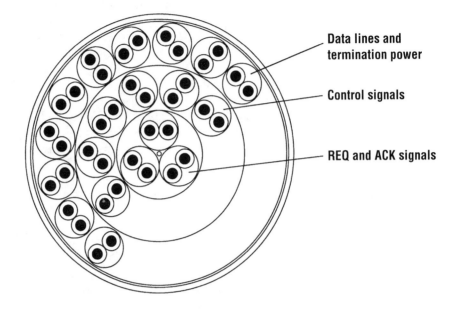

Data lines and
termination power

Control signals

REQ and ACK signals

CONNECTOR SPECS

Connectors are a continuing saga in the life of SCSI due to the various
interface widths and manufacturer preferences. We'll look at the standard connectors first. The cables are called by one-letter names like
A-cables or B-cables and so on, differentiated by bus width and cable/
connector layout. Normally, each letter names a typical combination of
cable layout and connector type. Only the A-cable comes in different
flavors, as defined in the SCSI-1 specification.

The official SCSI-1 connectors used are these:

- 50-pin flat cable connector called an IDC header (female for ribbon cables, male for devices)

- 50-pin Centronics-style connector "Alternative 2" (male for external cables, female for external devices)

(Sun Microsystems used the 50-pin Sub-D connector for their older
external devices, but they weren't used much elsewhere.)

SCSI-2 changed a few things. For one, it deleted the Alternative 1 SUB-D connector, and added the high-density connector as new Alternative 1. It also introduced the so-called B-cable with 68 pins for both 16-bit and 32-bit Wide SCSI, together with an internal 68-pin and an external 68-pin HD connector.

The B-cable wasn't very successful. It was expensive to implement, with two cables for each connection for bus widths greater than 8 bits. Also, most 16-bit devices didn't have enough space to fit two large connectors, and any attempt at setting up external cabling required four external connectors on the device's case. Not a pretty picture.

With this in mind, the SCSI-2 committee wised up by stating that "an alternate 16-bit single-cable solution and an alternate 32-bit solution is being defined and the B-cable definition will be removed in a future version of SCSI." During SCSI-2 development, the SCSI-3 committee designed a new, single 16-bit Wide SCSI cable, the P-cable, as their first project. Its major goal was the definition of a cheaper single-cable interface for 16-bit Wide SCSI and an extension of the bus arbitration to the 16-bit bus. As a result, the P-cable could address 16 devices instead of Wide SCSI's 8 devices. A 32-bit SCSI bus is accomplished by adding a Q-cable to the bus. It's actually just another P-cable with a different name. Of course, the same four-cable mess applies here for 32-bit devices, but when seeking the highest possible throughput in a high-end system, price often isn't a factor.

The P-cable came into existence very early in the history of SCSI-2 —so early that the B-cable never really got a chance to be a player. Some devices were implemented to use B-cables, but most manufacturers adopted the newer and cheaper P-cable.

A new variant called the L-cable, the 110-conductor cable for 8-, 16-, and 32-bit devices, is emerging as another type of cable/connector combo. The big advantage of the P- and L-cables are their compatibility with devices with smaller bus widths. A simple adapter connector allows the use of 8-bit devices on a P-cable and 8- and 16-bit devices on an L-cable.

For cost reasons, Future Domain and Apple defined two different and incompatible 25-pin connectors. Neither of them became an approved standard, but the Apple Macintosh SCSI connector became a defacto standard in the marketplace. The Macintosh, with its integrated SCSI port, was the first real mass market for SCSI devices. However, both Apple's and Future Domain's 25-pin connectors share a common problem. They don't have enough pins to provide a dedicated ground line for each signal, so signal quality is a major problem with those cables. Fast SCSI isn't even a remote possibility with such a configuration.

The following is a summary of the different connectors grouped by their type: official unshielded and shielded, and the unofficial types.

Unshielded Connectors — Defined Only for Internal Devices

- 50-pin flat cable connector ("IDC header") for 8-bit SCSI
- 68-pin for the Wide SCSI B-cable
- 68-pin for 16-bit Wide SCSI P- and Q-cables
- 110-pin Wide SCSI L-cable

External Shielded Connectors

- 50-pin "old-style" Centronics-style connector (A-cable)
- 50-pin high-density 8-bit SCSI-2 connector
- 68-pin high-density for the Wide SCSI B-cable
- 68-pin high-density for 16-bit Wide SCSI P- and Q-cables
- 110-pin high-density Wide SCSI L-cable

Non-official Standard SCSI Connectors

- 25-pin D-sub connectors (Apple and Future Domain pinouts)
- IBM 60-pin high-density PS/2 connector
- Apple 30-pin HDI connector ("PowerBook Connector")
- Sun 50-pin D-sub connector
- Novell/Procomp DCB SCSI connector

All official standard connectors are available in single-ended and differential versions, for a mind-boggling total of 24 connectors defined for SCSI (22, if you count the P- and Q-cables as the same type since the cables have identical layouts).

Unshielded Connectors

50-Pin 8-Bit SCSI

Figure B.3 shows the pinouts for the 50-pin IDC header connector. The upper connector with the female contacts is the cable connector, and the lower male part is the connector you will see on SCSI devices. If you're unsure of what you have, or if you have a connector without the keying notch, you can identify pin 1 on an arrow or a spot mark in the male connector's plastic body. Figures B.3 and B.4 are diagrams of the cable end and device end of a 50-pin IDC connector, respectively. The orientation of the pins is also illustrated.

FIGURE B.3 **IDC Header Connector, Cable End**

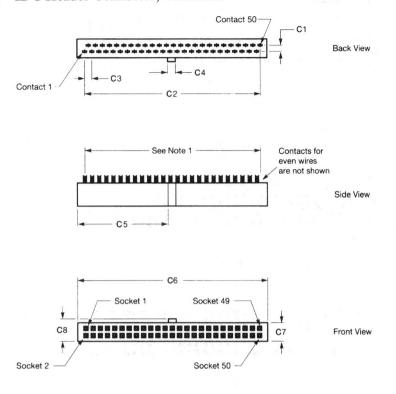

Dimension	Millimeters	Inches	Comments
C1	2.540	0.100	
C2	60.960	2.400	
C3	2.540	0.100	
C4	3.302	0.130	
C5	32.385	1.275	
C6	68.072	2.680	
C7	6.096	0.240	
C8	7.620	0.300	Maximum

Notes:
1. Fifty contacts on 1.27–mm (0.05–inch) staggered spacing = 62.23 mm (2.450 inch) [reference only].
2. Tolerances ±0.127 mm (0.005 inch) noncumulative, unless specified otherwise.
3. Connector cover and strain relief are optional.

FIGURE B.4 IDC Header Connector, Device End

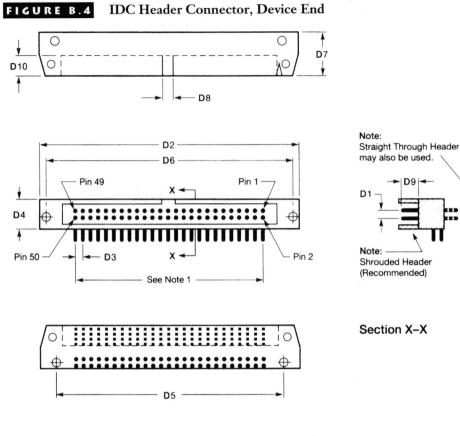

Note:
Straight Through Header may also be used.

Note:
Shrouded Header (Recommended)

Section X–X

Dimension	Millimeters	Inches	Comments
D1	2.54	0.100	
D2	82.80	3.260	Reference Only
D3	2.54	0.100	
D4	8.89	0.350	Reference Only
D5	72.64	2.860	Reference Only
D6	78.74	3.100	Reference Only
D7	13.94	0.549	Reference Only
D8	4.19$\pm$0.25	0.165$\pm$0.01	
D9	6.09	0.240	
D10	6.60	0.260	Reference Only

Notes:
1. Two rows of twenty-five contacts on 2.54–mm (0.100–inch) spacing = 60.96 mm (2.400 inch).
2. Tolerances ±0.127 mm (0.005 inch) noncumulative, unless specified otherwise.

Pinout Table for Single-Ended and
Differential IDC Header Connectors

Single-Ended SCSI Pinout, A-Cable				Differential SCSI Pinout, A-Cable			
Pin	Signal	Pin	Signal	Pin	Signal	Pin	Signal
1	GND	26	TERMPWR	1	GND	26	TERMPWR
2	−DB(0)	27	RESERVED	2	GND	27	RESERVED
3	GND	28	RESERVED	3	+DB(0)	28	RESERVED
4	−DB(1)	29	GND	4	−DB(0)	29	+ATN
5	GND	30	GND	5	+DB(1)	30	−ATN
6	−DB(2)	31	GND	6	−DB(1)	31	GND
7	GND	32	−ATN	7	+DB(2)	32	GND
8	−DB(3)	33	GND	8	−DB(2)	33	+BSY
9	GND	34	GND	9	+DB(3)	34	−BSY
10	−DB(4)	35	GND	10	−DB(3)	35	+ACK
11	GND	36	−BSY	11	+DB(4)	36	−ACK
12	−DB(5)	37	GND	12	−DB(4)	37	+RST
13	GND	38	−ACK	13	+DB(5)	38	−RST
14	−DB(6)	39	GND	14	−DB(5)	39	+MSG
15	GND	40	−RST	15	+DB(6)	40	−MSG
16	−DB(7)	41	GND	16	−DB(6)	41	+SEL
17	GND	42	−MSG	17	+DB(7)	42	−SEL
18	−DB(P)	43	GND	18	−DB(7)	43	+C/D
19	GND	44	−SEL	19	+DB(P)	44	−C/D
20	GND	45	GND	20	−DB(P)	45	+REQ
21	GND	46	−C/D	21	DIFFSENS	46	−REQ
22	GND	47	GND	22	GND	47	+I/O
23	RESERVED	48	−REQ	23	RESERVED	48	−I/O
24	RESERVED	49	GND	24	RESERVED	49	GND
25	NOT CONNECTED	50	−I/O	25	TERMPWR	50	GND

The pinout for single-ended and differential variants of this connector is shown in Table B.2. There is also a high-density version of
the 50-pin 8-bit SCSI connector. Figure B.5 shows the cable end and
Figure B.6 the device end. The pin assignment for the high-density
connectors is the same as that of the regular connectors.

50/68-Position Unshielded High-Density
Device Connector (A-, B-, P-, and Q-Cables)

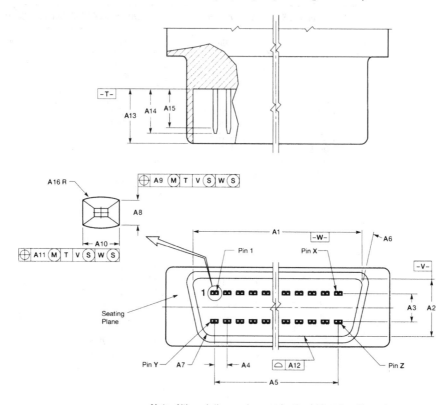

Note: Although the requirement for the A16 radius dimension was
added in SCSI-3 it is also recommended for SCSI-2 applications.

Dimensions	50 Position		68 Position	
	Millimeters	Inches	Millimeters	Inches
A1	34.85	1.372	46.28	1.822
A2	5.69	.224	5.69	.224
A3	2.54	.100	2.54	.100
A4	1.27	.050	1.27	.050
A5	30.48	1.200	41.91	1.650
A6	15°	15°	15°	15°
A7	1.04 R	.041 R	1.04 R	.041 R
A8	0.40±.010	.0156±.0004	0.40±.010	.0156±.0004
A9	0.23	.009	0.23	.009
A10	0.60±.03	.024±.001	0.60±.03	.024±.001
A11	0.23	.009	0.23	.009
A12	0.05	.002	0.05	.002
A13	5.15±.15	.203±.006	5.15±.15	.203±.006
A14	4.39 Max.	.173 Max.	4.39 Max.	.173 Max.
A15	3.02 Min.	.119 Min.	3.02 Min.	.119 Min.
A16	1.02±0.25	.040±.010	1.02±0.25	.040±.010
Pin X	25		34	
Pin Y	26		35	
Pin Z	50		68	

FIGURE B.6 50/68-Position Unshielded High-Density Cable Connector (A-, B-, P-, and Q-Cables)

Note: Dimension **B**8 and **B**10 are in the opening in the dielectric. The socket contacts (not shown) fit within the opening.

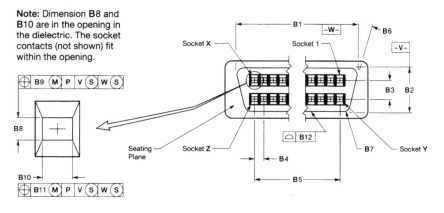

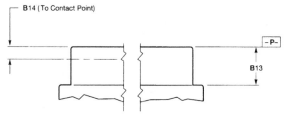

Dimensions	50 Position		68 Position	
	Millimeters	Inches	Millimeters	Inches
B1	34.70	1.366	46.13	1.816
B2	5.54	.218	5.54	.218
B3	2.54	.100	2.54	.100
B4	1.27	.050	1.27	.050
B5	30.48	1.200	41.91	1.650
B6	15°	15°	15°	15°
B7	1.00 R	.039 R	1.00 R	.039 R
B8	0.61±.05	.024±.002	0.61±.05	.024±.002
B9	0.15	.006	0.15	.006
B10	0.86±.10	.034±.004	0.86±.10	.034±.004
B11	0.15	.006	0.15	.006
B12	0.05	.002	0.05	.002
B13	5.00±.13	.197±.005	5.00±.13	.197±.005
B14	1.75 Max.	.069 Max.	1.75 Max.	.069 Max.
Socket X	25		34	
Socket Y	26		35	
Socket Z	50		68	

Single-Ended SCSI Pinout, B-Cable				Differential SCSI Pinout, B-Cable			
Pin	Signal	Pin	Signal	Pin	Signal	Pin	Signal
1	GND	35	GND		GND		GND
2	GND	36	−DB(8)		+DB(8)		−DB(8)
3	GND	37	−DB(9)		+DB(9)		−DB(9)
4	GND	38	−DB(10)		+DB(10)		−DB(10)
5	GND	39	−DB(11)		+DB(11)		−DB(11)
6	GND	40	−DB(12)		+DB(12)		−DB(12)
7	GND	41	−DB(13)		+DB(13)		−DB(13)
8	GND	42	−DB(14)		+DB(14)		−DB(14)
9	GND	43	−DB(15)		+DB(15)		−DB(15)
10	GND	44	−DB(P1)		+DB(P1)		−DB(P1)
11	GND	45	−ACKB		+ACKB		−ACKB
12	GND	46	GND		GND		DIFFSENS
13	GND	47	−REQB		+REQB		−REQB
14	GND	48	−DB(16)		+DB(16)		−DB(16)
15	GND	49	−DB(17)		+DB(17)		−DB(17)
16	GND	50	−DB(18)		+DB(18)		−DB(18)
17	TERMPWRB	51	TERMPWRB		TERMPWRB		TERMPWRB
18	TERMPWRB	52	TERMPWRB		TERMPWRB		TERMPWRB
19	GND	53	−DB(19)		+DB(19)		−DB(19)
20	GND	54	−DB(20)		+DB(20)		−DB(20)
21	GND	55	−DB(21)		+DB(21)		−DB(21)
22	GND	56	−DB(22)		+DB(22)		−DB(22)
23	GND	57	−DB(23)		+DB(23)		−DB(23)
24	GND	58	−DB(P2)		+DB(P2)		−DB(P2)
25	GND	59	−DB(24)		+DB(24)		−DB(24)
26	GND	60	−DB(25)		+DB(25)		−DB(25)
27	GND	61	−DB(26)		+DB(26)		−DB(26)
28	GND	62	−DB(27)		+DB(27)		−DB(27)
29	GND	63	−DB(28)		+DB(28)		−DB(28)
30	GND	64	−DB(29)		+DB(29)		−DB(29)
31	GND	65	−DB(30)		+DB(30)		−DB(30)
32	GND	66	−DB(31)		+DB(31)		−DB(31)
33	GND	67	−DB(P3)		+DB(P3)		−DB(P3)
34	GND	68	GND		GND		GND

68-Pin Wide SCSI B-, P-, and Q-Cables

The pinout for single-ended and differential B-cables is shown in Table B.3.

The P- and Q-cables use a much smaller high-density connector because the smaller 3¹/₂-inch devices don't have enough mounting space to fit an IDC connector with 68 pins. The connector is the same

P-Cable Single-Ended SCSI Pinout				P-Cable Differential SCSI Pinout			
Pin	Signal	Pin	Signal	Pin	Signal	Pin	Signal
1	GROUND	35	−DB(12)	1	+DB(12)	35	−DB(12)
2	GROUND	36	−DB(13)	2	+DB(13)	36	−DB(13)
3	GROUND	37	−DB(14)	3	+DB(14)	37	−DB(14)
4	GROUND	38	−DB(15)	4	+DB(15)	38	−DB(15)
5	GROUND	39	−DB(P1)	5	+DB(P1)	39	−DB(P1)
6	GROUND	40	−DB(0)	6	GND	40	GND
7	GROUND	41	−DB(1)	7	+DB(0)	41	−DB(0)
8	GROUND	42	−DB(2)	8	+DB(1)	42	−DB(1)
9	GROUND	43	−DB(3)	9	+DB(2)	43	−DB(2)
10	GROUND	44	−DB(4)	10	+DB(3)	44	−DB(3)
11	GROUND	45	−DB(5)	11	+DB(4)	45	−DB(4)
12	GROUND	46	−DB(6)	12	+DB(5)	46	−DB(5)
13	GROUND	47	−DB(7)	13	+DB(6)	47	−DB(6)
14	GROUND	48	−DB(P)	14	+DB(7)	48	−DB(7)
15	GROUND	49	GROUND	15	+DB(P)	49	−DB(P)
16	GROUND	50	GROUND	16	DIFFSENS	50	GND
17	TERMPWR	51	TERMPWR	17	TERMPWR	51	TERMPWR
18	TERMPWR	52	TERMPWR	18	TERMPWR	52	TERMPWR
19	RESERVED	53	RESERVED	19	RESERVED	53	RESERVED
20	GROUND	54	GROUND	20	+ATN	54	−ATN
21	GROUND	55	−ATN	21	GND	55	GND
22	GROUND	56	GROUND	22	+BSY	56	−BSY
23	GROUND	57	−BSY	23	+ACK	57	−ACK
24	GROUND	58	−ACK	24	+RST	58	−RST
25	GROUND	59	−RST	25	+MSG	59	−MSG
26	GROUND	60	−MSG	26	+SEL	60	−SEL
27	GROUND	61	−SEL	27	+C/D	61	−C/D
28	GROUND	62	−C/D	28	+REQ	62	−REQ
29	GROUND	63	−REQ	29	+I/O	63	−I/O
30	GROUND	64	−I/O	30	GND	64	GND
31	GROUND	65	−DB(8)	31	+DB(8)	65	−DB(8)
32	GROUND	66	−DB(9)	32	+DB(9)	66	−DB(9)
33	GROUND	67	−DB(10)	33	+DB(10)	67	−DB(10)
34	GROUND	68	−DB(11)	34	+DB(11)	68	−DB(11)

for internal and external cables, but the internal version is unshielded with a plastic body and without locking mechanisms. The male connector is the cable connector, and the device has the female connector.

Tables B.4 and B.5 list the pinouts for single-ended and differential P- and Q-cables.

Q-cable Single-Ended SCSI pinout				Q-cable Differential SCSI pinout			
Pin	Signal	Pin	Signal	Pin	Signal	Pin	Signal
1	GROUND	35	−DB(28)	1	+DB(28)	35	−DB(28)
2	GROUND	36	−DB(29)	2	+DB(29)	36	−DB(29)
3	GROUND	37	−DB(30)	3	+DB(30)	37	−DB(30)
4	GROUND	38	−DB(31)	4	+DB(31)	38	−DB(31)
5	GROUND	39	−DB(P3)	5	+DB(P3)	39	−DB(P3)
6	GROUND	40	−DB(16)	6	GND	40	GROUND
7	GROUND	41	−DB(17)	7	+DB(16)	41	−DB(16)
8	GROUND	42	−DB(18)	8	+DB(17)	42	−DB(17)
9	GROUND	43	−DB(19)	9	+DB(18)	43	−DB(18)
10	GROUND	44	−DB(20)	10	+DB(19)	44	−DB(19)
11	GROUND	45	−DB(21)	11	+DB(20)	45	−DB(20)
12	GROUND	46	−DB(22)	12	+DB(21)	46	−DB(21)
13	GROUND	47	−DB(23)	13	+DB(22)	47	−DB(22)
14	GROUND	48	−DB(P2)	14	+DB(23)	48	−DB(23)
15	GROUND	49	GROUND	15	+DB(P2)	49	−DB(P2)
16	GROUND	50	GROUND	16	DIFFSENS	50	GROUND
17	TERMPWRB	51	TERMPWRB	17	TERMPWRQ	51	TERMPWRQ
18	TERMPWRB	52	TERMPWRB	18	TERMPWRQ	52	TERMPWRQ
19	RESERVED	53	RESERVED	19	RESERVED	53	RESERVED
20	GROUND	54	GROUND	20	TERMINATED	54	TERMINATED
21	GROUND	55	TERMINATED	21	GROUND	55	GROUND
22	GROUND	56	GROUND	22	TERMINATED	56	TERMINATED
23	GROUND	57	TERMINATED	23	TERMINATED	57	TERMINATED
24	GROUND	58	TERMINATED	24	TERMINATED	58	TERMINATED
25	GROUND	59	TERMINATED	25	TERMINATED	59	TERMINATED
26	GROUND	60	TERMINATED	26	TERMINATED	60	TERMINATED
27	GROUND	61	TERMINATED	27	TERMINATED	61	TERMINATED
28	GROUND	62	TERMINATED	28	TERMINATED	62	TERMINATED
29	GROUND	63	TERMINATED	29	TERMINATED	63	TERMINATED
30	GROUND	64	TERMINATED	30	GROUND	64	GROUND
31	GROUND	65	−DB(24)	31	+DB(24)	65	−DB(24)
32	GROUND	66	−DB(25)	32	+DB(25)	66	−DB(25)
33	GROUND	67	−DB(26)	33	+DB(26)	67	−DB(26)
34	GROUND	68	−DB(27)	34	+DB(27)	68	−DB(27)

110-Pin 32-Bit Wide SCSI L-Cable

The L-cable uses the same connector model as the P- and Q-cables, but it has 110 pins. The purpose of each pin is listed in Table B.6. Both single-ended and differential versions are shown.

External Shielded Connectors

50-Pin Centronics-Style (A-Cable)

The Centronics-style is still the de-facto standard for external connections. While the connectors are usually secured with two spring clamps, they're sometimes secured with screws. Table B.7 lists the pinouts for 50-pin Centronics-style connectors. Figures B.7 and B.8 show 50-position shielded low-density device and cable connectors (A-cable).

TABLE B.6   Pinout Table for Single-Ended and Differential L-Cable

L-Cable Single-Ended SCSI Pinout				L-Cable Differential SCSI Pinout			
Pin	Signal	Pin	Signal	Pin	Signal	Pin	Signal
1	GROUND	56	GROUND	1	GROUND	56	GROUND
2	GROUND	57	−DB(24)	2	+DB(24)	57	−DB(24)
3	GROUND	58	−DB(25)	3	+DB(25)	58	−DB(25)
4	GROUND	59	−DB(26)	4	+DB(26)	59	−DB(26)
5	GROUND	60	−DB(27)	5	+DB(27)	60	−DB(27)
6	GROUND	61	−DB(28)	6	+DB(28)	61	−DB(28)
7	GROUND	62	−DB(29)	7	+DB(29)	62	−DB(29)
8	GROUND	63	−DB(30)	8	+DB(30)	63	−DB(30)
9	GROUND	64	−DB(31)	9	+DB(31)	64	−DB(31)
10	GROUND	65	−DB(P3)	10	+DB(P3)	65	−DB(P3)
11	GROUND	66	−DB(12)	11	+DB(12)	66	−DB(12)
12	GROUND	67	−DB(13)	12	+DB(13)	67	−DB(13)
13	GROUND	68	−DB(14)	13	+DB(14)	68	−DB(14)
14	GROUND	69	−DB(15)	14	+DB(15)	69	−DB(15)
15	GROUND	70	−DB(P1)	15	+DB(P1)	70	−DB(P1)
16	GROUND	71	−DB(0)	16	GROUND	71	GROUND
17	GROUND	72	−DB(1)	17	+DB(0)	72	−DB(0)
18	GROUND	73	−DB(2)	18	+DB(1)	73	−DB(1)
19	GROUND	74	−DB(3)	19	+DB(2)	74	−DB(2)
20	GROUND	75	−DB(4)	20	+DB(3)	75	−DB(3)
21	GROUND	76	−DB(5)	21	+DB(4)	76	−DB(4)
22	GROUND	77	−DB(6)	22	+DB(5)	77	−DB(5)
23	GROUND	78	−DB(7)	23	+DB(6)	78	−DB(6)
24	GROUND	79	−DB(P)	24	+DB(7)	79	−DB(7)
25	GROUND	80	GROUND	25	+DB(P)	80	−DB(P)
26	GROUND	81	GROUND	26	DIFFSENS	81	GROUND
27	TERMPWR	82	TERMPWR	27	TERMPWR	82	TERMPWR
28	TERMPWR	83	TERMPWR	28	TERMPWR	83	TERMPWR
29	TERMPWR	84	TERMPWR	29	TERMPWR	84	TERMPWR
30	GROUND	85	GROUND	30	GROUND	85	GROUND
31	GROUND	86	−ATN	31	+ATN	86	−ATN
32	GROUND	87	GROUND	32	GROUND	87	GROUND
33	GROUND	88	−BSY	33	+BSY	88	−BSY
34	GROUND	89	−ACK	34	+ACK	89	−ACK
35	GROUND	90	−RST	35	+RST	90	−RST
36	GROUND	91	−MSG	36	+MSG	91	−MSG
37	GROUND	92	−SEL	37	+SEL	92	−SEL
38	GROUND	93	−C/D	38	+C/D	93	−C/D
39	GROUND	94	−REQ	39	+REQ	94	−REQ
40	GROUND	95	−I/O	40	+I/O	95	−I/O
41	GROUND	96	−DB(8)	41	+DB(8)	96	−DB(8)
42	GROUND	97	−DB(9)	42	+DB(9)	97	−DB(9)
43	GROUND	98	−DB(10)	43	+DB(10)	98	−DB(10)
44	GROUND	99	−DB(11)	44	+DB(11)	99	−DB(11)
45	GROUND	100	GROUND	45	GROUND	100	GROUND
46	GROUND	101	−DB(16)	46	+DB(16)	101	−DB(16)
47	GROUND	102	−DB(17)	47	+DB(17)	102	−DB(17)
48	GROUND	103	−DB(18)	48	+DB(18)	103	−DB(18)
49	GROUND	104	−DB(19)	49	+DB(19)	104	−DB(19)
50	GROUND	105	−DB(20)	50	+DB(20)	105	−DB(20)
51	GROUND	106	−DB(21)	51	+DB(21)	106	−DB(21)
52	GROUND	107	−DB(22)	52	+DB(22)	107	−DB(22)
53	GROUND	108	−DB(23)	53	+DB(23)	108	−DB(23)
54	GROUND	109	−DB(P2)	54	+DB(P2)	109	−DB(P2)
55	GROUND	110	GROUND	55	GROUND	110	GROUND

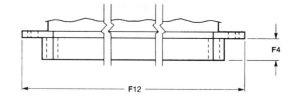

FIGURE B.7 50-Position Shielded Low-Density Device Connector (A-Cable)

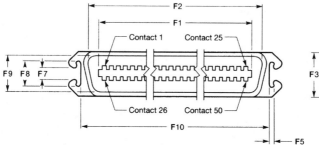

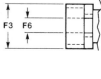

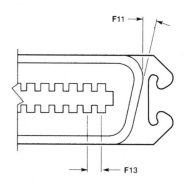

Dimension	Millimeters	Inches
F1	56.26 Maximum	2.215 Maximum
F2	64.29 Minimum	2.531 Minimum
F3*	15.24	0.600
F4	7.29 Minimum	0.287 Minimum
F5*	1.02	0.040
F6	4.09 Maximum	0.161 Maximum
F7*	5.08	0.200
F8*	6.10	0.240
F9	12.04 Minimum	0.474 Minimum
F10*	68.45	2.695
F11	15°±2°	15°±2°
F12*	76.71	3.020
F13	2.16	0.085

Notes:
1. Tolerances ±0.127 mm (0.005 inch) noncumulative, unless specified otherwise.
2. Dimensions listed with asterisks are shown for reference only.

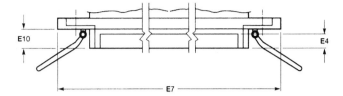

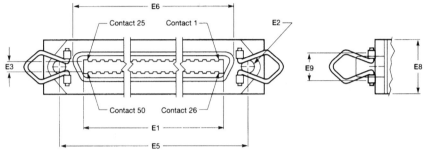

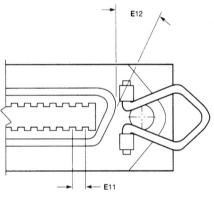

Dimension		Millimeters	Inches
E1		56.39 Minimum	2.220 Minimum
E2	(3)	2.62 Minimum	0.103 Minimum
E3		3.99 Minimum	0.157 Minimum
E4		5.84 Minimum	0.230 Minimum
E5		74.85	2.947
E6		64.29 Maximum	2.531 Maximum
E7*		83.06	3.270
E8*		15.24	0.600
E9		12.04 Maximum	0.474 Maximum
E10		9.78 Maximum	0.385 Maximum
E11		2.16	0.085
E12		15°±2°	15°±2°

Notes:
1. Tolerances ±0.127 mm (0.005 inch) noncumulative, unless specified otherwise.
2. Dimensions listed with asterisks are shown for reference only.
3. Dimension **E2** to accommodate 4–40 or 6–32 threaded screws.

TABLE B.7 Pinout Table for 50-Pin, Single-Ended and Differential, Centronics-Style Connector (A-Cable)

	Single-Ended SCSI Pinout				Differential SCSI Pinout		
Pin	Signal	Pin	Signal	Pin	Signal	Pin	Signal
1	GND	26	−DB(0)	1	GND	26	GND
2	GND	27	−DB(1)	2	+DB(0)	27	−DB(0)
3	GND	28	−DB(2)	3	+DB(1)	28	−DB(1)
4	GND	29	−DB(3)	4	+DB(2)	29	−DB(2)
5	GND	30	−DB(4)	5	+DB(3)	30	−DB(3)
6	GND	31	−DB(5)	6	+DB(4)	31	−DB(4)
7	GND	32	−DB(6)	7	+DB(5)	32	−DB(5)
8	GND	33	−DB(7)	8	+DB(6)	33	−DB(6)
9	GND	34	−DB(P)	9	+DB(7)	34	−DB(7)
10	GND	35	GND	10	+DB(P)	35	−DB(P)
11	GND	36	GND	11	DIFFSENS	36	GND
12	RESERVED	37	RESERVED	12	RESERVED	37	RESERVED
13	NOT CONNECTED	38	TERMPWR	13	TERMPWR	38	TERMPWR
14	RESERVED	39	RESERVED	14	RESERVED	39	RESERVED
15	GND	40	GND	15	+ATN	40	−ATN
16	GND	41	−ATN	16	GND	41	GND
17	GND	42	GND	17	+BSY	42	−BSY
18	GND	43	−BSY	18	+ACK	43	−ACK
19	GND	44	−ACK	19	+RST	44	−RST
20	GND	45	−RST	20	+MSG	45	−MSG
21	GND	46	−MSG	21	+SEL	46	−SEL
22	GND	47	−SEL	22	+C/D	47	−C/D
23	GND	48	−C/D	23	+REQ	48	−REQ
24	GND	49	−REQ	24	+I/O	49	−I/O
25	GND	50	−I/O	25	GND	50	GND

50/68-Pin Wide A- and B-Cables

Figures B.9 and B.10 offer a look at the 50/68-position shielded high-density cable connector and device connector (A- and B-cables). Table B.8 lists the pinouts for this connector.

FIGURE B.9 50/68-Position Shielded High-Density Cable Connector (A- and B-Cables)

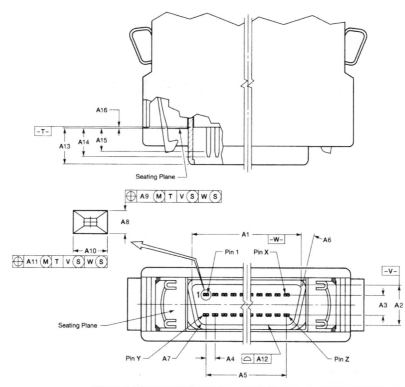

Dimensions	50 Position		68 Position	
	Millimeters	Inches	Millimeters	Inches
A1	34.85	1.372	46.28	1.822
A2	5.69	.224	5.69	.224
A3	2.54	.100	2.54	.100
A4	1.27	.050	1.27	.050
A5	30.48	1.200	41.91	1.650
A6	15°	15°	15°	15°
A7	1.04 R	.041 R	1.04 R	.041 R
A8	0.40±.01	.0156±.0004	0.40±.01	.0156±.0004
A9	0.23	.009	0.23	.009
A10	0.60±.03	.024±.001	0.60±.03	.024±.001
A11	0.23	.009	0.23	.009
A12	0.05	.002	0.05	.002
A13	4.90±.10	.193±.004	4.90±.10	.193±.004
A14	4.27 Max.	.168 Max.	4.27 Max.	.168 Max.
A15	2.64 Min.	.104 Min.	2.64 Min.	.104 Min.
A16	0.25±.13	.010±.005	0.25±.13	.010±.005
Pin X	25		34	
Pin Y	26		35	
Pin Z	50		68	

Note: Dimension B8 and B10 are in the opening in the dielectric. The socket contacts (not shown) fit within the opening.

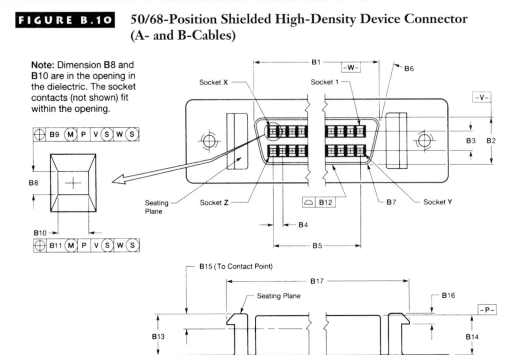

Dimensions	50 Position		68 Position	
	Millimeters	Inches	Millimeters	Inches
B1	34.70	1.366	46.13	1.816
B2	5.54	.218	5.54	.218
B3	2.54	.100	2.54	.100
B4	1.27	.050	1.27	.050
B5	30.48	1.200	41.91	1.650
B6	15°	15°	15°	15°
B7	1.00 R	.039 R	1.00 R	.039 R
B8	0.61±.05	.024±.002	0.61±.05	.024±.002
B9	0.15	.006	0.15	.006
B10	0.86±.10	.034±.004	0.86±.10	.034±.004
B11	0.15	.006	0.15	.006
B12	0.05	.002	0.05	.002
B13	5.10±.05	.201±.002	5.10±.05	.201±.002
B14	5.00±.13	.197±.005	5.00±.13	.197±.005
B15	1.85 Max.	.073 Max.	1.85 Max.	.073 Max.
B16	1.50±.03	.059±.001	1.50±.03	.059±.001
B17	42.29±.10	1.665 ±.004	53.72±.10	2.115 ±.004
Socket X	25		34	
Socket Y	26		35	
Socket Z	50		68	

Table for 68-Pin High-Density B-Cable

Single-Ended SCSI Pinout				Differential SCSI Pinout			
Pin	Signal	Pin	Signal	Pin	Signal	Pin	Signal
1	GROUND	35	GROUND	1	GROUND	35	GROUND
2	GROUND	36	−DB(8)	2	+DB(8)	36	−DB(8)
3	GROUND	37	−DB(9)	3	+DB(9)	37	−DB(9)
4	GROUND	38	−DB(10)	4	+DB(10)	38	−DB(10)
5	GROUND	39	−DB(11)	5	+DB(11)	39	−DB(11)
6	GROUND	40	−DB(12)	6	+DB(12)	40	−DB(12)
7	GROUND	41	−DB(13)	7	+DB(13)	41	−DB(13)
8	GROUND	42	−DB(14)	8	+DB(14)	42	−DB(14)
9	GROUND	43	−DB(15)	9	+DB(15)	43	−DB(15)
10	GROUND	44	−DB(P1)	10	+DB(P1)	44	−DB(P1)
11	GROUND	45	−ACKB	11	+ACKB	45	−ACKB
12	GROUND	46	GROUND	12	GROUND	46	DIFFSENS
13	GROUND	47	−REQB	13	+REQB	47	−REQB
14	GROUND	48	−DB(16)	14	+DB(16)	48	−DB(16)
15	GROUND	49	−DB(17)	15	+DB(17)	49	−DB(17)
16	GROUND	50	−DB(18)	16	+DB(18)	50	−DB(18)
17	TERMPWRB	51	TERMPWRB	17	TERMPWRB	51	TERMPWRB
18	TERMPWRB	52	TERMPWRB	18	TERMPWRB	52	TERMPWRB
19	GROUND	53	−DB(19)	19	+DB(19)	53	−DB(19)
20	GROUND	54	−DB(20)	20	+DB(20)	54	−DB(20)
21	GROUND	55	−DB(21)	21	+DB(21)	55	−DB(21)
22	GROUND	56	−DB(22)	22	+DB(22)	56	−DB(22)
23	GROUND	57	−DB(23)	23	+DB(23)	57	−DB(23)
24	GROUND	58	−DB(P2)	24	+DB(P2)	58	−DB(P2)
25	GROUND	59	−DB(24)	25	+DB(24)	59	−DB(24)
26	GROUND	60	−DB(25)	26	+DB(25)	60	−DB(25)
27	GROUND	61	−DB(26)	27	+DB(26)	61	−DB(26)
28	GROUND	62	−DB(27)	28	+DB(27)	62	−DB(27)
29	GROUND	63	−DB(28)	29	+DB(28)	63	−DB(28)
30	GROUND	64	−DB(29)	30	+DB(29)	64	−DB(29)
31	GROUND	65	−DB(30)	31	+DB(30)	65	−DB(30)
32	GROUND	66	−DB(31)	32	+DB(31)	66	−DB(31)
33	GROUND	67	−DB(P3)	33	+DB(P3)	67	−DB(P3)
34	GROUND	68	GROUND	34	GROUND	68	GROUND

68-Pin, 16-Bit Wide SCSI P- and Q-Cables

The pinouts and mechanical dimensions for the shielded P- and Q-cable connectors are the same as those of the internal connectors, except that they have a metal-shielded body and a locking mechanism with either spring clamps or screws. The connector diagram in Figure B.11 is for SCSI devices and the diagram in Figure B.12 is for cables. Table B.9 shows the pinouts for the single-ended and differential P-cable. Table B.10 shows the pinouts for the single-ended and differential Q-cable.

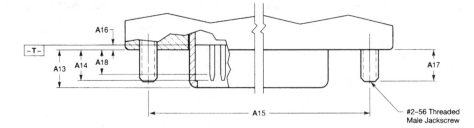

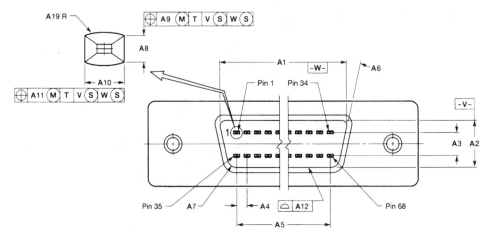

Dimensions	Millimeters	Inches
A1	46.28	1.822
A2	5.69	.224
A3	2.54	.100
A4	1.27	.050
A5	41.91	1.650
A6	15°	15°
A7	1.04 R	.041 R
A8	0.40±.01	.0156±.0004
A9	0.23	.009
A10	0.60±.03	.024±.001
A11	0.23	.009
A12	0.05	.002
A13	4.90±.10	.193±.004
A14	4.27 Max.	.168 Max.
A15	57.91±.13	2.280±.005
A16	0.25±.13	.010±.005
A17	3.43±.15	.135±.006
A18	2.64 Min.	.104 Min.
A19	1.02±.25	.040±.010

68-Pin, 16-Bit Wide SCSI Connectors (P- and Q-Cables)

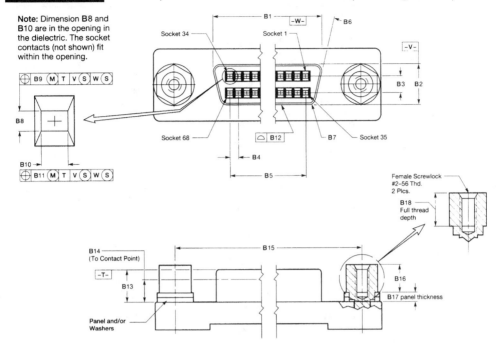

Note: Dimension B8 and B10 are in the opening in the dielectric. The socket contacts (not shown) fit within the opening.

Dimensions	Millimeters	Inches
B1	46.13	1.816
B2	5.54	.218
B3	2.54	.100
B4	1.27	.050
B5	41.91	1.650
B6	15°	15°
B7	1.00 R	.039 R
B8	0.61±.05	.024±.002
B9	0.15	.006
B10	0.86±.10	.034±.004
B11	0.15	.006
B12	0.05	.002
B13	5.00±.13	.197±.005
B14	3.30 Min.	.130 Min.
B15	57.91±.13	2.280±.005
B16	3.71±0.05	.146±.002
B17	1.52±.13	.060±.005
B18	3.58 Min.	.141 Min.

Pinout Table for Single-Ended and Differential P-Cable

	Single-Ended SCSI Pinout			Differential SCSI Pinout			
Pin	Signal	Pin	Signal	Pin	Signal	Pin	Signal
1	GROUND	35	−DB(12)	1	+DB(12)	35	−DB(12)
2	GROUND	36	−DB(13)	2	+DB(13)	36	−DB(13)
3	GROUND	37	−DB(14)	3	+DB(14)	37	−DB(14)
4	GROUND	38	−DB(15)	4	+DB(15)	38	−DB(15)
5	GROUND	39	−DB(P1)	5	+DB(P1)	39	−DB(P1)
6	GROUND	40	−DB(0)	6	GROUND	40	GROUND
7	GROUND	41	−DB(1)	7	+DB(0)	41	−DB(0)
8	GROUND	42	−DB(2)	8	+DB(1)	42	−DB(1)
9	GROUND	43	−DB(3)	9	+DB(2)	43	−DB(2)
10	GROUND	44	−DB(4)	10	+DB(3)	44	−DB(3)
11	GROUND	45	−DB(5)	11	+DB(4)	45	−DB(4)
12	GROUND	46	−DB(6)	12	+DB(5)	46	−DB(5)
13	GROUND	47	−DB(7)	13	+DB(6)	47	−DB(6)
14	GROUND	48	−DB(P)	14	+DB(7)	48	−DB(7)
15	GROUND	49	GROUND	15	+DB(P)	49	−DB(P)
16	GROUND	50	GROUND	16	DIFFSENS	50	GROUND
17	TERMPWR	51	TERMPWR	17	TERMPWR	51	TERMPWR
18	TERMPWR	52	TERMPWR	18	TERMPWR	52	TERMPWR
19	RESERVED	53	RESERVED	19	RESERVED	53	RESERVED
20	GROUND	54	GROUND	20	GROUND	54	GROUND
21	GROUND	55	−ATN	21	+ATN	55	−ATN
22	GROUND	56	GROUND	22	GROUND	56	GROUND
23	GROUND	57	−BSY	23	+BSY	57	−BSY
24	GROUND	58	−ACK	24	+ACK	58	−ACK
25	GROUND	59	−RST	25	+RST	59	−RST
26	GROUND	60	−MSG	26	+MSG	60	−MSG
27	GROUND	61	−SEL	27	+SEL	61	−SEL
28	GROUND	62	−C/D	28	+C/D	62	−C/D
29	GROUND	63	−REQ	29	+REQ	63	−REQ
30	GROUND	64	−I/O	30	+I/O	64	−I/O
31	GROUND	65	−DB(8)	31	+DB(8)	65	−DB(8)
32	GROUND	66	−DB(9)	32	+DB(9)	66	−DB(9)
33	GROUND	67	−DB(10)	33	+DB(10)	67	−DB(10)
34	GROUND	68	−DB(11)	34	+DB(11)	68	−DB(11)

110-Pin, 32-Bit Wide SCSI L-Cable

As with the P- and Q-cables, the L-cable has the same layout and mechanical connection for the external connector as for the internal one.
It's the same type of connector as the P-and Q-cables but has more
pins. The rather wide 110-pin connector makes a nut-and-bolt security

Pinout Table for Single-Ended and Differential Q-Cable

Q-Cable Single-Ended SCSI Pinout				Q-Cable Differential SCSI Pinout			
Pin	Signal	Pin	Signal	Pin	Signal	Pin	Signal
1	GROUND	35	−DB(28)	1	+DB(28)	35	−DB(28)
2	GROUND	36	−DB(29)	2	+DB(29)	36	−DB(29)
3	GROUND	37	−DB(30)	3	+DB(30)	37	−DB(30)
4	GROUND	38	−DB(31)	4	+DB(31)	38	−DB(31)
5	GROUND	39	−DB(P3)	5	+DB(P3)	39	−DB(P3)
6	GROUND	40	−DB(16)	6	GND	40	GROUND
7	GROUND	41	−DB(17)	7	+DB(16)	41	−DB(16)
8	GROUND	42	−DB(18)	8	+DB(17)	42	−DB(17)
9	GROUND	43	−DB(19)	9	+DB(18)	43	−DB(18)
10	GROUND	44	−DB(20)	10	+DB(19)	44	−DB(19)
11	GROUND	45	−DB(21)	11	+DB(20)	45	−DB(20)
12	GROUND	46	−DB(22)	12	+DB(21)	46	−DB(21)
13	GROUND	47	−DB(23)	13	+DB(22)	47	−DB(22)
14	GROUND	48	−DB(P2)	14	+DB(23)	48	−DB(23)
15	GROUND	49	GROUND	15	+DB(P2)	49	−DB(P2)
16	GROUND	50	GROUND	16	DIFFSENS	50	GROUND
17	TERMPWRB	51	TERMPWRB	17	TERMPWRQ	51	TERMPWRQ
18	TERMPWRB	52	TERMPWRB	18	TERMPWRQ	52	TERMPWRQ
19	RESERVED	53	RESERVED	19	RESERVED	53	RESERVED
20	GROUND	54	GROUND	20	TERMINATED	54	TERMINATED
21	GROUND	55	TERMINATED	21	GROUND	55	GROUND
22	GROUND	56	GROUND	22	TERMINATED	56	TERMINATED
23	GROUND	57	TERMINATED	23	TERMINATED	57	TERMINATED
24	GROUND	58	TERMINATED	24	TERMINATED	58	TERMINATED
25	GROUND	59	TERMINATED	25	TERMINATED	59	TERMINATED
26	GROUND	60	TERMINATED	26	TERMINATED	60	TERMINATED
27	GROUND	61	TERMINATED	27	TERMINATED	61	TERMINATED
28	GROUND	62	TERMINATED	28	TERMINATED	62	TERMINATED
29	GROUND	63	TERMINATED	29	TERMINATED	63	TERMINATED
30	GROUND	64	TERMINATED	30	GROUND	64	GROUND
31	GROUND	65	−DB(24)	31	+DB(24)	65	−DB(24)
32	GROUND	66	−DB(25)	32	+DB(25)	66	−DB(25)
33	GROUND	67	−DB(26)	33	+DB(26)	67	−DB(26)
34	GROUND	68	−DB(27)	34	+DB(27)	68	−DB(27)

B

mechanism the preferred method for attaching the connector. Normal spring clamps aren't as stable as they should be for the higher mechanical load of the L-cable. Table B.11 lists the pinout of the L-cable and the function of each pin.

Pinout Table for Single-Ended and Differential
L-Cable with the Function of Each Pin

L-Cable Single-Ended SCSI Pinout				L-Cable Differential SCSI Pinout			
Pin	Signal	Pin	Signal	Pin	Signal	Pin	Signal
1	GROUND	56	GROUND	1	GROUND	56	GROUND
2	GROUND	57	−DB(24)	2	+DB(24)	57	−DB(24)
3	GROUND	58	−DB(25)	3	+DB(25)	58	−DB(25)
4	GROUND	59	−DB(26)	4	+DB(26)	59	−DB(26)
5	GROUND	60	−DB(27)	5	+DB(27)	60	−DB(27)
6	GROUND	61	−DB(28)	6	+DB(28)	61	−DB(28)
7	GROUND	62	−DB(29)	7	+DB(29)	62	−DB(29)
8	GROUND	63	−DB(30)	8	+DB(30)	63	−DB(30)
9	GROUND	64	−DB(31)	9	+DB(31)	64	−DB(31)
10	GROUND	65	−DB(P3)	10	+DB(P3)	65	−DB(P3)
11	GROUND	66	−DB(12)	11	+DB(12)	66	−DB(12)
12	GROUND	67	−DB(13)	12	+DB(13)	67	−DB(13)
13	GROUND	68	−DB(14)	13	+DB(14)	68	−DB(14)
14	GROUND	69	−DB(15)	14	+DB(15)	69	−DB(15)
15	GROUND	70	−DB(P1)	15	+DB(P1)	70	−DB(P1)
16	GROUND	71	−DB(0)	16	GROUND	71	GROUND
17	GROUND	72	−DB(1)	17	+DB(0)	72	−DB(0)
18	GROUND	73	−DB(2)	18	+DB(1)	73	−DB(1)
19	GROUND	74	−DB(3)	19	+DB(2)	74	−DB(2)
20	GROUND	75	−DB(4)	20	+DB(3)	75	−DB(3)
21	GROUND	76	−DB(5)	21	+DB(4)	76	−DB(4)
22	GROUND	77	−DB(6)	22	+DB(5)	77	−DB(5)
23	GROUND	78	−DB(7)	23	+DB(6)	78	−DB(6)
24	GROUND	79	−DB(P)	24	+DB(7)	79	−DB(7)
25	GROUND	80	GROUND	25	+DB(P)	80	−DB(P)
26	GROUND	81	GROUND	26	DIFFSENS	81	GROUND
27	TERMPWR	82	TERMPWR	27	TERMPWR	82	TERMPWR
28	TERMPWR	83	TERMPWR	28	TERMPWR	83	TERMPWR
29	TERMPWR	84	TERMPWR	29	TERMPWR	84	TERMPWR
30	GROUND	85	GROUND	30	GROUND	85	GROUND
31	GROUND	86	−ATN	31	+ATN	86	−ATN
32	GROUND	87	GROUND	32	GROUND	87	GROUND
33	GROUND	88	−BSY	33	+BSY	88	−BSY
34	GROUND	89	−ACK	34	+ACK	89	−ACK
35	GROUND	90	−RST	35	+RST	90	−RST
36	GROUND	91	−MSG	36	+MSG	91	−MSG
37	GROUND	92	−SEL	37	+SEL	92	−SEL
38	GROUND	93	−C/D	38	+C/D	93	−C/D
39	GROUND	94	−REQ	39	+REQ	94	−REQ
40	GROUND	95	−I/O	40	+I/O	95	−I/O
41	GROUND	96	−DB(8)	41	+DB(8)	96	−DB(8)
42	GROUND	97	−DB(9)	42	+DB(9)	97	−DB(9)
43	GROUND	98	−DB(10)	43	+DB(10)	98	−DB(10)
44	GROUND	99	−DB(11)	44	+DB(11)	99	−DB(11)
45	GROUND	100	GROUND	45	GROUND	100	GROUND
46	GROUND	101	−DB(16)	46	+DB(16)	101	−DB(16)
47	GROUND	102	−DB(17)	47	+DB(17)	102	−DB(17)
48	GROUND	103	−DB(18)	48	+DB(18)	103	−DB(18)
49	GROUND	104	−DB(19)	49	+DB(19)	104	−DB(19)
50	GROUND	105	−DB(20)	50	+DB(20)	105	−DB(20)
51	GROUND	106	−DB(21)	51	+DB(21)	106	−DB(21)
52	GROUND	107	−DB(22)	52	+DB(22)	107	−DB(22)
53	GROUND	108	−DB(23)	53	+DB(23)	108	−DB(23)
54	GROUND	109	−DB(P2)	54	+DB(P2)	109	−DB(P2)
55	GROUND	110	GROUND	55	GROUND	110	GROUND

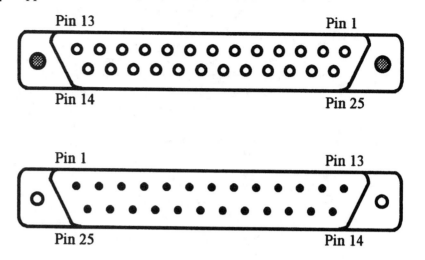

TABLE B.12 Pinout Table for Apple and Future Domain
Single-Ended SCSI Connectors Shown Above

Apple Single-Ended SCSI Pinout				Future Domain Single-Ended SCSI Pinout			
Pin	Signal	Pin	Signal	Pin	Signal	Pin	Signal
1	−REQ	14	RESERVED/GROUND	1	GND	14	−DB(0)
2	−MSG	15	−C/D	2	−DB(1)	15	−DB(2)
3	−I/O	16	RESERVED/GROUND	3	−DB(3)	16	−DB(4)
4	−RST	17	−ATN	4	−DB(5)	17	−DB(6)
5	−ACK	18	GROUND	5	−DB(7)	18	−DB(P)
6	−BSY	19	−SEL	6	GND	19	GND
7	GROUND	20	−DBP	7	−SEL	20	−ATN
8	−DB0	21	−DB1	8	GND	21	−MSG
9	GROUND	22	−DB2	9	SPARE	22	−ACK
10	−DB3	23	−DB4	10	−RST	23	−BSY
11	−DB5	24	GROUND	11	−C/D	24	−REQ
12	−DB6	25	Termination Power *	12	−I/O	25	GND
13	−DB7			13	GND		

* Pin 25 - Termination Power is not connected in the Mac Plus connector.

Non-Official Standard SCSI Connectors

For whatever reasons, some companies decided to introduce non-standard SCSI connectors. The most common are Future Domain's 25-pin D-sub connector, used on their early SCSI host adapters, Apple's 25-pin D-sub connector with a different and totally incompatible pinout scheme, and IBM's proprietary PS/2 SCSI connector. See Figures B.13 and B.14 and Tables B.12 and B.13.

Virtually all signal positions are incompatible in these two connectors. But the real dangerous part is pin 25. Apple's cables don't have a connection here so there isn't a problem, but most SCSI adapters with the Apple connector pinout do provide Termination Power at pin 25. So, connecting an Apple SCSI adapter with an old Future Domain cable will cause a short-circuit that will blow the host adapter's or device's terminator power fuse. The same thing could happen with a device providing terminator power via an old Future Domain adapter. If you have an older Future Domain SCSI adapter, look for the label "Apple layout" on the cover plate and/or an "M" in the model number. If it's a Future Domain pinout type, you need a special SCSI cable, type HCA-108, from Future Domain.

IBM 60-Pin High-Density PS/2

Early in the SCSI-2 draft process, a 60-pin high-density (HD) connector was used, but was later abandoned in favor of the 50-pin connector. IBM, on the other hand, kept the 60-pin connector for most of their systems. This connector is a high-density SCSI-2/SCSI-3 style connector, and its first 50 pins are identical to the standard SCSI-2 HD connectors. The remaining 10 conductors are simply defined as "reserved" without any mention as to their purpose. A reasonable guess would be

FIGURE B.14 **IBM 60-Pin High-Density PS/2 Connector**

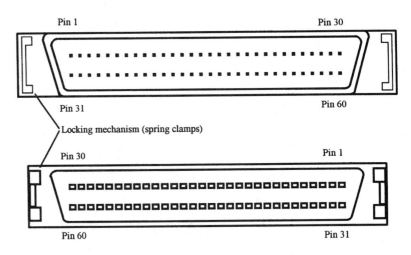

Pinout Table for IBM High-Density PS/2 Connector with the Function of Each Pin

Pin	Signal	Pin	Signal	Pin	Signal	Pin	Signal
1	GND	16	–DB(7)	31	GND	46	–C/D
2	–DB(0)	17	GND	32	–ATN	47	GND
3	GND	18	–DB(P)	33	GND	48	–REQ
4	–DB(1)	19	GND	34	GND	49	GND
5	GND	20	GND	35	GND	50	–I/O
6	–DB(2)	21	GND	36	–BSY	51	GND
7	GND	22	GND	37	GND	52	RESERVED
8	–DB(3)	23	RESERVED/GND	38	–ACK	53	RESERVED
9	GND	24	RESERVED/GND	39	GND	54	RESERVED
10	–DB(4)	25	NOT CONNECTED	40	–RST	55	RESERVED
11	GND	26	TERMPWR	41	GND	56	RESERVED
12	–DB(5)	27	RESERVED	42	–MSG	57	RESERVED
13	GND	28	RESERVED	43	GND	58	RESERVED
14	–DB(6)	29	GND	44	–SEL	59	RESERVED
15	GND	30	GND	45	GND	60	RESERVED

that they're reserved for additional signals, such as spindle synchronization necessary for RAID systems. (See Appendix I for more information about RAID.) IBM's pin configuration is shown in Figure B.14, and the pin assignments are shown in Table B.13.

Apple PowerBook 30-Pin HDI

The most recent addition to the growing list of non-standard SCSI connectors is Apple's HDI connector used in the PowerBook series of notebook computers. Its main feature is the very compact external connector and, in the internal version, the additional pins used to supply power to the internal hard disk (DISK +5 pins).

Apple's external HDI-30 SCSI connector's pinouts are listed in Table B.14.

Sun Microsystems' D-Sub Connector

Figure B.15 and Table B.15 show the Sun 50-pin D-sub connector. According to Sun, pin 1 is the pin in the upper-left corner. Remember that this means the male connector's pin 1 is on the upper-left as shown in Figure B.15. Pin 2 is the lower-left pin (in the third row of contacts, labeled pin 34). Pin 3 is the leftmost pin in the middle row (labeled pin 18). Pin 4 is the second-left pin in the upper row, and so on.

Table B.15 is the pinout scheme you will see if you look at a real Sun SCSI cable, not the one shown in their documentation.

TABLE B.14   Pinout Table for Apple's External HDI-30 Connector

Pin	Internal Connector	External Connector
1	DISK.+5	−LINK.SEL
2	DISK.+5	−DB(0)
3	GROUND	GROUND
4	GROUND	−DB(1)
5	GROUND	TERMPWR*
6	−DB(0)	−DB(2)
7	−DB(1)	−DB(3)
8	−DB(2)	GROUND
9	−DB(3)	−ACK
10	−DB(4)	GROUND
11	−DB(5)	−DB(4)
12	−DB(6)	GROUND
13	−DB(7)	GROUND
14	−DB(P)	−DB(5)
15	DISK.+5	GROUND
16	−BSY	−DB(6)
17	−ATN	GROUND
18	−ACK	−DB(7)
19	GROUND	−DB(P)
20	−MSG	GROUND
21	−RST	−REQ
22	−SEL	GROUND
23	−C/D	−BSY
24	−I/O	GROUND
25	−REQ	−ATN
26	GROUND	−C/D
27	GROUND	−RST
28	GROUND	−MSG
29	DISK.+5	−SEL
30	DISK.+5	−I/O

* Pin 5 - TERMPWR is not connected in Apple's original cable.

ALERT!   *When looking at Table B.15, keep in mind that the connector numbers shown in the table and in Figure B.15 are the ones that connector manufacturers, like AMP, use on the connectors. These are not the numbers used by Sun. For whatever reason, Sun used an unusual numbering scheme, which differs from the counting scheme the connector manufacturers use and print on the connector bodies. So, if you use an older Sun device, be extremely careful when supplying home-made cables.*

Sun Microsystems' 50-Pin D-Sub Connector

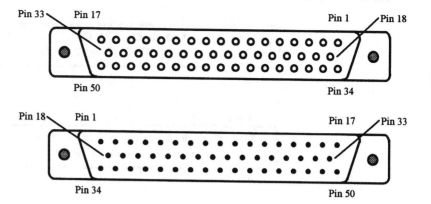

TABLE B.15 **Pinout Table for Sun Single-Ended SCSI Cable**

Pin	Signal	Pin	Signal	Pin	Signal	Pin	Signal
1	GND	14	−RST	26	RESERVED	39	GND
2	−DB(1)	15	GND	27	GND	40	GND
3	GND	16	−C/D	28	GND	41	RESERVED
4	−DB(4)	17	GND	29	−BSY	42	TERMPWR
5	GND	18	GND	30	GND	43	GND
6	−DB(7)	19	−DB(2)	31	−MSG	44	−ATN
7	GND	20	GND	32	GND	45	GND
8	GND	21	−DB(5)	33	−REQ	46	−ACK
9	NOT CONNECTED	22	GND	34	−DB(0)	47	GND
10	RESERVED	23	−DB(P)	35	GND	48	−SEL
11	GND	24	GND	36	−DB(3)	49	GND
12	GND	25	RESERVED	37	GND	50	−I/O
13	GND			38	−DB(6)		

Novell and Procomp DCB D-Sub 37 Connector

Years ago, Novell designed a proprietary connector for their DCB
SCSI boards. Procomp took the same connector for their F-DCB and
M-DCB host adapters to maintain 100 percent compatibility. This
connection uses a 37-pin D-sub connector. Unlike the 25-pin connectors, it has enough conductors to provide discrete wire pairs for each
signal. It's interesting to note that Novell's cable doesn't connect the
TERMPWR line so it needs to get TERMPWR from the terminated
device. Figure B.16 shows what the Novell connector looks like,
followed by a table of pin assignments (Table B.16).

Novell and Procomp DCB D-Sub 37 Connector

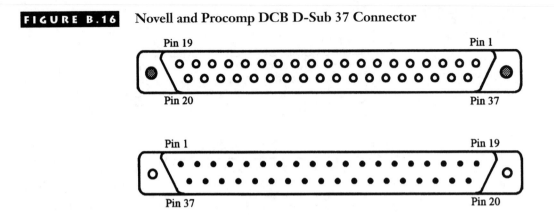

Novell and Procomp DCB External Pinout Table

Pin	Signal	Pin	Signal
1	GND	20	−DB(0)
2	GND	21	−DB(1)
3	GND	22	−DB(2)
4	GND	23	−DB(3)
5	GND	24	−DB(4)
6	GND	25	−DB(5)
7	GND	26	−DB(6)
8	GND	27	−DB(7)
9	GND	28	−DB(P)
10	GND	29	−ATN
11	GND	30	−BSY
12	GND	31	−ACK
13	GND	32	−RST
14	GND	33	−MSG
15	GND	34	−SEL
16	GND	35	−C/D
17	GND	36	−REQ
18	GND	37	−I/O
19	TERMPWR (possibly not connected)		

SCSI Bus Signals

The SCSI bus has eight (or more) data lines and a few control signals. Table B.17 is a basic explanation of what they are and how they're used.

- BSY, SEL, and RST are OR-tied, which means they can be asserted by multiple devices simultaneously.

- ACK and ATN are used only by the initiator for control purposes.

- C/D, I/O, MSG, and REQ are driven, or controlled, by the target.

TABLE B.17 An Explanation of the Data Lines
and Control Signals on the SCSI Bus

Signal	Meaning
BSY (Busy)	BSY indicates that the SCSI bus is in use.
SEL (Select)	SEL is used in the arbitration phase to select a target for communication. In this case, the term "target" could also stand for an initiator if it is set in a reselection phase.
C/D (Control/Data)	C/D indicates whether control or data information is on the data bus. If C/D is set, it indicates control information.
I/O (Input/Output)	I/O controls the direction of data movement on the data bus, as seen from the initiator. True indicates input to the initiator. I/O also distinguishes between selection and reselection phases.
MSG (Message)	MSG is used to indicate a message phase (together with C/D).
REQ (Request)	REQ is used by a target to request an ACK information transfer handshake.
ACK (Acknowledge)	ACK is used by an initiator to acknowledge the above REQ information transfer handshake request.
ATN (Attention)	ATN is set by an initiator to indicate the attention condition.
RST (Reset)	RST indicates the reset condition.
DB(0) to DB(7)	These are the data bits on the 8-bit SCSI data bus.
DB(P)	DB(P) is the parity bit for the first data byte.

TABLE B.18 Additional Data and Control Signals
Needed by the 16- and 32-Bit Buses

Signal	Meaning
REQB (RequestB)	REQB is the REQ signal for the B-cable if 16- or 32-bit data transfers are used.
ACKB (AcknowledgeB)	Similar to REQB, ACKB is the ACK signal for the B-cable if 16- or 32-bit data transfers are used.
DB(8) to DB(15)	These are the additional data bits for the 16-bit SCSI data bus.
DB(P1)	DB(P1) is the parity bit for the second data byte.
DB(16) to DB(31)	These are the additional data bits for the 32-bit SCSI data bus.
DB(P2) and DB(P3)	DB(P2) and DB(P3) are the parity bits for the third and fourth data bytes.

If a 16- or 32-bit bus is used, additional data and control signals are needed, as shown in Table B.18. Each data byte is accompanied by a parity bit (odd parity is used, so the parity bit is set to 1 when the number of logical 1 signals, including the parity bit, is an odd number).

TABLE B.19 SCSI Bus Phases

Phase	Definition
BUS FREE phase	The Bus Free phase indicates that no I/O process is running and the SCSI bus is available for a connection. The bus is in this state at the beginning of every transfer.
ARBITRATION phase	The Arbitration phase allows all attached SCSI devices to say "I need the bus" and eventually gain control over the SCSI bus so that an I/O process can be initiated or resumed.
SELECTION phase	In the Selection phase, the initiator (the arbitration winner) selects a target for its pending operation. When this target selection is complete, the target asserts the REQ signal to enter the information transfer phase.
RESELECTION phase	The Reselection phase is a special type of selection phase needed in case of an uncompleted operation. For example, if a target device disconnects itself (allows a bus free phase by releasing the BSY and SEL signals), the reselection process allows the target to reconnect to the initiator of the suspended operation. Contrary to the standard Selection phase, in a Reselection phase, the target of a former operation actively seeks a connection to the initiator.

TABLE B.20 Protocol Phases

Phase	Definition
COMMAND phase	The Command phase allows the target to request command information from the initiator.
DATA phase	The Data phase has two variants, Data In and Data Out, in which the target requests to send data to or from the initiator.
STATUS phase	The Status phase allows the target to request that status information be sent from the target to the initiator.
MESSAGE phase	The Message phase can be a Message In or a Message Out phase, during which the target can request a message to or from the initiator. A message can be either a single- or multiple-byte message, but the whole message must be contained in one Message phase. In other words, there must not be a change on the C/D, I/O, and MSG signals.

TABLE B.21 Information Transfer Phases

Phase	Definition
ATTENTION condition	The initiator can inform a target that it has a message ready. The target can then get this message by entering a Message Out phase. An attention condition is issued by asserting the ATN signal and can happen in any bus state except Arbitration and Bus Free.
RESET condition	Immediately clears all SCSI devices from the bus. The Reset condition has absolute priority over all other phases and conditions. And SCSI device can create the Reset condition by asserting the RST signal. On reset, all SCSI devices release all SCSI bus signals except RST. A Bus Free phase follows the Reset condition.

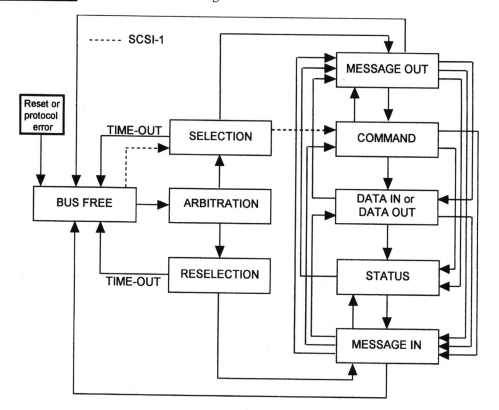

Bus Phases and Timing Diagrams

Bus Phases and Conditions

This section lists the bus phases defined in the SCSI specification (Tables B.19 through B.21) and a phase sequence diagram (Figure B.17) for quick reference.

FIGURE B.18   Arbitration and Selection Phases

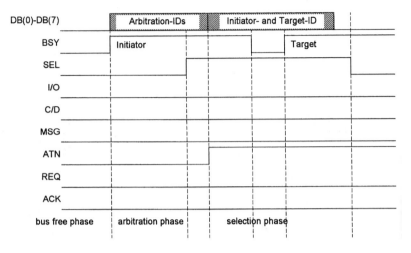

Bus Timing

SCSI bus timing is a very complex thing, but it can be broken down into some fundamental figures. The timing diagrams in this appendix are simplified. They do not include the various signal delays that actually occur on the SCSI bus. In reality, if an electrical signal changes its state, it never happens as cleanly as the timing diagrams would lead you to believe. To give the signals time to settle to their states, various delays are implemented. Table B.22 lists the various delays along with minimum or maximum times for defined changes to occur. The delays listed are for regular SCSI except where otherwise noted.

The timing diagrams included in this appendix illustrate the relationship between the various SCSI signals as follows:

- Arbitration and Selection phases (Figure B.18)
- Arbitration, Reselection, and Message In phases (Figure B.19)
- Message Out and Command phases (Figure B.20)
- Data I/O phases for asynchronous (Figure B.21) and synchronous (Figure B.22) transfer modes
- Status Message In phase followed by a Bus Free phase (Figure B.23)

SCSI Bus Delays

Timing Element	Time	Description
Arbitration Delay	2.4 µs	When a SCSI device has asserted BSY during the arbitration phase, it must wait at least one Arbitration Delay before deciding that it has won the arbitration.
Assertion Period	90 ns Fast SCSI: 30 ns	REQ/REQB and ACK/ACKB signals must be asserted for at least one assertion period.
Bus Clear Delay	800 ns	If a device detects a Bus Free phase, it has this time to release all signals.
Bus Free Delay	800 ns	After detection of a Bus Free phase, a device must wait one Bus Free Delay before starting the arbitration process.
Bus Set Delay	1.8 µs	A SCSI device may assert BSY and its ID bit for an arbitration not longer than one Bus Set Delay.
Bus Settle Delay	400 ns	After a phase change, signal levels should not be changed by devices during the Bus Settle Delay.
Cable Skew Delay	10 ns Fast SCSI: 5 ns	The signal run length between two SCSI signals on the bus shouldn't differ by more than a Cable Skew Delay. This is especially important when a signal is influenced by a ferrite core or similar damping measures.
Data Release Delay	400 ns	When I/O changes its state from true to false, the initiator must release the data lines for one Data Release Delay.
Deskew Delay	45 ns Fast SCSI: 20 ns	Time to decouple various signals.
Disconnection Delay	200 ns	When a target gets disconnected through the initiator, it must wait at least one Disconnection Delay before trying a new arbitration.
Hold Time	45 ns Fast SCSI: 10 ns	During a synchronous transfer, data must be asserted for at least one Hold Time to allow the receiving device to read them from the bus.
Negation Period	90 ns Fast SCSI: 30 ns	During a synchronous transfer, each REQ/REQB or ACK/ACKB pulse must be followed by at least one Negation Period.
Reset Hold Time	25 µs	The RST signal must be asserted for at least one Reset Hold Time before a reset is issued.
Selection Abort Time	200 ms	If a target doesn't react to a selection by asserting BSY during the Selection Abort Time, the initiator enforces a Bus Free phase (either through a reset condition, or by releasing the data lines and then releasing SEL and ATN).
Selection Timeout Delay	250 ms	During a Selection phase, a device should wait at least one Selection Timeout Delay for an answer before stopping the selection.
Transfer Period	Negotiated	The minimum time between two REQ/REQB or ACK/ACKB pulses. The possible Transfer Period is negotiated between the involved devices.
Power On to Selection	10 ns	A SCSI device should be able to answer to SCSI commands in this time after power-on. This is only a recommendation, but a meaningful one, as most host adapter drivers consider this the maximum time for a device to respond before its ID is skipped.
Reset to Selection	250 ms	Reset to Selection is the recommended maximum time a device is allowed to sit idle after a reset, before it is able to answer to commands.

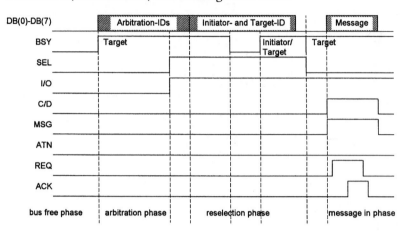

FIGURE B.19 Arbitration, Reselection, and Message In Phases

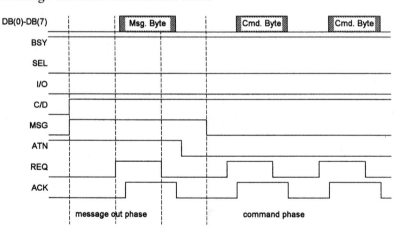

FIGURE B.20 Message Out and Command Phases

FIGURE B.21 Data In and Data Out Phases in Asynchronous Mode

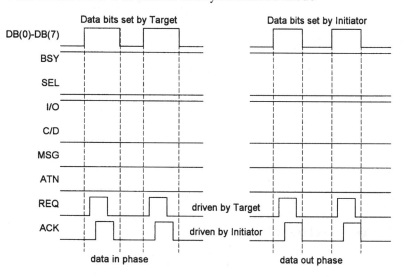

FIGURE B.22 Data In and Data Out Phases in Synchronous Mode, Offset = 4

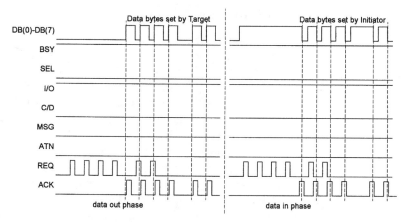

Status, Message In, and Bus Free Phases

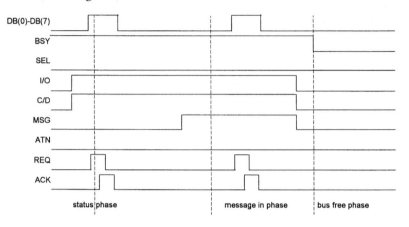

TERMINATION DIAGRAMS

Next to cabling, termination is the most crucial part of SCSI. The basic rule of termination is simple: both ends of the bus must be closed with termination circuits. However, in real life, termination and termination-related issues are the cause of at least 80 percent of all SCSI problems.

Termination Circuits

When the SCSI-1 specification was published, the established standard for termination was a passive terminator for each signal. Passive means that only passive parts were used, in this case two resistors, one with 220 ohm as a pull-up resistor against the TERMPWR line and the other a 330 ohm pull-down resistor to ground (0 V). This results in a standby signal level of about 3 volts if TERMPWR is at 5 volts. Passive termination has a few drawbacks. It draws a relatively high current and, although the specification stated that using resistors with +/−1 percent tolerance improves noise margins, most passive terminators use 5 percent resistor arrays just because they're about ten cents cheaper. Figure B.24 shows a schematic of single-ended passive termination. Figure B.25 shows the schematic of the differential version of the passive terminator.

SCSI-2 introduced active termination (shown in Figure B.26), also called Boulay-Terminator after Paul Boulay, who first designed it. Even with the historic card computer buses like S100 or the European ECB and SMP bus systems, active termination proved far superior to passive termination in signal quality and current draw. Active is far better than passive termination with respect to all signal quality issues, and it is

Single-Ended Passive Termination Circuit Diagram

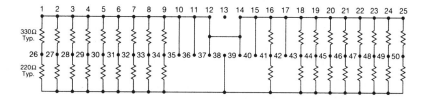

Differential Passive Terminator Circuit Diagram

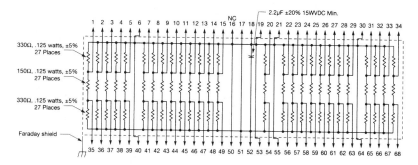

needed for Fast SCSI timing. However, one of active termination's biggest advantages is still underestimated. Specifically, it is far more forgiving of low voltage and noise on the TERMPWR line than passive termination. Unfortunately, as with many other advances in the high-tech industry, active termination's advantages make it more complex and more expensive to use than passive termination.

The official active termination specification recommends a voltage of 2.85 volts at the signal lines. Since good low-drop regulators need an input voltage of only 0.5 volts above the output, the terminator could be designed to work reliably with TERMPWR as low as 3.5 volts—far below the specification. To be on the safe side though, newer devices tend to use SCSI termination ICs (integrated circuits), like the Dallas Semiconductor DS2107A, that operates safely with TERMPWR from 4.0 to 5.25 volts.

As you can see in Figure B.26, the official active termination circuit needs a voltage regulator. Although this isn't an expensive part, many vendors tend to simplify this circuit and replace the voltage regulator with a simple green LED with 2.7 volts reverse breakdown voltage. In general, these cheap terminators work, but they are a bit on the risky side.

Single-Ended Active Termination Circuit Diagram

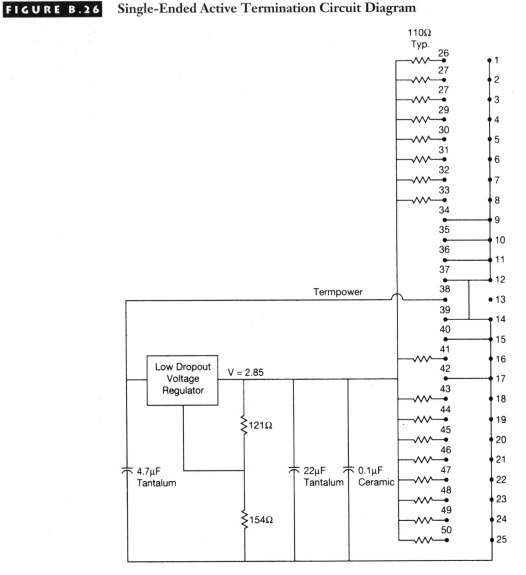

C

PC TECHNICAL
REFERENCE

The purpose of the three tables that follow, I/O Port Usage, Interrupt (IRQ) Usage, and DMA Channel Usage, is to give you a starting point for determining the possible configuration of add-on cards in your system. Due to the sheer number of add-on cards for the PC, these tables are by no means an exhaustive list of all possible devices and their resource uses. Be sure to check the installation or user manuals for the devices in your system to ensure that you don't introduce hardware conflicts when adding new cards.

| **TABLE C.1** | I/O Port Usage | | |

Hex Port Range	Defined Use	Other Uses	Comments
0–FF	Internal use only		Plug-in cards don't use I/O ports in this range.
100–1EF	<undefined>		
170–17F	<undefined>	Secondary floppy disk controller	Only 170–177 are used.
180–1EF	<undefined>	SCSI host adapters	A variety of ports can be used for SCSI.
1F0–1FF	Non-SCSI hard disk		Only 1F0–1F8 are used.
200–20F	Joystick port		
210–26F	<undefined>	Sound cards, SCSI host adapters	210, 220, 230, 240, 250, 260, 280 are typical for Sound Blaster and compatibles; SCSI can use any ports.
270–27F	Printer port		
280–29F	<undefined>	Sound cards	
2A0–2AF	<undefined>		
2B0–2DF	Alternative EGA		
2E0–2EF	GPIB interface card		
2F0–2FF	Serial port 2	Only 2F8–2FF are used.	
300–30F	Prototype card	MPU-401 MIDI, SCSI host adapter	MPU-401 uses 300–301
310–31F	Prototype card	SCSI host adapter, CD-ROM interface	
320–32F	<undefined>	SCSI host adapter, CD-ROM interface	
330–33F	<undefined>	MPU-401 MIDI, SCSI host adapter	MPU-401 uses 330–331
340–34F	<undefined>	SCSI host adapter, CD-ROM interface	
350–35F	<undefined>	CD-ROM interface	
360–36F	<undefined>		
370–37F	Parallel port 1	Only 378–37F are used.	
380–38F	SDLC or second bisync controller		
390–39F	Cluster adapter		
3A0–3AF	First bisync controller		
3B0–3BF	Monochrome video card and printer port	Printer port uses 3BC–3BF.	
3C0–3CF	EGA video card		
3D0–3DF	CGA video card		
3E0–3EF	<undefined>		
3F0–3FF	Floppy disk controller		Floppy disk uses 3F0–3F7; serial port 1 uses 3F8–3FF.
400–FFFF	EISA internal use		

TABLE C.2 Interrupt (IRQ) Usage

Interrupt Number	Defined Use	Other Uses	Comments
0	Timer		
1	Keyboard		
2	Cascade for IRQ 8-15	Sound card, MPU-401 MIDI	Devices on IRQ 2 are relocated to IRQ9.
3	Serial port 2	Sound card, CD-ROM	
4	Serial port 1		
5	Printer port 2	Sound card, serial port 3 or 4	
6	Floppy disk controller		
7	Printer port 1	Sound card	
8	Clock		
9	IRQ 2	SCSI host adapter	
10	<undefined>	Sound card, SCSI host adapter, CD-ROM	
11	<undefined>	Sound card, SCSI host adapter, network card, CD-ROM	
12	<undefined>	SCSI host adapter, network card	
13	Math coprocessor		
14	Non-SCSI hard disk controller	SCSI host adapter	
15	<undefined>	SCSI host adapter, network card	

TABLE C.3 DMA Channel Usage

DMA Channel	Defined Use	Other Uses	Comments
0	<undefined>	SCSI host adapter, sound card	8-bit DMA
1	<undefined>	Sound card	8-bit DMA
2	Disk		8-bit DMA
3	<undefined>	Sound card	8-bit DMA
4	Cascade for DMA 0-3		
5	<undefined>	SCSI host adapter, sound card	16-bit DMA
6	<undefined>	SCSI host adapter, sound card, CD-ROM	16-bit DMA
7	<undefined>	SCSI host adapter, sound card, CD-ROM	16-bit DMA

A PROFILE OF ASPI PROGRAMMING

ASPI stands for advanced SCSI programming interface. It is an Adaptec-developed interface specification for sending commands to SCSI host adapters. The interface provides an abstraction layer that insulates the programmer from considerations of the particular host adapter used.

With ASPI, software drivers can be broken into two components: the low-level ASPI manager, which is operating system and hardware dependent, and the ASPI module. The ASPI manager accepts ASPI commands and performs the steps necessary to send the SCSI command to the target. For example, although the Adaptec AHA-152x and AHA-274x host adapters have very different hardware, the ASPI interface to these boards is the same. (Obviously, Adaptec's code that implements the ASPI interface, e.g., ASPI2DOS.SYS, for each board is quite different.)

The ASPI module is tailored to the command set of a particular peripheral, such as CD-ROM. Although an ASPI-based CD-ROM driver would have to handle the differences between different CD-ROM drives, it would not have to handle host adapter differences.

I. ASPI DEVELOPER INFORMATION

In response to widespread demand for ASPI software, Adaptec provides the ASPI Software Developer's Kit (SDK), a complete toolkit for developing SCSI drivers for PC peripherals. This kit is designed to help you write your own ASPI device module that will work with any ASPI-compliant host adapter. The following sections describe the ASPI specifications for DOS, Windows, and OS/2. Updated information can be downloaded from the Adaptec BBS, 408-945-7727, in the ASPI Developer file library.

Adaptec also has a developer program (Adaptec Compatibility Advantage Program). To register, call 800-934-2766 and request the ACAP Developer Information Pack. You may also request the ACAP Program Application from an interactive fax system at 408-957-7150.

The ASPI Software Developer Kit (v2.2) contains the following documentation and tools.

- A copy of the ASPI specification document and programming guides for four major operating systems: DOS, Windows, OS/2, and NetWare.

- Sample assembler source code for DOS.

- A SCSI DOS disk driver, which can handle at most one SCSI partition on one SCSI drive.

- An ASPI demo program, which provides examples of how to use the ASPI programming interface. The main program obtains the ASPI entry point and calls subroutines for the different ASPI functions:

    ASPI Host Adapter Inquiry Command

    ASPI Get Device Type Command

    ASPI Execute SCSI I/O Command

    ASPI Reset SCSI Device Command using posting

- Sample C source code for Windows.

- An ASPI for Windows utility, which constantly scans the SCSI bus and displays the name of a device, if it finds one.

- Sample C source code for OS/2.

- An ASPI demo utility for OS/2, which scans the SCSI bus and displays information about the targets it finds. It is a 32-bit application created with Borland C++ for OS/2. A project file and makefile are included.

- An ASPI device driver for OS/2. This driver is intended for simple, single-threaded applications. If you need to support multitasking, you need to make your own modifications.
- A debugging utility for ASPI for Windows development.
- A complimentary copy of Adaptec EZ-SCSI, the latest version of DOS/Windows software managers, plus an installation program, CD-ROM drivers, and other utilities.

To use this kit, it is assumed that you have a solid understanding of system-level programming and are familiar at least with device driver development for the operating system you are targeting for SCSI. Prior to getting this kit, you should get the device driver kit from the appropriate operating system vendor.

To order in the U.S. and Canada, call 800-442-7274. To order internationally, call 408-957-7274. Price is US $150.00.

NOTE *Numerous tables of information appear throughout this chapter. For convenience, we have abbreviated certain column headings as R/W. In cases where R/W appears as a heading, the entries in that column indicate whether the field is sent to ASPI (W), returned from ASPI (R), or reserved (—).*

II. ASPI for DOS Specification

Two steps are involved in order for a driver to make use of ASPI: obtain the ASPI entry point, and call the ASPI driver. Typically, the entry point is obtained once, and then ASPI calls are made multiple times within a device driver. ASPI function calls are used to return data about the ASPI manager, host adapter, and SCSI devices, but they are mainly used to execute SCSI I/O requests. The ASPI layer is re-entrant and can accept function calls before previous calls have completed. A call will normally return immediately with zero status, indicating that the request has been successfully queued. In order to continue program flow after the function completes, the driver either polls ASPI status or enables the post bit, which turns control over to a specified routine upon completion of the ASPI call.

NOTE *When a program makes a call to an ASPI manager, the manager uses the caller's stack. It is therefore necessary for the program to allocate enough stack memory for itself as well as the ASPI manager. There is no fixed amount of stack needed by all ASPI managers; a programmer needs to be aware of this constraint and test code with individual managers for compatibility.*

Accessing ASPI

Device drivers wishing to access ASPI must open the driver by performing a DOS Int 21h function call OPEN A FILE as follows:

On Entry:

AX = 3D00h

DS:DX = Pointer to SCSIMGR$, 0

On Return:

AX = File handle if carry flag is not set

Error code if carry flag is set

Getting the ASPI Entry Point

Device drivers can get the entry point to ASPI by performing a DOS Int 21h function call IOCTL READ as follows:

On Entry:

AX = 4402h

DS:DX = Pointer to data returned (4 bytes)

CX = 4

BX = File handle

On Return:

AX = Nothing

Data returned in DS:DX contains the ASPI entry point:

Byte 0–1: ASPI Entry Point Offset

Byte 2–3: ASPI Entry Point Segment

Closing ASPI

Device drivers wishing to close ASPI must do it by performing a DOS Int 21h function call CLOSE A FILE as follows:

On Entry:

AH = 3Eh

BX = File handle

On Return:

> AX = Error code if carry flag is set
>
> Nothing if carry flag is not set

Calling ASPI

The following is an example of how to call the ASPI manager:

```
              .MODEL SMALL
              .STACK 100h               ;100h byte stack

              .DATA
SCSIMgrString db "SCSIMGR$"
              dw 0                       ;NULL-terminate string
ASPI_Entry    db 4 dup (?)
SRB           db 58 dup (0)             ;Initialize SRB for Host
                                        ;Adapter Inquiry
              .CODE
start:        mov  ax,@DATA
              mov  ds,ax                 ;Init DS
              mov  ax,03D00h
              lea  dx,SCSIMgrString
              int  21h                   ;Open ASPI Manager
              jc   NoASPIManager         ;Branch if none found
              push ax                    ;Save ASPI File Handle

              mov  bx,ax                  ;BX = File Handle
              mov  ax,4402h
              lea  dx,ASPI_Entry         ;Store entry point here
              mov  cx,4                   ;Four bytes to transfer
              int  21h                   ;Get ASPI entry point

              mov  ah,03Eh
              pop  bx                     ;BX = ASPI File Handle
              int  21h                    ;Close ASPI Manager

              push ds                     ;Push SRB's segment
              lea  bx,SRB
```

```
                push bx                              ;Push SRB's offset
                lea  bx,ASPI_Entry
                call DWORD PTR [bx]                  ;Call ASPI
                add  sp,4                            ;Restore the stack


ASPI_Exit:      mov  ax,4C00h                        ;Exit to DOS
                int  21h
                ret


NoASPIManager:                                       ;No ASPI Manager found!!
                jmp  ASPI_Exit                       ;Handle it.
                END
```

As shown in this sample code, the SRB's segment is first pushed onto the stack followed by its offset. ASPI is then called directly.

SCSI REQUEST BLOCK (SRB)

A SCSI request block (SRB) (see Table D.1) contains the command to be executed by the ASPI manager and is used by both drivers and application programs. An SRB consists of an SRB header followed by additional fields dependent on the command code. All request blocks have an eight-byte header.

Command Codes

The Command Code field is used to indicate which of the ASPI services is being accessed. Refer to Valid ASPI Command Codes in Table D.2.

TABLE D.1 **SCSI Request Block**

Offset	# Bytes	Description	R/W
00h (00)	01h (01)	Command Code	W
01h (01)	01h (01)	Status	R
02h (02)	01h (01)	Host Adapter Number	W
03h (03)	01h (01)	SCSI Request Flags	W
04h (04)	04h (04)	Reserved for Expansion = 0	—

Status

The Status Byte field is used to post the status of the command. Refer to ASPI Status Bytes in Table D.3.

Host Adapter Number

The Host Adapter Number field specifies which installed host adapter the request is intended for. Host adapter numbers are always assigned by the SCSI manager layer beginning with zero.

SCSI Request Flags

The SCSI Request Flags field definition is command code-specific.

Reserved for Expansion

The last four bytes of the header are reserved and must be zero.

ASPI COMMAND CODES

ASPI Command Code = 0: Host Adapter Inquiry

The status byte (defined in Table D.4) will always return with a nonzero status. A SCSI Request Completed Without Error (01h) status indicates that the remaining fields are valid. An Invalid Host Adapter Number (81h) status indicates that the specified host adapter is not installed.

This function is used to get information on the installed host adapter hardware, including number of host adapters installed. It can be issued once with host adapter zero specified to get the number of host adapters. If further information is desired, it can be issued for each individual host adapter.

The SCSI Request Flags field is currently undefined for this command and should be zeroed.

The SCSI Manager ID field contains a 16-byte ASCII string describing the SCSI manager.

The Host Adapter ID field contains a 16-byte ASCII string describing the SCSI host adapter.

The definition of the Host Adapter Unique Parameters field is left to implementation notes specific to a particular host adapter.

TABLE D.2	Valid ASPI Command Codes

Command Code	Description
00h	Host Adapter Inquiry
01h	Get Device Type
02h	Execute SCSI I/O Command
03h	Abort SCSI I/O Command
04h	Reset SCSI Device
05h	Set Host Adapter Parameters
06h	Get Disk Drive Information
07h-7Fh	Reserved for Future Expansion
80h-FFh	Reserved for Vendor Unique

TABLE D.3	ASPI Status Bytes

Status Byte	Description
00h	SCSI Request in Progress
01h	SCSI Request Completed Without Error
02h	SCSI Request Aborted by Host
04h	SCSI Request Completed With Error
80h	Invalid SCSI Request
81h	Invalid Host Adapter Number
82h	SCSI Device Not Installed

ASPI Command Code = 1: Get Device Type

This command (defined in Table D.5) will always return with nonzero status.

A SCSI Request Completed Without Error (01h) status indicates that the specified device is installed and the peripheral device type field is valid. A SCSI Device Not Installed Error (82h) indicates that the peripheral device type field is not valid.

This command is intended for use by various drivers, during initialization, for identifying the targets that they need to support. A CD-ROM driver, for example, can scan each target/LUN on each installed host adapter looking for the device type corresponding to CD-ROM devices. This eliminates the need for each driver to duplicate the effort of scanning the SCSI bus for devices.

The peripheral device type is determined by sending a SCSI Inquiry command to the given target. Refer to any SCSI specification to learn more about the Inquiry command.

The SCSI Request Flags field is currently undefined for this command and should be zeroed.

ASPI Command Code = 2: Execute SCSI I/0 Command

This command (defined in Table D.6) will usually return with zero status indicating that the request was queued successfully. Command com-

TABLE D.4 ASPI Command Code = 0: Host Adapter Inquiry

Offset	# Bytes	Description	R/W
00h (00)	01h (01)	Command Code = 0	W
01h (01)	01h (01)	Status	R
02h (02)	01h (01)	Host Adapter Number	W
03h (03)	01h (01)	SCSI Request Flags	W
04h (04)	04h (04)	Reserved for Expansion = 0	—
08h (08)	01h (01)	Number of Host Adapters	R
09h (09)	01h (01)	ID of Host Adapter	R
0Ah (10)	10h (16)	SCSI Manager ID	R
1Ah (26)	10h (16)	Host Adapter ID	R
2Ah (42)	10h (16)	Host Adapter Unique Parameters	R

TABLE D.5 ASPI Command Code = 1: Get Device Type

Offset	# Bytes	Description	R/W
00h (00)	01h (01)	Command Code = 1	W
01h (01)	01h (01)	Status	R
02h (02)	01h (01)	Host Adapter Number	W
03h (03)	01h (01)	SCSI Request Flags	W
04h (04)	04h (04)	Reserved for Expansion = 0	—
08h (08)	01h (01)	Target ID	W
09h (09)	01h (01)	LUN	W
0Ah (10)	01h (01)	Peripheral Device Type of Target/LU	R

pletion can be determined by polling for nonzero status or through the use of the Post Routine Address field (discussed later in the section ASPI Command Posting). Keep in mind that if you are going to use polling, interrupts must be enabled.

The SCSI Request Flags Byte Is Defined as Follows:

7	6	5	4	3	2	1	0
Rsvd	*Rsvd*	*Rsvd*	*Direction Bits*		*Rsvd*	*Link*	*Post*

The Post bit specifies whether posting is enabled (bit 0 = 1) or disabled (bit 0 = 0).

The Link bit specifies whether linking is enabled (bit 1 = 1) or disabled (bit 1 = 0).

The Direction Bits specify which direction the transfer is:

00 Direction determined by SCSI command. Length not checked.

01 Transfer from SCSI target to host. Length checked.

10 Transfer from host to SCSI target. Length checked.

11 No data transfer.

Offset	# Bytes	Description	R/W
00h (00)	01h (01)	Command Code = 2	W
01h (01)	01h (01)	Status	R
02h (02)	01h (01)	Host Adapter Number	W
03h (03)	01h (01)	SCSI Request Flags	W
04h (04)	04h (04)	Reserved for Expansion = 0	—
08h (08)	01h (01)	Target ID	W
09h (09)	01h (01)	LUN	W
0Ah (10)	04h (04)	Data Allocation Length	W
0Eh (14)	01h (01)	Sense Allocation Length (N)	W
0Fh (15)	02h (02)	Data Buffer Pointer (Offset)	W
11h (17)	02h (02)	Data Buffer Pointer (Segment)	W
13h (19)	02h (02)	SRB Link Pointer (Offset)	W
15h (21)	02h (02)	SRB Link Pointer (Segment)	W
17h (23)	01h (01)	SCSI CDB Length (M)	W
18h (24)	01h (01)	Host Adapter Status	R
19h (25)	01h (01)	Target Status	R
1Ah (26)	02h (02)	Post Routine Address (Offset)	W
1Ch (28)	02h (02)	Post Routine Address (Segment)	W
1Eh (30)	22h (34)	Reserved for ASPI Workspace	—
40h (64)		SCSI Command Descriptor Block (CDB)	W
40h+M	N	Sense Allocation Area	R

The Target ID and LUN fields are used to specify the peripheral device involved in the I/O.

The Data Allocation Length field indicates the number of bytes to be transferred. If the SCSI command to be executed does not transfer data (i.e., Rewind, Start Unit, etc.) the Data Allocation Length must be set to zero.

The Sense Allocation Length field indicates, in bytes, the number of bytes allocated at the end of the SRB for sense data. A request sense is automatically generated if a check condition is presented at the end of a SCSI command.

The Data Buffer Pointer field is a pointer to the I/O data buffer. You place the logical address here. ASPI will convert it to the physical address in the case of a bus master or DMA transfer.

The SRB Link Pointer field is a pointer to the next SRB in a chain. See the discussion on linking for more information.

The SCSI CDB Length field establishes the length, in bytes, of the SCSI command descriptor block (CDB).

The Host Adapter Status field is used to report the host adapter status as follows:

00h Host adapter did not detect any error

11h Selection timeout

12h Data overrun/underrun

13h Unexpected bus free

14h Target bus phase sequence failure

The Target Status field is used to report the target's SCSI status including:

00h No target status

02h Check status (sense data is in sense allocation area)

08h Specified target/LUN is busy

18h Reservation conflict

The Post Routine Address field, if specified, is called when the I/O is completed. See the discussion on posting below for more information.

The SCSI command descriptor block (CDB) field contains the CDB as defined by the target's SCSI command set. The length of the SCSI CDB is specified in the SCSI Command Length field.

The sense allocation area is filled with sense data on a check condition. The maximum length of this field is specified in the Sense Allocation Length field. Note that the target can return fewer than the number of sense bytes requested.

SCSI Command Linking with ASPI

ASPI provides the ability to use SCSI linking to guarantee the sequential execution of several commands. Note that the use of this feature requires the involved target(s) to support SCSI linking.

To use SCSI linking, a chain of SRBs is built with the SRB link pointer used to link the elements together. The link bit should be set in the SCSI request flags byte of all SRBs except the last in the chain. When a SCSI target returns indicating that the linked command is complete, the next SRB is immediately processed, and the appropriate CDB is dispatched. When using SCSI linking, make sure that the linking flags in the SCSI CDB agree with the link bit in the SCSI request flags. Inconsistencies can cause unpredictable results. For example, setting the CDB up for linking but failing to set the link bit may result in a random address being used for the next SRB pointer.

Any error returned from the target on a linked command will break the chain. Note that if linking without tags is used, as defined in SCSI, posting may not occur on any elements in the chain until the chain is complete. If you have the post bit set in each SRB's SCSI request flags byte, then each SRB's post routine will be called.

NOTE *It is strongly recommended that you do not use SCSI linking. There are many SCSI targets, as well as SCSI host adapters, which do not handle SCSI linking and will not work with your ASPI module.*

ASPI Command Posting

To use posting, the post bit must be set in the SCSI request flags. Posting refers to the SCSI manager making a FAR call to a post routine as specified in the SRB. The post routine is called to indicate that the SRB is complete. The specific SRB completed is indicated by a four-byte SRB pointer on the stack. It is assumed that all registers are preserved by the post routine.

The ASPI manager will first push the completed SRB's two-byte segment onto the stack followed by its two-byte offset. The following is a sample ASPI post handler:

```
ASPI_Post       proc far
                push bp
                mov  bp,sp


                pusha                   ;Save all registers
                push ds
                push es


                mov  bx,[bp+6]          ;BX = SRBs offset
                mov  es,[bp+8]          ;ES = SRBs segment
                     .                  ;ES:BX points to SRB


                     .

                     .

                pop  es
                pop  ds
                popa
                pop  bp                 ;Restore all registers
                retf                    ;and return to ASPI
ASPI_Post       endp
```

When your post routine is first entered, the stack will look as follows:

Top of Stack	[SP+0] —>	Return Address (Offset)
	[SP+2] —>	Return Address (Segment)
	[SP+4] —>	SRB Pointer (Offset)
	[SP+6] —>	SRB Pointer (Segment)
	...	
	...	
	...	

You may issue any ASPI command from within your post routine except for an Abort command. Your post routine should get in and out as quickly as possible.

ASPI Command Code = 3: Abort SCSI I/O Command

Offset	# Bytes	Description	R/W
00h (00)	01h (01)	Command Code = 3	W
01h (01)	01h (01)	Status	R
02h (02)	01h (01)	Host Adapter Number	W
03h (03)	01h (01)	SCSI Request Flags	W
04h (04)	04h (04)	Reserved for Expansion = 0	—
08h (08)	02h (02)	SRB Pointer to Abort (Offset)	W
0Ah (10)	02h (12)	SRB Pointer to Abort (Segment)	W

Posting can be used by device drivers and terminate and stay resident (TSR) programs, which need to operate in an interrupt-driven fashion.

ASPI Command Code = 3: Abort SCSI I/O Command

This command (defined in Table D.7) is used to request that an SRB be aborted. It should be issued on any I/O request that has not completed if the driver wishes to timeout on that request. Success of the Abort command is never assured.

This command always returns with SCSI Request Completed Without Error, but the actual failure or success of the abort operation is indicated by the status eventually returned in the SRB specified.

The SCSI Request Flags field is currently undefined for this command and should be zeroed.

The SRB Pointer to Abort field contains a pointer to the SRB that is to be aborted.

NOTE   *An Abort command should not be issued during a post routine.*

ASPI Command Code = 4: Reset SCSI Device

This command (defined in Table D.8) is used to reset a specific SCSI target. Note that the structure passed is nearly identical to the execute SCSI I/O SRB except that some of the fields are not used.

This command usually returns with zero status indicating that the request was queued successfully. Command completion can be determined by polling for nonzero status or through the use of posting.

The SCSI Request Flags Byte Is Defined as Follows:

7	6	5	4	3	2	1	0
Reserved							*Post*

The Post bit specifies whether posting is enabled (bit 0 = 1) or disabled (bit 0 = 0).

TABLE D.8 ASPI Command Code = 4: Reset SCSI Device

Offset	# Bytes	Description	R/W
00h (00)	01h (01)	Command Code = 4	W
01h (01)	01h (01)	Status	R
02h (02)	01h (01)	Host Adapter Number	W
03h (03)	01h (01)	SCSI Request Flags	W
04h (04)	04h (04)	Reserved for Expansion = 0	—
08h (08)	01h (01)	Target ID	W
09h (09)	01h (01)	LUN	W
0Ah (10)	0Eh (14)	Reserved	—
18h (24)	01h (01)	Host Adapter Status	R
19h (25)	01h (01)	Target Status	R
1Ah (26)	02h (02)	Post Routine Address (Offset)	W
1Ch (28)	02h (02)	Post Routine Address (Segment)	W
1Eh (30)	02h (02)	Reserved for ASPI Workspace	—

TABLE D.9 ASPI Command Code = 5: Set Host Adapter Parameters

Offset	# Bytes	Description	R/W
00h (00)	201h (01)	Command Code = 5	W
01h (01)	01h (01)	Status	R
02h (02)	01h (01)	Host Adapter Number	W
03h (03)	01h (01)	SCSI Request Flags	W
04h (04)	04h (04)	Reserved for Expansion = 0	—
08h (08)	10h (16)	Host Adapter Unique Parameters	W

ASPI Command Code = 5: Set Host Adapter Parameters

The definition of the host adapter unique parameters (shown in Table D.9) is left to implementation notes specific to a particular host adapter.

ASPI managers that support this command code always return with a status of SCSI Request Completed Without Error (01h). ASPI managers that do not support this command code always return with a status of Invalid SCSI Request (80h).

ASPI Command Code = 6: Get Disk Drive Information

This command (defined in Table D.10) is intended for use by SCSI disk drivers that need to determine which disk drives are already being controlled by some BIOS/DOS and which disk drives are available for use by the disk driver. It also provides a means to determine which drives are not under control of the BIOS/DOS yet are still accessible via Int 13h. This is useful because many disk caching utilities will cache Int 13h requests but not any disk driver requests. There are also some disk utility programs that will allow the user to access physical sectors on a disk via Int 13h.

The SCSI Requests Flags field is currently undefined for this command and should be zero.

ASPI Command Code = 6: Get Disk Drive Information

Offset	# Bytes	Description	R/W
00h (00)	01h (01)	Command Code = 6	W
01h (01)	01h (01)	Status	R
02h (02)	01h (01)	Host Adapter Number	W
03h (03)	01h (01)	SCSI Request Flags	W
04h (04)	04h (04)	Reserved for Expansion = 0	—
08h (08)	01h (01)	Target ID	W
09h (09)	01h (01)	LUN	W
0Ah (10)	01h (01)	Drive Flags	R
0Bh (11)	01h (01)	Int 13h Drive	R
0Ch (12)	01h (01)	Preferred Head Translation	R
0Dh (13)	01h (01)	Preferred Sector Translation	R
0Eh (14)	0Ah (10)	Reserved for Expansion = 0	—

The Drive Flags Byte Is Defined as Follows:

7	6	5	4	3	2	1	0
Rsvd	*Rsvd*	*Rsvd*	*Rsvd*	*Rsvd*	*Rsvd*	*Int 13 Info*	

All reserved (Rsvd) bits will return zeroed.

The Int 13 Info bits return information pertaining to the Int 13h drive field:

00 The given drive (HA #/target/LUN) is not accessible via Int 13h. If you wish to read/write to this drive, you will need to send ASPI read/write requests to the drive. The Int 13h Drive field is invalid.

01 The given drive (HA #/target/LUN) is accessible via Int 13h. The Int 13h Drive field contains the drive's Int 13h drive number. This drive is under the control of DOS.

10 The given drive (HA #/target/LUN) is accessible via Int 13h. The Int 13h Drive field contains the drive's Int 13h drive number. This drive is not under control of DOS and can be used, for example, by a SCSI disk driver.

11 Invalid.

The Int 13h Drive field returns the Int 13 drive number for the given host adapter number, target ID, and LUN. Valid Int 13 drive numbers range for 00-FFh.

The Preferred Head Translation field indicates the given host adapter's/disk drive's preferred head translation method. A typical value will be 64 heads.

The Preferred Sector Translation field indicates the given host adapter's/disk drive's preferred sector translation method. A typical value will be 32 sectors per track.

TABLE D.11	**Description of ASPI for Windows Functions**

Function	Description
GetASPISupportInfo	This function returns the number of host adapters installed and other miscellaneous information. You should call this function to make sure that ASPI is properly initialized before calling the SendASPICommand function.
SendASPICommand	This function allows you to send an ASPI for Windows command. All of your SRBs and data buffers must be in locked memory before being passed to ASPI.

ASPI for DOS Under Windows 3.x

Windows is a graphical user interface that runs under DOS as an application; however, writing a device driver or application capable of making ASPI calls in a Windows environment is not as simple as in the strictly DOS case. The problem arises because ASPI for DOS uses a real mode interface and Windows uses the DOS protected mode interface (DPMI). Whereas ASPI expects a real mode segment and offset for the SRB and the entry point of ASPI, Windows uses a selector and offset to address data and code. In order to program correctly in this environment, a consortium of companies, Microsoft and Intel among them, have written a specification called the DOS Protected Mode Interface Specification. The details of the specification are too complex to go into detail here, but it is recommended that a copy be obtained from the DPMI committee for programming purposes. As a brief overview, two steps need to be followed to access ASPI for DOS from a Windows application:

1. Allocate all SRBs and buffers down in real mode memory. This can be accomplished using Windows' GlobalDosAlloc routine or using DPMI interrupt 31h, function 100h. This makes it possible for the ASPI module and manager to locate the SRB and data buffers using segments and offsets.

2. Call the real mode procedure with Far Return Frame Function (interrupt 31h, function 0301h). This makes it possible to call the ASPI manager, which is a real mode procedure.

For more information on programming ASPI in the Windows environment, refer to the next section, "ASPI for Windows Specification."

III. ASPI for Windows Specification

ASPI for Windows is implemented as a dynamic link library (DLL). The name of this file is called winaspi.dll. ASPI function calls (shown in Table D.11) are used to return information about the ASPI manager, host adapter, and SCSI devices, but they are mainly used to execute SCSI I/O requests. The ASPI for Windows layer is fully multitasking and can accept function calls before previous calls have completed. There are two functions that need to be imported from winaspi.dll into your Windows application.

ASPI MANAGERS FOR WINDOWS

It is not the intent of this specification to define the protocol between winaspi.dll and any DOS ASPI managers that may be loaded. There are many reasons for this, including the following:

- Some hardware companies may decide to write an ASPI for Windows manager without concurrent ASPI for DOS support.

- Some may decide to have winaspi.dll communicate with a Windows 386 enhanced mode virtual device driver (VxD).

- Some may decide to only support Windows 3.1, which may or may not have improved hardware support.

It is also not the intent of this specification to define which modes of Windows need to be supported. We anticipate that most hardware companies will support ASPI for Windows in standard and 386 enhanced modes, and forego real mode support.

GetASPISupportInfo

WORD GetASPISupportInfo(VOID)

The GetASPISupportInfo function returns the number of host adapters installed and other miscellaneous information. It is recommended that this function be called first before issuing an ASPI command to ensure ASPI has been properly initialized. This function call does not perform any initialization itself, but rather confirms that everything is ready for processing.

This function has no parameters.

Returns

The return value specifies the outcome of the function. The LOBYTE returns the number of host adapters installed if the HIBYTE value equals SS_COMP. The HIBYTE returns whether ASPI for Windows is ready to accept ASPI commands. Refer to the sample code. The HIBYTE is defined as shown in Table D.12.

TABLE D.12	**HIBYTE Return Values for GetASPISupportInfo**

Value	Meaning
SS_COMP	SCSI/ASPI request has completed without error.
SS_OLD_MANAGER	One or more ASPI for DOS managers are loaded that do not support ASPI for Windows.
SS_ILLEGAL_MODE	This ASPI manager does not support this mode of Windows. You will typically see this error code when running Windows in real mode.
SS_NO_ASPI	No ASPI managers are loaded. This is typically caused by a DOS ASPI manager not being resident in memory.
SS_FAILED_INIT	For some reason, other than SS_OLD_MANAGER, SS_ILLEGAL_MODE, or SS_NO_ASPI, ASPI for Windows could not properly initialize itself. This may be caused by a lack of system resources.

Example

The following example returns the current status of ASPI for Windows:

```
WORD ASPIStatus;

BYTE NumAdapters;

HWND hwnd;

        .

        .

ASPIStatus = GetASPISupportInfo();

switch ( HIBYTE(ASPIStatus) )

{

  case SS_COMP:

    //ASPI for Windows is properly initialized

    NumAdapters = LOBYTE(ASPIStatus);

    break;

  case SS_NO_ASPI:

    MessageBox( hwnd, "No ASPI managers were found!!", NULL, MB_ICONSTOP );

    return 0;

  case SS_ILLEGAL_MODE:

    MessageBox( hwnd, "ASPI for Windows does not support this mode!!", NULL, MB_ICONSTOP );

    return 0;

  case SS_OLD_MANAGER:

    MessageBox( hwnd, "An ASPI manager which does not support Windows is resident!!",

     NULL, MB_ICONSTOP );

    return 0;
```

```
    default:

    MessageBox( hwnd, ASPI for Windows is not initialized!!",

     NULL, MB_ICONSTOP );

    return 0;

}
```

SendASPICommand—SC_HA_INQUIRY

WORD SendASPICommand(lpSRB)
LPSRB lpSRB;

The SendASPICommand function with command code
SC_HA_INQUIRY (defined in Table D.13) is used to get information
on the installed host adapter hardware, including the number of host
adapters installed.

Parameter	Description
lpSRB	Points to the following SCSI request block:

```
typedef struct
{
  BYTE   SRB_Cmd;               // ASPI command code = SC_HA_INQUIRY
  BYTE   SRB_Status;            // ASPI command status byte
  BYTE   SRB_HaId;              // ASPI host adapter number
  BYTE   SRB_Flags;            // ASPI request flags
  DWORD SRB_Hdr_Rsvd;          // Reserved, MUST = 0
  BYTE   HA_Count;             // Number of host adapters present
  BYTE   HA_SCSI_ID;           // SCSI ID of host adapter
  BYTE   HA_ManagerId[16];     // String describing the manager
  BYTE   HA_Identifier[16];    // String describing the host adapter
  BYTE   HA_Unique[16];        // Host Adapter Unique parameters
} SRB_HAInquiry;
```

Returns

The return value specifies the outcome of the function. One of the values shown in Table D.14 will be returned by ASPI for Windows.

SRB_HAInquiry Structure Definition

Member	Description	R/W
SRB_Cmd	This field must contain SC_HA_INQUIRY.	W
SRB_Status	On return, this field will be the same as the return status defined below.	R
SRB_HaId	This field specifies which installed host adapter the request is intended for. Host adapter numbers are always assigned by the SCSI manager layer beginning with zero.	W
SRB_Flags	The SRB Flags field is currently reserved for this function and must be zeroed before passed to the ASPI manager.	W
SRB_Hdr_Rsvd	This DWORD field is currently reserved for this function and must be zeroed before passed to the ASPI manager.	—
HA_Count	The ASPI manager will set this field with the number of host adapters installed under ASPI. For example, a return value of 2 indicates that host adapters #0 and #1 are valid. To determine the total number of host adapters in the system, the SRB_HaId field should be set to zero, or GetASPISupportInfo can be used.	R
HA_SCSI_ID	The ASPI manager will set this field with the SCSI ID of the given host adapter.	R
HA_ManagerId[..]	The ASPI manager will fill this 16-character buffer with an ASCII string describing the ASPI manager.	R
HA_Identifier[..]	The ASPI manager will fill this 16-character buffer with an ASPI string describing the SCSI host adapter.	R
HA_Unique[..]	The ASPI manager will fill this 16-byte buffer with host adapter unique parameters. The definition is left to implementation notes specific to a particular host adapter.	R

Values Returned by ASPI for Windows

Value	Meaning
SS_COMP	SCSI/ASPI request has completed without error
SS_INVALID_HA	Invalid host adapter number
SS_INVALID_SRB	The SCSI request block (SRB) has one or more parameters set incorrectly

Example

The following example retrieves host adapter hardware information from adapter #0:

```
SRB_HAInquiry MySRB;

WORD ASPI_Status;

        .

        .


MySRB.SRB_Cmd = SC_HA_INQUIRY;

MySRB.SRB_HaId = 0;

MySRB.SRB_Flags = 0;
```

```
MySRB.SRB_Hdr_Rsvd = 0;
ASPI_Status = SendASPICommand ( (LPSRB) &MySRB );
                        .
                        .
```

SendASPICommand—SC_GET_DEV_TYPE

WORD SendASPICommand(lpSRB)
    LPSRB lpSRB;

The SendASPICommand function with command code
SC_GET_DEV_TYPE (defined in Table D.15) is intended for use by
Windows applications for identifying the targets they need to support.
For example, a Windows tape backup package can scan each target/LUN
on each installed host adapter looking for the device type corresponding
to sequential access devices. This eliminates the need for each Windows
application to duplicate the effort of scanning the SCSI bus for devices.

NOTE *Rather than use this command, some Windows applications may favor scan-*
ning the SCSI bus themselves in case a SCSI device was not present during
ASPI initialization but was rather powered up after ASPI initialization.

Parameter	Description
lpSRB	Points to the following SCSI request block:

```
typedef struct
{
  BYTE   SRB_Cmd;                     // ASPI command code = SC_GET_DEV_TYPE
  BYTE   SRB_Status;                  // ASPI command status byte
  BYTE   SRB_HaId;                    // ASPI host adapter number
  BYTE   SRB_Flags;                   // ASPI request flags
  DWORD  SRB_Hdr_Rsvd;                // Reserved, MUST = 0
  BYTE   SRB_Target;                  // Target's SCSI ID
  BYTE   SRB_Lun;                     // Target's LUN number
  BYTE   SRB_DeviceType;              // Target's peripheral device type
} SRB_GDEVBlock;
```

Returns

The return value specifies the outcome of the function. One of the values shown in Table D.16 will be returned by ASPI for Windows.

SRB_GDEVBlock Structure Definition

Member	Description	R/W
SRB_Cmd	This field must contain SC_GET_DEV_TYPE.	W
SRB_Status	On return, this field will be the same as the return status defined below.	R
SRB_HaId	This field specifies which installed host adapter the request is intended for. Host adapter numbers are always assigned by the SCSI manager layer beginning with zero.	W
SRB_Flags	The SRB Flags field is currently reserved for this function and must be zeroed before passed to the ASPI manager.	W
SRB_Hdr_Rsvd	This DWORD field is currently reserved for this function and must be zeroed before passed to the ASPI manager.	—
SRB_Target	Target ID of device.	W
SRB_Lun	Logical unit number (LUN) of device.	W
SRB_DeviceType	The ASPI manager will fill this field with the peripheral device type. Refer to any SCSI specification to learn more about the SCSI Inquiry command.	R

Return Values for SendASPI Command SC_GET_DEV_TYPE

Value	Meaning
SS_COMP	SCSI/ASPI request has completed without error
SS_INVALID_HA	Invalid host adapter number
SS_NO_DEVICE	SCSI device not installed
SS_INVALID_SRB	The SCSI request block (SRB) has one or more parameters set incorrectly

Example

The following example retrieves the peripheral device type from host adapter #0, target ID #4, and LUN #0.

```
SRB_GDEVBlock MySRB;

WORD ASPI_Status;

        .

        .

MySRB.SRB_Cmd = SC_GET_DEV_TYPE;

MySRB.SRB_HaId = 0;

MySRB.SRB_Flags = 0;

MySRB.SRB_Hdr_Rsvd = 0;

MySRB.SRB_Target = 4;

MySRB.SRB_Lun = 0;

ASPI_Status = SendASPICommand ( (LPSRB) &MySRB );

        .
```

```
/**************************************************/
/* If ASPI_Status == SS_COMP, MySRB.SRB_DeviceType */
/* will contain the peripheral device type.       */
/**************************************************/
            .

            .
```

SendASPICommand—SC_EXEC_SCSI_CMD

WORD SendASPICommand(lpSRB)
    LPSRB lpSRB;

The SendASPICommand function with command code
SC_EXEC_SCSI_CMD (defined in Table D.17) is used to execute a
SCSI command, for example, send a SCSI Test Unit Ready command
to a tape drive, etc.

Parameter	Description
lpSRB	Points to one of the following SCSI request blocks:

```
typedef struct
{                                  // Structure for 6-byte CDBs
  BYTE   SRB_Cmd;                  // ASPI command code = SC_EXEC_SCSI_CMD
  BYTE   SRB_Status;               // ASPI command status byte
  BYTE   SRB_HaId;                 // ASPI host adapter number
  BYTE   SRB_Flags;                // ASPI request flags
  DWORD  SRB_Hdr_Rsvd;             // Reserved, MUST = 0
  BYTE   SRB_Target;               // Target's SCSI ID
  BYTE   SRB_Lun;                  // Target's LUN number
  DWORD  SRB_BufLen;               // Data Allocation LengthPG
  BYTE   SRB_SenseLen;             // Sense Allocation Length
  BYTE   far *SRB_BufPointer;      // Data Buffer Pointer
  DWORD  SRB_Rsvd1;                // Reserved, MUST = 0
  BYTE   SRB_CDBLen;               // CDB Length = 6
  BYTE   SRB_HaStat;               // Host Adapter Status
  BYTE   SRB_TargStat;             // Target Status
  FARPROC SRB_PostProc;            // Post routine
  BYTE   SRB_Rsvd2[34];            // Reserved, MUST = 0
```

```
  BYTE   CDBByte[6];                      // SCSI CDB
  BYTE   SenseArea6[SENSE_LEN];           // Request Sense buffer
} SRB_ExecSCSICmd6;


typedef struct
{                                         // Structure for 10-byte CDBs
BYTE   SRB_Cmd;                           // ASPI command code = SC_EXEC_SCSI_CMD
BYTE   SRB_Status;                        // ASPI command status byte
BYTE   SRB_HaId;                          // ASPI host adapter number
BYTE   SRB_Flags;                         // ASPI request flags
DWORD SRB_Hdr_Rsvd;                       // Reserved, MUST = 0
BYTE   SRB_Target;                        // Target's SCSI ID
BYTE   SRB_Lun;                           // Target's LUN number
DWORD SRB_BufLen;                         // Data Allocation Length
BYTE   SRB_SenseLen;                      // Sense Allocation Length
BYTE   far *SRB_BufPointer;               // Data Buffer Pointer
DWORD SRB_Rsvd1;                          // Reserved, MUST = 0
BYTE   SRB_CDBLen;                        // CDB Length = 10
BYTE   SRB_HaStat;                        // Host Adapter Status
BYTE   SRB_TargStat;                      // Target Status
FARPROC SRB_PostProc;                     // Post routine
BYTE   SRB_Rsvd2[34];                     // Reserved, MUST = 0
BYTE   CDBByte[10];                       // SCSI CDB
BYTE   SenseArea10[SENSE_LEN];            // Request Sense buffer
} SRB_ExecSCSICmd10;
```

NOTE *You can easily create a new structure for nonstandard CDB lengths.*

Returns

The return value specifies the outcome of the function. One of the values shown in Table D.18 will be returned by ASPI for Windows.

TABLE D.17 **ExecSCSICmd Structure Definition**

Member	Description	R/W
SRB_Cmd	This field must contain SC_EXEC_SCSI_CMD.	W
SRB_Status	On return, this field will be the same as the return status defined below.	R
SRB_Hald	This field specifies which installed host adapter the request is intended for. Host adapter numbers are always assigned by the SCSI manager layer beginning with zero.	W
SRB_Flags	The SRB Flags field is defined as follows:	W

Value	Meaning
SRB_DIR_SCSI	Direction determined by SCSI command. Length not checked.
SRB_DIR_IN	Transfer from SCSI target to host. Length checked.
SRB_DIR_OUT	Transfer from host to SCSI target. Length checked.
SRB_POSTING	If this value is ORed in with one of the previous three values, posting will be enabled. Refer to the section on ASPI posting.

Member	Description	R/W
SRB_Hdr_Rsvd	This DWORD field is currently reserved for this function and must be zeroed before passed to the ASPI manager.	—
SRB_Target	Target ID of device.	W
SRB_Lun	Logical unit number (LUN) of device.	W
SRB_BufLen	This field indicates the number of bytes to be transferred. If the SCSI command to be executed does not transfer data (i.e., est Unit Ready, Rewind, etc.), this field must be set to zero.	W
SRB_SenseLen	This field indicates the number of bytes allocated at the end of the SRB for sense data. A request sense is automatically generated if a check condition is presented at the end of a SCSI command.	W
SRB_BufPointer	This field is a pointer to the data buffer.	W
SRB_CDBLen	This field establishes the length, in bytes, of the SCSI command descriptor block (CDB). This value will typically be 6 or 10.	W
SRB_HaStat	Upon completion of the SCSI command, the ASPI manager will set this field with the host adapter status as follows:	R

Value	Meaning
HASTAT_OK	Host adapter did not detect an error
HASTAT_SEL_TO	Selection timeout
HASTAT_DO_DU	Data overrun/underrun
HASTAT_BUS_FREE	Unexpected bus free
HASTAT_PHASE_ERR	Target bus phase sequence failure

Member	Description	R/W
SRB_TargStat	Upon completion of the SCSI command, the ASPI manager will set this field with the target status as follows:	R

Value	Meaning
STATUS_GOOD	No target status
STATUS_CHKCOND	Check status (sense data is in SenseArea)
STATUS_BUSY	Specified target/LUN is busy
STATUS_RESCONF	Reservation conflict

Member	Description	R/W
SRB_PostProc	If posting is enabled, ASPI for Windows will post completion of an ASPI request to this function pointer. Refer to the section on ASPI Posting.	W
CDBByte[..]	This field contains the CDB as defined by the target's SCSI command set. The length of the SCSI CDB is specified in the SRB_CDBLen field.	W
SenseArea[..]	The SenseArea is filled with the sense data on a check condition. The maximum length of this field is specified in the SRB_SenseLen field. Note that the target can return fewer than the number of sense bytes requested.	R

D

Value	Meaning
SS_PENDING	SCSI request is in progress.
SS_COMP	SCSI/ASPI request has completed without error.
SS_ABORTED	SCSI command has been aborted.
SS_ERR	SCSI command has completed with an error.
SS_INVALID_SRB	SCSI request block (SRB) has one or more parameters set incorrectly.
SS_ASPI_IS_BUSY	ASPI manager cannot handle the request at this time. This error will generally occur if the ASPI manager is already using up all of its resources to execute other requests. You should try resending the command later.
SS_BUFFER_TO_BIG	ASPI manager cannot handle the given transfer size. Please refer to the "Miscellaneous" section for more information.

Example

The following example sends a SCSI Inquiry command to host adapter #0, target #0, and LUN #0:

```
SRB_ExecSCSICmd6 MySRB;

char InquiryBuffer[32];

FARPROC lpfnPostProcedure;

    .

    .

lpfnPostProcedure      = MakeProcInstance (PostProcedure, hInstance);

    .

    .

MySRB.SRB_Cmd = SC_EXEC_SCSI_CMD;

MySRB.SRB_HaId = 0;

MySRB.SRB_Flags = SRB_DIR_SCSI | SRB_POSTING;

MySRB.SRB_Hdr_Rsvd = 0;

MySRB.SRB_Target = 0;

MySRB.SRB_Lun = 0;

MySRB.SRB_BufLen = 32;

MySRB.SRB_SenseLen = SENSE_LEN;

MySRB.SRB_BufPointer = InquiryBuffer;

MySRB.SRB_CDBLen = 6;

MySRB.SRB_PostProc = lpfnPostProcedure;

MySRB.CDBByte[0] = SCSI_INQUIRY;

MySRB.CDBByte[1] = 0;
```

```
MySRB.CDBByte[2] = 0;

MySRB.CDBByte[3] = 0;

MySRB.CDBByte[4] = 32;

MySRB.CDBByte[5] = 0;

         .

/**************************************************/
/* Make sure all other reserved fields are zeroed */
/* before passing the SRB to ASPI for Windows     */
/**************************************************/

         .

SendASPICommand ( (LPSRB) &MySRB );

         .
         .
```

SendASPICommand—SC_ABORT_SRB

WORD SendASPICommand(lpSRB)
   LPSRB lpSRB;

The SendASPICommand function with command code
SC_ABORT_SRB (defined in Table D.19) is used to request that an
SRB be aborted. It should be issued on any I/O request that has not
completed if the application wishes to timeout on that request. Success
of the Abort command is never assured.

TABLE D.19 **SRB_Abort Structure Definition**

Member	Description	R/W
SRB_Cmd	This field must contain SC_ABORT_SRB.	W
SRB_Status	On return	R
SRB_Hald	This field specifies which installed host adapter the request is intended for. Host adapter numbers are always assigned by the SCSI manager layer beginning with zero.	W
SRB_Flags	The SRB flags field is currently reserved for this function and must be zeroed before passed to the ASPI manager.	W
SRB_Hdr_Rsvd	This DWORD field is currently reserved for this function and must be zeroed before passed to the ASPI manager.	—
SRB_ToAbort	This field contains a pointer to the SRB that is to be aborted. The actual failure or success of the abort operation is indicated by the status eventually returned in this SRB.	W

TABLE D.20	Return Values for SendASPICommand SC_ABORT_SRB	
Value	**Meaning**	
SS_COMP	SCSI/ASPI request has completed without error.	
SS_INVALID_HA	Invalid host adapter number.	
SS_INVALID_SRB	SCSI request block (SRB) has one or more parameters set incorrectly.	

Parameter	*Description*
lpSRB	Points to the following SCSI request block:

```
typedef struct
{
  BYTE   SRB_Cmd;                    // ASPI command code = SC_ABORT_SRB
  BYTE   SRB_Status;                 // ASPI command status byte
  BYTE   SRB_HaId;                   // ASPI host adapter number
  BYTE   SRB_Flags;                  // ASPI request flags
  DWORD  SRB_Hdr_Rsvd;               // Reserved, MUST = 0
  LPSRB  SRB_ToAbort;                // Pointer to SRB to abort
} SRB_Abort;
```

Returns

The return value specifies the outcome of the function. One of the values shown in Table D.20 will be returned by ASPI for Windows.

Example

The following example shows how to abort a stuck SCSI I/O:

```
SRB_ExecSCSICmd6 StuckSRB;

SRB_Abort AbortSRB;

WORD ASPI_Status;

         .
         .
         .

AbortSRB.SRB_Cmd = SC_ABORT_SRB;

AbortSRB.SRB_HaId = 0;

AbortSRB.SRB_Flags = 0;

AbortSRB.SRB_Hdr_Rsvd = 0;

AbortSRB.SRB_ToAbort = (LPSRB) &StuckSRB;
```

```
                    ASPI_Status = SendASPICommand ( (LPSRB) &AbortSRB );

                        .

                        .

                    while (StuckSRB.SRB_Status==SS_PENDING);

                        .

                        .

                    /****************************************************/
                    /* This sample code has no error handling, time-    */
                    /* out code, nor does it free up the processor.     */
                    /* Your application should be more robust.          */
                    /****************************************************/
```

SendASPICommand—SC_RESET_DEV

WORD SendASPICommand(lpSRB)
    LPSRB lpSRB;

The SendASPICommand function with command code
SC_RESET_DEV (defined in Table D.21) is used to send a SCSI bus
device reset to the specified target.

Parameter	Description
lpSRB	Points to the following SCSI request block:

```
typedef struct
{
  BYTESRB_Cmd;                        // ASPI command code = SC_RESET_DEV
  BYTE  SRB_Status;                   // ASPI command status byte
  BYTE  SRB_HaId;                     // ASPI host adapter number
  BYTE  SRB_Flags;                    // ASPI request flags
  DWORD SRB_Hdr_Rsvd;                 // Reserved, MUST = 0
  BYTE  SRB_Target;                   // Target's SCSI ID
  BYTE  SRB_Lun;                      // Target's LUN number
  BYTE  SRB_ResetRsvd1[14];           // Reserved, MUST = 0
  BYTE  SRB_HaStat;                   // Host Adapter Status
  BYTE  SRB_TargStat;                 // Target Status
  FARPROC SRB_PostProc;               // Post routine
  BYTE  SRB_ResetRsvd2[34];           // Reserved, MUST = 0
} SRB_BusDeviceReset
```

TABLE D.21 **SRB_BusDeviceReset Structure Definition**

Member	Description	R/W
SRB_Cmd	This field must contain SC_RESET_DEV.	W
SRB_Status	On return, this field will be the same as the return status defined below.	R
SRB_Hald	This field specifies which installed host adapter the request is intended for. Host adapter numbers are always assigned by the SCSI manager layer beginning with zero.	W
SRB_Flags	The SRB Flags field is currently reserved for this function and must be zeroed before passed to the ASPI manager.	W
SRB_Hdr_Rsvd	This DWORD field is currently reserved for this function and must be zeroed before passed to the ASPI manager.	—
SRB_Target	Target ID of device.	W
SRB_Lun	Logical unit number (LUN) of device. This field is ignored by ASPI for Windows since SCSI bus device resets are done on a per target basis only.	W
SRB_HaStat	Upon completion of the SCSI command, the ASPI manager will set this field with the host adapter status as follows:	R

Value	Meaning
HASTAT_OK	Host adapter did not detect an error
HASTAT_SEL_TO	Selection timeout
HASTAT_DO_DU	Data overrun/underrun
HASTAT_BUS_FREE	Unexpected bus free
HASTAT_PHASE_ERR	Target bus phase sequence failure

Member	Description	R/W
SRB_TargStat	Upon completion of the SCSI command, the ASPI manager will set this field with the target status as follows:	R

Value	Meaning
STATUS_GOOD	No target status
STATUS_CHKCOND	Check status (sense data is in SenseArea)
STATUS_BUSY	Specified target/LUN is busy
STATUS_RESCONF	Reservation conflict

Member	Description	R/W
SRB_PostProc	If posting is enabled, ASPI for Windows will post completion of an ASPI request to this function pointer. Refer to the section on ASPI Posting below.	W

Returns

The return value specifies the outcome of the function. One of the values shown in Table D.22 will be returned by ASPI for Windows. Refer to each ASPI command code definition for information on which ASPI commands return which errors.

Return Values for SendASPICommand SC_RESET_DEV

Value	Meaning
SS_COMP	SCSI/ASPI request has completed without error.
SS_INVALID_HA	Invalid host adapter number.
SS_INVALID_SRB	SCSI request block (SRB) has one or more parameters set incorrectly.
SS_ASPI_IS_BUSY	ASPI manager cannot handle the request at this time. This error will generally occur if the ASPI manager is already using up all of his resources to execute other requests. You should try resending the command later.

Example

The following example issues a SCSI bus device reset to host adapter #0, target #5:

```
SRB_BusDeviceReset MySRB;

WORD ASPI_Status;

        .

        .

MySRB.SRB_Cmd = SC_RESET_DEV;

MySRB.SRB_HaId = 0;

MySRB.SRB_Flags = 0;

MySRB.SRB_Hdr_Rsvd = 0;

MySRB.SRB_Target = 5;

MySRB.SRB_Lun = 0;

ASPI_Status = SendASPICommand ( (LPSRB) &MySRB );

        .

/***************************************************/

/* Make sure all other reserved fields are zeroed */

/* before passing the SRB to ASPI for Windows     */

/***************************************************/

        .

while (MySRB.SRB_Status==SS_PENDING);

        .

        .

/***************************************************/

/* This sample code has no error handling, time-  */

/* out code, nor does it free up the processor.   */

/* Your application should be more robust.         */

/***************************************************/
```

ASPI Polling

Once you send an ASPI for Windows SCSI request, you have two ways of being notified that the SCSI request has completed. The first and simplest method is called polling. After the command is sent, and ASPI for Windows returns control back to your program, you can poll the status byte waiting for the command to complete. For example, the following code segment sends a SCSI Inquiry command to target #2.

```
SRB_ExecSCSICmd6 MySRB;
char InquiryBuffer[32];

        .
        .

/**************************************************/
/* Code is entered with 'MySRB' zeroed.          */
/**************************************************/
MySRB.SRB_Cmd = SC_EXEC_SCSI_CMD;
MySRB.SRB_Flags = SRB_DIR_SCSI;
MySRB.SRB_Target = 2;
MySRB.SRB_BufLen = 32;
MySRB.SRB_SenseLen = SENSE_LEN;
MySRB.SRB_BufPointer = InquiryBuffer;
MySRB.SRB_CDBLen = 6;
MySRB.CDBByte[0] = SCSI_INQUIRY;
MySRB.CDBByte[4] = 32;

        .
        .

SendASPICommand ( (LPSRB) &MySRB );          // Send Inquiry command
while ( MySRB.SRB_Status == SS_PENDING );    // Wait till it's finished
/**************************************************/
/* At this point, the SCSI command has completed  */
/* with or without an error.                      */
/**************************************************/
if ( MySRB.SRB_Status == SS_COMP )
        ;                                    // Command completed without error
else
        ;                                    // Command completed with error
```

Since Windows is currently a nonpreemptive multitasking operating system, you should use polling with caution. The example above is not very good about freeing up the processor, nor does it have any timeout handler. Later in this specification, you will find sample code that does free up the processor while using polling.

ASPI POSTING

Most applications will use posting, rather than polling, to be notified that a SCSI request has completed. When posting is enabled, ASPI for Windows will post completion by calling your callback function. For example, the following code segment will send a SCSI Inquiry command to target #2 during the WM_CREATE message.

```
long FAR PASCAL WndProc (HWND, WORD, WORD, LONG);

void FAR PASCAL ASPIPostProc ( LPSRB );

HWND PostHWND;

HANDLE hInstance;


           .

           .

           .


//*************************************************************************
// ASPIPostProc - ASPI for Windows will post completion of a SCSI
//                request to this function. Note that this is most
//                likely during interrupt time so you can only use
//                a few Windows functions like 'PostMessage.' This
//                example post procedure is very simple. It will
//                wake up your application by posting a WM_ASPIPOST
//                message to your window handle.
//*************************************************************************
void FAR PASCAL ASPIPostProc ( LPSRB DoneSRB )
{
  PostMessage (PostHWND, WM_ASPIPOST,
    (WORD) ((SRB_ExecSCSICmd6 far *)DoneSRB)->SRB_Status,
    (DWORD) DoneSRB );
  return;
}
```

```
//************************************************************
// WndProc - Window message handler
//************************************************************
long FAR PASCAL WndProc ( HWND hwnd, WORD message, WORD wParam, LONG lParam)
{
  static SRB_ExecSCSICmd6 MySRB;
  static char InquiryBuffer[32];
  switch (message)
  {
    case WM_CREATE:
      /**************************************************/
      /* Code is entered with 'MySRB' zeroed.          */
      /**************************************************/
      lpfnASPIPostProc = MakeProcInstance (ASPIPostProc, hInstance);
      PostHWND = hwnd;
      MySRB.SRB_Cmd = SC_EXEC_SCSI_CMD;
      MySRB.SRB_Flags = SRB_DIR_SCSI|SRB_POSTING;
      MySRB.SRB_Target = 2;
      MySRB.SRB_BufLen = 32;
      MySRB.SRB_SenseLen = SENSE_LEN;
      MySRB.SRB_BufPointer = InquiryBuffer;
      MySRB.SRB_CDBLen = 6;
      ExecSRB.SRB_PostProc = lpfnASPIPostProc;
      MySRB.CDBByte[0] = SCSI_INQUIRY;
      MySRB.CDBByte[4] = 32;

            .

            .

      if ( SendASPICommand ( (LPSRB) &MySRB ) != SS_PENDING )
      {
          ;                     // Check return status for cause of failure!
          ;                     // Posting will NOT occur due to failure
      }
      else
      {
          ;                     // ASPI for Windows will post completion to
          ;                     // 'lpfnASPIPostProc' when command has completed.
      }
```

```
        return 0;

    case WM_ASPIPOST:

                        // Return status is in 'wParam'
                        // SRB Pointer is in 'lParam'
                        // We might want to send another ASPI request here.
                        // Look at 'ASPIPostProc' for more information.

        return 0;

    case WM_DESTROY:

        PostQuitMessage(0);

        return 0;

    }

    return DefWindowProc ( hwnd, message, wParam, lParam );

}
```

D

.
.
.

When the post routine gets called, the sample post handler will fill the wParam field and will contain the status of ASPI command (SRB_Status) while the lParam field will contain a far pointer to the SRB that has completed.

Miscellaneous

- Your ASPI for Windows program should never exit with pending SCSI I/Os. Doing so could lead to system instability. Send an ASPI Abort command if you need to.

- Your SRBs and data buffers must be in page-locked memory. Most SCSI host adapters are bus masters. This means that the data buffer must not move while the transfer is taking place. We recommend that you allocate your buffers using GlobalAlloc and then locking it first with GlobalLock and then with GlobalPageLock. This technique has been used to overcome some of the quirks that Windows 3.*x* seems to have with locking down buffers.

- It is a minimal requirement that all ASPI for Windows managers support transfers of 64K (64 kilobytes) or less. It is not possible for all SCSI host adapters to transfer data larger than this size. If the ASPI manager is unable to support your requested transfer size, you will be returned the SS_BUFFER_TO_BIG error from the SendASPICommand routine. No posting will occur. If this occurs, you should break the transfer down into 64K transfers or less. For maximum compatibility, it is recommended that you do not request transfer sizes larger than 64K if you do not need to.

- Do not forget to support the SS_ASPI_IS_BUSY return status when sending a SCSI command. Under extreme loads, some ASPI for Windows managers may not have enough resources to service each request.

- If you send an ASPI request with posting enabled, and the return value is not equal to SS_PENDING (in other words, the request is not in progress), then ASPI for Windows will not post completion to your specified window handle. (Refer to the specific return value for more information as to why the request is not in progress.)

- ASPI for Windows is fully multitasking. You can send a request to ASPI while another request is executing. Make sure you use a separate SRB for each ASPI request. It is also recommended that you only send one SRB at a time per target.

- If using posting, your post routine will most likely be called during interrupt time. Since most Windows routines are nonreentrant, you should call Windows routines with caution. One function you can call is PostMessage, which can be called during interrupt time.

- Make sure that you zero out all reserved fields before passing the SRB to ASPI for Windows.

ERROR CODES AND MESSAGES

All ASPI for Windows calls can fail. This specification has already defined which error codes can be returned by each ASPI routine. Table D.23 summarizes all of the error codes returned by ASPI routines.

IV. ASPI FOR OS/2 SPECIFICATION

Device drivers wishing to access ASPI must determine the address of the ASPI entry point through an OS/2 Attach Device Help call as follows:

```
SCSIMGR$             DB `SCSIMGR$',0
Return_Data_Buffer   DB 12 DUP(?)

                     MOV BX,OFFSET SCSIMGR
                     MOV DI,OFFSET Return_Data_Buffer
                     MOV DL,DevHlp_AttachDD


                     CALL [DevHlp]
```

TABLE D.23 **ASPI for Windows Error Codes**

Error Code	Value	Meaning
0x0000	SS_PENDING	SCSI request is in progress.
0x0001	SS_COMP	SCSI/ASPI request has completed without error.
0x0002	SS_ABORTED	SCSI command has been aborted.
0x0004	SS_ERR	SCSI command has completed with an error.
0x0080	SS_INVALID_CMD	Invalid ASPI command code.
0x0081	SS_INVALID_HA	Invalid host adapter number.
0x0082	SS_NO_DEVICE	SCSI device not installed.
0x00E0	SS_INVALID_SRB	SCSI request block (SRB) has one or more parameters set incorrectly.
0x00E1	SS_OLD_MANAGER	One or more ASPI for DOS managers are loaded that do not support Windows.
0x00E2	SS_ILLEGAL_MODE	This ASPI manager does not support this mode of Windows. You will typically see this error code when running Windows in real mode.
0x00E3	SS_NO_ASPI	No ASPI managers are loaded. This is typically caused by a DOS ASPI manager not being resident in memory.
0x00E4	SS_FAILED_INIT	For some reason, other than SS_OLD_MANAGER, SS_ILLEGAL_MODE, or SS_NO_ASPI, ASPI for Windows could not properly initialize itself. This may be caused by a lack of system resources.
0x00E5	SS_ASPI_IS_BUSY	ASPI manager cannot handle the request at this time. This error will generally occur if the ASPI manager is already using up all of his resources to execute other requests. You should try resending the command later.
0x00E6	SS_BUFFER_TO_BIG	ASPI manager cannot handle this larger than 64K transfer. You'll need to break up the SCSI I/O into smaller 64K transfers.

On return from the Attach Device Help call, a clear carry flag indicates that the SCSI manager SCSIMGR$ was found and that the return data is valid. A set carry flag indicates that the SCSI manager was not found.

The return data buffer has the following format:

```
ASPI_Real   DW Real Mode offset of ASPI entry point
            DW Real Mode CS segment of ASPI entry point
Real_DS     DW Real Mode DS of ASPI entry point
ASPI_Prot   DW Protected Mode offset of ASPI entry point
            DW Protected Mode CS selector of ASPI entry point
Prot_DS     DW Protected Mode DS of ASPI entry point
```

NOTE   *ASPI_Real and Real_DS are used by OS/2 1.x only. Information returned under OS/2 2.x is irrelevant.*

Calling ASPI

Once the ASPI entry point parameters have been successfully determined, calling ASPI is a matter of using the values appropriate to the mode of the processor. The address of the ASPI request block and the DS of the ASPI entry point must be pushed onto the stack before making a FAR call.

The following is an example of how to call ASPI:

```
             PUSH AX                           ;Save AX
             PUSH @ASPI_SRB                     ;Push pointer to ASPI SRB
             SMSW AX                            ;Check mode of processor
             TEST AX,PROTECT_MODE
             JNZ  PROT_CALL
             PUSH Real_DS
             CALL [ASPI_REAL]
             JMP  CALL_DONE


PROT_CALL:   PUSH Prot_DS
             CALL [ASPI_PROT]


CALL_DONE:   ADD  SP,6                          ;Restore the stack
             POP  AX
```

Accessing ASPI at Initialization Time

At initialization time, an OS/2 device driver lacks the privilege level for making a FAR call to the ASPI interface. To circumvent this restriction, the SCSI manager provides a special IOCTL that can be used by a driver to pass an ASPI request. To use the IOCTL, the driver must first use a DOSOPEN call to get a file handle for the SCSI manager. Having completed this successfully, the driver can call ASPI at initialization time as follows:

```
             PUSH @DATA_BUFFER        ;Not Applicable
             PUSH @REQUEST_BLOCK      ;Parameter List = SRB
             PUSH 40H                 ;Function Code
             PUSH 80H                 ;Function Category
             PUSH ASPI_Handle         ;File handle from DosOpen
             CALL DOSDEVIOCTL
```

Once the driver has returned from initialization, this access method is no longer valid.

ASPI AND OS/2 2.x

The device driver architecture for OS/2 2.x is divided into several basic layers. Device manager drivers (DMDs) receive requests from the file systems and other device drivers. These requests are passed on to an adapter device driver (ADD), which sends the appropriate command to the host adapter.

ASPI for OS/2 2.x is a translation layer, and it has been implemented as a device driver (os2aspi.dmd). An application can send SRBs to any SCSI adapter that has an ADD installed. It is no longer possible to set host adapter parameters, because OS2ASPI has no direct control over the host adapter.

TARGET ALLOCATION WITH OS/2 2.x

The device driver architecture for OS/2 2.x is structured so that targets controlled by an ADD must be allocated to an individual DMD. For example, when the system boots, os2dasd.dmd is normally the first device manager loaded, and it will automatically search for all available hard drives and permanently allocate them for use by the file systems. Other DMDs usually do something similar with targets that they assume should be controlled by them.

The standard method for preventing a DMD from allocating a particular target is through the use of command line switches on the ADD that handles the device. If you are planning on using ASPI to control a device that may be allocated by a DMD that loads before os2aspi.dmd, be sure to specify that the device manager in question is not allowed access to it.

1. If you are writing an ASPI application for a magneto-optical drive (target 6 on an AHA-1540) that returns device type 0 (DASD) in the Inquiry data, you must be sure to prevent OS2DASD from accessing it:

    BASEDEV=AHA154X.ADD /A:0 /!DM:6

2. If you are writing an ASPI application for a device that also may be controlled by a device driver through os2scsi.dmd (target 6 on an AHA-1540), you can also prevent OS2SCSI from accessing it:

    BASEDEV=AHA154X.ADD /A:0 /!SM:6

TABLE D.24 **SCSI Request Block Header**

Offset	# Bytes	Description	R/W
00h (00)	01h (01)	Command Code	W
01h (01)	01h (01)	Status	R
02h (02)	01h (01)	Host Adapter Number	W
03h (03)	01h (01)	SCSI Request Flags	W
04h (04)	04h (04)	Reserved for Expansion = 0	—

Currently, only os2dasd.dmd and os2scsi.dmd can be controlled in this manner, because they are the only DMDs mentioned in IBM's specification for ADDs. For a complete explanation of command line switches supported by the ADD that are provided with OS/2 2.1, consult the online help for SCSI.

The current ASPI specification does not provide a method for allocating targets, and there are no command line switches for os2aspi.dmd that can be used with the current ADD. The target for each SRB will be allocated and deallocated on a command basis until the first Execute I/O SRB is sent. At this point, the target will be permanently allocated to os2aspi.dmd and other DMDs will no longer have access to the target.

SAMPLE CODE FOR OS/2 2.x

The SDK (ASPI Software Developer's Kit) includes sample code for designing ASPI applications and device drivers to be used with OS/2 2.x.

ASPIAPP is a simple program that scans the SCSI bus and displays information about any targets that it finds on adapters in the system. This application is a single-threaded, character-based application intended to show you how ASPI can be used.

ASPIDRV is a simple device driver that passes requests from ASPI-APP to os2aspi.dmd after converting any virtual addresses to physical addresses. This driver is intended for handling single-threaded requests that are small enough not to require a scatter/gather list. If you are transferring large blocks of data, you may have to convert the virtual address of the buffer into a page table that can be used as a scatter/gather list.

SCSI REQUEST BLOCK (SRB)

A SCSI request block (SRB), defined in Table D.24, contains the command to be executed by the ASPI manager and is used by both drivers and application programs. An SRB consists of an SRB header followed by additional fields dependent on the command code. All request blocks have an eight-byte header.

| **TABLE D.25** | **Valid ASPI Command Codes** |

Command Code	Description
00h	Host Adapter Inquiry
01h	Get Device Type
02h	Execute SCSI I/O Command
03h	Abort SCSI I/O Command
04h	Reset SCSI Device
05h	Set Host Adapter Parameters
06h-7Fh	Reserved for Future Expansion
80h-FFh	Reserved for Vendor Unique

Command Code

The Command Code field is used to indicate which of the ASPI services is being accessed. Refer to Table D.25 for a description of valid ASPI command codes.

Status

The Status Byte field is used to post the status of the command. Refer to Table D.26 for a description of ASPI status bytes.

Host Adapter Number

The Host Adapter Number field specifies which installed host adapter the request is intended for. Host adapter numbers are always assigned by the SCSI manager layer beginning with zero.

SCSI Request Flags

The SCSI Request Flags field definition is command code-specific.

Reserved for Expansion

The last four bytes of the header are reserved and must be zero.

ASPI COMMAND CODES

Valid ASPI Command Codes

See Table D.25 for a list of valid ASPI command codes, and their descriptions.

TABLE D.26 **ASPI Status Bytes**

Status Byte	Description
00h	SCSI Request In Progress
01h	SCSI Request Completed Without Error
02h	SCSI Request Aborted By Host
04h	SCSI Request Completed With Error
80h	Invalid SCSI Request
81h	Invalid Host Adapter Number
82h	SCSI Device Not Installed

TABLE D.27 **ASPI Command Code = 0: Host Adapter Inquiry**

Offset	# Bytes	Description	R/W
00h (00)	01h (01)	Command Code = 0	W
01h (01)	01h (01)	Status	R
02h (02)	01h (01)	Host Adapter Number	W
03h (03)	01h (01)	SCSI Request Flags	W
04h (04)	04h (04)	Reserved for Expansion = 0	—
08h (08)	01h (01)	Number of Host Adapters	R
09h (09)	01h (01)	Target ID of Host Adapter	R
0Ah (10)	10h (16)	SCSI Manager ID	R
1Ah (26)	10h (16)	Host Adapter ID	R
2Ah (42)	10h (16)	Host Adapter Unique Parameters	R

ASPI Status Bytes

See Table D.26 for a list of ASPI status bytes, and their descriptions.

ASPI Command Code = 0: Host Adapter Inquiry

The status byte (defined in Table D.27) always returns with a nonzero status. A SCSI Request Completed Without Error (01h) status indicates that the remaining fields are valid. An Invalid Host Adapter Number (81h) status indicates that the specified host adapter is not installed.

This function is used to get information on the installed host adapter hardware, including number of host adapters installed. It can be issued once with host adapter zero specified to get the number of host adapters. If further information is desired, it can be issued for each individual host adapter.

The SCSI Request Flags field is currently undefined for this command and should be zeroed.

The SCSI Manager ID field contains a 16-byte ASCII string describing the SCSI manager.

ASPI Command Code = 1: Get Device Type

Offset	# Bytes	Description	R/W
00h (00)	01h (01)	Command Code = 1	W
01h (01)	01h (01)	Status	R
02h (02)	01h (01)	Host Adapter Number	W
03h (03)	01h (01)	SCSI Request Flags	W
04h (04)	04h (04)	Reserved for Expansion = 0	—
08h (08)	01h (01)	Target ID	W
09h (09)	01h (01)	LUN	W
0Ah (10)	01h (01)	Peripheral Device Type of Target/LUN	R

The Host Adapter ID field contains a 16-byte ASCII string describing the SCSI host adapter.

The definition of the Host Adapter Unique Parameters field is left to implementation notes specific to a particular host adapter.

ASPI Command Code = 1: Get Device Type

This command (defined in Table D.28) always returns with a nonzero status.

A SCSI Request Completed Without Error (01h) status indicates that the specified device is installed and the peripheral device type field is valid. A SCSI Device Not Installed Error (82h) indicates that the peripheral device type field is not valid.

This command is intended for use by various drivers, during initialization, for identifying the targets they need to support. A CD-ROM driver, for example, can scan each target/LUN on each installed host adapter looking for the device type corresponding to CD-ROM devices. This eliminates the need for each driver to duplicate the effort of scanning the SCSI bus for devices.

The peripheral device type is determined by sending a SCSI Inquiry command to the given target. Refer to any published SCSI specification to learn more about the Inquiry command.

The SCSI Request Flags field is currently undefined for this command and should be zeroed.

ASPI Command Code = 2: Execute SCSI I/O Command

This command (defined in Table D.29) usually returns with zero status indicating that the request was queued successfully. Command completion can be determined by polling for nonzero status or through the use of the Post Routine Address field in the ASPI Command Posting section (discussed later). Keep in mind that if you are going to use polling, interrupts must be enabled.

ASPI Command Code = 2: Execute SCSI I/O Command

Offset	# Bytes	Description	R/W
00h (00)	01h (01)	Command Code = 2	W
01h (01)	01h (01)	Status	R
02h (02)	01h (01)	Host Adapter Number	W
03h (03)	01h (01)	SCSI Request Flags	W
04h (04)	02h (02)	Length of Scatter/Gather List	W
06h (06)	02h (02)	Reserved for Expansion = 0	—
08h (08)	01h (01)	Target ID	W
09h (09)	01h (01)	LUN	W
0Ah (10)	04h (04)	Data Allocation Length	W
0Eh (14)	01h (01)	Sense Allocation Length (N)	W
0Fh (15)	04h (04)	Data Buffer Pointer	W
13h (19)	04h (04)	SRB Link Pointer	W
17h (23)	01h (01)	SCSI CDB Length (M)	W
18h (24)	01h (01)	Host Adapter Status	R
19h (25)	01h (01)	Target Status	R
1Ah (26)	02h (02)	Real Mode Post Routine Offset*	W
1Ch (28)	02h (02)	Real Mode Post Routine CS*	W
1Eh (30)	02h (02)	Real Mode Post Routine DS*	W
20h (32)	02h (02)	Protected Mode Post Routine Offset	W
22h (34)	02h (02)	Protected Mode Post Routine CS	W
24h (36)	02h (02)	Protected Mode Post Routine DS	W
26h (38)	04h (04)	Physical Address of SRB	W
2Ah (42)	16h (22)	Reserved for ASPI Workspace	—
40h (64)	M	SCSI Command Descriptor Block (CDB)	W
40h+M	N	Sense Allocation Area	R

Used by OS/2 1.x only. Fields are not used under OS/2 2.x.

The SCSI Request Flags Byte Is Defined as Follows:

7	6	5	4	3	2	1	0
Rsvd	*Rsvd*	*SGE*	*Direction Bits*		*Rsvd*	*Link*	*Post*

The Post bit specifies whether posting is enabled (bit 0 = 1) or disabled (bit 0 = 0).

The Link bit specifies whether linking is enabled (bit 1 = 1) or disabled (bit 1 = 0).

The Direction Bits specify which direction the transfer is:

00   Direction determined by SCSI command. Length not checked.

01   Transfer from SCSI target to host. Length checked.

10   Transfer from host to SCSI target. Length checked.

11   No data transfer.

The Scatter/Gather Enable (SGE) bit specifies whether scatter/gather is enabled (bit 5=1) or disabled (bit 5=0).

The Target ID and LUN fields are used to specify the peripheral device involved in the I/O.

The Data Allocation Length field indicates the number of bytes to be transferred. If the SCSI command to be executed does not transfer data (i.e., Rewind, Start Unit, etc.), the data allocation length must be set to zero.

The Length of Scatter/Gather List field is valid only when the scatter/gather enable bit in the flags is set. It contains the number of descriptors in the array pointed by the Data Buffer Pointer field.

The Sense Allocation Length field indicates, in bytes, the number of bytes allocated at the end of the SRB for sense data. A request sense is automatically generated if a check condition is presented at the end of a SCSI command.

The Data Buffer Pointer field is a pointer to the I/O data buffer. When scatter/gather is enabled, this field is a physical pointer to a scatter/gather list. A scatter/gather list is made up of one or more descriptors of the following format:

DWORD Buffer Pointer

DWORD Buffer Size

The SRB Link Pointer field is a pointer to the next SRB in a chain. See the section SCSI Command Linking with ASPI for more information.

The SCSI CDB Length field establishes the length, in bytes, of the SCSI command descriptor block (CDB).

The Host Adapter Status field is used to report the host adapter status as follows:

00h	Host adapter did not detect any error
11h	Selection timeout
12h	Data overrun/underrun
13h	Unexpected bus free
14h	Target bus phase sequence failure

The Target Status field is used to report the target's SCSI status, including:

00h	No target status
02h	Check status (sense data is in sense allocation area)
08h	Specified target/LUN is busy
18h	Reservation conflict

NOTE *The host adapter status and the target status are valid only when the status byte is either 2 or 4.*

The Post Routine Address field, if specified, is called when the I/O is completed. See the section ASPI Command Posting for more information.

The SCSI command descriptor block (CDB) field contains the CDB as defined by the target's SCSI command set. The length of the SCSI CDB is specified in the SCSI Command Length field.

The sense allocation area is filled with sense data on a check condition. The maximum length of this field is specified in the Sense Allocation Length field. Note that the target can return fewer than the number of sense bytes requested.

SCSI Command Linking with ASPI

ASPI provides the ability to use SCSI linking to guarantee the sequential execution of several commands. Note that the use of this feature requires the involved target(s) to support SCSI linking.

To use SCSI linking, a chain of SRBs is built with the SRB link pointer used to link the elements together. The link bit should be set in the SCSI request flags byte of all SRBs except the last in the chain. When a SCSI target returns indicating that the linked command is complete, the next SRB is immediately processed and the appropriate CDB is dispatched. When using SCSI linking, make sure that the linking flags in the SCSI CDB agree with the link bit in the SCSI request flags. Inconsistencies can cause unpredictable results. For example, setting the CDB up for linking but failing to set the link bit may result in a random address being used for the next SRB pointer.

Any error returned from the target on a linked command will break the chain. Note that if linking without tags is used, as defined in SCSI, posting may not occur on any elements in the chain until the chain is complete. If you have the post bit set in each SRB's SCSI request flags byte, then each SRB's post routine will be called.

NOTE *It is strongly recommended that you do not use SCSI linking. There are many SCSI targets, as well as SCSI host adapters, that do not handle SCSI linking and will not work with your ASPI module.*

ASPI Command Posting

Posting refers to the SCSI manager making a FAR call to a post routine as specified in the SRB. This can be used by a driver much like a hardware interrupt might be used. Post routines have all the same privileges and restrictions as a hardware interrupt service routine in OS/2. Posting is optional but should almost always be used in OS/2. To use posting, the post bit must be set in the SCSI request flags. The post routine is called to indicate that the requested I/O is complete. The specific SRB completed is indicated by the four-byte SRB pointer on the stack. The DS of the post routine as specified in the SRB is also passed to the stack.

The post routine will be called with interrupts enabled. It is assumed that all registers are preserved by the post routine.

```
ASPI_Post    proc far
             push bp                        ;Use bp as a reference
             mov  bp,sp
             pusha                          ;Save all registers
             push es                        ;Save ES
             mov  bx,[bp+6]                 ;Load DS of POST routine
             mov  ax,[bp+10]               ;Physical address of SRB->AX:BX
             mov  ax,[bp+8]
             .
             .
             .
             pop  es                        ;Restore registers
             popa
             pop  ds
             pop  bp
             retf
ASPI_Post    endp
```

When your post routine is first entered, the stack will look as follows:

Top of Stack	[SP+0] –>	Return Address (Offset)
	[SP+2] –>	Return Address (Segment)
	[SP+4] –>	SRB Pointer (Offset)
	[SP+6] –>	SRB Pointer (Segment)
	...	
	...	
	...	

You may issue any ASPI command from within your post routine except for an abort command. Your post routine should get in and out as quickly as possible.

ASPI Command Code = 3: Abort SCSI I/O Request

This command (defined in Table D.30) is used to request that an SRB be aborted. It should be issued on any I/O request that has not completed if the driver wishes to timeout on that request. Success of the Abort command is never assured.

This command always returns with SCSI Request Completed Without Error, but the actual failure or success of the abort operation is indicated by the status eventually returned in the SRB specified.

TABLE D.30 ASPI Command Code = 3: Abort SCSI I/O Request

Offset	# Bytes	Description	R/W
00h (00)	01h (01)	Command Code = 3	W
01h (01)	01h (01)	Status	R
02h (02)	01h (01)	Host Adapter Number	W
03h (03)	01h (01)	SCSI Request Flags	W
04h (04)	04h (04)	Reserved for Expansion = 0	—
08h (08)	04h (04)	Physical SRB Pointer	W

TABLE D.31 ASPI Command Code = 4: Reset SCSI Device

Offset	# Bytes	Description	R/W
00h (00)	01h (01)	Command Code = 4	W
01h (01)	01h (01)	Status	R
02h (02)	01h (01)	Host Adapter Number	W
03h (03)	01h (01)	SCSI Request Flags	W
04h (04)	04h (04)	Reserved for Expansion = 0	—
08h (08)	01h (01)	Target ID	W
09h (09)	01h (01)	LUN	W
0Ah (10)	0Eh (14)	Reserved	—
18h (24)	01h (01)	Host Adapter Status	R
19h (25)	01h (01)	Target Status	R
1Ah (26)	02h (02)	Real Mode Post Routine Offset*	W
1Ch (28)	02h (02)	Real Mode Post Routine CS*	W
1Eh (30)	02h (02)	Real Mode Post Routine DS*	W
20h (32)	02h (02)	Protected Mode Post Routine Offset	W
22h (34)	02h (02)	Protected Mode Post Routine CS	W
24h (36)	02h (02)	Protected Mode Post Routine DS	W
26h (38)	16h (22)	Reserved for ASPI Workspace	—

Used by OS/2 1.x only. Fields are not used under OS/2 2.x.

The SCSI Request Flags field is currently undefined for this command and should be zeroed.

The SRB Pointer to Abort field contains a pointer to the SRB that is to be aborted.

NOTE *An Abort command should not be issued during a post routine.*

ASPI Command Code = 4: Reset SCSI Device

This command (defined in Table D.31) is used to reset a specific SCSI target. Note that the structure passed is nearly identical to the execute SCSI I/O SRB except that some of the fields are not used.

This command usually returns with zero status indicating that the request was queued successfully. Command completion can be determined by polling for nonzero status or through the use of posting.

ASPI Command Code = 5: Set Host Adapter Parameters

Offset	# Bytes	Description	R/W
00h (00)	01h (01)	Command Code = 5	W
01h (01)	01h (01)	Status	R
02h (02)	01h (01)	Host Adapter Number	W
03h (03)	01h (01)	SCSI Request Flags	W
04h (04)	04h (04)	Reserved for Expansion = 0	—
08h (08)	10h (16)	Host Adapter Unique Parameters	W

The SCSI Request Flags Byte Is Defined as Follows:

7	6	5	4	3	2	1	0
Reserved							*Post*

The Post bit specifies whether posting is enabled (bit 0 = 1) or disabled (bit 0 = 0).

ASPI Command Code = 5: Set Host Adapter Parameters

The definition of the host adapter unique parameters (defined in Table D.32) is left to implementation notes specific to a particular host adapter.

V. ASPI FOR NETWARE SPECIFICATION

Before creating your NetWare loadable module (NLM), you must first create the object file and a definition file. In the definition file, you tell NetWare® what routines you wish to export to the operating system and what routines you wish to import into your NLM. You will need to import one ASPI routine. Sample definition file:

```
.
.
.
IMPORT
.
.
.
ASPI_Entry
.
.
.
```

Using the Novell linker, the object and definition files are linked together to create your NLM.

During load time, if NetWare 386 does not find this imported routine, it will not load your NLM. You must load the ASPI module before the other modules can access it.

SCSI Request Block Header

Offset	# Bytes	Description	R/W
00h (00)	01h (01)	Command Code	W
01h (01)	01h (01)	Status	R
02h (02)	01h (01)	Host Adapter Number	W
03h (03)	01h (01)	SCSI Request Flags	W
04h (04)	04h (04)	Reserved for Expansion = 0	—

ASPI ROUTINE: ASPI_ENTRY

This routine allows you to pass a SCSI request block (SRB) to ASPI.

Syntax

Void ASPI_Entry (void *ASPIRequestBlock)

Return Values

Returns nothing

Parameters

Parameter	Description
ASPIRequestBlock	This field contains a pointer to your SRB.

Assembly Example

```
push OFFSET ASPI_ReqBlock      ;Push SRB onto the stack
call ASPI_Entry                ;Call ASPI
lea  esp,[esp+(1*4)]           ;Restore the stack
```

Remarks

On entry, interrupts should be disabled. Returns with interrupts disabled.

SCSI REQUEST BLOCK (SRB)

A SCSI request block (SRB) contains the command to be executed by the ASPI manager and is used by both drivers and application programs.

Valid ASPI Command Codes

Command Code	Description
00h	Host Adapter Inquiry
01h	Get Device Type
02h	Execute SCSI I/O Command
03h	Abort SCSI I/O Command
04h	Reset SCSI Device
05h	Set Host Adapter Parameters
06h-7Fh	Reserved for Future Expansion
80h-FFh	Reserved for Vendor Unique

An SRB consists of an SRB header (shown in Table D.33) followed by additional fields dependent on the command code. All request blocks have an eight-byte header.

D

Command Code

The Command Code field indicates which ASPI service is being accessed. Table D.34 lists the valid ASPI command codes.

Status

The Status Byte field is used to post the status of the command. Refer to Table D.35 for a description of ASPI status bytes.

Host Adapter Number

The Host Adapter Number field specifies which installed host adapter the request is intended for. Host adapter numbers are always assigned by the SCSI manager layer beginning with zero.

SCSI Request Flags

The SCSI Request Flags field definition is command code-specific.

Reserved for Expansion

The last four bytes of the header are reserved and must be zero.

ASPI COMMAND CODES

Valid ASPI Command Codes

Table D.34 lists the valid ASPI command codes and their descriptions.

TABLE D.35   ASPI Status Bytes

Status Byte	Description
00h	SCSI Request In Progress
01h	SCSI Request Completed Without Error
02h	SCSI Request Aborted by Host
04h	SCSI Request Completed With Error
80h	Invalid SCSI Request
81h	Invalid Host Adapter Number
82h	SCSI Device Not Installed

TABLE D.36   ASPI Command Code = 0: Host Adapter Inquiry

Offset	# Bytes	Description	R/W
00h (00)	01h (01)	Command Code = 0	W
01h (01)	01h (01)	Status	R
02h (02)	01h (01)	Host Adapter Number	W
03h (03)	01h (01)	SCSI Request Flags	W
04h (04)	04h (04)	Reserved for Expansion = 0	—
08h (08)	01h (01)	Number of Host Adapters	R
09h (09)	01h (01)	Target ID of Host Adapter	R
0Ah (10)	10h (16)	SCSI Manager ID	R
1Ah (26)	10h (16)	Host Adapter ID	R
2Ah (42)	10h (16)	Host Adapter Unique Parameters	R

ASPI Status Bytes

Table D.35 lists the ASPI status bytes and their descriptions.

ASPI Command Code = 0: Host Adapter Inquiry

The status byte (defined in Table D.36) always returns with a nonzero status. A SCSI Request Completed Without Error (01h) status indicates that the remaining fields are valid. An Invalid Host Adapter Number (81h) status indicates that the specified host adapter is not installed.

This function is used to get information on the installed host adapter hardware, including number of host adapters installed. It can be issued once with host adapter zero specified to get the number of host adapters. If further information is desired, it can be issued for each individual host adapter.

The SCSI Request Flags field is currently undefined for this command and should be zeroed.

The SCSI Manager ID field contains a 16-byte ASCII string describing the SCSI manager.

ASPI Command Code = 1: Get Device Type

Offset	# Bytes	Description	R/W
00h (00)	01h (01)	Command Code = 1	W
01h (01)	01h (01)	Status	R
02h (02)	01h (01)	Host Adapter Number	W
03h (03)	01h (01)	SCSI Request Flags	W
04h (04)	04h (04)	Reserved for Expansion = 0	—
08h (08)	01h (01)	Target ID	W
09h (09)	01h (01)	LUN	W
0Ah (10)	01h (01)	Peripheral Device Type of Target/LUN	R

The Host Adapter ID field contains a 16-byte ASCII string describing the SCSI host adapter.

The definition of the Host Adapter Unique Parameters field is left to implementation notes specific to a particular host adapter.

ASPI Command Code = 1: Get Device Type

This command (defined in Table D.37) always returns with nonzero status.

A SCSI Request Completed Without Error (01h) status indicates that the specified device is installed and the peripheral device type field is valid. A SCSI Device Not Installed Error (82h) indicates that the peripheral device type field is not valid.

This command is intended for use by various drivers during initialization for identifying the targets that they need to support. A CD-ROM driver, for example, can scan each target/LUN on each installed host adapter looking for the device type corresponding to CD-ROM devices. This eliminates the need for each driver to duplicate the effort of scanning the SCSI bus for devices.

The peripheral device type is determined by sending a SCSI Inquiry command to the given target. Refer to any SCSI specification to learn more about the Inquiry command.

The SCSI Request Flags field is currently undefined for this command and should be zeroed.

ASPI Command Code = 2: Execute SCSI I/O Command

This command (defined in Table D.38) usually returns with zero status indicating that the request was queued successfully. Command completion can be determined by polling for nonzero status or through the use of the Post Routine Address field (discussed later in the section ASPI Command Posting). Keep in mind that if you are going to use polling, interrupts must be enabled.

TABLE D.38 ASPI Command Code = 2: Execute SCSI I/O Command

Offset	# Bytes	Description	R/W
00h (00)	01h (01)	Command Code = 2	W
01h (01)	01h (01)	Status	R
02h (02)	01h (01)	Host Adapter Number	W
03h (03)	01h (01)	SCSI Request Flags	W
04h (04)	04h (04)	Reserved for Expansion = 0	W
08h (08)	01h (01)	Target ID	—
09h (09)	01h (01)	LUN	W
0Ah (10)	04h (04)	Data Allocation Length	W
0Eh (14)	01h (01)	Sense Allocation Length (N)	W
0Fh (15)	04h (04)	Data Buffer Pointer	W
13h (19)	04h (04)	SRB Link Pointer	W
17h (23)	01h (01)	SCSI CDB Length (M)	W
18h (24)	01h (01)	Host Adapter Status	R
19h (25)	01h (01)	Target Status	R
1Ah (26)	04h (04)	Post Routine Address	W
1Eh (30)	22h (34)	Reserved for ASPI Workspace	—
40h (64)	M	SCSI Command Descriptor Block (CDB)	W
40h+M	N	Sense Allocation Area	R

The SCSI Request Flags Byte Is Defined as Follows:

7	6	5	4	3	2	1	0
Rsvd	*Rsvd*	*Rsvd*	*Direction Bits*		*Rsvd*	*Link*	*Post*

The Post bit specifies whether posting is enabled (bit 0 = 1) or disabled (bit 0 = 0).

The Link bit specifies whether linking is enabled (bit 1 = 1) or disabled (bit 1 = 0).

The Direction Bits specify which direction the transfer is:

    00   Direction determined by SCSI command. Length not checked.

    01   Transfer from SCSI target to host. Length checked.

    10   Transfer from host to SCSI target. Length checked.

    11   No data transfer.

The Target ID and LUN fields are used to specify the peripheral device involved in the I/O.

The Data Allocation Length field indicates the number of bytes to be transferred. If the SCSI command to be executed does not transfer data (i.e., Rewind, Start Unit, etc.) the Data Allocation Length must be set to zero.

The Sense Allocation Length field indicates, in bytes, the number of bytes allocated at the end of the SRB for sense data. A request sense is automatically generated if a check condition is presented at the end of a SCSI command.

The Data Buffer Pointer field is a pointer to the I/O data buffer. You place the logical address here. ASPI will convert it to the physical address in the case of a bus master or DMA transfer.

The SRB Link Pointer field is a pointer to the next SRB in a chain. See the discussion on linking for more information.

The SCSI CDB Length field establishes the length, in bytes, of the SCSI command descriptor block (CDB).

The Host Adapter Status field is used to report the host adapter status as follows:

00h	Host adapter did not detect any error
11h	Selection timeout
12h	Data overrun/underrun
13h	Unexpected bus free
14h	Target bus phase sequence failure

The Target Status field is used to report the target's SCSI status, including:

00h	No target status
02h	Check status (sense data is in sense allocation area)
08h	Specified target/LUN is busy
18h	Reservation conflict

The Post Routine Address field, if specified, is called when the I/O is completed. See the section ASPI Command Posting for more information.

The SCSI command descriptor block (CDB) field contains the CDB as defined by the target's SCSI command set. The length of the SCSI CDB is specified in the SCSI Command Length field.

The Sense Allocation Area is filled with sense data on a check condition. The maximum length of this field is specified in the Sense Allocation Length field. Note that the target can return fewer than the number of sense bytes requested.

SCSI Command Linking with ASPI

ASPI provides the ability to use SCSI linking to guarantee the sequential execution of several commands. Note that the use of this feature requires the involved target(s) to support SCSI linking.

To use SCSI linking, a chain of SRBs is built with the SRB link pointer used to link the elements together. The link bit should be set in the SCSI request flags byte of all SRBs except the last in the chain. When a SCSI target returns indicating that the linked command is complete, the next SRB is immediately processed, and the appropriate CDB is dispatched. When using SCSI linking, make sure that the linking flags in the SCSI CDB agree with the link bit in the SCSI request flags. Inconsistencies can cause unpredictable results. For example, setting the CDB up for linking but failing to set the link bit may result in a random address being used for the next SRB pointer.

Any error returned from the target on a linked command will break the chain. Note that if linking without tags is used, as defined in SCSI, posting may not occur on any elements in the chain until the chain is complete. If you have the post bit set in each SRB's SCSI request flags byte, then each SRB's post routine will be called.

NOTE *It is strongly recommended that you do not use SCSI linking. There are many SCSI targets, as well as SCSI host adapters, that do not handle SCSI linking and will not work with your ASPI module.*

ASPI Command Posting

To use posting, the Post bit must be set in the SCSI request flags. Posting refers to the SCSI manager making a call to a post routine as specified in the SRB. The post routine is called to indicate that the SRB is complete. The specific SRB completed is indicated by a four-byte SRB pointer on the stack.

If your post routine is written in assembly language, it must save the C registers: EBP, EBX, ESI, and EDI. Below is a sample ASPI post handler:

```
ASPI_Post  proc near

           Cpush                        ;Push 'C' required regs

           mov   eax, [esp+20]          ;EAX points to SRB
           .

           .                            ;Handle posted SRB

           .

           CPop                         ;Restore registers and
           ret                          ;  return to ASPI
ASPI_Post  endp
```

C example:

```
void ASPI_Post  ( SRB_Pointer )
void *SRB_Pointer;
{
       .

       .                                /* Handle posted SRB */

       .

}
```

ASPI Command Code = 3: Abort SCSI I/O Command

Offset	# Bytes	Description	R/W
00h (00)	01h (01)	Command Code = 3	W
01h (01)	01h (01)	Status	R
02h (02)	01h (01)	Host Adapter Number	W
03h (03)	01h (01)	SCSI Request Flags	W
04h (04)	04h (04)	Reserved for Expansion = 0	—
08h (08)	04h (04)	SRB Pointer to Abort	W

NOTE *On entry, interrupts will be disabled. You should return with interrupts disabled. You may issue any ASPI command from within your post routine except for an abort command. Your post routing should get in and out as quickly as possible.*

ASPI Command Code = 3: Abort SCSI I/O Command

This command (defined in Table D.39) is used to request that an SRB be aborted. It should be issued on any I/O request that has not completed if the driver wishes to timeout on that request. Success of the Abort command is never assured.

This command always returns with SCSI Request Completed Without Error (01h), but the actual failure or success of the abort operation is indicated by the status eventually returned in the SRB specified.

The SCSI Request Flags field is currently undefined for this command and should be zeroed.

The SRB Pointer to Abort field contains a pointer to the SRB that is to be aborted.

NOTE *An abort command should not be issued during a post routine.*

ASPI Command Code = 4: Reset SCSI Device

This command (defined in Table D.40) is used to reset a specific SCSI target. Note that the structure passed is nearly identical to the execute SCSI I/O SRB except that some of the fields are not used.

This command usually returns with zero status indicating that the request was queued successfully. Command completion can be determined by polling for nonzero status or through the use of posting.

The SCSI Request Flags Byte Is Defined as Follows:

7	6	5	4	3	2	1	0
Reserved							*Post*

The Post bit specifies whether posting is enabled (bit 0 = 1) or disabled (bit 0 = 0).

TABLE D.40 ASPI Command Code = 4: Reset SCSI Device

Offset	# Bytes	Description	R/W
00h (00)	01h (01)	Command Code = 4	W
01h (01)	01h (01)	Status	R
02h (02)	01h (01)	Host Adapter Number	W
03h (03)	01h (01)	SCSI Request Flags	W
04h (04)	04h (04)	Reserved for Expansion = 0	—
08h (08)	01h (01)	Target ID	W
09h (09)	01h (01)	LUN	W
0Ah (10)	0Eh (14)	Reserved	—
18h (24)	01h (01)	Host Adapter Status	R
19h (25)	01h (01)	Target Status	R
1Ah (26)	02h (02)	POST Routine Address	W
1Eh (30)	02h (02)	Reserved for ASPI Workspace	—

TABLE D.41 ASPI Command Code = 5: Set Host Adapter Parameters

Offset	# Bytes	Description	R/W
00h (00)	01h (01)	Command Code = 5	W
01h (01)	01h (01)	Status	R
02h (02)	01h (01)	Host Adapter Number	W
03h (03)	01h (01)	SCSI Request Flags	W
04h (04)	04h (04)	Reserved for Expansion = 0	—
08h (08)	10h (16)	Host Adapter Unique Parameters	W

ASPI Command Code = 5: Set Host Adapter Parameters

The definition of the host adapter unique parameters (defined in Table D.41) is left to implementation notes specific to a particular host adapter.

HANDLING GREATER THAN 16 MEGABYTES

Bus master ISA SCSI host adapters have a restriction in that they cannot perform DMA above 16 MB of RAM. This is because the ISA bus only receives 24 bits of the address bus (2^{24} = 16 MB). Thus, if you pass a buffer pointer above 16 MB to an ASPI manager/hardware that cannot handle it, you will most likely crash the file server. For these host adapters, you must make sure that both the ASPI SRBs and data buffers are below the first 16 MB of RAM. Adaptec's current host adapters handle this situation as detailed below:

Host Adapters Handling > 16 MB

AHA-1510

AHA-1520

AHA-1522

AIC-6260

AIC-6360

Host Adapters Handling PIO or Second-Party DMA Host Transfers

When in PIO mode, there is no restriction. When in second-party DMA mode, all ASPI SRBs and all data buffers must be below the first 16 MB of RAM.

AHA-1540

AHA-1542

Host Adapters Handling Bus Mastering ISA Mode Host Transfers

All ASPI SRBs and all data buffers must be below the first 16 MB of RAM.

AHA-1640

AHA-1740 (standard mode)

AHA-1740 (enhanced mode)

AHA-2740 series

Host Adapters Handling EISA Mode Host Transfers

Host adapters with no restrictions are the AHA-1740 in enhanced mode and the AHA-2740 series. These host adapters can directly access up to 4 GB of RAM.

For the AHA-1540/1542/1640/1740 (standard mode), you will need to run with an ASPI manager that can run with more than 16 MB of RAM. You will need aha1540.dsk v2.22 or later, or aha1640.dsk v2.22 or later for this.

NetWare 386 v3.11 (and above) has defined some new routines you can use to force a buffer allocation below the first 16 MB of RAM. Refer to the NetWare 386 Technical Specification for more information.

Scanning for New Devices

Most ASPI managers will not immediately scan the SCSI bus when first loaded. Rather, ASPI managers will wait for NetWare 386 to call its Scan for New Devices routine before the ASPI manager will scan the bus and update its internal ASPI device table. There may be some cases where you use ASPI's Get Device Type routine and your device does not appear although it is really there. In this case, you may want to request NetWare Force A Scan For New Devices, or you may want to scan the SCSI bus from within your own ASPI module. Refer to the appropriate NetWare 386 Technical Specification for more information.

VI. ASPI Specification Addendum

Adaptec has made minor additions to the ASPI specification to give greater flexibility to ASPI modules. The main addition is support for residual byte length reporting.

What Is Residual Byte Length?

Residual byte length is the number of bytes not transferred to, or received from, the target SCSI device. For example, if the ASPI buffer length for a SCSI Inquiry command is set for 100 bytes, but the target only returns back 36 bytes, this makes for a residual length of 64 bytes. As another example, if the ASPI buffer length for a SCSI write command is set for 514 bytes, but the target only takes 512 bytes, this makes for a residual length of two bytes.

How Do I Find Out If the ASPI Manager Loaded Supports This New Feature?

ASPI modules can determine if the loaded ASPI manager supports residual byte length by issuing an Extended Host Adapter Inquiry command. If you refer to the current ASPI for DOS specification, the standard Host Adapter Inquiry command is shown in Table D.42.

NOTE *The following discussion assumes you are already familiar with sending an ASPI Host Adapter Inquiry command to an ASPI manager. If not, refer to the section ASPI Command Codes for the operating system you are using.*

Host Adapter Inquiry Command

Offset #	# Bytes	Description	R/W
00h (00)	01h (01)	Command Code = 0	W
01h (01)	01h (01)	Status	R
02h (02)	01h (01)	Host Adapter Number	W
03h (03)	01h (01)	SCSI Request Flags	W
04h (04)	04h (04)	Reserved for Expansion = 0	
08h (08)	01h (01)	Number of Host Adapters	R
09h (09)	01h (01)	Target ID of Host Adapter	R
0Ah (10)	10h (16)	SCSI Manager ID	R
1Ah (26)	10h (16)	Host Adapter ID	R
2Ah (42)	10h (16)	Host Adapter Unique Parameters	R

TABLE D.43 **Extended Host Adapter Inquiry Command**

Offset	# Bytes	Description	R/W
00h (00)	01h (01)	Command Code = 0	W
01h (01)	01h (01)	Status	R
02h (02)	01h (01)	Host Adapter Number	W
03h (03)	01h (01)	SCSI Request Flags	W
04h (04)	01h (01)	Extended Request Signature = 55h	R/W
05h (05)	01h (01)	Extended Request Signature = AAh	R/W
06h (06)	01h (01)	Length of Extended Buffer (N),Low Byte	R/W
07h (07)	01h (01)	Length of Extended Buffer (N),High Byte	R/W
08h (08)	01h (01)	Number of Host Adapters	R
09h (09)	01h (01)	Target ID of Host Adapter	R
0Ah (10)	10h (16)	SCSI Manager ID	R
1Ah (26)	10h (16)	Host Adapter ID	R
2Ah (42)	10h (16)	Host Adapter Unique Parameters	R
3Ah (58)	N	Extended Buffer	R

The Extended Host Adapter Inquiry command is defined in Table D.43.

The user places the AA55h in bytes #4–5 of the structure. The Extended Buffer length (N) also needs to be initialized to the size of the extended buffer. A typical value would be four.

If the ASPI manager that is passed this new extended structure supports the Extended Host Adapter Inquiry command, the AA55h bytes will be flipped around to 55AAh. If this does not occur, the caller should assume that the ASPI manager does not support residual byte length or any of the other defined fields in the extended buffer. Note that it is possible to have multiple host adapters loaded where the ASPI manager loaded for one card supports this Extended call, while the ASPI manager for the other card does not. In certain situations, this

Extended Buffer Field Definition

Offset	# Bytes	Description	R/W
3Ah (58)	02h (02)	Features Word	R
	Bits 15-4 Reserved		
	Bit 3	0 = Not Wide SCSI 32 host adapter 1 = Wide SCSI 32 host adapter	
	Bit 2	0 = Not Wide SCSI 16 host adapter 1 = Wide SCSI 16 host adapter	
	Bit 1	0 = Residual byte length not reported 1 = Residual byte length reported	
	Bit 0	0 = Scatter/gather not supported 1 = Scatter/gather supported	
3Ch (60)	02h (02)	Maximum Scatter/gather list length	R
3Eh (62)	04h (04)	Maximum SCSI data transfer length	R

could cause the Extended Host Adapter Inquiry call to fail (i.e., default back to standard Host Adapter Inquiry call).

If the signature bytes are swapped (AA55h->55AAh), the Length of Extended Buffer field will also be modified to indicate how many bytes of the extended buffer were modified. This leaves us room to expand the meaning of the extended buffer in the future. For example, if an extended buffer size of ten is passed in, though the ASPI manager loaded only supports the first four bytes, then the value of four will be returned in the Length of Extended Buffer field.

Currently only the first eight bytes of the extended buffer are defined.

The extended buffer field is formatted as shown in Table D.44.

The Features Word bit fields defined above are self-explanatory. Note that if bit #2 is set, your ASPI module should scan SCSI IDs 0–15 on this host adapter for SCSI devices. The Scatter/Gather fields (including the scatter/gather list length) are currently only used by ASPI for OS/2.

A Maximum SCSI Data Transfer Length of zero indicates no data transfer length limitation. A nonzero value indicates the largest value you should specify in the ASPI SRB Data Allocation Length

IMPORTANT

Make sure you check the return value in the Length of Extended Buffer field to make certain that the field you are looking at is valid (e.g., if 4 is returned in the Length of Extended Buffer field, you should not use the value in the Maximum SCSI Data Transfer Length field).

Now That I Know My ASPI Manager Supports Residual Byte Length, How Do I Make Use of It?

The SCSI Request Flags Byte Is Currently Defined in the Various ASPI Specifications as Follows:

7	6	5	4	3	2	1	0
Rsvd	Rsvd	S/G	Direction Bits		Rsvd	Link	Post

NOTE *The S/G (scatter/gather) bit is currently used only under ASPI for OS/2.*

The New Definition for this Byte is as Follows:

7	6	5	4	3	2	1	0
Rsvd	Rsvd	S/G	Direction Bits		Residual	Link	Post

If bit #2 (Residual) is set to 1, and the ASPI manager supports residual byte length, then the residual byte length will be reported in the Data Allocation Length field within the SRB (bytes 0Ah–0Dh). On a typical command completion with all requested data transferred and no residual bytes, the Data Allocation Length field will contain the value zero.

NOTE *Adaptec EZ-SCSI v3.0 includes support for the residual byte feature.*

FUTURE/CAM™
DEVELOPER'S REFERENCE
MANUAL

for DOS and Windows™ Operating Systems

Introduction

Future/CAM™ is Future Domain's implementation of SCSI Common Access Method (CAM). Future/CAM™ is a software oriented interface designed to simplify writing device drivers for SCSI peripherals attached to SCSI controllers. Future/CAM™ allows all Future Domain SCSI controllers to be accessed in the same manner, allowing a single device driver to be written for all of the controllers.

Most often, device driver code is written to fill the gap between two interfaces. One interface is generally provided by the operating system, the other by the target hardware. In our case the target hardware is the Future Domain SCSI Controller in combination with some SCSI peripheral. A problem in past methods for bridging this gap was each time a new Future Domain Controller model was introduced a new driver had to be written. Such a new driver would take into account the differences between controllers. In well-structured code, this was laborious at best. In poorly structured code, this usually resulted in an almost completely new device driver for each new adapter. A second problem often encountered by device driver developers was a lack of knowledge both about how Future Domain hardware worked, and about the lowest levels of the SCSI protocol. A programmer had to expend considerable effort programming the host adapter hardware instead of

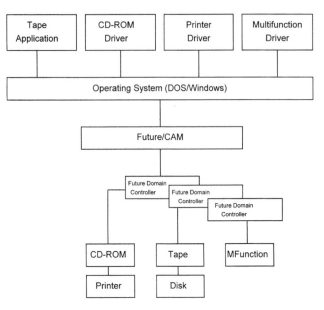

concentrating on programming his SCSI device. A final problem in developing SCSI drivers was that each driver usually attempted to control the hardware directly. This meant if two drivers were both loaded, one might try to take action while the other was already manipulating the hardware. This would cause both drivers to fail. The solution to all of the problems stated above is a single module that:

- Can handle the low level protocol issues of a host adapter
- Can be accessed by more than one device driver
- Can provide a consistent interface to device drivers despite the fact that the underlying hardware was completely different from one controller to another

This solution is Future/CAM™ which is meant to significantly simplify the SCSI device driver developer's job by handling all the low level SCSI details and providing a consistent interface across controllers. This lets the programmer concentrate on the important job of implementing a new driver for his new device. Since all the accesses to the hardware are handled by the Future/CAM™ module, multiple device drivers can use the same controller at the same time. This allows disks, tapes, CD-ROMs, WORMs, scanners, and other devices to share the same SCSI controller. Figure E.1 shows how Future/CAM™ fits in a typical SCSI environment.

The Future/CAM™ specification adheres as closely as possible to the proposed ANSI standard SCSI CAM specification by the accredited standards committee X3T9.2 (the SCSI Committee), but full functionality is not implemented. Please refer to *Future/CAM™ Commands* for the list of all the implemented CAM commands.

In an ideal world, one Future/CAM™ module is sufficient to support one kind of Future Domain controller across all commercial operating systems (DOS, Windows, OS/2, Novell, UNIX, etc.). Unfortunately, there are inherent differences on how each of the different operating systems handle software interfaces. This usually means that an application or driver written for one operating system (OS) will not work for another. Therefore, individual Future/CAM™ modules are provided for each of the currently available operating systems on the market, namely DOS, Windows, NOVELL, OS/2, and UNIX. This manual refers specifically to how to use Future/CAM™ on the DOS and Microsoft Windows™ operating systems. Reference manuals for Future/CAM™ on other operating systems are also available.

Essential Documents

This Future/CAM™ Developer's Reference Manual is not sufficient for developers to write good, workable applications and device drivers for SCSI devices. Other documents essential for a SCSI driver developer are the ANSI draft SCSI-2 Document X3.131-199x and the ANSI draft CAM Document X3T9.2/90-186. Recommended is a book from ENDL Publications called *The SCSI Bench Reference* (see address below). The SCSI-2 document presents the peripheral command sets that programmers will use to talk to SCSI peripherals. The draft CAM standard (X3T9.2/90-186) presents a detailed explanation of the different CAM Control Blocks that developers may use to write their applications or drivers. The *SCSI Bench Reference* is a shorthand reference of much of the information found in the SCSI-2 document. It contains general information and specifics for disk and tape drive peripherals.

The CAM and SCSI documents are available for purchase from:

Global Engineering Documents
15 Inverness Way East
Englewood, CO 80112-5704
800-854-7179
303-792-2181
FAX 303-792-2192

The *SCSI Bench Reference* is available from:

ENDL Publications
14426 Black Walnut Court
Saratoga, CA 95070
408-867-6630

Conventions

Wherever a number or combination of numbers and letters appears with an 'h' at the end, it means that the number is a hexadecimal (Base 16) number. For example, 2Ah is a hexadecimal number, which is equivalent to 42 in decimal.

INSTALLATION

Future/CAM™ for DOS and Future/CAM™ for Windows are part of the PowerSCSI!™ software that is distributed with the following Future Domain Controller Kits:

> TMC-850 MCD
>
> TMC-1670 SVP
>
> TMC-1680 SVP
>
> TMC-7000EX SVP
>
> MCS-700 SVP
>
> MCS-600 SVP
>
> FDU-DOSWIN Software Developer's Kit

The PowerSCSI!™ installation automatically detects which Future Domain controllers are present in the system and installs the corresponding Future/CAM drivers. Currently, there are some Future Domain ROM BIOS that already have embedded Future/CAM support. This support is functionally equivalent to Future/CAM™ for DOS minus the disconnect/reconnect and overlapped I/O capabilities of Future/CAM™ for DOS. By default, the PowerSCSI!™ installation will not install the Future/CAM™ for DOS drivers if any of the following ROM BIOS is detected:

> ROM BIOS Version 8.2 and later (for TMC-950 Controllers)
>
> ROM BIOS Version 3.2 and later (for TMC-1800 and 18C50 Controllers)

Refer to the table at the end of this appendix for a list of the different Future Domain controllers along with the latest BIOS versions used (subject to change without notice).

If desired, refer to the PowerSCSI!™ User's Manual for more information about Future/CAM™ installation.

DOS applications and device drivers can interface to Future/CAM by issuing CAM Control Blocks (CCB) via an interrupt call. The software interrupt 4Fh is used to access CAM in the DOS operating system. Currently, only real mode DOS applications are supported by Future/CAM™ for DOS. Protected mode Windows applications are handled by Future/CAM™ for Windows. Protected mode DOS applications that use a DOS Extender will be supported in a future version.

Refer to *Future/CAM™ Commands* for a discussion of all the CAM Control Blocks supported by Future/CAM™ for DOS.

Detecting the Presence of Future/CAM™

DOS applications and drivers can check for the presence of Future/CAM by performing the following Interrupt 4Fh call:

On entry:

AX	=	8200h
CX	=	8765h
DX	=	CBA9h

On return:

AH	=	0 (if successful)
CX	=	9ABCh
DX	=	5678h
ES:DI	=	address(segment:offset) of character string "SCSI_CAM"

All other registers unaffected.

Issuing CAM Control Blocks to Future/CAM™

After verifying that Future/CAM is present, DOS applications and drivers can issue a CCB by performing the following Interrupt 4Fh call:

On entry:

ES:BX	=	address (segment:offset) of the CCB
AX	=	8100h

On return:

AH = 0 if successful

  = any other value if an error occurred

All other registers unaffected

Using Future/CAM™ for Windows

Applications and device drivers can interface to Future/CAM™ for Windows by issuing CAM Control Blocks (CCB). Refer to *Future/ CAM Commands* for the different CCBs that Future/CAM supports.

Future/CAM™ for Windows is used specifically on the 386 Enhanced Mode of Windows. Standard and Real Mode applications can use Future/CAM™ for DOS. Under the 386 Enhanced Mode of Windows there are basically three (3) kinds of applications/drivers that can be executed, namely:

Windows Virtual Device Drivers

Windows Applications and Device Drivers

DOS Applications

Windows virtual device drivers or VxDs are 32-bit protected mode programs. Windows applications and device drivers are 16-bit protected mode programs. DOS applications which are executed within a DOS box/window are real mode programs and run in the Virtual 86 Mode (V86Mode) of Windows. To optimize the performance of these different types of programs, Future/CAM™ for Windows has provided different ways of accessing its "entry point." Please refer to the next sections on how to use Future/CAM™ for Windows depending on the type of program you are developing. For DOS applications refer back to *Using Future/CAM™ for DOS*.

Writing Windows Virtual Device Drivers

All Windows virtual device drivers (VxDs) are part of one, flat-model, 32-bit segment. This means that all the code and data are of the same group. VxDs do not need to export routines or data but instead call VxD services, which are public functions created by VxDs. To access VxD services, the VxDcall macro is used.

If you are developing a Windows virtual device driver and issue CCBs to Future/CAM you have to add the VMM.INC (included in your Microsoft Windows Device Driver Development Kit) file into your code and make a VxDcall to one of the VxD services available from Future/CAM™ for Windows. Refer to the next sections for the available VxD services.

TABLE E.1 Initialization Orders Used by Future/CAM™ for Windows

Future/CAM™ for Windows Driver	Initialization Order
VEXFCAMD.386	PageFile_Init_Order - 50h
V18FCAMD.386	PageFile_Init_Order - 40h
V9FCAMD.386	PageFile_Init_Order - 30h

Detecting the Presence of Future/CAM™

Windows virtual device drivers check for the presence of Future/CAM by performing the following VxDcall:

For the TMC-7000EX:

VxDcall   VEXFCAMD_Get_Version

For 1800 Series VLSI:

VxDcall   V18FCAMD_Get_Version

For 950 Series VLSI:

VxDcall   V9FCAMD_Get_Version

On entry:

None

On exit:

Carry flag is cleared

EAX = 0 if VEXFCAMD.386/V18FCAMD.386/V9FCAMD.386 is not initialized

EAX = 030Ah if VEXFCAMD.386/V18FCAMD.386/V9FCAMD.386 is initialized

Before calling this service, make sure that your Windows virtual device driver will be loaded after Future/CAM™ for Windows. To ensure this, you need to make the initialization order of your VxD to be greater than the ones used by Future/CAM. Table E.1 lists the current initialization orders used by Future/CAM™ for Windows.

The PageFile_Init_Order is defined in the VMM.INC file. The initialization order determines how Path IDs are assigned to each host bus adapter found. As a consequence of the predetermined initialization orders, Path IDs are assigned in the following order:

1.   All TMC-7000EX controllers

2.   All TMC-1800/18C50 based controllers

3.   All TMC-950 controllers

The assignment of Path IDs will not follow the above order if another Future/CAM (e.g., BIOS or DOS driver) had already assigned the Path IDs. Instead, the previously assigned Path IDs are used.

Getting the Number of Supported Controllers
A Windows VxD can get the total number of controllers supported by Future/CAM™ for Windows through the following VxD service:

For the TMC-7000EX:

    VxDcall   VEXFCAMD_Adapter_Count

For the 1800 Series VLSI:

    VxDcall   V18FCAMD_Adapter_Count

For the 950 Series VLSI:

    VxDcall   V9FCAMD_Adapter_Count

On entry:
    None

On exit:
    EAX = Total number of controllers supported by the specified Future/CAM driver

Getting the Highest Path ID of Supported Controllers
A Windows VxD can get the highest Path ID (the number assigned to each host adapter) assigned so far by Future/CAM™ for Windows through the following VxD service:

For TMC-7000EX:

    VxDcall   VEXFCAMD_Highest_Path_ID

For 1800 Series VLSI:

    VxDcall   V18FCAMD_Highest_Path_ID

For 950 Series VLSI:

    VxDcall   V9FCAMD_Highest_Path_ID

On entry:
    None

On exit:
    EAX = Highest Path ID assigned so far by the specified Future/CAM driver

Issuing CAM Control Blocks to Future/CAM™

A Windows virtual device driver can issue a CCB to Future/CAM™ for Windows through the following VxD service:

For the TMC-7000EX:

    VxDcall   VEXFCAMD_Send_CAM_Request

For the 1800 Series VLSI:

    VxDcall   V18FCAMD_Send_CAM_Request

For the 950 Series VLSI:

    VxDcall   V9FCAMD_Send_CAM_Request

On entry:

    EAX = 32-bit address of the CCB

On exit:

    Carry flag is cleared
    AH = 00

Writing Windows Applications and Device Drivers

Microsoft Windows applications (.EXE files) and device drivers (e.g., dynamic-link library DLL) using Graphics Device Interface (GDI) are 16-bit protected mode programs. Unlike Windows virtual device drivers, these programs do not have the capability to execute 32-bit instructions and cannot make VxD calls to Future/CAM for Windows.

For 16-bit Windows programs a software interrupt is provided to issue CCBs to Future/CAM™ for Windows. To adhere as closely as possible to the DOS CAM specifications the same software interrupt (4Fh) is used.

Detecting the Presence of Future/CAM™

Windows applications and device drivers can check for the presence of Future/CAM™ for Windows by performing the following Interrupt 4Fh call:

On entry:

AX	=	8200h
CX	=	8765h
DX	=	CBA9h

On return:

AH	=	0 (if successful)
CX	=	9ABCh
DX	=	5678h
ES:DI =		address(selector:offset) of character string "SCSI_CAM"

All other registers unaffected.

Issuing CAM Control Blocks to Future/CAM™

After verifying that Future/CAM is present, Windows applications and device drivers can issue a CCB by performing the following Interrupt 4Fh call:

On entry:

ES:BX =		address (selector:offset) of the CCB
AX	=	8100h

On return:

AH	=	0 if successful
	=	Any other value if an error occurred

All other registers unaffected

FUTURE/CAM™ COMMANDS

Currently, Future/CAM™ has support only for the following CAM Control Blocks (CCBs):

1. Get Device Type CCB
2. Path Inquiry CCB
3. Execute SCSI I/O Request CCB
4. Abort SCSI Command CCB
5. Reset SCSI Bus CCB
6. Reset SCSI Device CCB

You are strongly urged to study the next sections, which describe the supported CCBs the way Future/CAM had implemented it.

Each CCB has a CAM Status field and a CAM Flags field. Future/CAM does not use all of the status bytes and flag values defined in the ANSI CAM specifications. Refer to *Future/CAM™ Flags* and *Future/CAM™ Status Bytes* for the different flag values and status bytes used in Future/CAM.

Get Device Type CCB

Size in Bytes	Direction	Field Description
4	Out	Address of this CCB
2	Out	CAM Control Block Length = 15h
1	Out	Function Code = 02h
1	In	CAM Status
1	—	Reserved
1	Out	Path ID
1	Out	Target ID
1	Out	LUN
4	Out	CAM Flags
4	Out	Inquiry Data Pointer
1	In	Peripheral Device Type of Target/LUN

Finally, wherever a CCB field refers to an address or pointer, the format it uses depends on the kind of application/device driver that is being developed. The format *segment:offset* is used for DOS applications. The format *selector:offset* is used for Windows 16-bit protected mode programs. The 32-bit linear address format is used for Windows virtual device drivers.

Get Device Type CCB

The Get Device Type CCB (Table E.2) returns the SCSI Peripheral Device Type of a target device. The target device is identified by the combination of the Path ID, Target ID, and LUN fields in the CCB.

The ANSI draft CAM specifications has indicated that the Inquiry Data Pointer should return the inquiry data information if the value of the pointer field is not NULL. With Future/CAM, you have to set this field to NULL because Future/CAM will not return any inquiry data. If you need to get the inquiry information, you have to send an Inquiry SCSI command and retrieve the information from the data returned.

Path Inquiry CCB

The Path Inquiry CCB (Table E.3) has two functions. One is to obtain information about the controller and the second is to get the highest Path ID assigned so far. Path IDs are zero-based, which means that controllers are assigned with IDs in the order 0, 1, 2, 3, etc.

Size in Bytes	Direction	Field Description
4	Out	Address of this CCB
2	Out	CAM Control Block Length = 54h
1	Out	Function Code = 03h
1	In	CAM Status
1	æ	Reserved
1	Out	Path ID
1	Out	Target ID
1	Out	LUN
4	Out	CAM Flags
1	In	Version Number
1	In	SCSI Capabilities
1	In	Target Mode Support*
1	In	Miscellaneous
2	In	Engine Count*
14	In	Vendor Unique*
4	In	Size of Private Data Area*
4	In	Asynchronous Event Capabilities*
1	In	Highest Path ID Assigned
1	In	SCSI Device ID (of Initiator)
1	æ	Reserved
1	—	Reserved
16	In	Vendor ID of SIM-supplier
16	In	Vendor ID of HBA-supplier
4	Out	OSD Usage*

If an * appears beside a field, this indicates that the field is not used by Future/CAM. Values assigned to these fields that are write (Out Direction) fields are ignored by Future/CAM and the value zero (0) is assigned to those that are read (In Direction) fields.

The Version Number is the revision number of the ANSI draft CAM supported.

The value for the SCSI Capabilities field is currently 0 for the 950 Series VLSI, 10h for the 1800 Series VLSI and 91h for the TMC-7000EX. The 10h means that synchronous data transfers is supported and 91h means synchronous data transfers, modify data pointers, and soft reset features are supported.

The Miscellaneous field has a value of 20h meaning no inquiry data is kept by Future/CAM and therefore, the Get Device Type CCB will not have any inquiry data information on return.

The Highest Path ID Assigned field is valid on return only if the Path ID field has an FFh value.

The SCSI Device ID (of Initiator) field value is currently equal to 7 for the 1800/18C50 and 950 Series VLSI controllers. For the TMC-7000EX this value is dependent on what ID the adapter is configured to.

The Vendor ID of SIM-supplier field has the ASCII string "FUTURED 1800" for the 1800 Series VLSI, "FUTURED TMC-950" for the 950 Series VLSI and "FUTURED 7000EX" for the TMC-7000EX.

The Vendor ID of HBA-supplier field has the ASCII string "FUTURED 1800 0" for the 1800 Series VLSI, "FUTURED TMC-9500" for the 950 Series VLSI and "FUTURED 7000EX 0" for the TMC-7000EX.

Execute SCSI I/O Request CCB

The Execute SCSI I/O Request CCB (Table E.4) is used to issue SCSI commands to Future/CAM.

If an * appears beside a field, this indicates that the field is not used by Future/CAM. Values assigned to these fields that are write (Out Direction) fields are ignored by Future/CAM and the value zero (0) is assigned to those that are read (In Direction) fields.

The Callback on Completion field contains the address of the function to call after the CCB is completed. The address of the completed CCB is passed on the stack to inform the application/device driver which CCB has completed.

The Scatter/Gather List or Data Buffer Pointer field contains the address of either the Scatter/Gather List or a contiguous data buffer. The CAM Flags field must indicate if either a Scatter/Gather list is used or a contiguous data buffer is used. Scatter/Gather is supported only in Future/CAM™ for Windows. This feature is implemented to work only with 32-bit protected mode programs such as Windows VxDs. All data areas to be used for Scatter/Gather must be page locked before issuing the CCB.

The Data Transfer Length field indicates in number of bytes the total length of the data transfer.

The Sense Info Buffer Pointer field contains the address of the sense data returned by the Request Sense SCSI command issued immediately after a Check Condition Status has occurred on the SCSI bus. The Sense Info Buffer Length field indicates the length of the allocated sense buffer.

The CDB Length field indicates in number of bytes the length of the SCSI Command Data Block (CDB) to be sent.

The Number of Scatter/Gather Entries field indicates how many entries are in the Scatter/Gather list. Each entry contains two values, the Data Address and its corresponding Data Length. The format of the Scatter/Gather list is shown in Table E.5.

TABLE E.4 Execute SCSI I/O Request CCB

Size in Bytes	Direction	Field Description
4	Out	Address of this CCB
2	Out	CAM Control Block Length = 58h + n
1	Out	Function Code = 01h
1	In	CAM Status
1	—	Reserved
1	Out	Path ID
1	Out	Target ID
1	Out	LUN
4	Out	CAM Flags
4	Out	Peripheral Driver Pointer*
4	Out	Next CCB Pointer*
4	Out	Request Mapping Information*
4	Out	Callback on Completion
4	Out	Scatter/Gather List or Data Buffer Pointer
4	Out	Data Transfer Length
4	Out	Sense Information Buffer Pointer
1	Out	Sense Information Buffer Length
1	Out	CDB Length
2	Out	Number of Scatter/Gather entries
4	—	Vendor Unique Field*
1	In	SCSI Status
1	In	Auto Sense Residual Length*
2	—	Reserved
4	In	Residual Length
12	Out	CDB
4	Out	Timeout Value
4	Out	Message Buffer Pointer (Target only)*
2	Out	Message Buffer Length (Target only)*
2	Out	Vendor Unique Flags*
1	Out	Tag Queue Action*
3	—	Reserved
n	Out	Private Data*

The SCSI Status field contains the value of the byte returned during the Status Phase of the SCSI command.

The Residual Length field contains the length in bytes of the data that was not transferred. This value is zero for commands completed without error.

The CDB field contains either the address of the SCSI Command Data Block (CDB) or the actual CDB bytes. The CAM Flags field must indicate which one is used.

TABLE E.5 Scatter/Gather List Format

Size in Bytes	Description
4	Data Address 1
4	Data Length 1
4	Data Address 2
4	Data Length 2
:	:
4	Data Address n
4	Data Length n

TABLE E.6 Abort SCSI Command CCB

Size in Bytes	Direction	Field Description
4	Out	Address of this CCB
2	Out	CAM Control Block Length = 14h
1	Out	Function Code = 10h
1	In	CAM Status
1	—	Reserved
1	Out	Path ID
1	Out	Target ID
1	Out	LUN
4	Out	CAM Flags
4	Out	CCB to be Aborted Pointer

E

The Timeout Value field contains in seconds the total time allotted for the CCB to complete. If no value is specified, the default value of 60 seconds is used. A value of −1 means an indefinite timeout.

Abort SCSI Command CCB

The Abort SCSI Command CCB (Table E.6) is used to abort a previously issued Execute SCSI I/O CCB. This must be issued only to an I/O operation that has not completed.

The Abort SCSI Command CCB causes Future/CAM to search for the CCB to be aborted in the list of active CCBs. If the CCB is not found, a CAM Status of *Unable to Abort Request* will be returned. If the CCB to be aborted is found, a CAM Status of *Completed Without Error* is returned. The success and failure of aborting the CCB is never assured and the actual outcome is returned on the CAM Status byte of the aborted CCB.

Reset SCSI Bus CCB

Size in Bytes	Direction	Field Description
4	Out	Address of this CCB
2	Out	CAM Control Block Length = 10h
1	Out	Function Code = 11h
1	In	CAM Status
1	—	Reserved
1	Out	Path ID
1	Out	Target ID
1	Out	LUN
4	Out	CAM Flags

Reset SCSI Device CCB

Size in Bytes	Direction	Field Description
4	Out	Address of this CCB
2	Out	CAM Control Block Length = 10h
1	Out	Function Code = 12h
1	In	CAM Status
1	—	Reserved
1	Out	Path ID
1	Out	Target ID
1	Out	LUN
4	Out	CAM Flags

Reset SCSI Bus CCB

The Reset SCSI Bus CCB (Table E.7) is used to reset the SCSI bus corresponding to the specified Path ID. This always results to a SCSI RST signal being asserted and causes all the devices attached to the bus to be reset. This operation must be used with much care.

The Reset SCSI Bus CCB will always succeed and the CAM Status byte of *Completed Without Error* is returned. Any pending CCBs before the bus reset will have a CAM Status of *SCSI Bus Reset Sent/Received* on return.

Reset SCSI Device CCB

The Reset SCSI Device CCB (Table E.8) is used to reset the device specified in the Target ID field. This CCB will cause Future/CAM to attempt sending a Bus Device Reset Message over the SCSI bus. The success

Future/CAM Flags

Byte\Bit	7	6	5	4	3	2	1	0
0	Direction Bits		AutoS	SG	DClbck	0	0	CdbPtr
1	DCnct	0	0	0	0	0	0	0
2	0	0	0	0	0	0	0	0
3	0	0	0	0	0	0	0	0

of this operation is dependent on the target device and may not always result to a device reset. This operation must be used with much care.

If the Bus Device Reset Message is successfully sent, the CAM Status of *Completed Without Error* is returned, otherwise another status is returned depending on what caused the failure.

The actual success and failure of the Reset SCSI Device CCB may be known from the CAM Status returned for any previously pending I/O operation for the target. If the Bus Device Reset is successful, the CAM Status Byte of *Bus Device Reset Sent* will be returned for all pending I/O operations of the target.

FUTURE/CAM™ FLAGS

Each CCB has a CAM Flags field used to instruct Future/CAM on how the command is to be processed. The ANSI draft CAM specification has allocated 4 bytes for this field and defined the meaning of each of the 32 bits. Future/CAM does not recognize all the flags defined by the CAM specification and Table E.9 shows the ones used by Future/CAM.

The Direction Bits indicates the data movement direction. The following are the possible values:

01h = In Direction or a Read Operation

10h = Out Direction or a Write Operation

11h = No Data Transfer

If no data transfer is expected, the Data Transfer Length field of the Execute SCSI I/O Request CCB must be initialized to zero. Failure to do so will result in unpredictable system behavior. Also, the No Data Transfer direction bit must not be used with a CCB requiring data transfer on the TMC-7000EX Future/CAM.

Setting the AutoS bit disables sending of a Request Sense command whenever a Check Condition Status occurs on the SCSI bus.

Setting the SG bit indicates that the Scatter/Gather List or Data Buffer Length field in the Execute SCSI I/O CCB contains an address to a Scatter/Gather list. If the SG bit is 0, then the said field has the address of a contiguous data buffer.

Setting the DClbck bit indicates that Future/CAM must not call the callback function in the Callback on Completion field of the Execute SCSI I/O CCB. Assigning a NULL to the Callback on Completion field has the same effect.

Setting the CdbPtr bit indicates that the first 4 bytes of the CDB field in the Execute SCSI I/O CCB contains a pointer to the location of the CDB. If this bit is 0, the CDB field has the actual CDB bytes.

Setting the DCnct bit indicates that SCSI Disconnect/Reconnect must be disabled.

FUTURE/CAM™ STATUS BYTES

The CAM Status field of a CCB contains information on what had happened to the issued CCB. This field normally indicates success but in the few instances that the CCB was not successfully completed, the CAM Status byte returned can shed light on what went wrong.

Table E.10 *Future/CAM™ Status Bytes* lists all the status bytes that are returned by Future/CAM. If Auto Sense is enabled and sense data is available, CAM Status Byte 80H may be OR'd with another CAM Status byte on return.

TABLE E.10 Future/CAM™ Status Bytes

Status Byte Value	Status Byte Description
00h	Request in Progress
01h	Request Completed Without Error
02h	Request Aborted by Host
03h	Unable to Abort Request
04h	Request Completed with Error
07h	Invalid Path ID
08h	SCSI Device Not Installed
0Ah	Target Selection Timeout
0Bh	Command Timeout
0Eh	SCSI Bus Reset Sent/Received
0Fh	Uncorrectable Parity Error Detected
12h	Data OverRun/UnderRun
14h	Target Bus Phase Sequence Failure
16h	Cannot Provide Requested Capability
17h	Bus Device Reset Sent
80h	Auto Sense Data is Valid

To better understand the Future/CAM interface discussed in the previous sections, some simple program codes are provided here. Some of the codes are written in C, some are in BASIC, and some are in Intel's assembly language. These are not the required programming languages for developers to use Future/CAM. Other programming languages may be used as long as they are capable of issuing Interrupt calls and/or call VxD services.

For DOS and Windows Applications or Device Drivers

A majority of the development efforts for DOS and Windows applications and device drivers are either written in C, Assembly, or BASIC languages. The sample codes provided here are written in a combination of these three programming languages.

Using C Programming Language

```
//
// The following C code (Microsoft C/C++ V7.0) shows two functions that
// Windows or DOS applications/drivers (for VxD drivers, see the next
// section) developers may use as samples on how Future/CAM is called
// and used. The first function check_for_cam() tests for the presence
// of Future/CAM. This function must be called before any CCBs are
// issued. The second function issue_path_inquiry_ccb() is a very simple
// example of how a CCB is issued to Future/CAM.
//
#include <malloc.h>
#include <dos.h>
//
// check_for_cam();
// This routine checks for the presence of Future/CAM.
//
int check_for_cam()
{
    union _REGS inregs, outregs;
    struct _SREGS segregs;
    char label[] = "SCSI_CAM";
    char *scsi_cam_label = label;
    int cam_found=0;
```

```c
        inregs.x.ax = 0x8200;
        inregs.x.cx = 0x8765;
        inregs.x.dx = 0xCBA9;
        segread(&segregs);
        int86x(0x4F, &inregs, &outregs, &segregs);
        if (outregs.h.ah != 0x00 || outregs.x.dx != 0x5678
                || outregs.x.cx != 0x9ABC)
                return 0;
    asm{
            cld
            mov     es, segregs.es
            mov     di, outregs.x.di
            mov     cx, 8
            mov     si, WORD PTR scsi_cam_label
            repe    cmpsb
            je      its_present
            jmp     not_present
    its_present:
            mov     cam_found, 1
    not_present:
        }
        return (cam_found);
}
//
// The following is the structure declaration for the Path Inquiry CCB
//
struct path_inquiry_t{
        unsigned long       pi_ccb_addr;
        unsigned short      pi_total_length;
        unsigned char       pi_function_code;
        unsigned char       pi_cam_status;
        unsigned char       pi_reserved;
        unsigned char       pi_path_id;
        unsigned char       pi_target;
        unsigned char       pi_lun;
```

```c
    unsigned long        pi_flags;
    unsigned char        pi_cam_version_number;
    unsigned char        pi_scsi_capabilities;
    unsigned char        pi_target_mode_support;
    unsigned char        pi_misc;
    unsigned short       pi_engine_count;
    unsigned char        pi_vendor_unique[14];
    unsigned long        pi_private_data_size;
    unsigned long        pi_asynch_event_capability;
    unsigned char        pi_adapters_found;
    unsigned char        pi_adapter_id;
    unsigned char        pi_reserved_1;
    unsigned char        pi_reserved_2;
    unsigned char        pi_sim_vendor_id[16];
    unsigned char        pi_hba_vendor_id[16];
    unsigned long        pi_os_dependent;
};
//
// issue_path_inquiry_ccb()
// This function fills up the Path Inquiry CCB and issues it to
// Future/CAM via Interrupt 4Fh.
//
int issue_path_inquiry_ccb()
{
    union {
        unsigned char buf[4];
        unsigned int reg[2];
        unsigned long val;
    } long_convert;
    struct path_inquiry_t ccb;
    union REGS inregs, outregs;
    struct SREGS segregs;
    memset ((char *) (&ccb), 0x00, sizeof(ccb));
    ccb.pi_total_length = sizeof(struct path_inquiry_t);
    ccb.pi_function_code = 0x03;
```

E

```
    ccb.pi_flags |= 0xC0;               // No data transfer
    ccb.pi_path_id = 0xFF;              // get the highest path id
    long_convert.val = (char *)(&ccb);
    segread(&segregs);
    inregs.x.ax = 0x8100;
    inregs.x.bx = long_convert.reg[0];
    segregs.es = long_convert.reg[1];
    int86x(0x4F, &inregs, &outregs, &segregs);// issue it to Future/CAM
    return (!outregs.h.ah);
}
```

Using BASIC Programming Language

```
100        REM The following is an example of how to detect for the presence
110        REM of Future/CAM in BASIC.
120        DEF SEG = &H1800
130        SUBRT = 0
140        C = &H8765
150        D = &HCBA9
160        A = &H8200
170        CALL SUBRT (A,C,D)
180        IF A = 0, GOTO 1000
190        REM Future/CAM is present,  CCBs can now be issued
           :
           :
           :     (Continue Future/CAM processing)
           :
           :
1000       REM Future/CAM is not present. Process the exit procedure now.
           :
           :     (Exit procedure processing)
           :
```

At location 1800:0000 the following assembly language code must be loaded:

```
CSEG      SEGMENT
          ASSUME CS:CSEG
```

```
SUBRT      PROC    FAR
           PUSH    BP                          ; Save BP
           MOV     BP, SP                      ; Set Base Parameter List
           MOV     SI, [BP]+10                 ; Get address of parameter A
           MOV     AX, [SI]                    ; AX gets the value of parameter A
           MOV     SI, [BP]+8                  ; Get address of parameter C
           MOV     CX, [SI]                    ; CX gets the value of parameter C
           MOV     SI, [BP]+6                  ; Get address of parameter D
           MOV     DX, [SI]                    ; DX gets the value of parameter D
           INT     4FH                         ; perform Future/CAM call
           CMP     AH, 0                       ; Is the function supported?
           JNE     NOT_THERE                   ; If no, Future/CAM is not loaded
           CMP     DX, 5678H                   ; Check signature
           JNE     NOT_THERE                   ; Failed, Future/CAM not loaded
           CMP     CX, 9ABCH                   ; Check signature
           JNE     NOT_THERE                   ; Failed, Future/CAM not loaded
           CLD                                 ; Set direction flag
           MOV     CX, 8                       ; Load string length
           MOV     SI, OFFSET SCSI_CAM         ; Get string address
           REPE    CMPSB                       ; Compare strings
           JNE     NOT_THERE                   ; Failed, Future/CAM not loaded
           MOV     DI, [BP]+10                 ; Get address of parameter A
           MOV     [DI], 1                     ; Indicate success
           POP     BP                          ; Restore BP
           RET     6                           ; Far return to BASIC
NOT_THERE:
           MOV     DI, [BP]+10                 ; Get address of parameter A
           MOV     [DI], 0                     ; Indicate failure
           POP     BP                          ; Restore BP
           RET     6                           ; Far return tp BASIC
SUBRT      ENDP
SCSI_CAM           DB    'SCSI_CAM'            ; String to compare
CSEG       ENDS
           END
```

E

For Windows Virtual Device Driver

```
;---------------------------------------------------------------------
;
; The following procedure is a sample 386 assembly language code that
; calls the VxD services provided by Future/CAM. This does not
; represent any actual code that a developer must follow. It is
; provided only as an example on how VxD services are called.
;
;---------------------------------------------------------------------
AdapterEXCount      dd      0
Adapter18Count      dd      0
Adapter9Count       dd      0
HighestEXPath       dd      0
Highest18Path       dd      0
Highest9Path        dd      0
UserCCB             db      88 dup(?)                   ; Data area for the CAM
                                                        ;   Control Block (CCB)
BeginProc           VSampleD_Device_Init
    VxDcall             VEXFCAMD_Get_Version            ; Check for 7000EX Future/CAM
    jc                  VDI_Abort_loading              ; 7000EX Future/CAM not found

    cmp                 eax, 030Ah                     ; Verify the return value
    jne                 VDI_Abort_Loading              ; May not be 7000EX Future/CAM

    VxDcall             V18FCAMD_Get_Version           ; Check for 1800 Future/CAM
    jc                  VDI_Abort_loading              ; 1800 Future/CAM not found

    cmp                 eax, 030Ah                     ; Verify the return value
    jne                 VDI_Abort_Loading              ; May not be 1800 Future/CAM

    VxDcall             V9FCAMD_Get_Version            ; Check for 950 Future/CAM
    jc                  VDI_Abort_loading              ; 950 Future/CAM not found

    cmp                 eax, 030Ah                     ; Verify the return value
    jne                 VDI_Abort_Loading              ; May not be 950 Future/CAM

        .                                              ; Do other initialization code
        .
        .
        .
```

```
VxDcall VEXFCAMD_Adapter_Count            ; Get no. of 7000EX controllers
mov     [AdapterEXCount], eax             ; Store the value

VxDcall V18FCAMD_Adapter_Count            ; Get number of 1800 controllers
mov     [Adapter18Count], eax             ; Store the value

VxDcall V9FCAMD_Adapter_Count             ; Get number of 950 controllers
mov     [Adapter9Count], eax              ; Store the value


    .
    .                                     ; Do other initialization code
    .
    .


VxDcall      VEXFCAMD_Highest_Path_ID     ; Get the highest path id
                                          ; (7000EX)
mov          [Highest18Path], eax         ; Store the value

VxDcall      V18FCAMD_Highest_Path_ID     ; Get the highest path id (1800)
mov          [Highest18Path], eax         ; Store the value

VxDcall      V9FCAMD_Highest_Path_ID      ; Get the highest path id (950)
mov          [Highest9Path], eax          ; Store the value


    .
    .                                     ; Do other initialization code
    .
    .


; At this point, all the fields of the UserCCB data structure
; must be filled. The UserCCB (CAM Control Block) will be
; issued to Future/CAM (TMC-7000EX in this case) for processing
mov   eax, OFFSET32 UserCCB               ; Get the 32-bit address of CCB
VxDcall      VEXFCAMD_Send_CAM_Request    ; Issue it to Future/CAM (7000EX)
```

E

```
                                           ; Do other initialization code
        .

        .


; At this point, all the fields of the UserCCB data structure
; must be filled. The UserCCB (CAM Control Block) will be
; issued to Future/CAM (1800 Series VLSI in this case) for
; processing.

mov        eax, OFFSET32 UserCCB        ; Get the 32-bit address of CCB
VxDcall    V18FCAMD_Send_CAM_Request    ; Issue it to Future/CAM (1800)


        .
                                           ; Do other initialization code
        .

        .


; At this point, all the fields of the UserCCB data structure
; must be filled. The UserCCB (CAM Control Block) will be
; issued to Future/CAM (950 Series VLSI in this case) for
; processing.

mov        eax, OFFSET32 UserCCB        ; Get the 32-bit address of CCB
VxDcall    V9FCAMD_Send_CAM_Request     ; Issue it to Future/CAM (950)


        .
                                           ; Do other initialization code
        .

        .


    clc
    ret

VDI_Abort_Loading:

    ret

EndProc        VSample_Device_Init
```

Table of Future Domain
Controllers and Integrated Circuits

TABLE E.11 Future Domain Controllers and Integrated Circuits

Bus	Controller	IC Chip	ROM BIOS Version
ISA			
	TMC-850M	9C50	8.5
	TMC-1610	18C30	3.5
	TMC-1660	18C30	3.5
	TMC-1680	18C30	3.5
MCA			
	MCS-700	18C50	3.2
PCMCIA			
	SCSI2GO	18C30	3.2
PCI			
	TMC-3260	36C70	2.0
Plug and Play ISA			
	PNP-1630	18PNP300	4.0A

List of IRQ Levels, Memory Base Addresses, and
I/O Port Addresses for Future Domain Controllers

TABLE E.12 Allowable IRQ Levels for Future Domain Controllers

Controller	IRQ 3	IRQ 5	IRQ 10	IRQ 11	IRQ 12	IRQ 14	IRQ 15
TMC-850M	•	•					
TMC-1660	•	•	•	•	•	•	•
TMC-1680	•	•	•	•	•	•	•
MCS-600	•	•	•	•	•	•	•
MCS-700	•	•	•	•	•	•	•
TMC-1610	•	•	•	•	•	•	•
TMC-3260	•	•	•	•	•	•	•
PNP-1630		•	•	•			•
SCSI2GO	•	•	•	•	•	•	•

Allowable Memory Base Addresses for Future Domain Controllers

Controller	C000	C400	C800	CA00	CC00	CE00	D000	D200	D400	D600	D800	DA00	DC00	DE00	E800	EC00
TMC-850M														•	•	•
TMC-1660			•	•	•	•								•		
TMC-1680			•	•	•	•								•		
TMC-1610			•	•	•	•								•		
TMC-3260			•	•	•	•								•		
MCS-600			•	•	•	•								•		
MCS-700			•	•	•	•								•		
PNP-1630			•	•	•	•								•		
SCSI2GO			•	•	•	•								•		

I/O Port Addresses for Future Domain Controllers

Controller	140	150	160	170
TMC-850M	•	•	•	•
TMC-1660	•	•	•	•
TMC-1680	•	•	•	•
TMC-1610	•	•	•	•
TMC-3260	•	•	•	•
MCS-600	•	•	•	•
MCS-700	•	•	•	•
PNP-1630	•	•	•	•
SCSI2GO	•			

F

I D E   V E R S U S   S C S I

This section is an adaptation of written material provided by DPT (Distributed Processing Technology). DPT is a leading manufacturer of SCSI host adapters and RAID controllers, located in Maitland, Florida.

IDE Versus SCSI: Which Disk Interface Is Best?

The first PC/AT computers introduced by IBM in the early eighties used low-capacity, ST506 disk drives. The disk controller used in these early machines, a Western Digital WD1003, was quite unsophisticated by today's standards. The WD1003 controlled up to two ST506 drives and used the PC's processor to move the data to and from a buffer in the controller.

Demand for higher disk storage capacities soon reached the limits of ST506 drives. A new disk interface that offered a solution to this limitation was ESDI (enhanced small disk interface). Because of the large degree of similarity between the older ST506 and new ESDI interfaces, it was easy for controller manufacturers to build ESDI controllers that could emulate the original WD1003 ST506 controller register set and protocol. This avoided the necessity of writing a new BIOS, as well as new disk drivers for every PC operating system. As a result, ESDI was initially the interface of choice for high-capacity drives used in PCs.

Unfortunately, ESDI also had limitations. Like the ST506, it transferred data serially, one bit at a time. This placed practical limitations on the data transfer rate, and because of the fixed rotational speed, also the maximum number of bits that could be squeezed onto each track on the disk media. In the late eighties, drive manufacturers introduced the first fully intelligent SCSI disk drives by including an embedded disk controller in the drive electronics.

In addition to offering faster, parallel data transfer, SCSI drives offered significant architectural advantages over the previous ST506 and ESDI drives. Since each SCSI drive had its own embedded disk controller, it was now possible for the computer to issue simultaneous commands to every drive in the system. Each drive could then fully overlap its seek, rotational positioning and read or write operations with the other SCSI drives. The data could be fully buffered on the drive and transferred at high speed over the shared SCSI bus when a time slot was available.

The primary problem with SCSI drives was initially the lack of software support. Unlike ESDI, SCSI looked nothing like the old ST506 interface, and thus SCSI controllers that emulated the WD1003 ST506 disk controller were much more difficult to build. In the late eighties, DPT built such a controller—the PM2001. The PM2001 required no special software drivers since it emulated the old WD1003 ST506 controller register set. The drive companies also introduced an equivalent product by embedding a WD1003 register set compatible controller on the disk drive. These drives were called Integrated Drive Electronics, or IDE, drives.

In addition to requiring no special software, IDE drives offered the advantage of eliminating the need for any external controller or host bus adapter. Only a simple paddle card with a couple of ICs to implement the drive selection logic was required. Since the cost to build an IDE drive was identical to the cost of a SCSI drive, many low-end desktop PCs offered special connectors for one or two IDE drives, thereby freeing up a bus slot and reducing cost. However, because of a limitation of the original WD1003 controller register set, no more than two IDE drives are supported by the standard BIOS.

Each advantage of IDE, however, came with a cost. As PCs advanced beyond single-user applications, the ability to overlap the operation of multiple drives became instrumental in obtaining higher I/O rates from the disk subsystem. IDE drives, which were tied to the old WD1003 ST506 controller protocol, could only single-task I/O operations. Once a command had been issued to an IDE drive, the operating system had to wait until the command had been completed before issuing another command to any drive.

In addition, WD1003 protocol relied on the processor to move the data one word at a time between a buffer on the controller and the computer's RAM. This limited the speed of the data transfer, as well as precluding hardware scatter/gather support that can be implemented by bus-mastering SCSI controllers.

Although IDE drives do not require a host adapter card, more and more PCs require tape backup, CD-ROM, or optical drive support, and thus must still be configured with a SCSI host bus adapter.

In short, in the late eighties, IDE drives initially offered a high degree of software compatibility at a low cost. However, the incremental cost of supporting SCSI drives has dropped to zero in many cases since the SCSI host bus adapter can be shared with other devices like tape and optical drives. In addition, all major operating systems today include software support for a large range of SCSI devices. The disadvantages of IDE, although not as apparent under DOS, severely limit the performance of multiuser operating systems like Novell NetWare, UNIX, or Windows NT, which realize large benefits from multitasked, overlapped I/O, bus mastering, scatter/gather memory access, and I/O command queuing, all offered by SCSI drives with intelligent host bus adapters.

WHY ARE THE LIMITATIONS OF IDE NOT APPARENT UNDER DOS?

1. IDE does not support overlapped, multitasked I/O. Neither does DOS.
2. IDE does not support I/O command queuing. Neither does DOS.
3. IDE does not support bus mastering, thus data transfer must be done via slower PIO (processor I/O). However, unless the record size is quite large, reducing data transfer time through bus mastering produces little additional performance under single-user operating systems like DOS.
4. Since IDE supports only PIO data transfer, scatter/gather memory access is not possible. However, simple operating systems like DOS do not use virtual memory addressing that causes memory fragmentation, and thus DOS does not benefit from scatter/gather memory access.
5. No more than two IDE drives can be supported in a PC system without a special, nonstandard BIOS. However, most DOS users do not require more than two drives.
6. Because of limitations in the original WD1003 ST506 controller register set addressing, IDE imposes drive capacity limitations of 528 MB per drive without a special, nonstandard BIOS. However, few DOS systems require drive capacity greater than 528 MB.
7. Unlike SCSI, IDE does not support tape or optical drives. However, most DOS systems today are still not configured with tape or optical drives.

BUILDING FAST
SCSI SUBSYSTEMS

This section is an adaptation of written material provided by DPT (Distrib-uted Processing Technology). DPT is a leading manufacturer of SCSI host adapters and RAID controllers, located in Maitland, Florida.

Acknowledgments

Information for this paper is based upon testing conducted in the DPT labs as well as the work of many others. Much valuable research has been done under the auspices of the SCSI working committees and we are very appreciative for all their excellent publications. The major por-tion of the wording in this report has been copied directly from the SCSI specifications themselves or from papers and articles published by the committee membership, as well as others. In particular, we would like to thank Kurt Chan of Hewlett-Packard, Gordon Matheson of Hewlett-Packard, Paul Boulay of Laser Magnetic Storage International, James E. Schuessler of National Semiconductor Corp., Skip Jones of Emulex Corp., Peter Blackford of Cooper Industries, and John Lohmeyer of NCR Corp.

SCSI has become the interface of choice for high-performance storage subsystems. The original SCSI specification envisioned transfer rates of up to 5 MHz. The new SCSI-2 specification allows faster rates of up to 10 MHz. However, by pushing these original SCSI standards to their limits, system integrators have seen reliability problems mount. The dilemma is that signal quality problems, which have been present from the start, become more apparent as buses become more heavily loaded and are operated at faster data rates.

The SCSI electrical specification has two mutually exclusive transceiver specifications:

1. Differential RS-485 transceivers that allow for up to 10 MHz data transfer at a maximum cable length of 25 meters (82 feet).

2. Single-ended TTL transceivers, which allow

   - Slow synchronous data transfer up to 5 MHz at a maximum cable length of 6 meters (19 feet).

   - Fast synchronous data transfer up to 10 MHz at a maximum cable length of 3 meters (9 feet).

   - Asynchronous data transfer (no maximum transfer rate is given but typical rates are about 1.5 MHz to 2 MHz) at a maximum cable length of 6 meters (19 feet).

Each transfer may consist of one, two, or four bytes, depending on the bus width option implemented. However, today most implementations utilize only byte-wide data.

When 10 MHz Fast SCSI was first proposed, only differential SCSI transceivers were envisioned. However, many drive manufacturers have chosen to implement Fast SCSI with single-ended drivers because of savings in cost, size, and power consumption. This presents several problems to integrators, especially as systems increase in speed and size. A very common symptom of an unreliable single-ended interface is bus misoperation following the addition of devices or cabling to the system. The failures increase as the number of devices and length of the cable grow. The failures are also unpredictable and generally catastrophic in nature, and they are not necessarily the same from system to system.

Most data reliability problems stem from signal reflections and noise that are read by SCSI receivers as incorrect data or false SCSI bus phases. The SCSI cable is a transmission line that has a characteristic impedance whose value depends upon the type of cable used. Discontinuities in this impedance can cause signal reflections to occur. These impedance variations can be the result of extra capacitance internal to SCSI devices, connectors, improper terminators, mixing of different cable types, cable stubs, etc. At 10 MHz Fast SCSI rates, these reflections are much more prevalent than at the slower 5 MHz SCSI rates. Additional noise picked up from external devices, as well as from other signals on the SCSI cable, can add to these false signals. Unfortunately, a 10 MHz Fast SCSI bus is a more efficient transmitter of noise than a slower 5 MHz SCSI bus.

A carefully well-configured, single-ended SCSI bus can reliably transfer data at 10 MHz without a problem. However, good engineering practices should be followed in order to guarantee success:

Use as short a cable length as possible. The ANSI XT3T9.3 SCSI-3 Parallel Interface working group is currently recommending that for 10 MHz data transfers the total cable length should not exceed three meters (10 feet).

Avoid stub clustering. Do not space SCSI devices on the cable any closer than 0.3 meters (12 inches) apart. When devices are clustered closely together on the SCSI cable, their capacitances add together to create an impedance discontinuity and thus reflections. SCSI devices should be spaced as evenly as possible.

Cable stub length should not exceed 0.1 meters (4 inches). Some SCSI devices may create stubs internal to the device that exceed this value, resulting in excessive capacitive loading and signal reflections. This parameter is under the control of the SCSI device (e.g., tape drive or disk drive) manufacturer. The SCSI cabling itself should include no stubs.

Watch out for capacitance. As devices are added to a SCSI bus, capacitance is introduced to each signal from the connectors, receivers, and PC board traces. The SCSI-2 specification limits this capacitance to 25pF and this number will probably be lowered to 20pF in SCSI-3. The reason for this limit is that the added capacitance has the effect of lowering the impedance of the section of cable to which these devices are added, as well as adding delay. Both of these effects can be highly detrimental to a Fast SCSI bus. Look for input filters that may be attached to the SCSI front end of the printed circuit board. These filters add capacitance.

Avoid connector adapters. They are just another source of capacitance and signal degradation.

Route cable with care. Avoid practices such as rolling the cable up on itself, running the cable alongside of metal for long lengths, or routing the cable past noise generators (such as power supplies). Placing the cable near ground planes created by grounded metal cabinetry reduces its impedance. For example, the free air impedance of an unshielded 28 AWG, 0.050-inch center-ribbon cable is about 105 ohms, but direct contact with a metal ground plane cuts that by 61 ohms. Such an impedance discontinuity will cause signal reflections. The SCSI-3 working committee suggests that in order to minimize discontinuities due to local impedance variation, a flat cable should be spaced at least 1.27mm (0.050 inches) from other cables, any other conductor, or the cable itself when the cable is folded.

Use high-impedance cables wherever possible. This will allow for closer termination impedance matching, as well as provide more cushion against the impedance reduction normally experienced during cable routing.

Avoid mixing cable types. Select either flat or round, shielded or non-shielded. Typically, mixing cables mixes impedances. Cable impedance mismatch is a common problem resulting in signal reflections. If cable types must be mixed, use of 26 AWG wire in 0.050-inch pitch-flat cable will more closely match impedances of many round-shielded cables, resulting in fewer impedance discontinuities and therefore improved signal quality. Internal cables are typically flat-ribbon cables, while external cables should be shielded. Where they offer easier routing, size advantages, and better air flow, round cables can be used internally as well. This, in fact, may be desirable if it allows for better impedance matching to the external cable.

Ribbon cable shows fairly good cross talk rejection characteristics due to the GND-Signal-GND layout. However, more care needs to be taken to ensure adequate performance when round-shielded cable is employed. When round cable is used, select a cable that uses a wise placement of key lines within the cable. The following is suggested: In the case of a standard 25-pair round construction, pairs are arranged inside the cable in three layers. The closer the pair is to the outside shield, the lower the impedance. Conversely, pairs located closer to the center of the cable have higher impedances. Using centrally located high impedance pairs for speed-critical signals such as REQ and ACK is desirable. By locating data pairs in the outermost layer of the cable, cross talk between REQ, ACK, and the data lines is minimized. The middle layer might contain status lines such as C/D, I/O, MSG, ATN, etc. Another thing to look for in a round-shielded cable is to make sure that the lowest impedance wire in the cable is used for TERMPOWER to minimize transmission line effects on what is meant to be a voltage supply line. Some SCSI cable vendors have put a low-impedance conductor into the cable specifically for this purpose. Typically, a larger wire gauge along with a higher dielectric constant is used on this conductor.

SCSI CABLE TYPES

SCSI systems can utilize cabling both inside and outside the cabinet. Internal cables are typically flat unshielded ribbon cables, while external cables are generally round and shielded. The most common internal cable is the 50-conductor flat-ribbon cable, which typically uses 28 AWG conductors on 0.050-inch centers. Typical free air characteristic impedances for this type of cable runs about 105 ohms. DPT has had good success with the 3365 Round Conductor Flat Ribbon Cable manufactured by 3M Corp. It uses 28 AWG stranded wire on 0.050-inch centers and has a nominal free air characteristic impedance of 108 ohms.

External shielded 8-bit SCSI cables typically contain 25 twisted pairs (50-conductor) with an overall foil/braid composite shield. Typical free air characteristic impedances for this type of cable have run about 65 to 80 ohms. Higher single-ended round shielded cable impedances of 90 to 100 ohms are becoming available and should be strongly considered.

The SCSI-2 specification requires that systems employing the fast synchronous data transfer option shall use cables consisting of 26 AWG or 28 AWG conductors. Characteristic impedance is specified as between 90 and 132 ohms. In addition, signal attenuation should be 0.095 dB maximum per meter at 5 MHz. The pair-to-pair propagation delay delta should not exceed 0.2 ns per meter. Finally, the DC resistance is specified as 0.23 ohms maximum per meter at 20 degrees C.

PASSIVE TERMINATION

Passive termination (called Alternative-1 in the SCSI-2 specification) is the most common form of termination currently utilized today. A typical single-ended SCSI system will employ 18 sets of 220-ohm pull-up and 330-ohm pull-down, thick film resistors to equalize impedance and to absorb reflected signals. The Thevenin equivalent impedance for this type of termination is 132 ohms.

In order to maintain the largest possible high-level noise margin, it is advisable to use resistors with a maximum tolerance of 2 percent rather that 10 percent. In worst-case conditions, the difference could easily add up to 140 mV. Worst case occurs when the pull-up resistor is high and the pull-down resistor is low.

Consider the situation where TERMPOWER is being driven across a 6-meter (19 feet) cable. Due to power supply tolerances and to the 15 or so SCSI bus signals drawing current, it is possible for the remote end TERMPOWER to be sitting at 3.65 volts (see the "Where to Terminate" section for more details). If 2-percent resistors are used, the worst-case termination voltage divider will have a gain of 0.588 V/V and the quiescent signal bias will be 2.15 V. If 10-percent resistors are used, the worst-case termination voltage divider will have a gain of 0.551 V/V and the quiescent signal bias will be 2.01 V. In this worst-case example, given the SCSI mandated minimum V(ih) of 2.0 V, only 10 mV of high-end noise margin will remain.

ACTIVE TERMINATION

The preferred termination for 10 MHz Fast SCSI busses is active termination. This type of termination is known as Alternative-2 and uses only one 110 ohm resistor per signal per bus end pulled up to locally supplied, voltage-regulated 2.85 V. Features of this termination include

- Termination voltages, and therefore the currents flowing through the 100 ohm termination resistors are at least partly immune to IR voltage drops on the TERMPOWER line until TERMPOWER −2.85 V equals the dropout voltage of the voltage regulator, about 1.1 V.

- Closer match to the characteristic impedance of the cable (110 versus 132 for passive as compared to the typical 105–108 ohms free air impedance of the cable) minimizes reflections.

- Increased high-level noise margin of deasserted signals.

- Higher pull-down currents avoid rising "staircase" waveforms seen on weakly driven transmission lines.

Studies by Kurt Chan and Gordon Matheson, both of Hewlett-Packard, have shown that mixing termination types will yield better performance than using passive termination alone. Wherever possible, use SCSI devices that employ active termination.

WHERE TO TERMINATE

Termination should be installed only at the far ends of the cable. If the DPT controller is at one end of the bus and a SCSI device is at the other end, leave all three controller termination resistor packs in their sockets. If the DPT controller is supporting both internal and external SCSI devices and thus is located in the middle of the bus, the termination resistor packs must be removed from their sockets. In both cases, disable the termination of any SCSI devices that are not located at the cable ends. This can usually be done by jumper configuration, removal of resistor packs, or both.

Ideally, TERMPOWER should be located at the terminations, not in the middle of the cable. Interface error rates are lower if the termination voltage is maintained at the extreme ends of the cable. From strictly a signal quality perspective, it is best if terminators get power only from the device to which they attach, and not over the bus. Unfortunately, cable-ended devices may be powered-down and the bus would then be inoperative unless the terminators are supplied from the other voltage sources along the bus. This fact must be balanced against desired signal quality.

Most drives provide jumpers to select the manner in which TERM-POWER is supplied to their on-board termination. DPT recommends that drives be configured to supply their own isolated TERMPOWER unless accidental power-down concerns dictate otherwise.

The reason why TERMPOWER should be applied near terminations only is because TERMPOWER is a transmission line that shares many of the same characteristics as the signal lines. Current surges entering this line at the terminators will propagate and reflect exactly as they would on any signal line, except where there is a low-impedance voltage source. It follows, then, that current surge waveforms propagating down the bus from a point where many data lines are changing simultaneously will couple into other signals through the pull-up termination resistors if there is not a TERMPOWER voltage source right at the terminator to absorb or provide the current surge needed.

The worst real-life case is one in which data lines along with MSG, C/D, and I/O all change at the same time, causing noise on signals of opposite polarity (several signals going low causing a deasserted signal to also go low, or signals going high causing an asserted signal to also go high). This phenomenon has nothing to do with cross talk or driver skew rate, but is instead a function of where TERMPOWER is applied and where the drivers are.

Another reason to supply TERMPOWER locally is to prevent the loss of receiver noise margin due to TERMPOWER DC voltage drop across the cable. It is not uncommon to find TERMPOWER resistances of 2 ohms or more on maximally configured systems. When 15 to 18 signals conduct, the TERMPOWER line will carry nearly 300 mA to the far terminators, which would cause a voltage drop across the cable of about 0.6 V during these periods.

DPT controllers drive TERMPOWER onto the cable through a thermistor and a Schottky diode. Taking into account power supply tolerances, it is not inconceivable that under maximum loading conditions TERMPOWER at the controller connector may be lowered to 4.25 V. Subtract 0.6 V due to TERMPOWER DC resistance, and far-end TERMPOWER ends up at 3.65 V. This would bias a quiescent signal to 2.19 V ((330/220+330) × 3.65). Comparing this to the SCSI-specified minimum V(ih) of 2.0 V for single-ended inputs leaves a high-end noise margin of only 190 mV. This quick and dirty worst-case analysis does not even include termination resistor tolerances that could exacerbate the problem. It's a good thing that TTL receivers typically switch near 1.4 V to 1.5 V (the middle of the V(ih) range) rather than at 2.0 V.

For all the reasons discussed above, it is advised that TERM-POWER be maintained at as close to nominal voltage as possible. In the case of DPT controllers, this means that the voltage level to the controller be maintained at nominal and not be allowed to droop.

TERMPOWER Bypassing

The ANSI XT3T9.3 SCSI-3 Parallel Interface working group recommends that all TERMPOWER lines be decoupled at each terminator to minimize TERMPOWER glitch coupling.

The minimum recommended values are a 2.2 uF solid tantalum capacitor along with .01 uF ceramic capacitor in parallel to help with high-frequency, low-voltage noise. These capacitors, when utilized, will supply the high-frequency, low-impedance path to ground necessary to filter out glitches. Without the capacitors, TERMPOWER acts simply as a high-impedance node and couples noise from signal to signal. With the capacitors, an "AC ground" exists that filters this noise.

For cables of significant length and configurations without TERMPOWER at each terminator there is a high probability of signal corruption without adequate decoupling. Thus, DPT recommends that the system integrator inspect the system to ensure that all SCSI devices used are properly bypassed.

DPT controllers provide power to the on-board termination resistors directly from a highly decoupled power plane, thus ensuring minimal TERMPOWER glitch coupling. However, it is important to keep in mind that decoupling in the middle of the bus is not sufficient. If the DPT controller is supporting both the internal and external SCSI busses simultaneously, then the SCSI devices at the ends of the cable need to be bypassed at their terminations. This requirement applies to both passive and active termination.

FAST DIFFERENTIAL SCSI

When the total cable length of a fast, synchronous SCSI bus cable must exceed three meters (9.84 feet), DPT recommends the use of a differential-ended SCSI interface.

An important concern is cable selection. When twisted-pair cable is used, differential-ended SCSI busses provide greater signal integrity over longer distances than do single-ended, because noise coupled into a twisted-pair generally appears equally on both wires. Because differential receivers respond to differences between the conductors of the twisted-pair, the coupled common-mode noise is rejected.

On the other hand, the signal positioning of a differential SCSI on a flat nontwisted ribbon cable causes two problems. First, noise introduced into parallel conductors tends not to be common mode. Second, while the single-ended conductor arrangement naturally interleaves ground wires between signal wires, there are not enough conductors to interleave grounds between each differential signal pair. These factors lead to increased cross talk between adjacent conductors on a ribbon cable.

DPT strongly recommends the use of twisted-pair cable (either twisted-flat or discrete wire twisted-pairs) for differential-ended SCSI interfaces.

The maximum cumulative cable length permitted is 25 meters (82 feet) with devices not to be spaced any closer then 0.3 meters apart (12 inches) and stub lengths not to exceed 0.2 meters (8 inches). As in single-ended, SCSI bus terminators should be installed only at each end of the cable.

H

AN INTRODUCTION
TO RAID

This section on RAID is an adaptation of written material provided by DPT (Distributed Processing Technology). DPT is a leading manufacturer of SCSI host adapters, located in Maitland, Florida.

AN INTRODUCTION TO RAID

In 1987, the acronym RAID (redundant array of inexpensive disks) was introduced in a series of papers by Patterson, Gibson, and Katz at the University of California, Berkeley. The series, titled "A Case for Redundant Arrays of Inexpensive Disks (RAID)," outlines and defines various levels of fault-tolerant disk array architectures.

These papers define five types of array architectures, RAID-1 through RAID-5. Each type provides fault tolerance in case of a drive failure, and each offers different trade-offs in features and performance. Of the five types, only RAID-1, RAID-3, and RAID-5 are commonly used (RAID-2 and RAID-4 do not offer any significant advantages over these other types). RAID-3 is designed for single-user environments that access extremely large sequential records, such as imaging or data acquisition. This leaves RAID-1 and RAID-5 as the types applicable for multiuser applications such as UNIX platforms or fileservers.

The basic idea of RAID is to combine multiple small, inexpensive disk drives into an array of disk drives. The resulting performance exceeds that of a single disk drive (in RAID terminology, a single large expensive drive, or SLED). This array of drives appears to the computer as a single logical storage unit or drive.

In this discussion, we use the following definition: RAID is a method of combining hard disks into one logical storage unit, which offers disk fault tolerance and can operate at higher throughput levels than a single hard disk.

Fundamental to RAID is striping, a method of concatenating multiple drives into one logical storage unit. Striping entails partitioning each drive's storage space into stripes. These stripes are then interleaved round-robin, so that the combined space is comprised alternately of stripes from each drive. Stripes may be as small as one sector (512 bytes) or as large as several megabytes. The type of operating environment determines whether to use large or small stripes.

In order for striping to be effective you need an operating system that supports overlapped I/O. Most multiuser operating systems, like UNIX and Novell NetWare, support overlapped disk I/O operations across multiple disk drives. The key to maximizing throughput in the disk subsystem is to balance the I/O load across all the disk drives, in an attempt to keep each disk drive busy. Without striping, disk I/O is never perfectly balanced; while some disk drives will contain frequently accessed data files, others will seldom be accessed.

By striping the disk drives in the array with stripes large enough so that each record resides entirely within one stripe, the records are evenly distributed across all the disk drives and the I/O load is evenly balanced. This balancing allows each disk drive to satisfy a different I/O operation and thus maximize the number of simultaneous I/O operations that the array can perform.

In single-user systems that access large records, small stripes (typically one 512-byte sector in length) can be used so that each record spans across all the disk drives in the array. Thus, each disk drive stores a part of the data in the record. This speeds up the performance of long record accesses, since the data transfers occur in parallel on multiple disk drives. Medical imaging and data acquisition in single-user environments can typically achieve performance enhancements with small striped arrays.

One drawback to using small stripe sizes is that synchronized spindle disk drives are required to keep performance from degrading when short records are accessed. Without synchronized spindles, each disk drive in the array accesses its part of the data at different times. The disk drive that takes the longest to access its data determines when the

I/O completes. With synchronized spindles, the access time of the array equals the average access time of a single disk drive.

Unfortunately, small stripes reduce the benefit of multiple overlapped I/O operations, since each I/O will typically involve all disk drives. This small stripe configuration can be compared to a DOS environment, which does not allow overlapped disk I/O.

RAID-1 THROUGH RAID-5: PICKING THE RIGHT ARRAY FOR YOUR APPLICATION

The following sections describe the fundamental operation, as well as the benefits and drawbacks of each type of RAID. When discussing the five types of RAID architectures, we also need to take into account RAID-0, which commonly refers to an array of disk drives that doesn't offer disk fault tolerance.

RAID-0

RAID-0 is typically defined as a nonredundant group of striped disk drives without parity. It is the fastest and most efficient array type but offers no fault tolerance.

RAID-0 arrays are usually configured with large stripes, though they may be sector-striped with synchronized spindle drives for single-user environments that access long sequential records. If one drive in a RAID-0 array crashes, it brings the entire array down with it. However, RAID-0 arrays deliver the best performance and data storage efficiency of any array type.

Pros

- RAID-0 arrays deliver the best performance of any array type.
- Write operations can occur simultaneously on every disk drive in the RAID-0 array.
- Read operations can occur simultaneously on every disk drive in the RAID-0 array.
- RAID-0 arrays deliver the greatest data storage efficiency of any array type.

Cons

- RAID 0 offers no data redundancy.
- There is no parity in RAID-0, thus no fault tolerance.

RAID-1

RAID-1 arrays are probably the most commonly used arrays today. It is the array of choice for performance-critical, fault-tolerant environments, and it is the only choice for fault tolerance if no more than two drives are desired.

RAID-1 is always a pair of disk drives that stores duplicate data but appears to the operating system as a single drive. This feature of storing duplicate data, called disk mirroring, is characteristic only of RAID-1.

RAID-1 arrays can be combined into larger groups by "striping" the arrays together to appear as a single large drive. RAID-1 arrays may be configured with either large stripes or with sector stripes.

One large array created from the combination of smaller arrays is sometimes called a dual-level array. In this scheme, writes must go to both drives in a mirrored pair so that the information on the drives is kept identical. Each individual drive, however, can perform simultaneous read operations. Mirroring thus doubles the read performance of an individual drive and leaves the write performance unchanged.

RAID-1 has been popularized at the system level by Tandem Computers, through software by Novell Corporation, and in a hardware implementation on the disk controller by DPT.

Pros

- RAID-1 delivers the best performance of any redundant array type in multiuser environments.
- RAID-1 doubles read performance of an individual disk drive.
- Read operations can occur simultaneously on every disk drive in the RAID-1 array.

Cons

- RAID-1 requires twice as many disk drives to reach the same usable storage space as that of non-RAID systems.

RAID-2

RAID-2 arrays sector-stripe data across groups of drives, with some drives relegated to storing ECC (error correction code) information. It is seldom used today, since most modern disk drives embed ECC information within each sector. RAID-2 offers no significant advantages over RAID-3 architecture.

RAID-3

As with RAID-2, RAID-3 sector-stripes data across groups of drives, but one drive in the group is dedicated to storing parity information. It can be used to speed up data transfer in single-user environments that access long sequential records. Records typically span all drives, thereby optimizing disk transfer rate. However, it does not allow multiple I/O operations to be overlapped and it requires synchronized spindle drives in order to avoid performance degradation with short records.

RAID-3 relies on the embedded ECC in each sector for error detection. In the case of a hard drive failure, RAID-3 accomplishes data recovery by calculating the exclusive OR (XOR) of the information recorded on the remaining drives.

Pros

- RAID-3 uses the embedded ECC already present in the drive rather than dedicating an extra drive.
- With RAID-3, records span all drives, optimizing transfer rate.

Cons

- RAID-3 requires synchronized spindle drives.
- RAID-3 does not allow overlapping of multiple I/O operations.

RAID-4

RAID-4 is largely identical to RAID-3, except that it uses large stripes so that records can be read from any individual drive in the array (except the parity drive). This allows RAID-4 to overlap read operations. Write operations, on the other hand, cannot be overlapped, since they must update the parity drive. This architecture offers no significant advantages over RAID-5, especially since it does not support multiple, simultaneous write operations.

RAID-5

RAID-5 arrays, although not as frequently used as RAID-1, have received much attention in the trade press. Sometimes called a rotating parity array, RAID-5 avoids the write bottleneck caused by the single dedicated parity drive of RAID-4. It is the best choice in multiuser environments that are not performance-sensitive or that do little or no write operations. However, RAID-5 arrays require at least three, and more typically five, drives.

H

Like RAID-4, RAID-5 uses large stripes so that multiple I/O operations can be overlapped. However, unlike RAID-4, each drive takes turns storing parity information for a different series of stripes. Since RAID-5 does not require a dedicated parity drive, all drives contain data, and read operations can be overlapped on every drive in the array. Write operations will typically access a single data drive, plus the parity drive for that record. Since, unlike RAID-4, RAID-5 specifies that different records store their parity on different drives, write operations can be overlapped.

RAID-5 arrays, like RAID-1, store redundant information, enabling them to survive a disk failure and continue to operate. However, RAID-5 offers improved storage efficiency over RAID-1 by storing parity information rather than a complete redundant copy of all data. This parity information is generated by calculating the XOR of the data stored on every drive in the array. The result is that any number of drives can be combined into a RAID-5 array, with the effective storage capacity of only one drive sacrificed to store the parity information.

Greater storage efficiency comes at the cost of a corresponding loss in performance. When data is written to a RAID-5 array, the parity information must be updated. There are two ways to accomplish this. The first is straightforward but very slow. As we said before, the parity information is the XOR of the data on every drive in the array. Therefore, when one drive's data is changed, the other drives in the array holding data are read and XORed to create the new parity. This method requires accessing every drive in the array for each write operation.

The second method of updating parity, which is usually more efficient, is to find out which data bits were changed by the write operation and then change the corresponding parity bits. This is accomplished by first reading the old data to be overwritten. This data is then XORed with the new data to be written. The result is a bit mask that has a one in the position of every changed bit. This bit mask is then XORed with the old parity information read from the parity drive. This results in the corresponding bits being changed in the parity information. The new, updated parity is then written back to the parity drive. Although this method may seem more convoluted, it results in only two reads, two writes, and two XOR operations, rather than a read or write and XOR for every drive in the array.

So the cost of storing parity, rather than redundant data, is the extra time taken during write operations to regenerate the parity information. This additional time results in a degradation of write performance for RAID-5 over RAID-1 arrays by a factor of between 3:5 and 1:3 (i.e., RAID-5 writes are between three-fifths and one-third the speed of RAID-1 write operations). Because of this, RAID-5 arrays are not recommended for applications in which performance is important.

Applications that never write data are the exception to this recommendation, since their parity information never has to be regenerated.

Pros

- RAID-5 is best suited for multiuser environments that are not performance-sensitive or for those environments with a high read-to-write ratio.
- Read operations can occur simultaneously on every disk drive in the RAID-5 array.

Cons

- RAID-5's performance is slightly less than other RAID levels, due to the complexity of the algorithm used to update parity.

In summary, RAID-1 is the array of choice for performance-critical, fault-tolerant environments. In addition, RAID-1 is the only choice if not more than two drives are desired. RAID-5 is the best choice in environments that either are not performance sensitive or do not perform write operations. However, at least three, and more typically five drives are required for RAID-5 arrays.

Q & A FROM DISTRIBUTED PROCESSING TECHNOLOGY

DISTRIBUTED PROCESSING TECHNOLOGY Q & A

The following commonly asked questions and answers about Distributed Processing Technology (DPT) products is courtesy of DPT's technical services department, namely Pete Bolliger, Technical Support Manager, and John Kearney, Technical Support Supervisor.

In preparation for this section, each DPT technical support engineer contributed the ten most commonly asked questions about DPT products. That list was, in turn, compiled and edited. For updates to this list or late-breaking news or tips on using DPT controllers, be sure to consult the DPT BBS at 407-831-6432 (for 2400- to 9600-baud access) or 407-830-1070 or 407-830-0852 (for 1200- to 9600-baud access). You can also reach DPT technical support directly by voice at 407-830-5522 or fax 407-260-5366.

Frequently Asked Questions

Q If DPT Storage Manager reports that a SCSI peripheral's transfer rate is 4 MB/second, do I need to lower the host bus adapter's (HBA) transfer rate?

A DPT adapters will negotiate with each SCSI peripheral on the SCSI bus during POST. During the negotiation period, the adapter will determine the maximum transfer rate supported by each peripheral and operate at the maximum supported rate for each peripheral.

Q If my EISA DPT adapter is configured for Primary (WD1003) I/O port and IRQ 14, is it operating in emulation mode?

A To configure the DPT adapter for WD1003 emulation mode, you must not only set the I/O port and IRQ, but you must also be sure that a hard disk drive type is defined in the system CMOS. Further, whenever a DPT adapter is configured for emulation mode, the DPT SmartROM will display the word "EMULATED" to the right of the hard disk parameters.

Q Can I modify any of the DPT adapter settings in DPT Storage Manager?

A No. The information displayed by DPT Storage Manager cannot be modified. The settings represent the hardware's current configuration.

Q How much DPT hardware cache should I install on my DPT adapter?

A The recommended amount of hardware cache varies from system to system. Your cache requirements will vary depending on your operating system, the number of active users, the load that your applications place on the disk subsystem, and the type of load that your applications place (that is, whether they are read-intensive or write-intensive). As a rule of thumb, the CM4000 should have 0.5 MB of cache for each active user on the system. Typically, more cache is recommended for systems with many active users or large data files. However, if your system has a large number of users who access the same data, you may need less cache.

Q When I boot my DOS system, the message "Warning: SCSI BIOS ROM version is later than this driver" is displayed. What does this message mean?

A You will receive this message when your version of the SCSI BIOS ROM is newer than your version of DPTDDL.SYS driver. The version of DPTDDL.SYS must be equal to or newer than the SCSI BIOS ROM version. Should you encounter this problem, download the latest version of DPTDDL.SYS from the DPT BBS.

Q I'm using Novell NetWare 3.*x* or higher, and the message "DPT CRTL *h* DISK *d* resetting controller" appears on my server console (where *h* = host adapter number and *d* = SCSI device ID). What does this mean?

A Whenever a SCSI peripheral does not respond to a request from the SmartCache III adapter within the allotted time period of nine seconds, the adapter will reset the peripheral, retry the request, and display the message above. You will typically encounter this message in a heavily loaded system that has a cabling or a termination problem. Also, a faulty SCSI peripheral or adapter may cause this error, so be sure to check your bus connections.

Q How do I perform a low-level format on a SCSI hard disk attached to the SmartCache III adapter?

A To perform a low-level format on a SCSI hard disk attached to the SmartCache III adapter, you would first load the DPTMGR program and then double-click on the hard disk icon to be formatted. Now, click on the Format button and select either Format Only or Format And Certify. Format Only writes new sector IDs to the hard disk and erases all existing data. Format And Certify reads each and checks the CRC fields after each track is formatted. Regardless of the option you choose, the DPT adapter does not perform the low-level format; it simply sends a command to the hard disk controller and tells it to format itself.

Q I am receiving the message "Notice: Sdsk unrecoverable error reading SCSI disk 0 dev 1/42 (ha=0 id=0 lun=0) blk=149154 command aborted:" on the console of my SCO UNIX 3.2.4.*x* system several times (and some with different block numbers). The message occurs intermittently.

A This error is normally related to a hardware or, more specifically, a single hard disk (non-RAID) problem. However, you may try the following steps, which have proved beneficial in some instances:

1. Disable scatter/gather by following these steps:
   a. Enter the following commands at the Unix prompt:
      ```
      # cd /etc/conf/pack.d/Sdsk
      # vi space.c
      ```
   b. Find the line that reads
      ```
      /*If true, disable scatter/gather on all units */
      int Sdsk_no_sg = 0;
      ```
   c. Make true by changing the '0' to '1' for the Sdsk_no_sg value.
   d. Now save the file.
   e. Relink the kernel using the following steps:
      ```
      # cd /etc/conf/cf.d
      # ./link_unix
      ```
   f. Issue the following command to reboot the system:
      ```
      # shutdown -g5 -y
      ```
2. Obtain and install Maintenance Supplement Version 4.1 for SCO UNIX System V/386 Release 3.2 Version 4.0 (MSV4.1).

TABLE I.1   LEDs on the DPT Adapter

LED number	Meaning
1	BUSY
2	COMPUTER BUS TRANSFER TO ADAPTER
3	COMPUTER BUS TRANSFER FROM ADAPTER
4	CACHE HIT
5	DISK READ-AHEAD ACTIVE
6	DISK READ
7	DISK WRITE
8	ADAPTER RESET
9	ADAPTER IRQ PENDING TO COMPUTER
10	DRQ ASSERTED TO COMPUTER

3.   Run scsibadblk by typing the following:

```
# scsibadblk
```

This scans SCSI hard disks for defective blocks and attempts to re-allocate them. For further details and options, go to the man page for scsibadblk by typing the command

```
# man scsibadblk
```

If the above options do not resolve the error, your hard disk may be the cause.

Q   Which LED on the DPT adapter is LED 1?

A   There are ten LEDs on the DPT adapter, each one representing a different adapter status. LED 1 is farthest away from the SCSI ribbon cable connector. The meaning of each LED is shown in Table I.1.

Q   I've successfully installed SCO UNIX 3.2.4.0 or 3.2.4.1 on my Smart-Cache III adapter, but when I attempt to boot UNIX from the hard disk I receive the message "NO OS." What's causing this problem?

A   SCO UNIX 3.2.4.0 and 3.2.4.1 both have a driver included in the kernel for the DPT adapters. However, DPT adapters were not included in the UNIX /boot table until SCO UNIX 3.2.4.2. The UNIX /boot table contains the list of adapters that SCO searches for at boot time. If a software adapter is found, then SCO will load/boot using the adapter's BIOS ROM parameters. Since the DPT adapter is not listed in the /boot table, the OS cannot load.

With the previously listed versions of UNIX, the DPT adapter must be configured for WD1003 emulation mode prior to the installation of UNIX. Upon rebooting after installing UNIX, the system BIOS is used to boot the UNIX kernel. Once the kernel loads, the DPT driver, which is included in the kernel, transfers the DPT adapter into EATA mode. To set up the DPT adapter for WD1003 emulation mode, follow these steps:

1. Set the I/O port to Primary (EISA), 1F0h (ISA).
2. Set the interrupt to IRQ 14 EDGE (EISA), 14 (ISA).
3. Set the DMA to channel 5 (ISA only).
4. Load Storage Manager (DPTMGR.COM) and run the Initial System Installation option. Select SCO UNIX 3.2.4.0/ODT 2.0 as your OS. Then save, exit, and reboot off the SCO UNIX N1 disk and begin your installation.
5. Upon rebooting, ensure that the word "EMULATED" appears to the right of the hard disk parameters displayed by the DPT SCSI BIOS ROM. If "EMULATED" appears, the HBA is configured for WD1003 emulation mode.
6. If "EMULATED" doesn't appear, reverify the settings in steps 1, 2, and 3 above. Load Storage Manager again and choose the Initial System Installation option. When the prompt "You have selected SCO UNIX 3.2.4.0/ODT 2.0, is this correct?" appears, respond NO. Then reselect SCO UNIX 3.2.4.0/ODT 2.0 as the OS. Save, exit, and reboot. If the word "EMULATED" still fails to appear, contact DPT Technical Support for further assistance.

J

Q & A FROM FUTURE DOMAIN CORPORATION

FUTURE DOMAIN CORPORATION Q&A

The following commonly asked questions and answers about Future Domain Corporation (FDC) products is courtesy of Future Domain Corporation.

For the latest news or tips on using FDC controllers, be sure to consult the FDC BBS at 714-253-0432. You can also reach FDC technical support directly by voice at 714-253-0440.

Top Ten Questions About FDC SCSI Controllers

Q What operating systems do Future Domain SCSI controllers work under?

A Future Domain controllers support almost all the major operating systems, including DOS, all versions of Windows, OS/2, NetWare 386, SCO UNIX, and so on.

DOS and Windows: Fixed disk drive support is built into the BIOS on Future Domain controllers, so there's no need to load any device drivers. CD-ROM, MO (magneto-optical), removable hard disk, WORM (write-once read-many), and multifunction drives are all supported by FDC PowerSCSI!™ software.

Other major operating systems (Windows NT, Windows 95, NetWare 386, OS/2, SCO UNIX, etc.): Most of the major operating systems come with Future Domain controller support. FDC controllers support all SCSI devices supported by each operating system.

Q How do I low-level format my hard disk drive?

A To low-level format your hard disk, use FDDSU, a menu-driven utility that performs a low-level format and surface analysis of your hard drive. FDDSU is included in FDC PowerSCSI! software, or it can be downloaded from the FDC BBS (714-253-0432).

Q I upgraded the BIOS on my controller, and now my hard drive doesn't work. What should I do?

A The FDC onboard BIOS controls the drive geometry, which governs the way data is written to and read from the hard disk. Whereas older versions use a proprietary FDC format, the newer BIOS supports the industry-standard geometry. Your problem is probably due to the presence of the older BIOS version. In order to resolve your problem, you should update your BIOS as follows:

1. Install the old BIOS on your controller.
2. Back up the data on your SCSI drive(s).
3. Replace the old BIOS with the new one.
4. Run FDISK to delete the old partition(s) and create a new one(s) if you wish to change the size of your partition(s).
5. Run FORMAT (high-level format) to set up the new geometry on your SCSI hard disk drive(s).

Q How do I make my SCSI hard disk drive bootable?

A If you have an IDE hard drive in your system and it is active or usable, you will not be able to boot the system from your SCSI hard drive. If you do not have an active IDE drive in your system, you can make a SCSI hard drive bootable by setting the C drive to "not installed" in your CMOS SETUP. Then, create a primary DOS partition of any size on the drive, and assign it as *active*. Finally, type **FORMAT C:/S** to do a high-level format on the C drive with the system's boot files.

Q What software do I need to have installed in my system in order to use a CD-ROM drive under DOS and Windows?

A If you want to use a CD-ROM drive, you need Future Domain's CD-ROM driver, FDCD.SYS. To load this driver, run the automatic installation program in PowerSCSI!. (See your user manual for further details.)

| **TABLE J.1** | **Tape Backup Software Programs** |

Software	Vendor
Backup Exec for DOS/Windows	Arcada Software
ARCsolo for DOS/Windows	Cheyenne
NovaBack for DOS/Windows	NovaStor Corporation
Backup Director for DOS	Palindrome
FastBack Plus for DOS/Windows	Symantec/Fifth Generation
Central Point Backup	Symantec/Central Point Software
Sytos Plus	Sytron

The FDCD.SYS driver works with all Future Domain SCSI controllers (with or without a BIOS on the controller), and it supports almost all the SCSI CD-ROM drives in the industry.

Q What software do I need to use a tape drive(s) under DOS and Windows?

A Follow these steps to load the software you'll need to support your tape drive:

1. Load PowerSCSI! and make sure that the highlighted lines listed under the appropriate heading below are in your CONFIG.SYS file.

   If you have an 8-bit controller

   ```
   DEVICE=C:\PWRSCSI!\DCAM950.EXE /CA00 5
        (Default memory address and IRQ)
   DEVICE=C:\PWRSCSI!\ASPIFCAM.SYS /D
   ```

   If you have a 16-bit controller

   ```
   DEVICE=C:\PWRSCSI!\DCAM18XX.EXE
   DEVICE=C:\PWRSCSI!\ASPIFCAM.SYS /D
   ```

2. Having checked for the appropriate lines in your CONFIG.SYS, install any of the following tape backup software programs listed in Table J.1 (make sure your tape drive is supported by the software).

Q I installed a CD-ROM drive and FDC controller, but now I can't load FDCD.SYS, a CD-ROM driver included in PowerSCSI!. What's the answer?

A To solve this particular problem and to load FDCD.SYS, follow these steps:

1. First confirm that Future Domain's logo and your SCSI device ID information are displayed during POST. If they are, your hardware is set up properly and you can go to step 5. If they do not display, go to step 2.

TABLE J.2	**Controller Drivers**		
	Your Controller Type	**Under NetWare V3.x**	**Under NetWare V4.x**
	TMC-8xx	SIM950_3.DSK	SIM950_4.DSK
	TMC-16xx/3260, MCS-xxx	SIM18_3.DSK	SIM18_4.DSK

NOTE *If your controller does not have a BIOS on it, the device ID information will not appear even if your hardware is set up properly. In this case you should go to step 2.*

2. Make sure that the termination settings on your controller and drive(s) are correct. See the user manuals for your FDC controller and CD-ROM drive for the correct settings.

NOTE *Some of FDC's new controllers have no termination jumpers or switches on them. Their termination is configured automatically.*

3. If the termination settings are correct (according to your manuals), change the memory address setting on your controller (see an FDC controller user manual for the address-setting combinations). If none of the address settings work, try disabling your shadow RAM in your CMOS SETUP.

4. Make sure that your CONFIG.SYS file has as its last line

   ```
   DEVICE=C:\PWRSCSI!\FDCD.SYS /D:MSCD001
   ```

5. Be sure that the first line in your AUTOEXEC.BAT reads

   ```
   C:\DOS\MSCDEX.EXE /D:MSCD001 /M:10
   ```

Q Can I use my CD-ROM or tape drive under Novell NetWare V3.x or 4.x?

A Yes, by following these steps:

1. Load the appropriate driver (according to Table J.2) found in PowerSCSI! in the STARTUP.NCF. Here's a sample line in STARTUP.NCF:

   ```
   Load SIM950_3.DSK
   ```

   After running PowerSCSI! the following lines will be automatically added to your STARTUP.NCF file:

   ```
   FUTD_3.DSK  (for NetWare V3.x use)
   FUTD_4.DSK  (for NetWare V4.x use)
   FUTXPT.DSK  (for both NetWare V3.x and 4.x use)
   ```

TABLE J.3	Tape Drive Software	

Software	Vendor
Backup Exec for NetWare	Arcada Software
ARCserve	Cheyenne
Networker for NetWare	Legato Systems
NovaNet-NLM	NovaStor Corporation
SBACKUP	Novell
FastBack Plus Network's	Symantec/Fifth Generation
Central Point Backup	Symantec/Central Point Software
ProServe/ProServe Lite	Sytron

2. **For CD-ROM drive(s):** If you want to install a CD-ROM drive, add the following lines to AUTOEXEC.NCF:

   :Load CDROM.NLM

   :CD HELP (For help files: Optional)

   :CD DEVICE LIST

   :CD VOLUME LIST

   :CD MOUNT [DEVICE#] [VOLUME NAME]

   Use the MAP command to assign a drive letter to the CD volume name after mounting.

   For tape drive(s): If you want to install a tape drive, add the line FUTASPI.DSK to STARTUP.NCF, and then use any of the software listed in Table J.3. Make sure that your tape drive is supported by the software.

Q I want to connect an external SCSI device to my FDC controller. What kind of cable do I need and where do I get it?

A Table J.4 on the following page will help you find the right cable. Cables are available through Future Domain's distribution center at 1-800-879-7599.

Q How do I take advantage of Microsoft Windows 32-bit disk and file access with my FDC controller?

A Future Domain's WINDISK (32-bit disk access driver) is included in PowerSCSI!. When you install PowerSCSI! from Windows, the setup program will automatically install the WINDISK drivers, V18FCAMD.386 for the TMC-16xx/3260 controllers, INT13.386 to replace the Windows Int13 driver, and FDSCSI.386 to replace the Windows 32-bit driver. They are loaded in the 386[ehn] section of the SYSTEM. INI.WINDISK will improve your hard disk drive's performance.

TABLE J.4 — SCSI Cables

Your Controller Model	Cable Model	Description
TMC-1680/1660 MCS-700 TMC-3260	HCA-112	48-inch round shielded and jacketed cable with one external 50-pin high-density connector and one external 50-pin centronics SCSI-2 connector
TMC-850M TMC-1610M TMC-1650/1670 MCS-600	HCA-120	36-inch round shielded and jacketed cable with one external 25-pin Apple Macintosh pin-out connector and one external 50-pin centronics SCSI connector
TMC-830/845 TMC-850/860/885	HCA-108	36-inch round shielded and jacketed cable with one external 25-pin FDC proprietary pin-out connector and one external 50-pin centronics SCSI connector
TMC-7000EX	HCA-117	36-inch round shielded and jacketed cable with two external 50-pin centronics connectors
TMC-1660/1680 MCS-700 TMC-3260	HCA-113	Two 50-pin high-density connectors

(For NEC's 3X CD-ROM drive that comes with 50-pin high-density connectors.)

Q & A FROM ADAPTEC

ADAPTEC, INCORPORATED Q & A

The following commonly asked questions and anwers about Adaptec
products are courtesy of Adaptec, Incorporated.

I. SOFTWARE AND DRIVER COMMON QUESTIONS AND ANSWERS

Q What are Adaptec's ASPI Managers used for?

A Loading the Manager allows you to use a wide assortment of SCSI devices that have the appropriate ASPI-compliant device drivers for them. aspi4dos.sys also gives you Virtual DMA Services (VDS) support and enhances the performance of your system.

Q How can I download the ASPI device drivers and managers from your BBS?

A Since these items are product offerings by Adaptec with an associated cost, they are not found on the BBS. They are available through your dealer, as part of an Adaptec kit or through our Software Hotline at 800-442-7274. If you already have an older version, you can download a file from the upgrade library in the BBS and then expand it. It will replace the older drivers with up-to-date software.

Q My DOS ASPI Manager does not install, but my Adaptec board initializes and installs OK. How can I fix this?

A The usual reason for this behavior is incorrect jumper settings on the Adaptec host adapter. Check the jumpers for I/O port address, IRQ, and DMA channel conflicts with other boards. Also check for correct termination on the board and other devices. Make sure that there is also enough memory to load the driver.

Q Why am I unable to load any of my device drivers high without hanging my computer?

A You must have the ASPI Manager loaded for bus mastering boards in the config.sys file before the memory management device drivers can be loaded.

Q Why can't I get my Windows 3.1 to run in enhanced mode? It seems to run just fine in standard mode.

A Be sure to load aspi4dos.sys, which will supply Virtual DMA Services (VDS) support to the application. This applies to any protected mode application. With the ASPI Manager loaded, remove the double buffering from the config.sys file. Look for the line shown below and remove it. This only applies to the AHA-1540/42B, AHA-1640, and AHA-1740 in standard mode.

```
device=smartdrv.exe /double_buffer
```

Q Why is my floppy drive taking so long to do a backup using SCSI devices?

A You need to make an adjustment on the ASPI Manager device line in the config.sys file. Add the following switches to the ASPI Manager statement: /n04/f11.

Q Do I need a double buffer statement on my SMARTDRV entry if I am loading aspixdos.sys in my config.sys?

A No, the ASPI Manager supplies the double buffering.

Q What does the message that reads "BIOS not intended to run with this card" mean?

A This can happen when the BIOS or aspixdos.sys loads. This message indicates a conflict between our host adapter I/O port address and another card in the system. Change our port address to one of the alternate settings, or change the other card that is conflicting.

Q When should I disable the BIOS on the adapter?

A The BIOS should be disabled when the adapter is not to be used to operate a SCSI hard disk drive.

Q When aspidisk.sys loads, I get an error of "too many block devices." Why?

A The error indicates that there are not enough drive letters available. Increase the LASTDRIVE statement in config.sys.

Q Can aspidisk.sys be revised to assign logical drive letters?

A No.

Q When running NetWare with drives that are greater than 1 GB, do I enable the Extended BIOS Option?

A No. You do not enable that option when running under NetWare for any of our cards. You also need to ensure that on the AHA-154xC and AHA-154xCF the Dynamic Scan of the SCSI Bus is disabled. Press F6 for default settings in the SCSI Select utility. If greater than 1 GB is enabled upon installation, download the latest NetWare drivers from the NetWare directory on the BBS.

Q I added a CD-ROM drive to my NetWare v3.11 server, and the BIOS sees the drive. Why can't I access the drive on the network?

A You need a third-party device driver package, such as COREL SCSI, SCSI Express by Micro Design International, OptiNet by Optisys, or CDNET by Meridian Data.

Q Can I use aspi4dos.sys, aspi2dos.sys, or aspiedos.sys under OS/2?

A No, these ASPI drivers are only for DOS operating systems. Instead, we have os2aspi.dmd, which can be used in the config.sys file to handle ASPI calls. We also have a beta version of virtual DOS ASPI on the BBS.

II. HARDWARE COMMON QUESTIONS AND ANSWERS

Q Which host adapter contains floppy controllers and which do not?

A Any Adaptec host adapter that has a "2" as the last number in the product name has an on-board floppy controller. For example, the AHA-1542CF has floppy support, but the AHA-1540CF does not.

Q Is there a way to disable the floppy controller on the host adapter?

A Yes. Check your user's guide or installation manual for details. Installation manuals can be obtained by calling our Interactive Fax System at 408-957-7150.

K

Q What if I already have a controller I am booting from?

A All Adaptec host adapters will coexist with another controller (IDE, ESDI, RLL, etc.). Any hard drive not connected to the host adapter must be the primary (or booting) drive controller (IDE, ESDI, RLL, etc.).

Q How many host adapters can you have in one system?

A You can have two AHA-152*x* host adapters in your system at one time. You can have up to four AHA-154*x* host adapters in your system at one time. You can have up to four AHA-174*x* host adapters in standard mode; in enhanced mode, you are limited to the number of bus mastering slots in your system. With the AHA-274*x* series, you are limited by the number of available bus mastering slots. With AHA-284*x*, you are limited by the number of available VL-Bus master slots. Most systems have two or three VL-Bus slots, but they may not all be capable of bus mastering. Check your motherboard documentation to determine this.

Q Is technical documentation available for Adaptec hardware and software products? How do I get it?

A You can call Adaptec's Literature Hotline at 800-934-2766 and request technical reference manuals or user guides for our hardware. Software manuals are available with the purchase of Adaptec software.

Q Is target mode supported by Adaptec host adapters?

A Target mode has been implemented in Adaptec's bus mastering host adapter firmware for the AHA-154*x*, AHA-164*x*, and AHA-174*x*. However, our ASPI software managers do not currently support target mode. To get target mode to work, you would need to write your own host adapter software manager, which is not a trivial effort. Adaptec cannot provide you with any assistance in this effort. You can request a technical reference manual by calling our Literature Hotline at 800-934-2766.

Q Why does my computer or SCSI think that I have seven hard drives (or CD-ROMs, or some other device) when I only have one drive connected?

A When installing an Adaptec SCSI host adapter, SCSI bus protocol must be observed. The host adapter should be SCSI ID 7, always the highest ID number, so that the host adapter will always win SCSI arbitration. SCSI bus theory dictates that each device (the host adapter is a device) must have a unique and separate SCSI ID number. If a hard drive or other device is attached to the SCSI bus with the same ID as the host adapter, then the host adapter will see a response for "Phantom" devices at IDs where no device exists. To solve this problem, simply set the device ID to something other than that of the host adapter's SCSI ID. If the device is a boot drive, then the SCSI ID should be set at 0.

Q Why can't I use my new CD-ROM/tape/WORM drive with my Adaptec host adapter?

A Most Adaptec SCSI host adapters are designed to support two hard drives and, on some models, floppy drives with just a bare board. Additional devices require the use of a device driver. For more information on what your particular host adapter/kit should support, contact your dealer or distributor, or download kits.txt from the Adaptec BBS for an overview. Specification sheets are available on Adaptec's Interactive Fax System.

Q When I boot, why do I see a message that says something like "SCSI BIOS not installed", "Drive C already installed", or "Searching for Target 0"?

A The BIOS on Adaptec host adapter is used primarily for installing and booting from attached SCSI hard drives set to ID 0 (target 0). SCSI ID of the hard drive is set with jumpers or switches located on the hard drive. If the host adapter you are using is not being used to control a SCSI hard drive, and the host adapter has been working with the attached devices and their associated drivers, then disable the BIOS on the host adapter you are using. Consult your host adapter user guide or installation pamphlet for the jumper that enables the BIOS or the software switch that needs to be set to disable the BIOS. AHA-152*x* and AHA-154*x* boards can have the BIOS disabled with jumpers. The AHA-1640, AHA-174*x*, and AHA-274*x* boards BIOS enabling is controlled by software. The AHA-154*x*C and AHA-2840 boards BIOS address is controlled by DIP switches, located at the top edge of the board, or through CTRL–A for SCSI Select. AHA-2940 BIOS is controlled through CTRL–A for SCSI Select only.

Q When running NetWare with drives that are greater than 1 GB, do I enable the Extended BIOS Option for drives greater than 1 GB?

A No. You do not enable that option when running under NetWare for any of our cards. You also need to ensure that on the AHA-154*x*C/CF the dynamic scan of the SCSI bus is disabled. Press F6 for default settings in the SCSI Select utility.

Q Do Adaptec host adapters support RAID software?

A Yes. The AHA-154*x*, AHA-164*x*, AHA-174*x*, and the AHA-274*x* support RAID levels 0, 1, and 5 with the help of third-party software.

Q I added an external CD-ROM drive, and now my server won't boot from the hard disk. What should I do?

A Terminate the drive and remove the termination on the host adapter.

Q I was using a non-Adaptec host adapter. I replaced it with an Adaptec host adapter, but it won't boot. What should I do?

A Boot from a floppy. Back up your data. Low-level format the drive, then restore your data.

Q Why does NetWare report volume sizes larger than the drive's capacity?

A This is due to extraneous bytes in the FAT (file allocation table) area of the disk drive. This problem is easily resolved by performing a low-level format of the drive. Use scsifrmt.exe from the Adaptec BBS. The format utility is also in the BIOS of all the adapters (except the AHA-1740).

Q Why are there seven identical hard drives on my screen?

A There is a SCSI ID conflict on the SCSI bus. Make sure that the SCSI ID is 7 for the Adaptec host adapter and the SCSI ID for the hard drive is 0.

Q When do I need to install the drivers?

A The Adaptec adapters that are equipped with a BIOS are set to run with two to seven SCSI hard disk drives. If the adapter is for operating SCSI hard disks only, then no drivers are required. The drivers are required for operating CD-ROMs, tape drives, scanners, and removable media drives, such as Bernoulli, Syquest, and magneto-optical drives.

Q My system hangs on boot after I installed the SCSI adapter. What should I do?

A Make sure there are no address conflicts between the SCSI adapter and other cards in the system. Possible conflicts are the port address, DMA channel, interrupt, and BIOS address. Disconnect all SCSI peripherals from the adapter and try rebooting the system. If the adapter no longer hangs, then check for proper termination cable quality or SCSI ID.

Q My system works great with the adapter, but when I load the drivers the system hangs. What should I do?

A Run with the minimum config.sys to verify there is no conflict with another driver or TSR. Run the driver as the first device driver in config.sys. Make sure you are running the latest driver for the adapter. Most drivers can be upgraded via the Adaptec Technical Support BBS at 408-945-7727.

Q When I install the SCSI host adapter, my floppy no longer works. The error message says "FDD controller failure." What is happening?

A Some adapters have a floppy interface included on the adapter. If you are running the floppy from another controller or from the motherboard, make sure that you disable the floppy controller on the

SCSI adapter. If you are running the floppy from the SCSI host adapter, then make sure your have disabled any other floppy controller in the system.

Q   The adapter recognizes the drive on bootup but gives "Drive not ready." What should I do?

A   Make sure that the drive is jumped for "spinup on power-up." You may also enable the Send Start Unit command on many different models of Adaptec host adapters.

Q   What does the message "BIOS not intended to run with this card" mean?

A   This can happen when the BIOS or aspixdos.sys loads. This message indicates a conflict between our host adapter I/O port address and another card in the system. Change our port address to one of the alternate settings, or change the other card that conflicts.

Q   When should I disable the BIOS on the adapter?

A   The BIOS should be disabled when the adapter is not operating a SCSI hard disk drive.

Q   Can I replace my non-Adaptec SCSI adapter with one from Adaptec and read the data from the disk?

A   SCSI is standard, but how data is translated onto the drive is not. Each manufacturer uses its own translation scheme. The drive will have to be low-level formatted once it is connected to the Adaptec host adapter.

Q   I have UNIX installed on my ESDI (or IDE) drive. Can I add an Adaptec host adapter to install a SCO tape drive and do backups under UNIX?

A   Yes. Disable the host adapter BIOS. Use the mkdev tape command to configure the tape drive. The backup can be done using the cpio command or other UNIX commands. Consult your UNIX documentation for details.

Q   When I boot up, I get the message "hdd controller failure." Why?

A   If you are only using a SCSI hard disk drive in your system, you need to enter the CMOS SETUP in your system and ensure that "Hard disk" is marked as "not installed" or "none."

Q   My CD-ROM is supposed to support synchronous negotiation, but when I have synchronous negotiation enabled on the Adaptec card, it won't work. Why not?

A   It is often necessary to turn this setting to "disable" on the Adaptec board. This *does not* mean that the devices won't communicate synchronously. This setting only determines who *initiates* the dialogue.

III. AHA-154x COMMON QUESTIONS AND ANSWERS

Q I disabled the BIOS via the switches, and now I can no longer make changes to the adapter. Why?

A Once the BIOS is disabled via the switches, the CTRL–A SCSI Select will no longer function. An alternative for disabling the BIOS and still allowing for the CTRL–A to function would be to use the CTRL–A to disable the BIOS. This is done in the Advanced Configuration Options menu found under the Configure/View Host Adapter Settings menu. Set the option Host Adapter BIOS (Configuration Utility Reserves BIOS Space) to DISABLE. This will disable the BIOS but still allow access to SCSI Select using CTRL–A.

Q I have the AHA-1542B with the greater than 1 GB BIOS, and my system doesn't see the hard drive or just hangs there when I run Novell's SERVER program. What is the problem?

A The greater than 1 GB BIOS is a DOS solution and should not be used with NetWare 386, since greater than 1 GB support is built in. Remove the jumper at J6, position 2.

Q How do I correct the message "command port full" when installing an AHA-154xC and Novell 2.x?

A Ensure the hard disk drive is at SCSI ID 0 and the AHA-1540C advanced features has extended BIOS translation disabled and dynamic scan disabled.

Q Under install.nlm with the AHA-1542C card there is a message "The Host Adapter appears to be hung…" or "There are no accessible hard drives…" What should I do?

A After you reboot your system, press CRTL–A, select Configure/View Host Adapter Settings, then press F6 to reload the defaults. (The greater than 1 GB option was enabled, and this will not work under Novell.)

Q While installing NetWare 3.11 with an AHA-1540 host adapter, I load the driver AHA-1540.DSK. Then I load, install, and select disk options. The system "beeps" and the console displays a message that says "Host adapter appears to be hung. Resetting Host Adapter." What should I do?

A Press F6 in the SCSI Select utility to reset to defaults, or disable the "Dynamically Scan SCSI Bus" option in the advanced configurations setup.

Q What do you do when you have an AHA-154xC, Novell 3.11, and Toshiba hard disk drive, and Novell INSTALL reports "no accessible disk drives"?

A Remove "unit attention" jumper from the Toshiba hard drive, and check the version of AHA-1540.DSK to ensure it's current. Ensure the AHA-1540C advanced features has the dynamic scan option disabled.

IV. AHA-174x COMMON QUESTIONS AND ANSWERS

Q Why does my AHA-174x board always come up in the configuration as being in standard mode, and what is the difference between standard mode and enhanced mode?

A The default standard mode is the most compatible mode. Standard mode requires IRQ, DMA, and I/O port definitions by the installer. Only four AHA-174x's can be used if all are in standard mode, because of the number of available DMA channels for use in this mode. Enhanced mode allows the installer the luxury of not having to worry about the DMA, IRQ, and I/O addresses. This is all taken care of by the EISA motherboard. Enhanced mode also is the only mode that supports Fast SCSI (up to 10 MB/second). Up to 4 GB of RAM is supported, with up to 12 host adapters being allowed, the limit being imposed by the number of EISA slots. Both standard and enhanced modes support 32-bit addressing.

Q Why can't I configure an AHA-174x in enhanced mode in my EISA Computer? I get the error "Unable to initialize host adapter" or the system hangs after the Adaptec BIOS scans the SCSI devices.

A These errors are usually limited to motherboards that do not support LEVEL INT triggering. These chipsets, such as the Hint and SIS, require that a few modifications be made to the host adapter's EISA configuration (.cfg) file.

Make the following changes to the !ADP000X.CFG file beginning at line 117:

```
CHOICE = "Enhanced Mode"
FREE
INT=IOPORT(1) LOC (7 6 2 1 0) 10000B
LINK
IRQ=11|12|10|15|14|9
SHARE = "AHA-1740" —> Change to:  SHARE = NO
TRIGGER = LEVEL ——-> Change to: TRIGGER = EDGE
INIT=IOPORT93) LOC(4 3 2 1 0) 10010B | 10011B | 10001B | 1011B | 10101B |
100000B —> Change first zero in each binary number to a one.
Example:  10010B = 11010B
```

Another option is to download the latest CFG file for this card, (aswc174.exe). Reconfigure the card with new CFG file and select edge-triggered IRQ.

Q I have the AHA-1742A with the greater than 1 GB BIOS, and my system doesn't see the hard drive or just hangs when I run Novell's SERVER program. What is the problem?

A The greater than 1 GB BIOS is a DOS solution. NetWare 386 has greater than 1 GB support built in. Disable greater than 1 GB support with the EISA configuration utility.

Q If I have already installed the AHA-174x in standard mode in SCO UNIX v3.2.4 or ODT v2.0, how can I configure the AHA-174x to enhanced mode without reloading the operating system?

A The five major steps for this process are

1. Use the VI editor to edit the file /etc/conf/sdevice.d/ad. Change Y to N to disable the standard mode driver (named ad).

2. Use the VI editor to edit the file /etc/conf/sdevice.d/eiad. Change N to Y to enable the enhanced mode driver (named eiad).

3. Use the VI editor to edit the file /etc/conf/cf.d/mscsi. Change all occurrences of ad to eid on the leftmost column of this file.

4. Rebuild the kernel and shut down the system.

5. Use the EISA configuration utility to configure the AHA-174x from standard to enhanced mode. Save the changes and reboot to complete the process.

Q I'm trying to install the AHA-174x. After I run EISA configuration and reboot, I get "EISA configuration slot mismatch" or "board not found in slot x." Why?

A This error is caused by the fact that your board is not completely seated in the slot. You can verify this by booting to a floppy disk and running the DOS debug command.

DEBUG ENTER

i Xc80 ENTER   (where "X" is the slot where your board is physically installed.)

If "04" is returned, the board is correctly seated and the problem lies elsewhere. If "FF" is returned, the board needs to be pushed down further. Power-down your system before reseating your board.

V. AHA-274x COMMON QUESTIONS AND ANSWERS

Q   I am running an AHA-2742T, and when I load ASPI7DOS.SYS, the system hangs. Why?

A   If channel B is set as the primary channel and you are booting from the hard disk at target ID 0, then this problem will occur. Update the ASPI7DOS.SYS driver by downloading the file upgrade.exe from our BBS at 408-945-7727.

Q   When loading AIC7770.DSK, NetWare reports "Unable to find loader $ public symbol." What should I do?

A   Ensure the appropriate driver is loading for each supported version of NetWare. NetWare 2.x and 3.10 are not supported. Novell 3.11 requires AIC7770.DSK version 1.0x. Novell 4.0 requires AIC7770.DSK ver 2.0x.

Q   Why do I have problems with the AHA-274xT under Novell 3.1x and 4.0x?

A   Run the EISA configuration utility and disable greater than 1 GB support and disable support for more than two drives. Load AIC7770.DSK slot=x (where x is the slot number).

VI. AHA-284x COMMON QUESTIONS AND ANSWERS

Q   When I plug my AHA-2842VL into my system, the system hangs on boot up. Why?

A   The AHA-2842VL is a bus mastering device and requires that the VL slot support full 32-bit bus mastering. Most VLB systems have either slave slots and/or master slots. The adapter must be inserted in a master slot. If you are not sure if the system supports bus mastering, or if you do not have a master slot, contact the system manufacturer.

VII. AHA-294x COMMON QUESTIONS AND ANSWERS

Q   Why wouldn't an AHA-2940 BIOS banner be displayed when installing the AHA-2940?

A   Either the board is not in a bus mastering slot, or the PCI slot is not enabled for bus mastering in the CMOS setup. Check your motherboard manual to find out if the slot is bus mastering, or how to enable bus mastering for that slot.

K

Q On bootup, I get the error message "Host Adapter Configuration Error." What should I do?

A In CMOS setup, enable IRQ for the PCI slot. Alternatively, you can mark one of the IRQs as free. Be aware that there may be an IRQ conflict with a built-in controller on the motherboard. For CMOS settings, refer to your PC user manual.

Q On bootup, I get a message "BIOS installed successfully," but my system hangs. What should I do?

A Verify that the CMOS interrupt structure is set to "INTA" and the CMOS IRQ level matches the jumper setting on the motherboard. Refer to your PC user manual.

Q When I invoke the CTRL–A option, the message "Cannot locate host adapter" is displayed. What should I do?

A Update the AHA-2940 BIOS to version 1.11 (checksum 8200). If you have an EPROM burner, download the file 2940.exe from the BBS. Otherwise, call Adaptec Technical Support at 408-934-7274.

Q My Intel P90 system hangs during bootup, while displaying "Starting MS-DOS…" What should I do?

A Contact the system vendor to obtain the latest system BIOS.

Q When loading aspi8dos.sys, the system hangs and then displays the error message "Read BIOS Parameter Failed." What should I do?

A Update aspi8dos.sys manager to version 1.10 (EZ-SCSI 3.03).

Q The ATI (Mach 64) video card installed with my AHA-2940 shows no video or causes intermittent hangs during boot under DOS or Windows. Why?

A There are known compatibility issues between the two PCI cards. Contact ATI for possible resolution of these issues.

Q The EZ-SCSI installation hangs on installing the AIC-7870.DLL driver.

A Update to EZ-SCSI version 3.03.

Q Upon bootup, a 486 AMI BIOS system displays the "Device Name Not Available" message. What should I do?

A Contact your system vendor to obtain the latest system BIOS.

Q How do I determine which AHA-2940 is the primary card if I am duplexing under Novell?

A During bootup, check the LED on the AHA-2940 cards to see which one illuminates first.

Q I recently upgraded from a previous SCSI host adapter to an AHA-2940 PCI adapter and the 78xx.SYS driver. When I removed the old adapter from the system, I connected the hard drive to the AHA-2940 and rebooted. Now the system will not boot. What's wrong?

A A possible cause is that when the new driver was added to the ntbootdd.sys, the old driver was also there and was configured to be activated at BOOTUP time. The new driver must be set to start at BOOTUP. This can be done in the Device section of the Control Panel. The old driver needs to be deleted from the ntbootdd.sys if the card is no longer in the system. If the old card is still in the system but is not controlling the boot device, choose the Service section in the Control Panel and select the original driver to be started at SYSTEM time, not BOOTUP.

VIII. APA PRODUCT COMMON QUESTIONS AND ANSWERS

Q What is the purpose of Cardsoft Socket Services? Why do I need it?

A It is the software enabler to "wake up" the PCMCIA chip in the computer. Use the enabler that comes with your PC, if one exists.

Q Why does my Notebook computer hang and report "no COMMAND.COM" when the MA460.SYS loads?

A This is a known problem with the MA460.SYS v1.12 and v1.15 when used with the Databook chipset. MA460 scans addresses 360h through 230h. When we scan address 250, the power management on the Notebook shuts down the hard drive.

Q Can I use devices with high transfer rates on MiniSCSI adapters?

A The APA-348 MiniSCSI Plus and bi-directional specifications only support a maximum burst rate of 260K per second. The APA-358 MiniSCSI EPP and enhanced parallel port specifications only support a maximum burst rate of 1 MB/sec. If you require higher transfer rates, then consider getting a 16-bit or 32-bit SCSI host adapter.

Q I have a Media Vision Pro Audio sound card, and I want to utilize the SCSI port to run a hard disk and tape drive. How do I do this?

A SCSIWorks! software contains the drivers and software necessary to run additional SCSI devices on the Media Vision Pro Audio series of sound cards. The software can be ordered from our software order line at 800-442-7274.

K

Q I have a CD-ROM connected to a T-130. The driver loads fine, and I get my drive letter E:. When I do a dir E:, I get "CDR-101 not ready reading..." error, or it just hangs. What should I do?

A Try removing the JP2 jumper (0 wait state) from the T-130.

IX. AMM PRODUCT COMMON QUESTIONS AND ANSWERS

Q My Audio CD Player works fine in DOS, but why can't I play Windows CD Player?

A To play an audio CD under Windows, either using the Adaptec CD Player or Windows' Media Player, an MCI CD Audio driver is required. The most common error message displayed when the MCI driver is not present is "NO CD." You can add it yourself, and you will need your Microsoft Windows disks available before taking the following steps. In Windows, under Control Panel, click on the Drivers icon, then click on ADD, and select the MCI CD Audio driver from the list. Click OK, and exit the Control Panel.

Q My CD-ROM drive is XA-compliant, so why does aspicdxa.exe not load during boot up?

A XA (Mode 2 Form 2) is a newer technology that supports both audio and data on the same track of CD-ROMs. There are few XA CD titles on the market that support this technology yet. Currently this driver only supports certain CD-ROMs, including Chinon (CDS-535), Hitachi (CDR-6750), Panasonic (CR-532), Plextor (or Texel) (DM-3028, DM-5028), Sony (CDU-541), Teac (CD-50), and Toshiba (XM-3301, XM-3401). More information can be found in the readme.txt or the EZ-Audio installation disk.

Q Why can't I hear any sound from the speakers when the CD Player in DOS and Windows seems to be working okay?

A In order to use Audio CDs or play games and utilities with analog audio, a four-pin CD Audio cable is required. This cable is connected from the CD Audio-In connector of AMM-157X to the CD Audio connector of your internal CD-ROM. You can purchase this cable from your local computer supply store or order it directly from TTS Multimedia Systems at 800-887-4968.

Q I am replacing a previously installed sound card. Do I need to remove any drivers first?

A Yes. If you had a sound card previously installed in your system, there are drivers and configuration parameters that must be removed. Remove all the sound card drivers and parameters from autoexec.bat, config.sys, and system.ini before installing the AMM-157X. For further information, download othersnd.txt from the Adaptec BBS.

Q During Windows bootup, why do I get warning messages like "no Adaptec AMM-157X detected" or "Roland MPU-401 driver not installed"?

A To resolve this configuration error, install the EZ-Audio disk and continue installing up to Windows Sound System, disk 1. Under Windows Sound System, select the AMM-157*x* driver. When it asks you to "install software" or "restart Windows," select restart Windows. Also, if you have any IRQ or port address conflicts in Windows, you can change them in Windows' Control Panel, under the Drivers icon (by clicking on SETUP).

X. TRANTOR COMMON QUESTIONS AND ANSWERS

Q Why do I get "No SCSI Functions in use" when loading tscsi.sys?

A tscsi.sys is for hard drives. Make sure the hard drive is attached, powered on, and formatted.

Q I get "no Host Adapter found" with T-338, T-348, or T-358. What should I do?

A Make sure the SCSI device provides termination power and the ASPI manager (MA3##) loads in config.sys. Try another SCSI device.

Q How can I check for TERMPWR when using the T-338, T-348, or T-358?

A Try attaching the printer cable to the printer-pass-through on the T-338, T-348, or T-358. If it prints, then the SCSI device has termination power. Otherwise, call the manufacturer, or measure pin 38 (5-volts) and pin 37 (ground).

Q Why do I get "No SCSI $MGR Found"?

A Make sure you are loading the correct ASPI manager (ma###.sys) for the Trantor-brand adapter. If using the T-338, T-348, or T-358 adapters, make sure the SCSI device supplies 5-volt termination power.

Q What does it mean when the mscdex.exe loads and I receive the error message "Incorrect DOS Version"?

A DOS 6 contains its own version of mscdex.exe located in the DOS directory. There are two solutions. You can overwrite Trantor's mscdex.exe with the DOS version. Or you can change the path in the autoexec.bat to the DOS directory.

K

Q During the TFORMAT process the drive reports a "CMD failure ##" message. Why?

A The TFORMAT program may have a conflict with a TSR or MEMORY resident program. Create a boot floppy with the correct ASPI manager in the config.sys. Here's an example of the config.sys line: "device=ma13b.sys". Copy the manager and TFORMAT to the floppy. Reboot the computer from the floppy and run TFORMAT. Answer Y to make the drive bootable, even if you are not booting from the drive. Once completed, reboot from the normal C: drive. If the procedure does not work, try TFORMAT/560.

Q My T-338, T-348, or T-358 driver fails to load, and it says "No host adapter present." Why?

A The T-338, T-348, or T-358 requires that the SCSI device provide termination power. The T-338, T-348, or T-358 receives its power from the SCSI device connected. To conduct a quick test to verify termination power, connect a printer to the T-338, T-348, or T-358 pass-through-port and execute a print screen. If the printer fails to print, then the T-338, T-348, or T-358 lacks termination power. Verify that the SCSI device provides termination power.

Q My T-338, T-348, or T-358 devices will not operate when connected to a Iomega Bernoulli drive. Why not?

A The T-338, T-348, or T-358 receives power from the device. Iomega drives such as the 90 or 150 ship from the factory with the termination power jumper removed. As a result, they will not work as stand-alone devices with the T-338, T-348, or T-358. You will have to daisy chain the Iomega with another device that supplies termination power, or have an Iomega approved service center install the termination power jumper on the jumper block marked TRM.

L

INTERNET AND ONLINE RESOURCES

Are you looking for files, documents, and other information about SCSI but don't know where to begin your search? If so, this section lists the addresses for the major SCSI-related Internet sites, online services, and BBSs so that you'll be able to find what you're looking for quickly.

NOTE *If you're looking for a BBS number or Internet site for a particular manufacturer, see the directory of SCSI vendors in Appendix A.*

INTERNET: WORLD WIDE WEB

Following are the major SCSI-related Internet Web pages. The page's sponsor is listed first, followed by its Web page address.

Apple Computer

To reach the Apple Computer Web page, type in your Web browser:

```
http://www.apple.com
```

Buslogic

To reach the Buslogic home page, type the following:

```
http://www.buslogic.com
```

To reach the Buslogic FTP sites, type the following:

```
ftp://199.182.164.5
```

```
ftp://ftp.buslogic.com
```

CERN Fibre Channel Homepage

To reach the CERN Fibre Channel Homepage, type in your Web browser:

```
http://www.amdahl.com/ext/carp/fca
/fca.html
```

Fibre Channel Association

To reach the Fibre Channel Association home page, type in your Web browser:

```
http://www.amdahl.com/ext/carp/fca
/fcsi.html
```

Interphase Corporation

To reach the Interphase Corporation home page, type in your Web browser:

```
http://www.iphase.com
```

NCR

To reach the NCR home page, type in your Web browser:

```
http://www.ncr.com
```

SCSI FAQs (Frequently Asked Questions)

For a compilation of frequently asked questions and answers about SCSI, read or download the latest SCSI FAQs (there should be at least two parts). You can find the SCSI FAQs in this newsgroup:

```
comp.periphs.scsi
```

Or, type the following into your Web browser:

```
http://www.cis.ohio-state.edu/
hypertext/faq/usenet/scsi-faq/
top.html
```

```
http://scwww.ucs.indiana.edu/faq/
Windows/
```

SCSI Newsgroup

The SCSI newsgroup is the only place to go for constant discussions and help with SCSI. To read it, type the following into your newsgroup reader:

```
comp.periphs.scsi
```

SCSI under Linux

If you use SCSI under Linux, you should download Drew Eckhardt's Linux SCSI How-To, a terrific compilation of Linux SCSI information that is posted as a public service. To download this document, type in your Web browser:

```
ftp://sunsite.unc.edu/pub/Linux/
docs/howto/scsi-howto
```

Note: This site limits logons to the first 250 users. If you can't get it, you'll get a "Could not login to FTP server" message followed by a list of mirror sites that you can also go to for Linux information.

SCSI-2 Home Page

In addition to its various other tidbits of information, the SCSI-2 home page has the X3T9.2 committee's draft ANSI specification for the SCSI-2 standard, revision 10L. You can reach it by typing into your Web browser:

(US site)

`http://abekas.com:8080/SCSI2/`

(UK site)

`http://www.abekrd.co.uk/SCSI2/`

Standards Committee Documents

To find the SCSI Standards Committee's documents, type into your Web browser:

`http://www.ncr.com/pub/standards/io/`

Add the following to your address to retrieve these specific documents:

`/cam/`	*CAM*
`/pnpscsi/`	*Plug-and-Play SCSI*
`/scsi1/`	*SCSI-1*
`/scsi2/`	*SCSI-2*
`/scsi3/`	*SCSI-3*
`/fc/`	*Fibre Channel*
`/x3t10/`	*X3T10 Committee information*

Sun Microsystems

To reach Sun Microsystems, type into your Web browser:

`http://www.sun.com`

Symbios Logic Incorporated

Symbios Logic Incorporated (formerly NCR Microelectronics) posts a Web page with draft and final ANSI committee standards drafts, as well as a variety of other SCSI-related information. To reach their page, type into your Web browser:

`http://ftp.hmpd.com`

INTERNET: FTP

The following lists Internet FTP sites with SCSI related information.

American Megatrends

To reach American Megatrends, where you'll find chipset guides and general SCSI tips, ftp to

`american.megatrends.com`

NCR

NCR (National Cash Register), one of the leading manufacturers of SCSI host adapters, has a variety of SCSI specification documents. To access these documents, ftp to

`ncrinfo.ncr.com`

The various documents are available in the following directories:

`/pub/standards/io/ata`
                    `/ata2`
                    `/cam`
                    `/fc/profiles`
                    `/pnpscsi`
                    `/scsi1`
                    `/scsi2`
                    `/scsi3`
                    `/xet10`

Standards Documents

A variety of standards documents—including those for ATA-2, ATAPI, Plug-and-Play, SSA, IEEE 1394, Fibre Channel, SPI, and SCSI-2—are available by ftp to

`fission.dt.wdc.com`

Look in the /pub/ and /pub/standards/ directories.

Institute of Electrical and Electronics Engineers (IEEE)

The IEEE promotes many standards, including those used for SCSI-3. To access their files, ftp to

`ftp.fidonet.org`

L

Library of Congress

If you still can't find what you're looking for and you know that the document is a published work, you can search the Library of Congress for it. To get there, ftp to

`ftp.loc.gov`

Read the README file for information on the Library of Congress search software for the Internet.

National Institute for Standards and Technology (NIST)

NIST hosts a variety of standards documents, including Plug-and-Play, and can be reached by ftp to

`enh.nist.gov`

Sun Microsystems, Inc.

For FCSI Fibre Channel Profiles from Sun, ftp to

`playground.sun.com`

Symbios Logic Inc.

Symbios Logic Inc. (formerly NCR Microelectronics) is also available for ftp access of its draft and final ANSI committee standards drafts, as well as a variety of other SCSI-related information. To reach their site, ftp to

`ftp.hmpd.com`

Tulane University

For files from the SCSI BBS and information about ESDI, Fiber Channel, IPI, and SCSI, ftp to

`ftp.cs.tulane.edu`

University of Amsterdam

To reach the University of Amsterdam and its SCSI documents and information, ftp to

`ftp.fwi.uva.nl`

University of Heidelberg

For Linux, MS-DOS, OS/2, Novell, UNIX, Windows, and SCSI files from the University of Heidelberg, ftp to

`ftp.urz.uni-heidelberg.de`

Walnut Creek CD-ROM

To reach Walnut Creek CD-ROM, where you'll find SCSI files, source code, and public domain and shareware programs, ftp to

`freefall.cdrom.com`

Wolfenbuettel Polytechnical Institute

To reach Wolfenbuettel for SCSI documents, ftp to

`ftp.fh-wolfenbuettel.de`

COMMERCIAL ONLINE SERVICES

Commercial online services—like CompuServe, America Online, and Prodigy—all have a number of resources for information or help with SCSI installations. Try the areas listed below for ongoing help with SCSI.

America Online

Macintosh Hardware Forum

Keywords: mhw, mac hardware

Services: Message boards, software libraries, real-time conferences, and industry personalities

PC Hardware Forum

Keywords: phw, pc hardware

Services: Message boards, software libraries, weekly live conferences, and a Hardware Reference Guide with answers to many common hardware questions

PC Vendors Database

Keyword: Vendors

Services: Database of hardware vendors with contact information and product listings

CompuServe

Computer Database Plus

Go: COMPDB

Services: A comprehensive collection of over 370,000 computer-related abstracts and/or full text from leading computer industry publications

Computer Directory

Go: COMPDIR

Services: Information on over 74,000 computer-related products and more than 13,000 manufacturers of hardware, software, peripher-als, and data communications and telecommunications equipment

Hardware

Go: HARDWARE for various hardware forums and extensive software libraries

CD-ROM

Go: CDVENB

Services: Access to leading CD-ROM publishers and manufacturers, updated drivers, and help with your questions

Plug-and-Play

Go: PLUGPLAY

Services: Discussion of hardware and software issues concerning Plug-and-Play on PCs

Manufacturers

Adaptec Inc.

Go: ADAPTEC

Services: Drivers, software, configuration help, and support

Apple Computer

Go: APPLE for Apple sites

Go: MAC for Macintosh sites

Go: MACINTOSH for various Macintosh forums

Go: MACHW for the Macintosh Hardware Forum

Canon USA Inc.

Go: CANON

Services: Technical support, information, and troubleshooting assistance

Cheyenne

Go: CHEYENNE

Services: Information on ARCserve SCSI Express, drivers, and compatibility issues

L

Corel Corp.

Go: COREL

Services: CorelSCSI updates and compatibility lists

Creative Labs, Inc.

Go: BLASTER

Services: Help with the Sound Blaster 16 SCSI board and software updates

Logitech Inc.

Go: LOGITECH

Services: Technical support, updates on product development, software, and answers to commonly asked questions about Logitech products

Seagate Technology Inc.

Go: SEAGATE

Services: Specifications for Seagate SCSI drives

Storage Dimensions Inc.

Go: PCVENF

Services: Technical support

Prodigy

Computer BBS

Jump: Computer BB

Choose "Hardware: Peripherals" or scan the message listings for relevant topics.

Computer Support

Jump: Support BB

Choose the Hardware BB or the Software BB and scan the message postings for SCSI-related discussions.

THE SCSI BBS

The SCSI BBS is *the* place to visit for SCSI standards documents, discussions, and messages. To reach the BBS, dial 719-574-0424.

Glossary

A

A-cable A 50-wire cable used for 8-bit SCSI-1 buses. There are two types of A-cable connectors: high- and low-density. The low-density A-cable connector is also known as a Centronics-type connector.

active terminator A terminator that can compensate for variations in the terminator power supplied by the host adapter through means of a built-in voltage regulator. *See also* forced-perfect terminator; passive terminator

adapter A card that communicates with and controls a device or system.

add-on Something added to the computer to expand its functionality. Commonly refers to cards that are plugged into the computer.

address The numbers used to identify particular locations in memory.

Advanced SCSI Programming Interface *See* ASPI

American National Standards Institute *See* ANSI

ANSI American National Standards Institute. The organization that promotes standards for hardware and software including those used in PCs. SCSI is an ANSI standard.

API Application Programming Interface. A software module that provides a consistent set of commands that programs can use to perform tasks. ASPI and CAM are examples of SCSI APIs.

Application Programming Interface *See* API

ASPI Advanced SCSI Programming Interface. Formerly called the Adaptec SCSI Programming Interface, ASPI was developed by Adaptec as a standard way for programs to send commands and data between SCSI host adapters and devices.

asynchronous transfer A method of sending data that requires an acknowledgment from the receiver for each byte of data that is sent before the next one is sent. Asynchronous transfers are slower than synchronous transfers.

autodetection The ability of the computer to check the identity and configuration of a device without user intervention.

B

B-cable A 68-wire cable used for 16-bit SCSI-2 buses.

backup A copy of files used on a computer system that is stored on disk, tape, or other medium for safekeeping in case of a system failure.

backward compatibility The ability of newer technology to work with older technology without any modification.

BBS Bulletin Board System. A computer or group of computers that provide services such as E-mail and file transfer via modem or the Internet. There are commercial (CompuServe, America Online, Prodigy) as well as private BBSs.

BIOS Basic Input/Output System. Software stored in a chip used for a variety of purposes. In a PC, the BIOS contains code that communicates with devices such as the floppy drive, keyboard, and video output.

BIOS address The memory address that is used to access code stored in the BIOS chip.

bit Binary digit. The smallest unit of data used by digital computers and devices. A bit can be either on or off. These two states are referred to as 1 and 0, true and false, high and low, to name a few.

boot The process of starting the computer. Also called bootup.

built-in A peripheral or device that is manufactured as a part of the computer, not added by the user.

Bulletin Board System *See* BBS

burst speed   The rate at which data can be transferred for a short period of time. Burst speeds are generally higher than sustained speeds.

bus   A collection of wires in a cable or copper traces on a circuit board used to transmit data, status, and control signals. ISA, EISA, VL-Bus, and PCI are examples of PC buses. SCSI is also a bus.

bus mastering   A method of transferring data through a bus in which the device takes over the bus and directly controls the transfer of data to the computer's memory. Bus mastering is a method of DMA transfer. Also known as first-party DMA.

bus slots   Also known as expansion slots or simply slots, bus slots are connectors inside the computer that are used for attaching add-on cards and devices to a bus.

byte   A unit of data consisting of eight bits.

C

cache   Memory used as a high-speed temporary storage place for frequently used data.

CAM   Common Access Method. The proposed ANSI software interface for SCSI devices and a part of the SCSI-3 standard.

cascading drivers   Drivers that can connect to, and thereby work with, other drivers.

CCS   *See* Common Command Set

CD   *See* compact disc

CDB   *See* command descriptor block

CD-R   Compact Disc Recordable. A special type of CD that can be written to one time. It is primarily used for making a master disc to be mass-produced.

CD-ROM   Compact Disc Read-Only Memory. A storage medium using the same technology as audio CDs and used to store large amounts of data.

command chaining   Combining multiple SCSI commands into a single group in order to reduce the overhead of many individual commands.

command descriptor block (CDB)   A block of SCSI information containing the command, parameter, and address information needed by the target to carry out a certain task.

Common Access Method   *See* CAM

Common Command Set (CCS)　A standard set of commands for communicating with SCSI devices.

compact disc　An optical disc capable of storing the equivalent of hundreds of floppy disks. *See* CD-ROM

controller card　A circuit board that plugs into the motherboard on the computer. Controller cards allow the computer to communicate and control devices. SCSI and IDE cards are examples of hard disk controller cards. Some printers and scanners also require controller cards, called printer controller cards and scanner controller cards, respectively.

CPU　Central Processing Unit. The main microprocessor in a computer. The CPU carries out the primary functions of the computer. The Intel 486 and Pentium are examples of CPUs.

cross-platform　Cross-platform hardware or software can function on more than one type of computer (e.g., PC, Macintosh, or Sun) or operating system (e.g., DOS, Windows, or UNIX).

cross section　An illustration that shows what something looks like after being cut.

cross talk　Interference between two wires caused by the signal from one wire appearing on the other.

D

D-sub connector　A widely used family of connectors probably deriving its name from its "D" shape. Specific connectors are denoted by a letter for its size and a number for its pin configuration. For example, a DB-15 connector is a D-sub connector of size B with pin configuration number 15.

data transfer rate　A measure of how quickly information can be passed between the computer and another device or between devices. The higher the data transfer rate, the less you'll have to wait for data to get where it needs to go.

device　Generally refers to equipment that can be connected to the computer, such as printers, hard disks, scanners, and modems. Devices can also be interface cards, such as video cards, SCSI cards, and sound cards. The computer itself may also be referred to as a device.

device driver　A software module that communicates with and transfers data to a controller or other device.

device ID　*See* SCSI ID

differential A SCSI bus configuration in which each signal is sent on two wires. The signal is derived by taking the difference in voltage between the two wires, effectively eliminating unwanted noise in the wire. *See* also single-ended

Direct Memory Access *See* DMA

disconnect/reconnect The ability of a device to remove itself from a bus to perform a task (such as a tape drive fast-forwarding) and then connecting itself back to the bus after completion of the task.

disk cache Memory used to temporarily store data read from and/or written to a floppy or hard disk to increase performance.

DLL Dynamic Link Library. A Windows file, that contains code that can be added to a Windows program while it is running.

DMA Direct Memory Access. A method of transferring data from a device to the computer's memory without intervention by the CPU. DMA is handled by a DMA controller chip in the computer (third-party DMA) or by the device itself (bus mastering or first-party DMA).

DOS Disk Operating System. A single-tasking operating system for the PC. The most common version of DOS is developed by Microsoft.

DOS Protected Mode Interface *See* DPMI

double-click Pressing a mouse button twice in rapid succession.

DoubleSpeed SCSI *See* Fast-20

DPMI DOS Protected Mode Interface. An API that allows programs to use memory beyond the 640K limitation imposed by DOS.

driver *See* device driver

dynamic link library *See* DLL

E

E-mail Electronic mail. Messages sent by modem or other electronic means, which enables people to communicate over long distances in minutes as opposed to days. *See also* snail-mail

ECC Error Correction Code. A method used on hard disks to determine if an error has occurred in the data stored on the drive.

EIDE Enhanced IDE. The second generation of IDE technology that improves the data throughput of IDE hard disks and adds the capability of connecting CD-ROM drives to the same interface card as hard disks.

EISA   Extended Industry Standard Architecture. A 32-bit computer bus introduced in 1988 that enhanced the capabilities and performance of the ISA bus standard.

end user   You. A person who uses hardware and software.

Enhanced IDE   *See* EIDE

Enhanced Small Disk Interface   *See* ESDI

error checking   Any one of a number of methods used to verify that data sent from one place to another arrives at its destination without errors.

ESDI   Enhanced Small Disk Interface. A high-speed hard disk bus interface used in the 1980s that has been superseded by SCSI due to ESDI's limitation of supporting only hard drives.

even parity   *See* parity checking

exclusive OR   *See* XOR

F

face plate   The front cover (usually plastic) of a device such as a hard disk or CD-ROM drive.

Fast-20   A SCSI-3 transfer mode that is capable of sending data at 20 MB/sec. Also known as DoubleSpeed SCSI and UltraSCSI.

Fast-40   A SCSI-3 transfer mode that is twice as fast as Fast-20, capable of sending data at 40 MB/sec.

Fast SCSI   A SCSI-2 transfer mode that operates at 10 MB/sec, twice as fast as regular SCSI.

Fast Wide SCSI   Wide SCSI operating at twice the rate of regular Wide SCSI.

fault tolerance   Able to recover from errors or other failures without loss or corruption of data.

Fibre Channel   A new ANSI standard that specifies high-speed serial communication between devices. Fibre Channel is used as one of the bus architectures in SCSI-3.

fileserver   A computer used primarily for storing files on a network.

Firewire   *See* IEEE 1394

first-party DMA   *See* bus mastering

flat-ribbon cable   *See* ribbon cable

floppy disk   A magnetic disk used to store computer data.

forced-perfect terminator   A type of terminator containing a sophisticated circuit that can compensate for variations in the power supplied by the host adapter, as well as variations in bus impedance of complex SCSI systems. *See also* passive terminator; active terminator

FPT   *See* forced-perfect terminator

free-air characteristic impedance   The average impedance of air.

G

GB   Gigabyte. One gigabyte equals 1,073,741,824 bytes.

GPP   Generic Packetized Protocol. A method for transferring groups of data that is independent of the type of hardware used, hence the name generic.

H

handshake   The communication that occurs between devices in order to determine the method and speed of data transfer to be used.

HD (high-density) connector   A connector in which the pins are closely packed in order to save space. High-density A-cable connectors have just as many pins as low-density A-cable connectors but are smaller than the low-density ones.

host   The computer that contains the SCSI host adapter.

host adapter   The controller card used to communicate with and control devices. A SCSI host adapter is used to attach and communicate with SCSI devices.

I

I/O   Input/Output.

IDE   Integrated Drive Electronics. A hard disk technology that puts the communication control and related circuitry on the drive itself (integrated). Older technologies such as MFM had some of the electronics on the drive and the rest on the interface card. *See also* EIDE

IEEE   Institute of Electrical and Electronics Engineers. An organization that promotes electrical and electronics standards.

IEEE 1394   Called Firewire by Apple, IEEE 1394 is a serial bus that runs at 100 MB/sec and doesn't require any terminators. A special feature of IEEE 1394 is isochronous transfer mode.

impedance   A measure of a material's resistance to the transfer of electricity.

initiator   A device that is in control of the bus and sends commands to a target.

Integrated Drive Electronics   *See* IDE

interrupt   *See* IRQ

IRQ   Interrupt Request. A signal used by devices to indicate that they need attention from the CPU. Computers have several IRQ channels so that many devices can be attached, each one to its own IRQ, and serviced by the CPU.

ISA   Industry Standard Architecture. An 8-bit computer bus introduced by IBM (International Business Machines) in 1983 and later expanded to 16-bit for the IBM AT computer. The ISA bus is also known as the AT bus.

isochronous transfer   A method of sending data that guarantees that the data will arrive at its destination at a specified period of time. Isochronous transfers are important for sending data such as video and audio, since they are dependent on time.

J

jumper   A small plastic and metal connector used to bridge the gap between two or more pins. Jumpers are commonly used for configuring devices and add-on cards.

K

Kb   Kilobit. One kilobit equals 1,024 bits or 128 bytes.

KB   Kilobyte. One kilobyte equals 1,024 bytes.

L

L-cable   A 110-wire cable used for 32-bit SCSI-3 buses.

LADDR   Layered Device Driver. A SCSI device driver architecture used in early versions of OS/2.

local bus   A computer bus that allows devices to transfer data directly to the CPU. VL-Bus and PCI are common types of local bus.

logical unit   Usually the medium used by a device to store or retrieve data. A CD-ROM drive is a device and the disc in the drive is a logical unit.

logical unit number   *See* LUN

low-level format   The process of writing special markers and other tracking information on a storage medium such as a floppy disk or hard disk.

LUN   Logical Unit Number. A 3-bit value identifying a logical unit in a device.

M

magneto-optical (MO)   A storage medium similar to CD-ROM, except that magneto-optical discs can be erased and rewritten thousands of times.

mainframe   An extremely large (occupying the space of entire rooms) and costly computer used for supporting many users running programs simultaneously. The IBM S370/3031 is an example of a mainframe.

max out   Slang term meaning to use fully.

Mb   Megabit. One megabit equals 1,048,576 bits or 131,072 bytes.

MB   Megabyte. One megabyte equals 1,048,567 bytes.

MCA   Micro Channel Architecture. *See* Micro Channel

Micro Channel   A 32-bit computer bus developed by IBM for its PS/2 series of computers.

microcomputer   A computer that is small enough to fit on a desktop and consisting of very few microchips. The PC and Macintosh are examples of microcomputers.

MiniCAM   A scaled-down, limited-functionality version of NCR's DOSCAM driver.

minicomputer   A term coined in the early 1970s to describe a small, low-priced computer (relative to the humongous and extremely expensive mainframe computers). The PDP-11, VAX-11, and HP3000 are examples of minicomputers.

MO   *See* magneto-optical

motherboard   The main circuit board in a computer on which the CPU, main memory, system BIOS, and any other built-in electronics reside.

multitasking   Multitasking is simply performing more than one function simultaneously. Multitasking operating systems, such as Windows 95, OS/2, and UNIX, can run many programs simultaneously.

N

NetWare   A network operating system developed by Novell Corporation.

nexus   The link between initiator, target, and logical unit used to identify an I/O process. An I_T_L (initiator, target, logical unit) nexus is the most basic type of SCSI link. To send multiple I/O processes to the same target and logical unit, an I_T_L_Q (initiator, target, logical unit, queue) nexus is used.

noise   Unwanted and usually interfering electrical signals.

O

odd parity   *See* parity checking

online   Existing on a BBS.

operating system   A set of commands and programs used to interact with and operate a computer.

OR   A binary operation that compares two bits and yields a 1 if at least one of the bits being compared is set to 1, as shown in the table below. *See also* XOR

First Bit	Second Bit	Result
0	0	0
1	0	1
0	1	1
1	1	1

OS/2   A multitasking operating system for the PC developed by IBM Corporation.

overhead   Time lost during an operation due to error checking or other tasks that hinder the completion of the operation.

P

P-cable   A 68-wire cable used for 16-bit SCSI-3 buses. P-cables can be used with Q-cables for 32-bit SCSI-3 buses.

P-to-A transition cable   An adapter used to connect 8-bit SCSI-1 devices using A-cables to a 16- or 32-bit SCSI-3 device using P-cables.

parallel   Sending bits in groups. *See also* serial

parity checking   A simple error-checking method that looks for the number of bits in a byte that are set to 1. Odd parity requires that all data bytes have an odd number of bits set to one; even parity requires an even number set to one.

passive terminator   A terminator that provides a fixed-value impedance match between the end of the SCSI bus and the cable. Passive terminators are comprised only of resistors and are susceptible to variations in the power supplied by the host adapter. *See also* active terminator; forced-perfect terminator

PCI   *See* Peripheral Component Interconnect

Peripheral Component Interconnect (PCI)   A 32-bit local bus developed by Intel that allows peripherals to communicate directly with the CPU.

PIO   Programmed Input/Output. A method of transferring data from a device to the host computer's memory that requires the CPU to perform the transfer. PIO is slower than DMA.

pipeline   A channel used to transfer commands, data, or signals.

Plug-and-Play   An Intel/Microsoft standard for configuring add-on cards and other devices so that user intervention is minimized. No more switches, jumpers, and wheels to fiddle with.

plug-in card   *See* add-on

PostScript   A printer language used to describe the text and graphics to be printed.

programmed input/output   *See* PIO

Q

Q-cable   A 68-wire cable used in conjunction with a P-cable for 32-bit SCSI-3 buses.

QIC   Quarter-Inch Cartridge. A tape format used for backing up data. QIC tape is 1/4-inch wide.

queuing   Grouping a series of commands in order to send them as a single command, thereby reducing data transfer overhead.

R

RAID   Redundant Array of Inexpensive Drives. A collection of storage devices configured to provide higher data transfer rates and/or data recovery capability.

read-intensive   A process that requires a lot of reading of data from a device such as a hard disk.

read-only   Something that can only be read from, not written to.

regular SCSI   8-bit SCSI.

RF   Radio Frequency.

ribbon cable   A group of wires arranged in rows that comprise a single flat cable resembling a ribbon.

round-robin   A method of guaranteeing that a number of devices will have an opportunity to be serviced. The round-robin method simply requires that every device is serviced in turn. After the last device is serviced, the first one is serviced, and the process starts again.

S

SASI   Shugart Associates Systems Interface. The predecessor to SCSI.

SC   Selector Channel. An intelligent bus used on the IBM 360 mainframe.

SCAM   SCSI Configured Auto-Magically. A pending standard that will give SCSI devices the ability to automatically select their SCSI IDs.

SCO UNIX   A version, or flavor, of UNIX developed by Santa Cruz Operations.

SCSI   Small Computer System Interface. An intelligent bus for transmitting data and commands between a variety of devices. There are many implementations of SCSI, including Fast SCSI, Wide SCSI, Fast Wide SCSI, Fast-20, and Fast-40.

SCSI-2   The second generation of SCSI; includes many improvements to SCSI-1, including Fast SCSI, Wide SCSI, and mandatory parity checking.

SCSI-3   The third generation of SCSI; introduces Fast-20 and Fast-40 as improvements to the parallel bus. The standard also includes a number of specifications for high-speed serial bus architectures such as SSA, Fibre Channel, and IEEE 1394.

SCSI BIOS   A chip on the host adapter that contains programs for communicating with the adapter and the bus.

SCSI Configured Auto-Magically   *See* SCAM

SCSI ID   A number used on SCSI devices to uniquely identify them among other devices on the bus. Also referred to as a device ID.

Selector Channel   *See* SC

serial   Sending bits individually, one after the other. *See also* parallel

Serial Storage Architecture   *See* SSA

setup   A computer or device configuration.

shielded   Containing a metal cover to keep out unwanted interference from the environment. A shielded connector has a metal cover. A shielded cable has a foil wrapping or braided metal sleeve under the plastic covering.

shrouded header connector   A device connector with a plastic guard around its perimeter. The shroud ensures that all the pins on a cable are plugged into the device. Shrouded connectors also have a notch on one side so that the cable can only be inserted in one direction.

Shugart Associates Systems Interface   *See* SASI

single-ended   A SCSI bus configuration in which each signal is carried by a signal wire. Single-ended buses are more susceptible to noise than differential buses.

single-tasking   The ability to perform only one process at a time. DOS is a single-tasking operating system.

snail-mail   Regular old, lick the stamp, seal the envelope, and then wait several days mail. *See also* E-mail

solid-state   Electronics not utilizing vacuum tubes.

sound card   An add-on card use to play and/or record audio.

SSA   Serial Storage Architecture. A high-speed serial communication bus developed by IBM for sending commands, data, and status signals between devices.

stand-alone   Able to operate without support.

sustained speed   The rate at which data can be transferred continuously. *See also* burst speed

sync   Shortened form of synchronized. Events that happen at the same time.

synchronous transfer   A method of sending data that allows many bytes of data to be sent before acknowledgment is received from the target. Only data can be sent in synchronous mode. Commands, messages, and status must be transmitted in asynchronous mode.

synchronous transfer negotiation   The process of determining if a target is able to send/receive data using synchronous transfers.

T

target   A device that responds to commands from a device (the initiator).

techno-babble   The reason for this glossary. Jargon used by people in technical fields.

terminal   A screen and keyboard combination device used to interact with a computer. Terminals are usually used to access a mainframe computer.

terminate and stay resident   *See* TSR

terminator   An electrical circuit attached to each end of a SCSI bus to minimize signal reflections and extraneous noise. SCSI defines passive, active, and forced-perfect termination schemes.

TERMPWR   Terminator power.

third-party DMA   *See* DMA

TSR   Terminate and Stay Resident. A program that resides dormant in the computer's memory until triggered by another program or by a device.

twisted pair   Two wires twisted together to reduce susceptibility to RF noise.

twisted-pair flat cable   A group of twisted pairs of wires arranged in rows that comprise a single flat cable. Twisted-pair flat cables are less susceptible to noise than are ribbon cables.

U

UltraSCSI   *See* Fast-20

UMB   Upper Memory Block. *See* upper memory

UNIX   A multitasking operating system used on a variety of computer types, including PCs.

upper memory   Memory in the PC that is between 640K and 1 MB. This memory area is used for BIOS addresses and can be used to store TSRs and other drivers. Upper memory is divided into 64K subsections called upper memory blocks (UMBs).

Usenet   A collection of message areas accessed via Internet.

V

VESA   Video Electronics Standards Association. A standards body that promotes video hardware and software specifications. VESA is also the organization governing the VL-Bus.

VL-Bus (VLB)   VESA Local Bus. A 32-bit local bus promoted by VESA for communicating directly to the CPU rather than through the ISA or EISA bus.

W

Wide SCSI   A SCSI-2 bus that is 16 or 32 bits wide. Regular SCSI is 8-bit.

Windows   A multitasking operating system for the PC developed by Microsoft Corporation.

Windows NT   A high-end, cross-platform, multitasking operating system developed by Microsoft.

word   A unit of data consisting of two bytes (16 bits).

WORM   Write-Once Read-Many. A storage medium that can be written to only once but read from many times.

write-intensive   A process that requires a lot of writing of data to a device such as a hard disk.

write-once read-many   *See* WORM

X

XOR   A binary operation that compares two bits and yields a 1 only if the bits being compared are different, as shown in the table below. *See also* OR

First Bit	Second Bit	Result
0	0	0
1	0	1
0	1	1
1	1	0

X3.131-1986   The document describing the specifications of the SCSI-1 standard.

X3.131-1994   The document describing the specifications of the SCSI-2 standard.

X3T10   The ANSI committee responsible for organizing, realizing, and promoting SCSI standards.

INDEX

Note: *Italic* page numbers indicate illustrations.

NUMBERS

8-bit SCSI devices, connecting with 16-bit and 32-bit devices, 40, 57

8mm tape backup drives, 13

25-pin D-sub connectors, 34, 173, 195–196, *195*

50/68-pin Wide SCSI A-cable and B-cable external shielded connectors, 186–189, *187, 188*

50-pin 8-bit (IDC header) connectors, 175–180, *175, 176*

50-pin Centronics-style (A-cable) connectors, 34, 182–186, *184, 185*

60-pin high-density PS/2 connector, 34, 196–197, *196*

68-pin 16-bit Wide SCSI P-cable and Q-cable external shielded connectors, 34, 189–193, *190, 191*

68-pin Wide SCSI B-cable, P-cable, and Q-cable unshielded connectors, 34, 178, 179, 180–181

110-pin 32-bit Wide SCSI L-cable connectors, 182, 183, 192–194

A

A-cables
    50/68-pin Wide SCSI external shielded connectors, 186–189, *187, 188*
    50-pin Centronics-style connectors, 34, 182–186, *184, 185*
    overview of, 33, 40, 91–92, *92*
    See also cables

Abort SCSI Command CAM Control Block, 295

Abort SCSI I/O Command command code
    in ASPI for DOS, 227
    in ASPI for NetWare, 271

Abort SCSI I/O Request command code, in ASPI for OS/2, 261–262

Acculogic Inc., 134–135

active termination, 22, 23, 208–209, *210*, 318

Adaptec Inc., 135–136, 343–358
    address and telephone information, 135–136
    AHA-154*x* questions and answers, 350–351
    AHA-174*x* questions and answers, 351–352
    AHA-274*x* questions and answers, 353
    AHA-284*x* questions and answers, 353
    AHA-294*x* questions and answers, 353–355
    AMM product questions and answers, 356–357
    APA product questions and answers, 355–356
    hardware questions and answers, 345–349
    software and driver questions and answers, 343–345
    Trantor questions and answers, 357–358
    See also ASPI

adapter cards. *See* controller cards; SCSI controller cards

Add Hardware Wizard, in Windows 95, 63

addresses
    I/O port address settings for SCSI controller cards in PCs, 51–52
    for SCSI devices, 16
    for SCSI vendors, 129–167

Advanced Integration Research (AIR), 136

Advanced SCSI Programming Interface. *See* ASPI

Advanced Storage Concepts, 136

Advanced System Products Inc. (AdvanSys), 136–137

Aeronics Inc., 137

Alpha Research Corporation, 165

Always Technology Corporation, 137

America Online, 363

American Digital Systems, 137

Boulay, Paul, 208
Buffalo Inc., 141
bulletin board systems (BBSs)
    downloading ASPI managers and drivers,
        343–344
    downloading SCSI drivers, 58–59,
        129–130
    for SCSI-3 information, 7
    SCSI BBS, 364
    See also Internet resources; online services
bus mastering DMA SCSI controllers, 55, 71
bus phases, 97, 98–101, *98*, 103, 202–208
    ARBITRATION phase, 98–101, *98*, 106,
        107, 202, *204, 206*
    BUS FREE phase, 98–101, *98*, 104–105,
        107, 111, 202, *208*
    bus phase diagram, 203, *203*
    overview of, 202
    RESELECTION phase, 98–101, *98*,
        106, 107, 202, *206*
    SELECTION phase, 98–101, *98*, 107,
        202, *204*
    See also SCSI protocol
bus slots, 1
bus timing, 204–208
buses
    defined, 1
    See also SCSI buses
BusLogic Inc., 141, 360

C

cables, 20–21, 29–34, 90–93, 171–172
    A-cables, 33, 40, 91–92, *92*
    for attaching external SCSI devices
        through sound cards, 49–50
    B-cables, 33, 40, 91–92, *92*, 173
    connecting regular and Wide SCSI de-
        vices, 40, 57
    connecting SCSI devices to SCSI buses,
        35–37, *35, 36, 37*
    electrical specifications, 171, *172*
    external cables, 31, 33, *33*, 36, 73,
        171, *172*

    in Fast SCSI subsystems, 315–317
    flat-ribbon SCSI cables, 31, 32, *32*, 171
    internal cables, 31, 32, *32*, 36, *36*
    internal versus external cable connectors,
        33–34, *34*, 74
    L-cables, 173
    length of, 30–31
    overview of, 17, 19, 20–21, 90
    P-cables, 33, 40, 90, 92–93, *93*, 173
    performance and quality of, 29–30
    Q-cables, 33, 40, 92–93, *93*
    repeaters for long cables, 31
    SCSI-1, SCSI-2, SCSI-3 cabling
        diagram, 92–93, *93*
    selecting cables, 31
    specifications, 171–172, *172*
    troubleshooting, 69–70, 72–74, 75, 76
    See also connectors; SCSI devices
caching SCSI controller cards for PCs,
    47–49, 332, 333
CAM (Common Access Method) drivers,
    58, 61–62, 82–83
    ASPI-to-CAM translation drivers, 62
    See also Future/CAM interface
CAM Control Blocks (CCBs), 290–297
    Abort SCSI Command, 295
    Execute SCSI I/O Request, 293–295
    Get Device Type, 291
    issuing to Future/CAM for DOS,
        285–286
    issuing to Future/CAM for Windows,
        289, 290
    overview of, 290–291
    Path Inquiry, 291–293
    Reset SCSI Bus, 296
    Reset SCSI Device, 296–297
    See also Future/CAM interface
Canon USA Inc., 141
CD (Custom Design) Technology Inc., 142
CD ROM Inc., 142
CDBs (command descriptor blocks),
    115–117
CD-ROM drives, 13, 66
CD-ROM writers, 13
Centronics-style 50-pin (A-cable) connec-
    tors, 34, 182–186, *184, 185*
CERN Web site, 360

Corel Corp., 145
CorelSCSI! driver installation tool, 59
Corporate Systems Center, 145
cost of SCSI controller cards, 11
Creative Labs, Inc., 145
Cristie Electronics Ltd., 145
Curtis Inc., 145
Custom Design (CD) Technology Inc., 142

D

daisy-chaining SCSI devices, 35–42
   connecting devices, 35–37
   SCSI IDs and, 41–42
   terminating devices, 38–41
   See also SCSI devices; termination
DAT (digital audio tape) backup drives,
   12–13
data bus signals, 94, 200–201
data clock signals, 94–95
Data General Corporation, 145
DATA IN and DATA OUT phases, in
   SCSI protocol, 110, 114
Data Technology Corporation (DTC), 146
data transfer rates
   caching and, 47–49
   defined, 2
   for Fast SCSI standard, 5
Dataquest, 146
DBM Associates, 146
DC2000 minicartridges, for SCSI tape
   backup drives, 12
definition files, in ASPI for NetWare, 263
Dekka Technologies, 146
device drivers
   defined, 57
   See also SCSI device drivers
devices
   defined, 2
   See also SCSI devices
diagnostic programs, 52, 53–54
differential passive terminator circuit diagram, 208–209, *209*

differential SCSI buses, 18–19, 32, 169–171,
   169, 320–321
Digi-Data Corporation, 146
digital audio tape (DAT) backup drives,
   12–13
dirty cache blocks, 47, 49
disconnect process, in SCSI protocol,
   27–28, 104–105, 108, *108*
Disk Emulation Systems, 146
Distributed Processing Technology (DPT),
   146, 331–335
DMA (direct memory access)
   bus mastering DMA SCSI controllers,
      55, 71
   DMA channel and transfer speed
      settings, 47, 54–56, 69, 70, 71
   DMA channel usage, 213
   first-party DMA, 55
   handling DMA above 16 MB of RAM in
      ASPI for NetWare, 272–273
   third-party DMA, 55
DOS
   ASPI device driver configuration, 60–61,
      81–82, 83
   ASPI for DOS, 217–230
      accessing ASPI, 218
      ASPI command codes, 221–229
      ASPI command code 0: Host Adapter
         Inquiry, 221
      ASPI command code 1: Get Device
         Type, 222
      ASPI command code 2: Execute SCSI
         I/O Command, 222–226
      ASPI command code 3: Abort SCSI
         I/O Command, 227
      ASPI command code 4: Reset SCSI
         Device, 227–228
      ASPI command code 5: Set Host
         Adapter Parameters, 228
      ASPI command code 6: Get Disk
         Drive Information, 228–229
      ASPI command posting, 225–227
      calling ASPI manager, 217, 219–220
      closing ASPI, 218–219

external cables, 31, 33, *33*, 36, 73, 171, *172*
external SCSI devices
    attaching through sound cards, 49–50
    physical terminators for, 40–41, *41*
    SCSI support for, 10
    troubleshooting, 73
    See also SCSI devices
external shielded connectors, 33–34, 174,
    182–194
    50/68-pin Wide SCSI A-cable and B-
        cable connectors, 186–189, *187, 188*
    50-pin Centronics-style (A-cable) con-
        nectors, 34, 182–186, *184, 185*
    68-pin 16-bit Wide SCSI P-cable and Q-
        cable connectors, 189–193, *190, 191*
    110-pin 32-bit Wide SCSI L-cable con-
        nectors, 192–194
    overview of, 33–34, *34*
    See also connectors

F

FAQs (frequently asked questions), 360
Fast SCSI standard
    A-cables for, 33
    cable length, 30–31
    compatibility problems, 5
    overview of, 5
    See also SCSI-2 standard; SCSI standards
Fast SCSI subsystems, 313–321
    active termination and, 318
    cables and, 315–317
    differential SCSI and, 320–321
    overview of, 314–316
    passive termination and, 317
    TERMPOWER bypassing, 320
    where to terminate, 318–319
Fast-20 SCSI standard, 6, 124–125
Fast Wide SCSI standard
    cables for, 33
    overview of, 6
    See also SCSI-2 standard; SCSI standards
faxback services, 130

Fiber Channel standard, 125
Fiber SCSI standard, 127
Fibre Channel Association, 360
Fintec Peripheral Solutions, 147
Firewire serial SCSI standard, 126
first-party DMA (direct memory access), 55
flags, in Future/CAM interface, 297–298
flat-ribbon SCSI cables, 31, 32, *32*, 171
flushing dirty cache blocks, 47, 49
forced perfect termination (FPT), 22–23
FOREX Computer Corporation, 147
freezes, troubleshooting, 75–76
FTP SCSI resources, 361–362
Future Domain Corporation
    25-pin D-sub connectors, 34, 173,
        195–196, *195*
    addresses and telephone numbers, 148
    SCSI controllers, 307–308, 337–342
        integrated circuits and, 307
        IRQ levels, memory base addresses,
            and I/O port addresses, 307–308
        questions and answers, 337–341
Future/CAM interface, 279–306
    CAM Control Blocks (CCBs), 290–297
        Abort SCSI Command, 295
        Execute SCSI I/O Request, 293–295
        Get Device Type, 291
        issuing to Future/CAM for DOS,
            285–286
        issuing to Future/CAM for Windows,
            289, 290
        overview of, 290–291
        Path Inquiry, 291–293
        Reset SCSI Bus, 296
        Reset SCSI Device, 296–297
    documentation, 283
    flags, 297–298
    Future/CAM for DOS, 284–286,
        299–303
        detecting presence of, 285
        installing, 284
        issuing CAM Control Blocks to,
            285–286
        sample code, 299–303

I

I/O port address settings
  programmed input/output (PIO), 55
  for SCSI controller cards in PCs, 51–52,
    69, 70
I/O port usage, 212
I/O process, SCSI devices and, 86–88, *87*
IBM
  60-pin high-density PS/2 connector, 34,
    196–197, *196*
  ASPI for OS/2, 250–263
    accessing ASPI at initialization,
      252–253
    ASPI command codes, 255–263
    ASPI command code 0: Host Adapter
      Inquiry, 256–257
    ASPI command code 1: Get Device
      Type, 257
    ASPI command code 2: Execute SCSI
      I/O Command, 257–261
    ASPI command code 3: Abort SCSI
      I/O Request, 261–262
    ASPI command code 4: Reset SCSI
      Device, 262–263
    ASPI command code 5: Set Host
      Adapter Parameters, 263
    ASPI command posting, 261–262
    calling ASPI, 252
    Command Code field, 255
    Host Adapter Number field, 255
    obtaining ASPI entry point, 250–251
    OS/2 2.*x* and, 253
    sample code for OS/2 2.*x*, 254
    SCSI command linking with ASPI, 260
    SCSI request blocks (SRBs), 254–255
    SCSI Request Flags field, 255,
      258–260, 263
    Status Byte field, 255
    target allocation with OS/2 2.*x*,
      253–254
  LADDR (Layered Device Driver), 65
  MCA (Micro Channel Architecture)
    SCSI controller cards, 46

OS/2 SCSI device drivers, 65
  See also PC computers
ID numbers
  overview of, 16, 41–42, *42*, 90, 91
  for SCSI controller cards in PCs, 56–57
  troubleshooting, 72, 74, 76–77
IDC header 50-pin connectors, 175–180,
  175, 176
IDE (Integrated Drive Electronics) standard
  defined, 2
  versus SCSI standard, 8–10, *8*, 309–311
  using SCSI drives with IDE drives,
    50–51
IEEE 1394 (Firewire) standard, 126
Industrial Computer Source, 149
Industry Standard Architecture (ISA) SCSI
  controller cards, 46, 47, 56
information transfer control signals, 94–95
information transfer phases, 109–119, 202,
  206–208
  command descriptor blocks (CDBs) and,
    115–117
  COMMAND phase, 108, 109, 115–117,
    118, 202, *206*
  DATA IN and DATA OUT phases, 110,
    114, 202, *207*
  MESSAGE IN phase, 104–105, 106,
    109, 112, 202, *206, 208*
  MESSAGE OUT phase, 107, 109, 111,
    112, 202, *206*
  overview of, 109–111, *109, 111*, 202
  STATUS phase, 108, 109, 117–119,
    202, *208*
  synchronous data transfer request
    (SDTR) negotiation example,
    112–115
  See also SCSI protocol
initiators, 15–16, 86–89, *89*
  See also SCSI protocol
input/output. *See* I/O
installing
  DOS ASPI Manager, 344
  SCSI CD-ROM drives, 66
  SCSI controller cards, 10–11
  SCSI controller cards in PCs, 51–57

M

P

P-cables
  68-pin 16-bit Wide SCSI external
      shielded connectors, 34, 189–193,
      190, *191*
  68-pin Wide SCSI unshielded connec-
      tors, 34, *178*, *179*, 180–181
  overview of, 33, 40, 90, 92–93, *93*, 173
  See also cables
Pacific Electro Data, 157
Palindrome Corporation, 157
parity checking, 23–25, 43
Parity Systems Inc., 157
partitioning SCSI hard disk drives, 67
passive termination, 22, 79, 208–209,
      209, 317
Path Inquiry CAM Control Block, 291–293
PC computers, 211–213
  DMA channel usage, 213
  I/O port usage, 212
  interrupt (IRQ) usage, 213
  See also SCSI controller cards for PCs
PCI SCSI controller cards, 46–47, 56
Perceptive Solutions Inc., 157
performance
  cables and, 29–30
  caching and, 47–49, 332
  speed of SCSI versus IDE/Enhanced
      IDE devices, 9
Perifitech Inc., 157
Peripheral Interface Ltd., 157–158
Peripheral Land Inc. (PLI), 158
phase sequence diagram, in SCSI protocol,
      98–99, *98*, 203–204, *203*
Philips Consumer Electronics, 158
phone numbers, for SCSI vendors, 129–167
physical terminators, 40–41, *41*
PIO (programmed input/output), 55
Plexstor Corporation, 158
Plug-and-Play interface
  SCAM (SCSI configured automatically)
      standard and, 7
  SCSI controller card installation and,
      10–11, 51

polling
  in ASPI for Windows, 246–247
  defined, 53
ports
  I/O port address settings for SCSI con-
      troller cards in PCs, 51–52, 69, 70
  I/O port usage, 212
posting
  command posting in ASPI for DOS,
      225–227
  command posting in ASPI for OS/2,
      261–262
  command posting in ASPI for Windows,
      247–249
PowerBook 30-pin HDI connector, 34,
      197, 198
PowerSCSI! Future/CAM installation, 284
Prima Storage Solutions, 158
printers, 14
Procom Technology Inc., 159
Procomp USA Inc., 159, 199–200, *200*
Prodigy, 364
programmed input/output (PIO), 55
PS/2 60-pin high-density connector, 34,
      196–197, *196*

Q

Q-cables
  68-pin 16-bit Wide SCSI external
      shielded connectors, 34, 189–193,
      190, *191*
  68-pin Wide SCSI unshielded connec-
      tors, 34, *178*, *179*, 180–181
  overview of, 33, 40, 92–93, *93*
  See also cables
QLogic Corporation, 159
Quantum, 159–160
quarter-inch cartridge (QIC) tape backup
      drives, 12
Quatech Inc., 160
Queue Tag Message, 107

R

RAID (redundant array of inexpensive disks), 127–128, 323–329
  overview of, 323–325
  RAID architectures, 323–324, 325–329
  RAID controllers, 127–128
  striping and, 324–325
Raidtec Corporation, 160
Rancho Technology Inc., 160
reconnect process, in SCSI protocol, 27–28, 105–106, 108, *108*
Relax Technologies Inc., 160
Relisys Corporation, 160
repeaters for long cables, 31
RESELECTION bus phase, 98–101, *98*, 106, 107
Reset SCSI Bus CAM Control Block, 296
Reset SCSI Device CAM Control Block, 296–297
Reset SCSI Device command code
  in ASPI for DOS, 227–228
  in ASPI for NetWare, 271–272
  in ASPI for OS/2, 262–263
residual byte length reporting, in ASPI, 274–277

S

SASI (Shugart Associates Systems Interface), 2–3
SC&T International Inc., 160–161
SC_ABORT_SRB command code, 241–243
SCAM (SCSI configured "automagically") standard, 7
scanners, 14
scanning for new devices in ASPI for NetWare, 274
SC_EXEC_SCSI_CMD command code, 237–241
SC_GET_DEV_TYPE command code, 235–237

SC_HA_INQUIRY command code, 233–235
SC_RESET_DEV command code, 243–245
SCSI-1 standard
  cable length, 30
  cabling and bus options, 92–93, *93*
  connectors, 172
  ID numbers, 41
  overview of, 3–4, 5
  See also SCSI standards
SCSI-2 standard
  cable length, 30
  cabling and bus options, 92–93, *93*
  command sets, 127–128
  compatibility problems, 4
  connectors, 173
  Fast SCSI standard
    A-cables for, 33
    cable length, 30–31
    compatibility problems, 5
    overview of, 5
  Fast SCSI subsystems, 313–321
    active termination and, 318
    cables and, 315–317
    differential SCSI and, 320–321
    overview of, 314–316
    passive termination and, 317
    TERMPOWER bypassing, 320
    where to terminate, 318–319
  Fast Wide SCSI standard, 6, 33
  ID numbers, 41
  overview of, 4
  Wide SCSI standard
    cables for, 33
    compatibility problems, 6
    connecting regular and Wide SCSI devices, 40, 57
    ID numbers, 41
    overview of, 5–6
    SCSI IDs and LUNs and, 16, 17
  See also SCSI standards
SCSI-3 standard
  BBS for information about, 7
  cabling and bus options, 92–93, *93*
  command sets, 127–128

with SC_EXEC_SCSI_CMD command
code, 237–241
with SC_GET_DEV_TYPE command
code, 235–237
with SC_HA_INQUIRY command
code, 233–235
with SC_RESET_DEV command code,
243–245
serial SCSI, 7, 125–127, 128
Fiber Channel, 125
Fiber SCSI, 127
IEEE 1394 (Firewire), 126
overview of, 7, 125
Serial Storage Architecture (SSA),
125–126
See also SCSI-3 standard
Set Host Adapter Parameters command
code
in ASPI for DOS, 228
in ASPI for NetWare, 272
in ASPI for OS/2, 263
Shugart Associates Systems Interface
(SASI), 2–3
Silicon Composers Inc., 162
single-ended active terminator circuit diagram, 208–209, *210*
single-ended passive terminator circuit diagram, 208–209, *209*
single-ended SCSI buses, 18, 19, 169–170,
169
SmartDrive caching program, 48
software caching, 48–49
Sony Electronics Inc., 162
sound cards, SCSI controller cards for PCs
with, 49–50
Spectrum Engineering Inc., 163
speed
of SCSI versus IDE/Enhanced IDE devices, 9
See also performance
SPI (SCSI-3 Parallel Interface), 124–125
SRBs (SCSI request blocks)
in ASPI for DOS, 220–221
in ASPI for NetWare, 264–265
in ASPI for OS/2, 254–255

SSA (Serial Storage Architecture), 125–126
ST506 disk drives, 309–310
Staffstall Corporation, 162
Status Byte field
in ASPI for DOS, 221, 222
in ASPI for NetWare, 265, 266
in ASPI for OS/2, 255
status bytes, in Future/CAM interface, 298
STATUS phase, in SCSI protocol, 108,
109, 117–119
Storage Dimensions Inc., 163
striping disk drives in RAID architectures,
324–325
Sun Microsystems, Inc.
addresses and phone numbers, 163
D-sub connector, 172, 197, 199, *199*
Internet resources, 361, 362
Symbios Logic Incorporated, 163–164,
361, 362
synchronous data transfer request (SDTR)
negotiation, 112–115
synchronous handshaking, 25–27, 121–
122, *122*
SYSTEM.INI files, 62–63
system lockups, 75–76

T

tagged command queuing, in SCSI protocol, 107
tape backup drives, 12–13
Targa Electronics Systems Inc., 164
targets
overview of, 15–16, 86–90, *89*
target allocation in ASPI for OS/2,
253–254
See also SCSI protocol
Teac America Inc., 164
Tecmar Inc., 164
Teknor Microsystems Inc, 165
Tekram Technology, 165
telephone numbers, for SCSI vendors,
129–167

W

Walnut Creek CD-ROM, 362
Wangtek Inc., 166
Western Automation Labs Inc., 166
Western Digital Corporation, 166–167
Western Systems, 167
Wide SCSI standard
 cables for, 33
 compatibility problems, 6
 connecting regular and Wide SCSI
  devices, 40, 57
 ID numbers, 41
 overview of, 5–6
 SCSI IDs and LUNs and, 16, 17
 See also SCSI-2 standard; SCSI standards
Winchester Systems Inc., 167
Windows. *See* Microsoft Windows
Wolfenbuettel Polytechnical Institute, 362
World Wide Web SCSI resources, 360–361
WORM (write-once read-many) drives, 14
write caching, 47

X

Xirlink Inc., 167

ABOUT SOLUTION TECHNOLOGY

Since its formation in 1984, Solution Technology has focused exclusively on the design and presentation of seminars covering complex computer systems and technologies. Our company provides services for the electronics industry ranging from course design and implementation to operating, on a subcontractual basis, as a complete training department.

> *Solution Technology's objective is to concentrate on course design and delivery, and to provide you with the highest quality and most technically accurate educational experience.*

Dave Deming, an independent consultant and founder of Solution Technology, is a graduate of the Devry School System and holds a degree in Electronics Engineering Technology. Using his 15 plus years of experience, he has designed many software and hardware courses covering a wide variety of program languages and operating systems for test and development systems. Mr. Deming is also an active participant and member of the X3T10 and X3T10.1 Standards Committees.

Mr. Deming's accomplishments include assisting industry leaders in successfully debugging firmware, consulting with engineers who write SCSI drivers and firmware, and writing numerous lines of SCSI test code.

He has personally conducted hundreds of training courses and trained thousands of engineers on SCSI-related topics.

In 1994 Solution Technology conducted over 80 SCSI, Fibre Channel and SSA seminars training over 2000 SCSI engineers.

World wide recognition and prestigious clients: We have delivered courses around the world and 90% of our training courses are from repeat customers. The effectiveness of Solution Technology's instructional methodology is also attested to by the company's numerous prestigious clients.

Interactive training approach: Solution Technology seminars are distinguished by a highly interactive training approach. This student-centered technique, which encourages discussion and intensive question-answer exchanges, insures that each attendee completes the training with a thorough understanding of the subject matter.

Live demonstrations: In our "In-Depth" courses, we make available the most recent state-of-the-art test equipment and logic analyzers. We use this equipment interactively, via an overhead display, which allows the participants to see each interface in action.

Published documentation: Each seminar participant receives our published documentation which is unequaled in the SCSI community. Most seminar participants replace their X3 standards with our documentation because of its ease of use, thoroughness and additional information.

On-site corporate seminars: On-site seminars are available at a discounted corporate rate. Call for details.

A REPRESENTATIVE LIST OF SOLUTION TECHNOLOGY CLIENTS:

Adaptec • Advanced Micro Devices • Analog Devices • Apple Computer • AST • AT&T • Burr Brown Cipher • Compaq • Conner Peripherals • DEC • Diagsoft • EMC • Exabyte • Fujitsu America • Hewlett-Packard Hitachi • Honeywell • Hughes Aircraft • IBM • Integrated Systems • Intel • Intellistor • Kodak • Laser Magnetic Storage • Maynard • Maxtor • Micropolis • Motorola • National Semiconductor • NCR N-Cube • NEC • Photometrics • Pyramid Technology • Quantum • Samsung • Seagate Technology • Sequent Silicon Graphics • Sony • Storage Dimensions • Storage Tek • Sun Microsystems • Syquest • Tandem Computers T.I. • Toshiba • Unisys • University of California at Davis • Western Digital

SOLUTION TECHNOLOGY

P.O. Box 104 • Boulder Creek, CA, USA 95006
(408) 338-4285 • Fax (408) 338-4374

$50 Discount Coupon

**Mail in this form and receive a $50.00 discount
on any of the following training seminars:**

❏ 1 Introduction to SSA

❏ 2 In-Depth Exploration of SSA

❏ 3 Introduction to SCSI

❏ 4 In-Depth Exploration of SCSI

❏ 5 SCSI: The Physical Interface
(Additional discount for both In-
Depth Exploration SCSI & SCSI
The Physical Interface)

❏ 6 Introduction to Fibre Channel

❏ 7 Fibre Channel-Arbitrated Loop
(Additional discount if also
attending Fibre Channel)

❏ 8 SCSI-3 Architecture

❏ 9 SCSI-3 Interface Comparison:
Fast-20, SSA, and Fibre Channel

❏   Please keep me informed
of future seminars.

✍ **Group discounts & on-site courses available.
Please call for details.**

Please complete and return this form.
We will send you additional information.

Name: _____

Title: _____

Company: _____

Address: _____

Mail Stop: _____

City: _____

State/Zip: _____

Phone: _____

Fax: _____

SOLUTION
TECHNOLOGY

P.O. Box 104 • Boulder Creek, CA • 95006
Tel: 408/338-4285 • Fax: 408/338-4374

Give Us a Piece of Your Mind

Did *The Book of SCSI* meet your expectations? (Why or why not?)

....

....

How could this book be improved?

....

....

Any suggestions for other computer books?

....

....

❏ **Add me to your mailing list** ❏ **Send me your catalog**

Name ....

Title ....

Company name ....

Address ....

City .... **State** ....

Zip .... **Country** ....

Phone ....

Fax ....

E-mail ....

HOW TO REACH US

no starch press

1903 Jameston Lane
Daly City, CA 94014-3466
415-334-7200
Fax: 415-334-3166
E-mail: nostarch@ix.netcom.com

Place
First Class Stamp
Here

No Starch Press

1903 Jameston Ln

Daly City CA 94014-3466